MULTIPLE JOYCE

ONE HUNDRED SHORT ESSAYS ABOUT JAMES JOYCE'S CULTURAL LEGACY

GW00566745

DAVID COLLARD

Set in Minion with LaTeX.

ISBN: 978-1-952386-32-9 (paperback)
ISBN: 978-1-952386-33-6 (ebook)
Library of Congress Control Number: 2021953000

Sagging Meniscus Press
Montclair, New Jersey
saggingmeniscus.com

For Edwin

Contents

Illustrations

FOREWORD BY RÓNÁN HESSION

Perhaps more than any other author, James Joyce encapsulates all that is good and bad about the idea of greatness in literature. To his admirers he is a writer whom it is impossible to ever know fully; to the rest he is a writer whom it is difficult to get to know at all. Big thick books full of genius and cleverness have a habit of dividing the dance floor into those who dig it and those who don't—with the latter suspecting the former of faking it.

My introduction to James Joyce came through the inclusion of *A Portrait of the Artist as a Young Man* on the school curriculum. I went to O'Connell School on North Richmond Street in Dublin's working class inner city. Joyce went there too, albeit for a brief time, as did his brother Stanislaus. He also lived on North Richmond Street, where my grandparents later lived, and where my parents spent the first few years of their marriage, before I was born.

I recall my mother saying that my father had recommended *Ulysses* to her father (his father-in-law) who later returned it to him quietly on account of the filth in it. This impressed me doubly: first, that my father had read it, and knowing what was in it, had the temerity to recommend it to the father of the woman he was sleeping with; and second, that my grandfather had the frankness to return the book—presumably unread—as though doing so were some sort of virtue test he had passed.

There were bits of *Portrait* that spoke to me, bits that bored me, but mostly it struck me that I didn't see what was so great about this writer. As a self-doubting teenager, I figured the problem was with me. I read *Dubliners* after that, but still didn't feel the juice in Joyce.

I parked Joyce until adulthood, when I revisited him as part of the *Ulysses* anniversary commotion in 2004. I had prepared myself for a monumental effort: I would have to read it aloud; I would need a companion volume of footnotes; I would need to study the book, not just read it; it could take me months—all year perhaps. Instead, what I found was a book of incantatory beauty and intelligence and wizardry, that I simply let flow through and ignite my imagination. I felt grateful that Joyce had made himself accessible after all, and rued that I had listened to all those who created such needless resistance by over-preparing me for difficulty, in much the same way that teenage virgins talk to other teenage virgins about how complicated sex is.

Thinking back, I wish the first person I had asked about Joyce had been David Collard, who coincidentally started reading Joyce in the year I was born (which was nice of him). I wish that the first time anyone heard about Joyce was from David Collard. And I especially wish my grandfather had had a David Collard available to him when he first opened—and closed—*Ulysses*.

I first met David through his hosting and curation of the lockdown online literary salon 'A Leap in the Dark', and its anagrammatic successor, 'Carthorse Orchestra'. Whether in person or on the page, David is good company. He has that quality of a great host: an enthusiasm about drawing your attention so that he can direct it elsewhere—never towards himself. He uses his curiosity boundlessly, his scepticism sparingly, and his sense of humour unrepentantly. Most of all, he just has that knack for knowing what's interesting.

I say all this not to embarrass David, nor to win the reader over with adjectival blurby fluff. I think of a book's foreword as a sort of safety demonstration before the book proper gets underway. It is for the benefit of those wavering over whether they are in good hands. After all, the question of whose hands Joyce should be left in has been perennially to the fore in decisions about the Joyce estate ever since his death.

In the dense thicket of writing about Joyce, the essays in *Multiple Joyce* are the pickable wildflowers that help us make the journey our own. Within its pages are the kitsch, the serious, the scholarly, the creative, the playful and the heartfelt—qualities that are found in abundance in Joyce, though none of them alone could lay claim to defining his work. For the serious Joyce reader, there is much here to enrich the reading—or no doubt, rereading—experience. For the newcomer, it is reassurance that Joyce is in fact interesting and rooted in the real life of his time and the time since. But most of all, it speaks to the Joycean-in-progress. The half-finished reader; the reader who needs some encouragement to keep going; or the reader who, like, me is Joyce-fluid—who feels Joyce is like a posh restaurant, where I would enjoy the meal so much better if I didn't feel like I was doing things wrong all the time.

I'm not sure I'll ever start *Finnegans Wake,* but at least with *Multiple Joyce,* the idea feels more welcoming to me. *Multiple Joyce* reaffirms the idea that Joyce is not there, Everest-like, to be conquered. He is not a reading challenge. He is not a '1001 books to read before you die' (though you'll die anyway). Rather, he is, like all great literature, full of life. And like Life, he is there to be experienced, even if not understood.

—Rónán Hession

INTRODUCTION

'From the sublime to the ridiculous is but a step. Pyjamas, let us say?'

—*Ulysses*

'We are still learning to be James Joyce's contemporaries' wrote Richard Ellmann at the start of his magnificent 1959 biography and now, more than sixty years later, that's still the case. James Joyce is also learning to be ours, and his cultural presence today takes countless forms, many of them reflecting the values and priorities of our hyper-consumerist, late capitalist times.

You need pyjamas? Of course you do. But do you need *Joyce* pyjamas? Then check out the online retailer Cafe Press which—at the time of writing—offers not only branded Joycean nightwear but also mugs, hip flasks, shot glasses, face masks, baby clothes (a cute onesie with 'yes I will' printed on the front), bumper stickers, bookmarks, tote bags, badges, fridge magnets, sweat shirts, hoodies, flip flops, posters, mousepads and greetings cards. There's also a t-shirt for dogs, although Joyce feared and hated dogs. You name it, the chances are Cafe Press have stuck a Joyce quote on it.

Other online retailers offer Joyce shower curtains, iPhone covers, scented candles, quilts, teabags, finger puppets, articulated paper dolls, pendants, etchings, framed quotations and . . . but you get the idea. That all this merchandise has nothing much to do with the author and his works amply demonstrates Walter Benjamin's notion of the 'aura' that surrounds a work of art, and of the many cultural rituals attached to it, something he called the 'fabric of tradition'. In Joyce's case this aura exists because of the work and the life, but has only an intermittent and haphazard connection with either. No other great writer is more commemorated and commodified, and no other great writer is less read and understood.

Joyce's colossal literary reputation derives from a modest tally of books published during his short lifetime: *Chamber Music* (poems, 1907), *Dubliners* (short story collection, 1914), *A Portrait of the Artist as a Young Man* (novel, 1916), *Exiles* (play, 1918), *Ulysses* (novel, 1922), *Pomes Penyeach* (poems, 1927) and *Finnegans Wake* (novel, 1939).

Taken together these seven volumes amount to around two thousand pages which, along with a *Collected Poems* (1936) and *Stephen*

Hero (the early draft of *A Portrait*), take up about eight inches of my bookshelves. Alongside them are several more shelves of correspondence, biography, criticism, commentaries, concordances, a bibliography, a few academic volumes (mostly unexplored), topographical studies of Dublin and sundry Joyceana. That's the lot. By the standards of most Joyce enthusiasts I'm a featherweight. A true Joycean with money to burn is likely to acquire dozens of new books every year, many of them linking our man with another literary figure and with titles such as *Beckett and Joyce, Shaw and Joyce, Derrida and Joyce, Joyce and Aquinas, Joyce and Lacan, Joyce et Mallarmé, Vico and Joyce, Joyce and Jung, Virgil and Joyce, Joyce/Shakespeare, Joyce/Foucault* and so, endlessly, on. With *Multiple Joyce* my aim is not so much to lower the bar as remove it entirely.

This book was written in London during a period of pandemic lockdown, without access to libraries or archives and without any opportunity to travel beyond my immediate neighbourhood so, apart from my very basic library, I had to rely entirely on the internet for my researches. This unexpected constraint became a liberating advantage because, as I soon realised, Joyce is a ghost in the machine with, at the time of writing, more than 130,000,000 online citations. Only Shakespeare, with a head start, beats that. To get a sense of his astonishing ubiquity all you have to do is enter 'James Joyce' on a search engine then add any other word or phrase that occurs to you, randomly: 'James Joyce + Beyoncé'* for instance, or 'James Joyce + entropy' or 'James Joyce + Freud' or 'Spongebob Squarepants'† or 'Jürgen Habermas' or 'pornography' or 'whiskey' or 'Sontag' or 'football' or 'feminism'. There's a prize every time, or nearly, and many of these essays arose from my casually entering the two elements, clicking 'Search' and exploring whatever seam was exposed. As a methodology this lacks academic rigour, and is warmly recommended.

---

*www.facade.com is 'the first and most popular web site devoted to Tarot, Runes, I Ching, Biorhythms, Numerology, and other forms of spiritual introspection. offering statistical evidence of celebrity compatibility'. As matchmaker to the stars it gives James Joyce and Beyoncé a surprisingly high 'compatibility' rating of 64%, which breaks down thus: Physical 17%, Emotional 99%, Intellectual 77%.

†Reviewing *The Spongebob Movie: Sponge Out of Water* for the *Santa Barbara Independent* (11th Feb 2015), the film critic D.J. Palladino wrote: 'This whole movie would make James Joyce happy; it's brimming with puns, narrative loops, and complicated satirical references to philosophical issues.'

In setting out to navigate Joyce's vast cultural legacy I found myself looking less and less at the author and his works and more and more at everything else. My first essay begins in a retail warehouse, where the chance discovery of a plastic action figure prompted the line of speculation that led to to this book. What other unregarded, unrecorded examples of Joyce's cultural aura were out there? Could I attempt a preliminary audit? What would I find?

Multiple Joyce won't much appeal to the purist or the doctrinaire and that's fine, because the purist and the doctrinaire don't much appeal to me. I'm not an academic and not, come to that, much of a scholar. My approach throughout is *partial* in both senses of the word: incomplete, and biased. And I'm not at all ashamed to be a literary hack or, as Joyce put it in a letter to his friend George Antheil on 3rd January 1931:

> I am quite content to go down to posterity as a scissors and paste man.

MULTIPLE

JOYCE

1. Meet Finnegan Wake™

They hailed him cheeringly, their encient, the murrainer, and wall-ruse, the merman, ye seal that lubs you lassers.

—*Finnegans Wake*

For James Joyce an epiphany was a brief spiritual manifestation that offered an insight into the truth of things. This could take the form of something overheard or glimpsed in daily life, something quite mundane. Joyce applied the term to a series of prose sketches he wrote between 1898 (when he was 16) and 1904. These have been described as 'snapshots', or perhaps a more accurate comparison would be with magic lantern slides (and we'll return to these towards the end of this book).

Joyce himself never defined the meaning of epiphany but his character Stephen Daedalus in *Stephen Hero* (the earlier version of *A Portrait of the Artist as a Young Man*, in which Stephen would become the more familiar Dedalus) describes it as 'a sudden and momentary showing forth or disclosure of one's authentic inner self.' These were 'the most delicate and evanescent of moments,' to be scrupulously recorded by the artist. Stephen's first experience of an epiphany occurs, significantly, in Eccles Street, later home to Leopold and Molly Bloom in

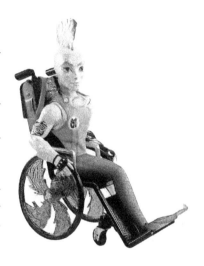

Finnegan Wake™

Ulysses. One misty evening he overhears an exchange between a young woman standing on the steps of 'one of those brown brick houses which seem the very incarnation of Irish paralysis' and a young man 'leaning on the rusty railings of the area.' The words spoken are entirely inconsequential but make an intense impression on young Stephen's sensibility. (It would be a nice metatextual moment if the young woman overheard by Stephen turned out to be Milly

Bloom, flirting with a local lad while her parents prepare supper in the basement kitchen.)

My epiphanic moment happened in a North London branch of the now-defunct retail chain Toys "R" Us. Trips to this cavernous warehouse involved a joyless immersion in the aesthetic and commercial priorities of the corporations behind the multi-million dollar global franchises responsible for Thomas the Tank Engine, Peppa Pig, Bob the Builder, Fireman Sam and—here's the Joyce connection—Finnegan Wake™, the wheelchair-using teenage punk merman who once featured in a television cartoon series called *Monster High*. He sits on my desk as I write this.

Not so much an epiphany, more of a lightbulb moment. An idea flickered dimly, briefly, when I first set eyes on this foot-high plastic figure and, a few minutes later, in the mild trance that comes with gratuitous acquisition, I took my place in the line of grown-ups at the check-out counter with Finnegan Wake™ in my basket. I had, to quote the *Wake*, found my vacation in life. If Joyce's work could percolate into the wider world in such an indirect and possibly unacknowledged way there must, I thought, be many other examples out there, 'ringsome on the aquaface', awaiting discovery and annotation.

The Monster High brand ('Be Yourself, Be Unique, Be a Monster') was created in 2010 by the designer Garrett Sander, who had noticed that lots of young girls were interested in something darker and edgier than the wholesome Barbie. Monster High fashion dolls—around 70 different designs—were the main product and, quite astonishingly, more than 700 million were produced before the range was discontinued in 2018, a figure equivalent to the combined populations of Indonesia, Pakistan and Brazil. The merchandise was linked to an animated web series, which appeared on YouTube in 185 episodes and 15 feature films between 2010 and 2017.

The student cohort at Monster High is arranged on binary lines. There are 'Ghouls' (i.e. girls) and 'Mansters' and, despite the gothic undertow and gestures towards transgressive behaviour, they all seem equally bright, aspirational and full of co-operative high spirits.

The character of Finnegan Wake™ was introduced—or launched—in 2013.* Here's the product description taken from the Amazon website (and quite possibly run through a translation engine at some point):

> The son of a mermaid sits in the wheelchair and is always "ready to go, free and capable" for everything—except for standing still! Finnegan makes his debut as a monster doll in his cool sports outfit, sitting in his typical wheelchair. Shimmering in different shades of blue, he wears a yellow muscle shirt with the number 01, which brings out his tattoos and makes his scale-studded, articulated tail fin competitors. Axe [*sic*] accessories include Finnegan's swimming goggles, racing gloves and a backpack that can be attached to the wheelchair. In it, his monster-crass diary with spooky information about his life in the water and on land is perfectly stored. The wheelchair has flames instead of spokes, a coating with structure and silver armrests. All monster friends can roll off with the favourites of the Monster High fans, the Aquarius with Moha's cut, who pushes the door to monster-grassy fun with handicap with his passion for speed!

Finnegan Wake™ is, if you will, the *Finnegans Wake* of toys—a complex, cryptic, multi-layered bundle of signifiers, not all of them comprehensible. First of all, what on earth is a 'monster-crass diary'? Next—why the wheelchair? A merman on dry land is a fish out of water and his tail, whether fully functional or not, would be a disabling impediment. One of the many fan websites explains that 'he needs a wheelchair due to a condition he was born with, a motor disability in his tail which he justifies as "I was just born this way. My tail just never worked." '†

---

*In Series 3, episode 45 *Ready, Wheeling and Able*. 'When Rider rolls into Monster High, the ghouls learn there's more to this wheelchair-bound new student body than meets the eye.'
†Perhaps the creative team who came up with Finnegan Wake™ were aware of the British comedy film *Miranda the Mermaid* (1948), in which Glynis John (Miranda) is disguised as an invalid patient by the London doctor she has captivated. At one unsettling point we see her vacant wheelchair parked in the street, its implied fishy aroma sniffed at enquiringly by some cats.
　But this does prompt a question. Any mermaid or merman out of their natural element would need to use a wheelchair, or some other mobility aid, to get around. The fact is that our hero is doubly disabled, unable to swim in water *or* walk on

So his immobility is not down to being out of his natural element. By way of compensation he has some lexical zingers at his disposal, although they're all quite humdrum by Joycean standards. He's a self-styled 'scaredevil', the things he approves of are 'spoketastic' and 'clawsome' and his 'skultimate pet' would be a ghost cheetah 'because they're the fastest creature in the monster world . . . but they're too wild to be tamed.' He is endowed with a range of upbeat, mildly rebellious attitudes, which feature on the Monster High™ website:

> If it isn't extreme and it isn't now, it has very little chance of getting Finnegan's attention. Adrenaline rushes are what he lives for and suggesting he should be more careful does little but seriously tick him off.

The Scaredevil cultivates his inner Hipster by 'going for cardio exercises and making himself some healthy smoothies.' How the hell did we get here?

Well for a start it's quite possible that our merman is actually named after the traditional (and apostrophised) ballad *Finnegan's Wake* rather than the unapostrophised novel (and we'll be tackling that problematic apostrophe later, and more than once). The websites run by fans of Monster High come down equivocally on either origin, or both.

Did Garrett Sander or his creative associates settle on the name as a way of showing that their intellectual allegiances extended beyond the world of dolls and cartoons, that they aspired to something now increasingly remote in their lives but which, for a while, when they were younger, had value and meaning—the search for beauty and truth?

Is Finnegan Wake™ beautiful? Is he—or it—*true*?

We can rope in Thomas Aquinas here, or rather Stephen Daedalus's brisk exposition of Thomas Aquinas in *Stephen Hero*:

land. Interestingly enough the show's creator insists that the character is 'pansexual', although all his close friendships (with Lorna McNessie, Rebecca Steam and especially Gigi Grant, an unbottled djinn) appear to be heteronormative, or whatever the Monster High equivalent to that is. Finnegan Wake™ is one of 11 'Mansters' in the franchise. As they are unlikely to have pinged your radar I'll name them here: Clawd Wolf, Deuce Gorgon, Garrott DuRocque, Gillinton "Gil" Webeber, Heath Burns, Invisi Billy, Jackson Jekyll/Holt Hyde, Neighthan Rot, Porter Geiss and Sloman "Slo-Mo" Mortovich. Any one of which, or of whom, might have leapt from the pages of the original *Finnegans Wake*.

The three things requisite for beauty are, integrity, a wholeness, symmetry and radiance. Some day I will expand that sentence into a treatise.

In fact Stephen pretty much does so on the spot, and we can follow his lead. Confronted with a hypothetically beautiful object—a plastic toy punk merman in this case—the mind contemplates the form of the object, and its symmetry, and immediately recognises the object as a *thing*, or as a 'definitely constituted entity', which is to say an organised structure. The term 'radiance' initially baffles young Stephen but then he hits on it—in the moment which he calls the 'epiphany'— namely, the recognition of the object's soul, or 'whatness'.

The soul of the commonest object, the structure of which is so adjusted, seems to us radiant. The object achieves its epiphany.

Now it's a big ask to expect my readers to recognise Finnegan Wake™ as an object of beauty or symmetry or epiphanic 'whatness', but here I can rope in Aquinas once again, who defined beauty as something 'the contemplation of which pleases'.

I'm looking at my model of Finnegan Wake™ right now, and I have to say it pleases me, so I guess it's beautiful, or at least attractive. Of course 'looking at' is not quite the same thing as 'contemplation', but cut me some slack here—it's a plastic toy.*

In 'Jouets', the short essay in *Mythologies* (1957), Roland Barthes compared the simple wooden toys of his childhood and the plastic ones of the present day (or his present day, in the middle of the last century). The former are, he says, the product of nature, the latter of chemistry. He was among the first commentators to write about, and question, the function and influence and legitimacy of gendered toys, and the way they shape children into their roles as adults:

French toys always mean something, and this something is always entirely socialised, constituted by the myths or the techniques of modern adult life.†

---

* *Finnegans Wake* has a shoal of mermen references: 'Yussive smirte and ye mermon answerth from his beelyingplace below the tightmark, Gotahelv!' (262.F1), 'Enjoy yourself, O maremen!' (312.10), 'And still a light moves long the river. And stiller the mermen ply their keg.' (399.16) and 'One two moremens more' (628.06—at the end of the novel, when the river meets the sea).

† *'la matière plastique y a une apparence à la fois grossière et hygiénique.'*

Not only French toys, surely? The fact is that most toys literally prefigure the adult world and all that's in it.* Dolls, for instance, prepare or condition girls to 'the causality of house-keeping' and a future role as a mother, while other toys equip boys to be soldiers, mechanics, engineers and so on. Faced with more complex plastic playthings, says Barthes, the child is an owner or a user but never a *creator*, unable to do more than implement 'actions without adventure, without wonder, without joy.' There is no comparable sense of discovery in ready-made plastic toys as there is in a simple set of building blocks. Barthes laments the disappearance of the wooden toys of his own childhood, carved by craftsmen from 'a familiar and poetic substance, which does not sever the child from close contact with the tree, the table, the floor'. This is not nostalgia merely, but a sense of real loss, and not only on behalf of today's children. Of the now-forgotten plastic ancestors of Finnegan Wake™, he observes:

> These toys die in fact very quickly, and once dead, they have no posthumous life for the child.†

Joyce's novels have something in common with Barthes' wooden toys. They are a product of the past, expertly crafted, timeless, inexhaustible and, in common with other great novels, communicate to the reader '*le plaisir, la douceur, l'humanité du toucher*' (the pleasure, the sweetness, the humanity of touch). They have a posthumous life. They are radiant.

Is there, speaking of toys, a market for a range of Joycean action figures? Buck Mulligan in a yellow dressing gown, ungirdled, with shaving accessories; Stephen Dedalus with Latin Quarter hat, detachable ashplant and brothel chandelier; lonely Miss Emily Sinico with a

---

* '*l'Armée, la Radio, les Postes, la Médecine (trousses miniatures de médecin, salles d'opération pour poupées), L'École, la Coiffure d'Art (casques à onduler), L'Aviation (parachutistes), les Transports (Trains, Citroëns, Vedettes, Vespas, Stations-Services), la Science (Jouets martiens).*' (The Army, Broadcasting, the Post Office, Medicine (miniature instrument-cases, operating theaters for dolls), School, Hair-Styling (driers for permanent- waving), the Air Force (Parachutists), Transport (trains, Citroëns, Vedettes, Vespas, petrol-stations), Science (Martian toys). Translated by Annette Lavers (Hill and Wang, New York, 1984)
† '*Ces jouets meurent d'ailleurs très vite, et une fois morts, ils n'ont pour l'enfant aucune vie posthume.*'

carrier bag full of empties, Shem the Penman, Anna Livia Plurabelle, Humphrey Chimpden Earwicker?

The journalist Frank McNally has thought along these lines. Writing in *The Irish Times* in 2014 he suggested that there might be a niche market for a Lego version of Joyce's Dublin, which would come with a copy of *Ulysses* as an instruction manual. 'Then, finally,' he concluded, 'enthusiasts could test Joyce's claim that, if it ever proved necessary, the 1904 city could be reconstructed from his pages, brick by brick.'

Since 2015 the German dramatist and director Michael Sommer has been using Lego Playmobil® figures to create more than sixty short films based on novels and plays, from Antigone to Büchner's Woyzeck. His choice of texts is impressively highbrow (for the most part) and includes an engaging take on *Ulysses*.* Perhaps he's the man to develop McNally's whimsical proposal.

It's too late to attempt any reconstruction of Toys "R" Us. In 2018 the company declared bankruptcy and announced that it would close all of its U.S. and British stores. If you're keen to acquire a Finnegan Wake™ of your own you'll have to look elsewhere.

---

*http://mwsommer.de/ulysses-english/

2. JJ FROM A TO B

Here's the opening sentence of Graham Greene's novel *Brighton Rock* (1938):

> Hale knew, before he had been in Brighton three hours, that they meant to murder him.

Who wouldn't read on? Here's another opening sentence, from another novel:

> A man called Berg, who changed his name to Greb, came to a seaside town intending to kill his father . . .

On the face of it this is a similar first line, but something trickier is happening, as the self-conscious and artificial reversal of 'Berg' to 'Greb' suggests, and the vague setting of 'a seaside town'. This is the opening sentence of *Berg*, a novel written by Ann Quin (1936–1973), published in 1964. Quin wrote three more novels—*Three* (1966), *Passages* (1969) and *Tripticks* (1972)—before walking into the sea to end her life near her home town, which happened to be Brighton, at the age of 36. She is among the vanishingly small cohort of women experimental writers, and one of the most compelling. She is not to be valued simply because she's rare, of course, but because she's a thrilling and original talent. (By the way I tend to avoid the term 'experimental' when referring to contemporary fiction, not least because it suggests something provisional, unformed, contingent and—for the ordinary reader—*daunting*. Lucy Ellmann, on winning the Goldsmiths Prize for her novel *Ducks, Newburyport*, said that she preferred the term 'adventurous fiction', and so do I.) Quinn and Ellmann are both exemplary 'B-writers'.

That certainly doesn't mean they're second-rate. It was Anthony Burgess (whose shade will haunt the pages of *Multiple Joyce*) who proposed that novelists could be divided into two classes, as 'A-writers' and 'B-writers'. The A-writer, he said, is essentially a storyteller, concerned above all with plot and character and psychological motivation. Most novelists throughout history fall into this category—Daniel Defoe and Jonathan Swift and Jane Austen and George Eliot and Harper Lee. Think of *Robinson Crusoe*, *Gulliver's Travels*, *Pride and Prejudice*, *Middlemarch* and *To Kill a Mockingbird*, and then think of E.L. James's best-selling *Fifty Shades of Grey* (the two categories have nothing to do with literary merit). A-writers are part of a long tradition, and add to that tradition without much changing it. They are part of the literary mainstream and tend to work within popular forms, or genres—the crime novel, the horror story, romantic fiction, science fiction and so on. Not all A-writers are great writers, or even good ones, but some certainly are.

B-writers, on the other hand, often employ plot and character and so on to a high degree of sophistication and accomplishment, but their real interest is in language and form and structure, and the potential of the novel to say new things in a new way. They are explorers, and they are seldom if ever popular in the way that some A-writers are popular. Burgess saw himself with good reason as a B-writer, but often managed to be both.

B-writers tend to be highly original, adventurous, 'difficult' even, and do not as a rule attract a large readership. Not all B-writers are great writers, or even good ones, but many are.

Anyone aware of the Burgess categories will think twice before dismissing a novel that doesn't deliver the consolations of character and a page-turning plot, a novel that aims elsewhere, and perhaps higher. Joyce is certainly the greatest of B-writers and *Ulysses* the very greatest of all B-novels and, while we're at it, let's agree that it's the greatest novel of all *full stop*, and to hell with categories. I shall not be taking any questions at this time.

Finnegans Wake is the most extreme example of B-writing, a book in which language 'is not about anything but is the thing itself' as Samuel Beckett put it in his essay on the novel in *Our Exagmination Round His Factification for Incamination of Work in Progress* (1929).

Beckett's take sums up the challenge that faces any reader of adventurous writing, and can be applied not only to books but also to films and music and theatre and art. It's a line I tend to quote whenever I'm faced with something new that I like and admire, or want to like and admire but don't understand, which is often the case.[*]

We might also consider the corresponding categories of 'A-readers' and 'B-readers'—those who find what they need in the literary mainstream (and there's nothing wrong with that) and those who seek elsewhere (and there's nothing wrong with that either).

In 'Fail Better', an incisive essay published in *The Guardian* newspaper in 2007, Zadie Smith wrote:

---

[*]Brendan Behan once said: 'I like *Waiting for Godot*. I don't know what it's about. I like a swim in the sea. I don't know what that's about either.'

> Readers fail writers just as often as writers fail readers. Readers fail
> when they allow themselves to believe the old mantra that fiction
> is the thing you relate to and writers the amenable people you seek
> out when you want to have your own version of the world con-
> firmed and reinforced.

This is well said, I think, although I'm unaware of the 'old mantra'
she mentions. I absolutely agree that fiction should function as a
window to other worlds, not as a mirror to our own, and readers
who favour only novels that reflect their own experiences, or that
endorse their personal tastes and values, or feature 'relatable' characters, hardly qualify as readers at all. Misogyny and envy aside, it
seems to me that the critical ire directed at the immensely popular
novelist Sally Rooney, author of *Conversations with Friends*, *Common People* and *Beautiful World Where Are You*, is aimed at her readers as much as it is at her. But we'll be taking a look at Rooney later
on. She manages to be both an A and B writer, and neither, and all
at the same time.

B-readers, sympathetic to the aims of B-writers, are better
equipped to navigate the challenges of fictions that do not offer
the traditional consolations of plot and character. They are not necessarily better readers, but they do have different expectations. Some
A-readers tend to react with suspicion and hostility to B-writers and,
indeed, to B-readers. Hey-ho.

When it comes to fiction I'm like the character played by Isabelle
Huppert in Hal Hartley's film *Amateur* (1994), a former nun and now
an erotic writer who is also, we learn, a nymphomaniac virgin. When
invited to explain how it's possible to be both, she explains with a
shrug: 'I'm choosy.'

I'm choosy too. I prefer the work of a brilliant A-writer to that of a
merely average B-writer, and that of a brilliant B-writer to a merely
competent A-writer. Now what constitutes 'brilliant' or 'average' or
'competent' is very much a matter of taste and judgement, and I'm not
setting myself up as any kind of arbiter or gatekeeper here, although
if you rate (say) Terry Pratchett above V.S. Pritchett we're unlikely to
find much common ground. But we can still be friends and, in the
handy phrase attributed online to Ezra Pound, Winston Churchill
and many others, 'when two people agree about everything, one of
them is unnecessary.'

3. Degrees of celebrity

How famous is James Joyce?

The website famousbirthdays.com tells me that, of those born in 1882 and deemed worthy of mention, Joyce (born on 2nd February) is 'the 6th most popular for the year' after Franklin D. Roosevelt, A.A. Milne, Virginia Woolf, Bela Lugosi and Igor Stravinsky. Popularity is based, apparently, on 'user activity'.

Joyce is also the '18th most popular Aquarian named James' in a list headed by the actor James Dean, and the 12th most famous Irish author of all time, beaten by the likes of 'award-winning fashion, beauty and lifestyle blogger' Cliona Kelly and Suzanne Jackson (another blogger, with a particular interest in wedding planning). Beckett comes in 26th.

In 2014, when I first started gawping at this website, Joyce was the fifteenth most famous Irish person on a list headed by Liam Neeson, Oscar Wilde, Saoirse Ronan, Siva Kaneswaran and Colin Farrell. Our man came just after Bono. By the time I came to check the site again while editing this book I discovered with a sinking heart and rising gorge that practically every category was now dominated by bloggers and vloggers and stars of YouTube or TikTok or other social media platforms. Of the current 'top fifty famous Irish people', the only names on the list who are *not* bloggers or TikTok stars or reality TV celebrities are Cillian Murphy (12th), Pierce Brosnan (28th), Bono (32nd), Michael Gambon (35th), Richard Harris (41st) and the singer Enya (43rd).

As for the other 44, a chap called Jacksepticeye can stand for them all. He's an 'energetic video game commentator whose YouTube channel has over 26 million subscribers,' which is more than the population of Australia.

There are at the time of writing and, one fears, for the rest of history, no authors at all in the top fifty famous Irish people, unless you include Graham Norton. When you filter for Irish writers—or rather 'writers born in Ireland'—Joyce comes nowhere in a list headed by Oscar Wilde and, in second place, Cecilia Aherne, author of *A Place Called Here, Thanks for the Memories* and *P.S., I Love You.* She happens to be the daughter of Bertie Aherne, the Taoiseach (Prime Minister) of Ireland between 1997 and 2008 and her books, we learn, 'have won numerous accolades.'

Joyce has never been and never will be popular in the sense that, say, Cecilia Aherne is popular. But he is unquestionably famous, at least to the extent that describing him as famous is, or should be, tautologous. Everyone used to know the story of Lord Reith, the rather terrifying Director-General of the British Broadcasting Corporation who, on hearing somebody described on the wireless as 'a famous lawyer' fired off this peppery memorandum to his subordinates:

> The word famous. If a person is famous, it is superfluous to point out the fact; if he is not, then it is a lie. The word is not to be used by the BBC.

Reith died on Bloomsday, in 1971.

4. HOW MANY POETS ARE THERE?

There's an episode in Tom Stoppard's play *Travesties* (1974), based on events in real life, in which Henry Carr, a minor British embassy official in Zürich, sues James Joyce over a pair of trousers used in an am-dram production of *The Importance of Being Earnest.* Goaded beyond endurance by an imagined insult, he launches into an underdog outburst:

> For every thousand people there's nine hundred doing the work, ninety doing well, nine doing good, and one lucky bastard who's the artist.

Applying the Stoppard-Carr ratio to the Republic of Ireland's population of 4.7 million (in the 2016 census) we get 23,420 artists, roughly equal to the population of Tralee in County Kerry.

But how many of these lucky bastards are poets? Let's say 5% might, at a stretch, be described as poetry practitioners, which is to say poets who are published and read, if only by other poets. That would amount to 1,171 poets, which seems quite a low figure to me, given that the population is likely to be closer to 5 million by now. So I contacted Poetry Ireland to see if they could shed any light and they very sensibly suggested that I should go to the website of each of the main poetry publishers in the Republic—around a dozen—and tot up the number of poets on their roster. Then be sure to add the Irish poets published outside Ireland, in the UK and the US and elsewhere.

I started to do this but soon gave up, because there's not much to be said for counting poets. And of course these are just the *published* poets, and therefore the tip of a very large cultural iceberg. Let's just say that the answer to my question (How many poets are there?) is: a lot. Which isn't much of an answer.

Travesties was written in 1974 and we are in a position to make some very rough estimates. I have before me the hefty *Directory of Contemporary Poets*, published by Macmillan in 1970, when the UK population was 55.5 million. Limited to the UK (and we'll get back to the Irish Republic in a moment), it lists around 1,100 poets from Abse, Dannie to Zurndorfer, Lotte, so either the Stoppard-Carr formula is flawed or my 5% estimate overgenerous, and should hover somewhere between one and two per cent. The 1970s turned out to be the boom years and subsequent editions of the *Directory* give lower figures—787 in 2001, rising slightly to 840 in 2014. So let's say that Britain sustains a population of under a thousand poets. Not that any of them can earn a living as such, but that's another matter.

Let's look at the bigger picture. How many poets are working actively in the English language today? The *International Who's Who of Poetry* (Routledge, 2011 and the most recent edition I could find) confirms that there are around 4,000 practitioners, all of them apparently with proper jobs to fall back on, from Aalfs, Janet ('American writer, poet and martial arts instructor') to Zyck, Adam ('Polish psychologist, gerontologist, poet and translator'). The publishers make no claim to be comprehensive and there are likely to be many omissions, but 4,000 poets in a global anglophone population of 375 million (assuming that the readership of poetry is likely to be almost entirely made up of native speakers) is a vanishingly small proportion—around 0.0001%.

And of those four thousand poets, how many are any good? Not necessarily popular, just *good* (and I hope you'll agree with what I mean by that). Could it be as many as a few hundred? And what of the even smaller cohort of *great* poets, past and (theoretically) present, whose work has lasted and will continue to circulate? Perhaps a dozen in all, writing in English in the twentieth century. Who are, or were, they? Hardy, Yeats, Pound, Eliot, Auden, Robert Lowell and . . . how many is that? Seven, and I do realise that 'greatness' and the very idea of a canon is old hat, and patrician, and elitist, and barely worth considering. A few years ago I met a bright young English graduate with a degree from a reputable university who insisted she had never even *heard* of T.S. Eliot because (as she quite reasonably pointed out) he wasn't on the syllabus, and you can't be expected to read *everything*. Which seems fair enough, although Eliot doesn't strike me as optional and surely a graduate in any subject who hasn't read *The Waste Land* is by any objective measure culturally impoverished. To her credit she wasn't at all uncomfortable with her admission and to my credit neither was I. But still.

We used to care more, or some folk did. According to Julian Symons in his 1960 account *The Thirties: a dream revolved*, the interwar audience for poetry in Britain took the form of a pyramid, the broad base of which was formed by a million-strong intelligentsia. Above them a group numbering 50,000 subscribed to the handful of little magazines featuring the most recent work of new writers. This section of the pyramid was generally younger than the base and the social composition more complex, including working-class intellectuals, members of the lower-middle class educated at state or grammar schools (and in some cases at red-brick universities), and a general sampling of professional men and women (doctors, architects, lawyers, dons, economists etc). The artists themselves, around a thousand in number, lived, often precariously, at the top. Not, it should hardly be necessary to point out, that they were all wealthy, or even solvent. By 'artists' Symons meant novelists, poets, painters, composers and the like, and clearly wasn't concerned with the applied arts, or with such popular media as the music hall and cinema—both of which would surely bump up the numbers. The UK population in the mid-1930s being around 46 million, that thousand-strong cohort represents a percentage too small to bother about, although it's those very painters and poets and novelists, who today stand for the age—they are what we know of the period.

Not everyone at the time agreed with the proportions of Symons' pyramid, and a jaundiced contemporary of his reckoned the population of serious poetry readers in Britain numbered around a hundred.

Symons admits that the image of a pyramid is over-simple and the set of assumptions on which his model was based now seems very old-fashioned, but what interests me most, and still, are his estimated numbers. The overall population has increased since 1935 by around twenty million (and let's for the sake of argument assume that there has been a corresponding growth in the 'intelligentsia', not that such a label would be employed in a positive way today), but the greatest increase must surely have been in the number of artists. Post-war access to higher education, the growth of art schools, state sponsorship, the Arts Council, lottery funding and the wide-scale commodification of culture through new media—all have led to an enormous boom in practitioners to the extent that today one gets the impression that more people write poetry than read it. So what shape, metaphorically, are things in today? No longer a pyramid but perhaps a wonky sort-of oblong?

There are workshops and festivals and readings and signings and book clubs, and competitions (some even free to enter), and little magazines and big anthologies and reviews. There's a radio presence, online activity and a handful of public poets who scrape a living through the practice of poetry and associated 'poetic' activities. Not much of this is very good, of course, but then not much of anything is very good. Poetry is, we are constantly reassured, 'for everyone'— the nine hundred doing the work, the ninety doing well and the nine doing good. This is nonsense, of course, because poetry, like Matisse and Mozart and Miles Davis, like ragtime, rap and reggae, like ballet, baseball and baba ganoush, like *Ulysses* and *Finnegans Wake* and every other novel ever written, is not for everyone, and should never be for everyone. Poetry is for *anyone*.

5. CALL OF THE WILDE

At 11:45 p.m. on Friday July 6th 1923 the Irish medium Hester Travers Smith (1868–1949) conducted the tenth of eighteen seances in which she interrogated the ghost of Oscar Wilde, who had died in 1900.

She mediated his thoughts through automatic writing and a ouija board, later publishing the results in a strange little book called *Oscar Wilde from Purgatory* (1924). His eternal slumber rudely interrupted, Wilde is initially invited to pass critical judgement on such contemporary writers as Thomas Hardy and John Galsworthy, but eventually the talk turns to a particular book the medium claims never to have read, but with which Wilde seems surprisingly familiar.

> What is your opinion of "Ulysses," by James Joyce?
>
> *Yes, I have smeared my fingers with that vast work. It has given me one exquisite moment of amusement. I gathered that if I hoped to retain my reputation as an intelligent shade, open to new ideas, I must peruse this volume. It is a singular matter that a countryman of mine should have produced this great bulk of filth. You may smile at me for uttering thus when you reflect that in the eyes of the world I am a tainted creature. But, at least, I had a sense of the values of things on the terrestrial globe. Here in "Ulysses" I find a monster who cannot contain the monstrosities of his own brain. The creatures he gives birth to leap from him in shapeless masses of hideousness, as dragons might, which in their foulsome birth contaminate their parent . . . This book appeals to all my senses. It gratifies the soil which is in everyone of us. It gives me the impression of having been written in a severe fit of nausea. Surely there is a nausea fever. The physicians may not have diagnosed it. But here we have the heated vomit continued through the countless pages of this work. The author thought no doubt that he had given the world a series of ideas. Ideas which had sprung from out his body, not his mind!*

Clearly Wilde's punishment in the afterlife was to be stripped of quicksilver wit while condemned to chronic loquacity. His denunciation continues for some time, and Hester Travers Smith doesn't let Joyce's 'great bulk of filth' off the hook after Oscar has had his say, returning to the subject in her conclusion. She cannot resist a final dig:

> I feel it is quite natural that Wilde should be revolted by a work like "Ulysses." It is entirely out of harmony with his time and ideas.

He might easily fail to see what the admirers of Joyce call the "vastness of the book." It is completely ugly; that is enough. His horror of probing into the "inside" of a human being would naturally be aroused by a book which, I believe, practically deals with nothing else.

No personal animus there, no axe to grind. Joyce knew Smith's book and, a good sport, incorporated a version of her supernatural dialogue with Wilde in *Finnegans Wake*:

Tell the woyld I have lived true thousand hells. Pity, please, lady, for poor O.W. in this profundust snobbing I have caught. Nine dirty years mine age, hairs hoar, mummeries failend, snowdrift tomy elpow, deff as Adder. I askt you, dear lady, to judge on my tree by our fruits. I gave you of the tree.

J.P. Mahaffy (1839–1919), the Irish classicist and Provost of Trinity College, held very low opinions of the dead Oscar Wilde and the living James Joyce, writing:

Thank God, they have both cleared out of Dublin, but not before they had squirted stink like a pair of skunks on all the decent people with whom they came in contact. It's an ill bird that fouls its own nest. James Joyce is a living argument in defence of my contention that it was a mistake to establish a separate university for the aborigines of this island—for the cornerboys who spit into the Liffey.[*]

A question for any practising spiritualist: would it still be possible, theoretically, to summon up the shade of Oscar Wilde and see how he's getting on? I mean, the afterlife is supposed to be unending, isn't it? Perhaps he's had second thoughts about *Ulysses* and would like to share them.

---

[*] Quoted by Gerald Griffin in *The Collegians* (1938).

6. Their hospitality

Martin Amis once told a Moscow literary gathering that Joyce was 'a huge genius and no talent,' a variant on what Harold Bloom said of John Updike: 'a minor novelist with a major style.' Amis, one might slice back, is a huge talent and no genius, but I enjoyed what he then went on to say about Joyce's relation to his readers:

> If you go to Nabokov's house, metaphorically speaking, you get his best chair, in front of his fire, with his best wine. If you go to James Joyce's house, you come into this big drafty edifice, and there's no one there. And then you find him tinkering around in some scullery. And he offers you two slabs of peat around a conger eel, and a glass of mead.

This is in fact a buffed-up version of something Clive James had written about Seamus Heaney (or 'Seamus Feamus' as he is renamed) in his satirical epic *Peregrine Prykke's Pilgrimage through the London Literary World* (1976):

> These were the *Belfast* poets—all called *Seamus*–
> Of whom the leading light was Seamus Feamus,
> Who even now attacked his midday meal:
> Two slabs of peat around a conger eel.

Martin Amis continued to repeat his version on the circuit, but it became baggier and less amusing as the years went by. In 2018 he wearily delivered the following, straight to camera:

> The writer is like a host and the reader is a guest. When you visit a Nabokov novel it's as if he has given you the best chair nearest the fire and given you his best wine ... If you went round to Joyce's house, you'd find the address didn't exist. Then you would find some sort of outbuilding where Joyce lives, and then he wouldn't be in. You'd shout for him and eventually a figure would appear and he would talk to you in a language you'd never heard of before. And instead of giving you a delicious dinner, as Nabokov does, Joyce would give you two slabs of peat around a conger eel and some repulsive drink he'd made himself.[*]

[*]https://www.facebook.com/BigThinkScience/videos/1493171714128281

The bright bloom of the original has by now long faded. But speaking of food, Joyce was a great diner out and spent vast quantities of his patron Harriet Shaw Weaver's money in fancy restaurants where, by all accounts, he drank gallons of white wine but rarely touched his grub:

> Joyce ate obviously without appetite, he always toyed with his food as if searching for something, and would push back his plate with a disgusted look: he could put up with almost no food [. . .] He enjoyed entertaining his friends at restaurants, finding nothing too expensive and too refined for them; he was a regular customer of the Trianon and Fouquet's where the luxury pleased him as a relaxation after his daily work, but at all these places he barely picked at his food, merely nibbling from his plate some leaves of salad or a piece of cake. He seemed to live on air.*

In *Ulysses* Stephen Dedalus has practically no interest in food at all. After tucking into a 'plate of fry' for breakfast in the opening 'Telemachus' episode he appears to eat nothing else for the rest of the day. Mr Bloom, on the other hand, is something of a trencherman— his budget for the day includes the purchase of a pork kidney, two Banbury cakes, lunch at Davy Byrne's, a pig's foot, a sheep's trotter, some Fry's plain chocolate, a square of soda bread, and coffee and a bun which he offers to Stephen in the cabman's shelter in the early hours of the 17th June, and which Stephen flatly refuses.

*Louis Gillet, 'The Living Joyce', 1941, published in *Portraits of the Artist in Exile* (ed. Potts), p. 170.

7. JOYCE . . . WOMEN. WOMEN . . JOYCE

In a Bloomsday blog about our man for the *Times Literary Supplement* (16th June 2016), Adrian Tahourdin noted what he believed was 'the large gender imbalance in those who have published books about the writer'. He cited a broad selection of recent Joyce books, and he seemed to have a point.

But, as many dissenting correspondents were quick to point out, there is a large cohort of women who have published books about Joyce, including, among many others, Adaline Glasheen (who wrote the magnificent *Census of Finnegans Wake*), Jeri Johnson ('perhaps THE eminent Joyce scholar'), Katherine Mullin ('*James Joyce, Sexuality and Social Purity* is fantastically good'), Maud Ellmann (daughter of Joyce biographer Richard and sister of the novelist Lucy), Jennifer Levine, Katherine Mullin, Margot Norris, Vike Plock and Vicky Mahaffey. There is clearly no shortage of female Joycean academics, and there are presumably just as many female readers. I hardly need add that Joyce was loyally and tirelessly supported by women throughout his writing career, including his publisher Sylvia Beach, his patron Harriet Shaw Weaver and *The Little Review* co-editors Jane Heap and Margaret C. Anderson. Among the earliest critics to recognise Joyce was Mary Colum (1884–1957), who wrote an influential review of *Ulysses* for *The Freeman* in 1922, followed by two memoirs including *Our Friend James Joyce* (1959). And then there was Nora. But that's a whole other story.

Responding to Tahourdin's observation, Professor Margot Backus of the University of Houston, author of *Scandal Work: James Joyce, the New Journalism, and the Home Rule Newspaper Wars* (University of Notre Dame Press, 2013) added, sardonically:

> I ritually scan the TLS in hopes of finding that my recent book on James Joyce and the new journalist sex scandal has been reviewed. My heart leapt with joy when I saw "James Joyce" in a subject heading and I looked with interest to see if maybe my book was at last mentioned as case of scholarship on Joyce by a woman, but alas, no.

Another gender-related issue connected with Joyce scholarship is even more troubling. In January 2019 the people who run the Twitter account @JoyceanWomen ('Celebrating women's scholarship on

Joyce since July 2018') published an Open Letter in *The Modernist Review* with 130 signatories calling for 'meaningful action to reduce the incidents of sexual harassment, inappropriate behaviour, abuse, and even assault at conferences, workshops, summer schools and any other events affiliated with the community.'

The 'Concerned Joyceans' cited cases of misogyny, voyeurism, abuse of power, harassment, assault and even rape at Joyce-related events. They were, they said, 'tired of sending graduate and undergraduate students to conferences or summer schools with a list of unsafe individuals to avoid and/or behaviour of which to be wary or, conversely, tolerant.'

Not being part of any Joycean community, academic or otherwise, I had naively and complacently assumed that such things simply didn't go on at such events, that somehow this aspect of the literary world (if no other) was exempt from such behaviour, so I read the Open Letter with alarm, dismay and despondency. It began thus:

> The works of James Joyce are remarkable in their frankness about sexuality and their sensitivity to the value of women's experience. Women's scholarship within Joyce Studies is justly respected and celebrated. The spirit of Joyce's works themselves, as well as the critical tradition emerging from it (which includes an important branch of feminist scholarship), is in sympathy with making the academic and social events that are central to the life of the community more accessible, more inclusive, and safer for women who are trying to make a name in the field.

To what extent this is down to a malignant handful of (presumably) male academics is unclear but it's evidently a long-standing, embedded and institutional problem. Given the gravity of the claims, the signatories' demands were perfectly reasonable: they called on the boards of Joyce societies, foundations, and journals to issue official statements condemning such behaviour, and to implement codes of conduct for workshops and the design and content of summer school materials, membership forms, and websites. Three months after it was published the Covid-19 pandemic began to bite, lockdowns began and travel was restricted. Workshops, summer schools, conferences and other academic gatherings became a thing of the future.

This needs fixing before things get back to normal. Or rather, we need a far better normal to get back to.

8. WRITE LIKE A KARDASHIAN

> This is really random, but I thought it was kind of cool!!! The International Bowling Museum in Texas are doing a poll to see who should be inducted into the bowling hall of fame and I have been nominated! I probably shouldn't admit it, but I'm not the best bowler haha. But that doesn't stop me going and having a great time! Bowling to me is about spending time with friends and family! Where's the fun in getting perfect strikes every time!? I'd rather have some fun trying and laugh at myself than get a perfect score.

That's a sample of Kim Kardashian's writing taken from a blog post attributed to her which, when run through an online app* confirms that the author whose style her writing most closely resembles is that of our man Joyce. The app, launched in 2010, is a statistical analysis tool created by a 27-year-old Russian software developer called Dmitry Chestnykh.

Of course there's nothing remotely Joycean about Kardashian's prose style, even if its fragmentary inconsequentiality does have distant echoes of Molly Bloom's soliloquy. If Kim Kardashian writes like anyone it's the plastic merman Finnegan Wake™.

But interest was snagged so I took part of the essay you're currently reading and ran it through the same app and it seems that I, too, write like James Joyce and therefore like Kim Kardashian, which gets us nowhere much. Next I ran the opening paragraph of my introduction to this book, and it came up as James Joyce *again*. But when, with low cunning, I removed all references to Joyce from the same paragraph and re-entered it in the app I was told I wrote like David Foster Wallace.

Here's the badge I printed off to prove it:

I write like
David Foster Wallace
About David Foster Wallace : **Analyze your text**

---

*"I Write Like" (iwl.me)

Now thoroughly alarmed, I cut and pasted other bits and pieces from *Multiple Joyce* and came up with H.P. Lovecraft, Bram Stoker and Edgar Allan Poe. (I am large. I contain multitudes.) Hooked, I carried on, feverishly cutting and pasting random fragments and clicking for an adjudication:

— the lyrics for *Teddy Bear's Picnic*: Margaret Atwood;
— a passage from Gertrude Stein's *Tender Buttons*: Oscar Wilde;
— the chorus from Joy Division's *Love Will Tear Us Apart*: Charles Dickens;
— a paragraph from Lionel Shriver's execrable novel *The Mandibles*: Jane Austen;
— Rónán Hession's generous foreword to *Multiple Joyce*: James Fenimore Cooper.

Finally I cut and pasted the opening paragraph of Eimear McBride's *A Girl Is a Half-formed Thing*. She writes like Ernest Hemingway, apparently.

A footnote. While researching this essay I came across the twitter account @KimKierkegaard, which blends Søren Kierkegaard's philosophy with Kim Kardashian's inanity, producing such magnificent mind-numbing aberrations as:

> I have majorly fallen off my workout-eating plan! AND it's summer. But to despair over sin is to sink deeper into it.

Late to this party, I noticed that around 30 writers and critics and poets I admire were already following the account, so I signed up immediately. There's also a book: *My Beautiful Despair: The Philosophy of Kim Kierkegaardashian* (Gallery Books, 2018), of which a nameless reviewer in the *Washington Post* said this:

> Basically what you have is profound ideas that exercise your brain, combined with mindless comments that lower your IQ. Put the two together and they cancel each other out, allowing your mind to do exactly nothing . . . it's pretty entertaining.

I printed this off and stuck it above my desk while writing *Multiple Joyce*.

9. PALINURUS HAS HIS SAY

> Daydream: a golden classical house, three stories high, with attic windows and a view over water. Outside a magnolia growing up the wall, a terrace for winter, a great tree for summer and a lawn for games; behind it a wooded hill and in front a river, then a sheltered garden, indulgent to fig and nectarine.

'Indulgent to fig and nectarine.' It's Cyril Connolly, writing anonymously as 'Palinurus', in *The Unquiet Grave* (1944).

Connolly was marooned unhappily in London during the Blitz when he wrote this, and yearning for a bolt hole in the Lot region of France. My own lockdown dreams tended less to property than to books, and this essay was prompted by media reports that a winner of a huge National Lottery payout had announced to the press his plans to buy 'a really good pair of shoes for about £200.'

I've never spent that much on shoes but, in the event of a colossal windfall coming my way (like Bloom's 'independent discovery of a goldseam of inexhaustible ore'), an early priority would be to splash out on what's known to booksellers as 'The Connolly 100', being the books, actually numbering 106 in all, listed in Cyril Connolly's 1965 volume *The Modern Movement: One Hundred Key Books from England, France, and America 1880–1950*.

The title is misleading because some of the books are from South Africa, New Zealand and Ireland, but that doesn't detract in the slightest from a magisterial and entertaining series of short, incisive assessments of modernist literary benchmarks, ranging from Flaubert's *Bouvard et Pécuchet* (1881) to Orwell's *Nineteen Eighty-Four* (1949).

The most recent Connolly 100 auction was in 2007, but there was nothing in the catalogue I could afford then and it's less likely that I could afford any of the items now, even if they came up for grabs. Given the funds I'd prefer signed first editions, of course, and ideally with some fabulous association—Beckett's annotated copy of Huysmans, for instance, if such a thing even exists. How much would that set me back? And how much would it cost to bag the lot? I spent an absorbing afternoon online to find out, looking first at abe.com and then various bookseller websites, mostly in Britain, France—many of Connolly's choices are French—and the United States. The price

I settled on in each case was that of the best copy I could find—fine first editions, in the original dust wrapper where called for, ideally signed, sometimes inscribed. In many cases signed copies were also the costliest available: *Bouvard et Pécuchet* was £10,200 and *Nineteen Eighty-Four* £9,400, but the prices for the volumes in between varied wildly, with Joyce's *Portrait* (£100k) and *Ulysses* (£170k) among the most expensive.*

The total cost of acquiring the Connolly 100 came to £1,616,512 in all, rounded up to £1,620,000 to cover postage and packing. That's around $2,245,000 at current exchange rates, or 1,873,530 Euros. So, goldseam of inexhaustible ore aside, or a collapse in the market for first edition modernist benchmarks, I'm stuck for now with my tatty paperbacks.

Even if I had the dosh at my disposal, would the Connolly 100 be a sound investment? In these days of Non-Fungible Tokens who can tell? I'd certainly enjoy gloating over a bookcase with all the volumes arranged side by side, and that would be a pleasure beyond price. But here's a thing: should I organise my imaginary collection in my hypothetical glass-fronted bookcase chronologically (as they appear in Connolly's survey) or alphabetically, by author? There's a first-world problem for you.

Despite its many shortcomings and omissions Connolly's list provides a snapshot of an educated reader's taste in the 20th century. Not all the works he includes are canonical and, to be sure, the very idea of a canon is these days problematic, but those works that were canonical for Connolly mostly remain so for us today. There will no doubt in the years ahead be new standards, new critical approaches, new gatekeepers (or none), and new novels from new writers. Will there be celebrations to mark the bicentenary of Joyce's birth in 2082?

---

*Although the copy of *Ulysses* I chose was a first edition in pretty good nick, it's priced far lower than the record-breaking $275k paid for a particularly fine example in 2009, at that time the highest price recorded for a 20th-century first edition. The copy was number 45 of the first 100 is printed on fine Dutch handmade paper, with most of the pages uncut. It was also one of only four copies accounted for of the first edition print run to be signed by the author. The dealer who made the sale was Pom Harrington, who said 'The colour is amazing—this lovely Aegean Sea, Greek flag blue which would normally have darkened into a more dirty blue but because it has been in a box it is a complete thing of beauty.' Desirable yes, but I'd happily settle for a Shakespeare and Company *Ulysses* inscribed 'To H.G. Wells respectfully James Joyce, 5 November 1928 Paris.' Auctioned by Bonham's in London on 24th June 2021, it went for £25,250.

Or the 200th anniversary of the publication of *Ulysses*, forty years later? Does anybody dare to think that far ahead, with any degree of certainty? Not just in terms of literary reputations, but of our very existence as a species?

Giambattista Vico (1668–1744) the Neapolitan philosopher and author of *Principi di Scienza Nuova* (*The New Science*, 1725) proposed a cyclical version of history of three consecutive Ages in which nations and civilisations rise and fall and rise again. This informed the recursive structure of *Finnegans Wake* and I expect some of you will already have skipped to the next essay. In Viconian terms we have come through the three Ages of Theocracy, Aristocracy and Democracy and are about to enter, or have already entered, a period of chaos that will follow the collapse of democratic society, after which a new cycle will begin with a return to the Theocratic Age. Which really is the last thing I need.

10. 'THERE ONCE WAS A WRITER CALLED JOYCE'

When *The Poetry of James Joyce Reconsidered* (edited by Mark C. Connor) was published by the University of Florida Press in 2012, the series editor Sebastian D.G. Knowles wrote in his foreword, almost apologetically, that this was 'quite improbably, the first book of essays on Joyce's poetry' and that all of the content drew on the 'exiguous extant scholarship.'

The two collections of poetry published in Joyce's lifetime—*Chamber Music* (1907) and *Pomes Penyeach* (1927)—were brought together as *Collected Poems* in 1936. There were also two satirical broadsides 'The Holy Office' (1904) and 'Gas from a Burner' (1912), as well as various bits and pieces. None of it has aged very well. With a distinct whiff of the *fin de siècle*, Joyce's poetry seems out of step with the modernism of his contemporaries Eliot and Pound and Gertrude Stein and, come to that, with his own achievements in prose. Joyce's poetry has always been, and will always be, entirely overshadowed by his novels, and there isn't a line in any of his poems to match 'the heaventree of stars hung with humid night blue fruit' in *Ulysses*.

Joyce enjoyed making up limericks, and Ellmann's biography lists around twenty examples, most of them appearing in letters to friends. J.C.C. Mays included five limericks in his 1992 edition of Joyce's poems, all but one of them dating from 1917 and therefore unrepresentative of what amounted to a lifelong practice.[*] They are not widely known, have rarely appeared in print and it's quite astonishing that no publisher has to date brought out a comprehensive, lavishly illustrated *edition de luxe*, complete with full critical apparatus and an introduction by Colm Tóibín.

Limericks tend to be vulgar, trivial, formally predictable and not, in literary terms, particularly respectable. As the scholar Tim Conley points out, 'the body of criticism dealing with limericks is on the whole both small and shallow. Their repetition is more common than any commentary: limericks speak for themselves, and criticism does not like to be made to feel superfluous.'[†] Some may argue that Joyce's

---

[*] *Poems* and *Exiles* by James Joyce, edited by J.C.C. Mays (Penguin books, 1992)
[†] See http://hjs.ff.cuni.cz/archives/v14_1/essays/conley.htm

limericks detract from his reputation as a serious writer, but such is his canonical status that they will never dent his reputation, and in any case his worst limericks are not as excruciatingly bad as Eliot's racist 'King Bolo' verses or as flat as Auden's dull, donnish Clerihews.

Joyce's limericks do not, in general, bear close analysis, being quite conventional in form and entirely lacking in pornographic, scatological or anti-clerical content. But as a recurring feature throughout his writing career, like doodles in the margins of a manuscript, they are intriguing and potentially revealing.* The most interesting of them is, I think, the one he wrote to mark the publication in 1938 of Beckett's novel *Murphy*:

> There's a maevusmarked maggot called Murphy
> Who would fain be thought thunder-and-turfy.
>   When he's out to be chic he
>   Sticks on his gum dicky
> And worms off for a breeze by the surfy.†

There are two limericks in *Ulysses*. One is recalled, eventually, by Bloom in 'Lestrygonians' as he waits for his lunchtime sandwich to be served in Davy Byrne's. It concerns the reverend Mr MacTrigger (whose name rhymes with the n-word) and eventually comes back to him in full, or nearly:

> His five hundred wives
> Had the time of their lives
> It grew bigger and bigger and bigger.

Enough of that. But since we're on the subject of limericks here's a memory I'd like to share with you.

---

*Oliver St. John Gogarty, in his memoir *As I Was Going Down Sackville Street* (London: Sphere Books, 1968), recalls a limerick Joyce composed as a student:

> There was a kind Lady called Gregory,
> Said, "Come to me poets in beggary."
>   But found her imprudence
>   When thousands of students
> Cried, "All we are in that catégory!"

†Every version of the limerick I could find online had 'maevusmarked' as (presumably) a misprint for 'naevusmarked'—Murphy is revealed after his death to have a large naevus, or flat mole, as a birthmark on his backside. 'Gum dicky' is a reference to Murphy's celluloid yellow 'dicky bow' or bow-tie.

One sunny Thursday evening in June 2009 I found myself at the London Review of Books bookshop in Bloomsbury celebrating the launch of Zachary Leader's *The Movement Reconsidered.* This was a sprightly collection of essays about the pre-eminent group of post-war poets assembled in the 1956 *New Lines* anthology by Robert Conquest (who doubled as editor and contributor) along with Kingsley Amis, Thom Gunn, Philip Larkin and illustrious others.

As sole survivor of What-Was-Never-Really-a-Movement, Conquest (1917–2015) was to be guest of honour at the launch. I had long admired his deadpan *New Lines* introduction in which he said that all the poets were linked by 'a negative determination to avoid bad principles', a shapely phrase that meant quite a lot and nothing at all. I was excited at the prospect of seeing in person a literary and cultural hero who had, quite incredibly, first appeared in print over seventy years before, in 1937. I was also curious. What, I wondered, did a Thirties writer look like? What did a Thirties writer *sound* like?

To complicate matters he was at the time widely regarded as one of the finest living historians, on the strength of *The Great Terror* (1968), his account of Stalin's show trials, purges and all-round wickedness. Conquest's view, that Stalin's grim tyranny was not a ghastly and anomalous perversion of Lenin's political theories but their inevitable outcome, rattled a generation of Marxist intellectuals and provoked furious debate, although it is now a widely-accepted orthodoxy. He was also (and remains) a master of pungent and instantly memorable limericks, his two fields of expertise combining thus:

> There was a great Marxist named Lenin
> Who did two or three million men in.
> > That's a lot to have done in,
> > But where he did one in
> That grand Marxist Stalin did ten in.

So I found a seat and hung around for half an hour as the room quickly filled, mostly with celebrated (though not celebrity) poets. The famous writer Martin Amis arrived late, looking like a famous writer and this was, I realised, the only place to be. Conquest sat in a wheelchair, looking spry and quietly amused, or possibly aghast. It was hard to tell. He was dapper in a dark blue open-collar shirt and olive-green sports jacket, cool in the timeless way that very old people can sometimes appear to be. Things kicked off. After the usual

launch flummery and speeches and readings by a cohort of admirers
I mentally labelled *los Conquestadores*, Leader wound things up by
reciting Conquest's miraculous condensation of Jacques' speech in
As You Like It:

> Seven ages, first puking and mewling
> Then very pissed off with one's schooling;
>   Then fucks and then fights;
>   Then judging chaps' rights;
> Then sitting in slippers; then drooling.

The author sat imperturbably throughout this impromptu tribute
and the warm applause that followed. I remember thinking that in
Shakespearean terms he had already been once around the block, so
to speak, was now experiencing the third age for the second time,
and therefore likely to be very pissed off. He had written *The Great
Terror*. He knew *Solzhenitsyn*, for pity's sake. Would he, would anyone, choose to be remembered for an admittedly magnificent limerick? As the audience clustered around Leader and his readers, I made
a nervous bee-line for Conquest who, temporarily overlooked by the
rest of the room, was now sitting quietly alone and apparently happy
to be ignored.

Closing in on him with all the queasy assurance that comes from
a second glass of publisher's plonk I blabbered some complimentary
preamble and, prompted by his earlier recital of a very fine poem
about a lamented basset hound named Bluebell, we chatted about
dogs. Conquest likes dogs and writes very well about them. I don't,
so I don't, but we hit it off just fine. He had by far the quietest voice
of anyone I've ever met, little more than a murmur compared with
which his barely-audible reading had been delivered at a roar. Standing, I had to crane solicitously in his direction so as not to to miss a
word.

Our conversation turned to the once-notorious opening lines of
an unfinished limerick by Aldous Huxley that featured in his novel
Antic Hay:

> There was a young man of East Anglia
> Whose loins were a tangle of ganglia

Huxley reportedly promised that all royalties from the novel
would go to anybody who could polish off the next three lines, given

that (in his view) no third rhyme was possible after 'ganglia'. It so happened that a few weeks earlier I had risen to the challenge and come up with:

> When touched by a tart
> He awoke with a start
> And said: 'Do that again and I'll stranglia.'

Conquest smiled faintly. This, I immediately convinced myself, was not only a clear indication of his approval but the overture to a profound and lasting friendship. He would leave the venue that evening buoyed by our encounter, his wavering faith in the cultural values of my generation agreeably and definitively boosted. 'There was one fellow over there,' he would murmur, back at home in Palo Alto, 'who seemed the right sort. I should be sorry not to hear from him again.' A mutually-enriching correspondence would ensue. He would read my poetry, I would read his and I might in time get to call him 'Old Bob' as Kingsley used to do.

Our first encounter had reached an end, and we shook hands. Not having a business card I scribbled my address on a bookstore flyer so we could continue our burgeoning relationship, but Bob was now surrounded, hemmed in by his admirers. They were all craning solicitously in his direction so as not to miss a word. It was getting late. I stuffed the flyer in my pocket and left.

11. CARRY ON DRAWING

Back in the 1970s the edition of *Dubliners* most readily available in British bookshops, the one we all read, was a paperback published variously by such imprints as Grafton, Flamingo and Triad Panther. It featured fifteen attractive illustrations by the artist Robin Jacques (1920–1995), and I've long wondered why this book, along with *A Portrait*, was given such treatment and not, say, *Ulysses* or *Finnegans Wake*. I suspect the Estate had a say in the matter.

Jacques ('rhymes with cakes' he used to say) was a self-taught artist with a distinctive 'stippling' technique and a prolific illustrator, mostly of books for children. His sister, the lovely comic actress Hattie Jacques, was born just five days after the publication of *Ulysses*. They were both originally named Jaques, but when she added a 'c' to her name for professional reasons he loyally did the same.

Many other illustrators and fine artists have been attracted to Joyce. Foremost among them is the English painter and collage artist Richard Hamilton (1922–2011), who designed the James Joyce exhibition at London's Institute of Contemporary

Robin Jacques, 'Two Gallants' from *Dubliners*

Arts in 1950 and would spend half a century illustrating *Ulysses* after first reading it while doing National Service at the age of 25. A series of eight etchings and aquatints and heliogravures are part of an unfinished project to illustrate all eighteen episodes of the novel. In a 2002 interview Hamilton said:

> I thought of doing some etchings. But then I realised that nothing is described in *Ulysses*. There's no visual sense in the whole book.

And yet I had an image of the book in my head—somehow Joyce had put it there without any of the usual textual devices. Just as everyone has the same picture of Leopold Bloom in their heads, although he's never described.*

Joyce is not a visual writer and Hamilton has a point—what does Bloom *actually* look like? We have a clear sense from the novel of his height, his build, his complexion and so on, but the overall impression remains vague, which of course is how it should be for an Everyman. Molly Bloom tends to be portrayed in film and illustrations as a latter day Moll Flanders—the clue may be in the name—while I expect most of us visualise Stephen Dedalus as a young Joyce lookalike. Of the other characters it is Buck Mulligan who has the most memorable physical presence, with his Wildean plumpness, yellow nightgown and booming theatrical eloquence.

Joyce's caricature of Mr Bloom

We know what his creator thought Bloom looked like. In January 1926, while visiting the Montparnasse studio of an American painter called Myron C. Nutting, Joyce took a thick black pencil and dashed off a caricature of a moustachioed Bloom *(left)* in bowler hat and big-buttoned overcoat, along with the opening line of Homer's Odyssey ἄνδρα μοι ἔννεπε, μοῦσα, πολύτροπον, ὃς μάλα πολλὰ ('Tell me, muse, of that man of many turns, who wandered far and wide' in Robert Fitzgerald's 1961 translation). This included 'a minor error in spelling and characteristically skewed accents' according to R.J. Schork in *Greek and Hellenic Culture in Joyce*. I'm sure I'm not the first to notice that Joyce's portrait is quite possibly his version of Milly Bloom's drawing of her father,

*'Richard Hamilton: Revealing the face (and body) of Leopold Bloom' by Tom Rosenthal (*The Independent*, 22nd March 2014)

34

kept in the unlocked drawer in his bedroom (and the buttons are particularly suggestive):

> A Vere Foster's handwriting copybook, property of Milly (Millicent) Bloom, certain pages of which bore diagram drawings marked Papli, which showed a large globular head with 5 hairs erect, 2 eyes in profile, the trunk full front with 3 large buttons[.]

In the same interview with John Walsh, Richard Hamilton said that the fragmentations of *Ulysses*, the multiple styles and voices and genres, had a direct influence on his own work, which supports my claim that without *Ulysses* there would be no Pop Art.

My favourite Joyce illustrations feature in Herbert Gorman's *James Joyce: a definitive biography* (The Bodley Head, 1941). As well as a frontispiece drawing of Joyce by Augustus John there are eight surrealist photo-montages 'especially made by G.R. Morris,' two of which are reproduced here.

At the time Gorman's book was published Morris was working for the high street shoe retailers Clark's, but the company archive has no information whatever about him.

Photomontages by G.R. Morris from Herbert Gorman's *James Joyce: a definitive biography*

He was a poster designer for the National Safety First Association between the 1920s and 1950s and worked for London Transport intermittently between 1937 and 1948, but nothing much is known about him. His collage illustrations for the Gorman biography are wonderful, anticipating Richard Hamilton's celebrated collage *Just what is it that makes today's homes so different, so appealing?* (1965), one of the earliest works of pop art. I wonder what's become of the originals.

Finally there's thecrackedlookingglass.com where Jacob Trunk, an American artist, graphic designer, printmaker, and web designer, is slowly illustrating Joyce's prose in a charmingly naive style, one page at a time. Since he began the project in 2015 he's completed the *Dubliners* story 'An Encounter' (see the next essay) and, to date, the first eight episodes of *Ulysses*. Below is the opening scene from 'Telemachus' with Buck Mulligan, Stephen and the cracked looking-glass from which the website takes its name.

Jacob Trunk, 'Telemachus'

12. 'A QUEER OLD JOSSER'

Among the gifts reserved for age—in my case, at least—is a belated realisation that Joyce's first book, *Dubliners*, a collection of fifteen short stories published in 1914, may well be his best. My favourite story in the collection is 'An Encounter', which opens thus:

> The summer holidays were near at hand when I made up my mind to break out of the weariness of school life for one day at least.

This opening sentence makes equal sense whether delivered by a schoolboy or schoolmaster. The narrator is either a precociously literate schoolboy or an older man recalling an earlier time—it's hard to tell. He describes 'a day's miching' with another boy, Mahoney, in which the pair bunk off school together, walking along the quays, eating currant buns and enjoying 'the spectacle of Dublin's commerce'. They cross the Liffey by ferryboat and head for The Pigeon House (with it implications of flight and return), roaming around the impoverished backstreets of Ringsend. As the day grows sultry they feast on biscuits and chocolate and bottles of raspberry lemonade. Too tired to reach their destination they rest in a field where they are approached by an old man 'shabbily dressed in a suit of greenish-black,' a Beckettian tramp-like figure with a refined accent who embarks on a series of monologues, first and innocuously about literature and then, unsettlingly, about 'girls'.

> He gave me the impression that he was repeating something which he had learned by heart or that, magnetised by some words of his own speech, his mind was slowly circling round and round in the same orbit.

Like a priest reciting the liturgy? After this eerie monologue he retreats to the end of the field. The narrator does not see what happens next, but his companion Mahoney does:

> "I say! Look what he's doing!"

> As I neither answered nor raised my eyes, Mahony exclaimed again:

> "I say . . . He's a queer old josser!"

Jacob Trunk, 'An Encounter'

Most readers will assume the old man is masturbating, as Bloom does on Sandymount Strand in *Ulysses*, although on first reading the story I assumed he was either urinating or defecating, or perhaps both. Surely, I thought, if he'd actually been *wanking* the boys would have fled in horror, perhaps hurling insults and rocks. So it's left to the reader to imagine the scene. Perhaps he's doing something perfectly innocent, like dancing or praying. In his recollection of the real-life encounter many years later, Joyce's brother Stanislaus calls the man a 'juggins', which means a simple-minded or gullible person, or a simpleton; the equivalent American term might be 'doofus'.

An English professor once told me that 'josser' was a slang term for God, a claim I've never been able to verify but am happy to pass on for your consideration. It's also circus slang for an outsider.*

---

* *Green's Dictionary of Slang* (2010) offers five definitions of 'josser': (1) an ageing roué, (2) a swell, a grandee, (3) a clergyman, a minister (Joyce having another swipe at the Church?), (4) one who begs for loans, a 'sponge' and (5) a simpleton, a fool; a victim for criminal gamers. Joss' is Chinese pidgin for god, so a missionary was called a 'joss-pidgin-man'. The druid in *Finnegans Wake* is called the 'archdruid of Irish chinchinjoss' and since 'chin-chin' is pidgin for talking (as Peter Chrisp pointed out to me) he's 'the top man in Irish God-talking—or theology'.

If the episode offers an epiphany, or sudden spiritual illumination, it is a particularly downbeat one, and this may be why 'An Encounter' has become my favourite story in *Dubliners*.

Fourteen other short stories make up Joyce's first book—surely the greatest of all short story collections—each exploring themes of loss, inertia, indecision and flight. They were published when the author was, quite astonishingly, 26 years old. There are no duds. You could read one a day for two weeks.

13. Dubliners 100

The last decade has seen a spectacular renaissance of Irish writing both north and south of the border which coincides with the emergence of new independent publishers. Among the best of these is Dublin's Tramp Press, founded and run by Sarah Davis-Goff and Lisa Coen. They have an impressive backlist, including fine novels by Sara Baume, Arja Kajermo, Mike McCormack and Doireann Ní Ghríofa. To mark the 2014 centenary of the publication of *Dubliners* they published *Dubliners 100*, an anthology in which the editor Thomas Morris assembled a company of new and established Irish writers to create 'cover versions' of their favourite stories in Joyce's original collection.

Among the contributors was Eimear McBride, who updated 'Ivy Day in the Committee Room', singled out by several reviewers as the best in a strong collection. McBride has been compared regularly, favourably and (perhaps, for her, annoyingly) with Joyce, for whom she has enormous admiration and to whom she is happy to admit she owes a debt. I happened to be at the London launch of her debut novel *A Girl Is a Half-formed Thing* in June 2013, a few weeks after it had been published in Norwich by the tiny independent Galley Beggar Press. The venue was the London Review of Books bookshop in Bury Place, near the British Museum in Bloomsbury and a stone's throw from the offices of Faber and Faber, Joyce's publishers, who would later snap up the rights for McBride's novel.

A crowd of friends, family and supporters packed the ground floor room after the shop closed on a very sultry summer's evening. There were short speeches by the co-founders of Galley Beggar, Henry Layte, Sam Jordison and Eloise Millar, and I made a few carefully-prepared off-the-cuff remarks. Eimear read beautifully, first from the opening pages of the book and then from the 'grandfather's wake' episode. Then we chatted, clumsily passing a big microphone from hand to hand and both of us failing to remember the correct wording of Joyce's well-known note to his patron Harriet Shaw Weaver explaining the language of *Finnegans Wake* which, McBride said, she kept pinned above her desk throughout the writing of *A Girl Is a Half-formed Thing*:

> One great part of every human existence is passed in a state which cannot be rendered sensible by the use of wideawake language, cutanddry grammar and goahead plot.

Once the formal part of the launch was over, as the drink flowed and the hubbub grew, a young woman introduced herself to the author, saying that she had grown up 'surrounded by modernist writing' because her maternal grandmother, she explained, was the aforementioned Harriet Shaw Weaver—patron of Joyce, Eliot and other less illustrious beneficiaries. In the 1920s Weaver owned a suffragist publication that, improbably, employed Ezra Pound as its literary critic. He changed its name to *The Egoist* and they published *A Portrait of the Artist* in serial form. How's that for an auspicious connection? Harriet Shaw Weaver bankrolled Joyce and his family to the equivalent £1.5 million in today's money, and I'd say she got a bargain.

14. THE FALL OF THE HOUSE OF USHER

As I write this in late September 2021, dispiriting news from Dublin confirms that Joyce's cultural legacy is apparently more secure on the internet than in the real world.

In October 2020 An Bord Pleanála (Ireland's national independent planning body) approved plans to develop a derelict Georgian townhouse on the southern side of the River Liffey at 15 Usher's Island into a 54-room tourist hostel, the best way (they insisted) to secure the long-term conservation of this historic building.

Here's the full entry from Ireland's National Inventory of Architectural Heritage:

> Terraced three-bay four-storey over basement former house, built c.1775, now in use as museum. Hipped M-profile roof hidden behind parapet to front (north) having granite capping, and red brick chimneystacks. Red brick walls laid in Flemish bond to front having rusticated cut granite quoins and cut granite plinth course. Lined-and-ruled rendered wall to basement level. Rendered walls to east elevation. Square-headed window openings having granite sills. Six-over-six pane timber sash windows to basement, ground and first floors, six-over-three pane timber sash windows to second floor. Three-over-three pane timber sash windows to third floor. Elliptical-headed door opening having carved masonry surround with engaged Ionic columns and respondent pilasters. Plain sidelights and fanlight surrounding timber-panelled door, approached by granite steps and entrance platform. Cast-iron railings on granite plinth flanking steps and enclosing basement area to front. Flagstones and later metal staircase to basement area.

There was a national and international outcry led by the author Colm Tóibín and other public figures, with 99 signatories adding their names to an open letter to Josepha Madigan, the Minister for Culture, Heritage and the Gaeltacht, and Owen Keegan, Dublin City Manager, which went as follows:

> 15, Usher's Island is not just another house connected with Joyce. Built in 1775, its upper floors were rented by Joyce's great-aunts in the 1890s and the writer himself often visited them there. Most importantly, it is the setting of 'The Dead', widely considered Joyce's and indeed the world's greatest short story. The atmosphere in the house and the way the rooms are configured are mostly untouched

since Joyce's time. Turning it into a 56-room hostel would destroy the uniquely valuable interior which still maintains the character of the house so splendidly described in the story.

The setting of 'The Dead' is the annual gathering organised by Joyce's great aunts on January 6th, the feast of the Epiphany. As such the address on Usher's Island has as much literary and cultural significance as 7, Eccles Street and the Martello Tower in Sandycove.

Despite petitions and online campaigning and so on, which were hard to organise during the pandemic lockdowns, the decision was taken to convert the historic building into 'a high quality tourist offering' to the dismay of all those who hate to see the historic fabric of the city swept away and, worse, turned into something crass both in purpose and execution.

The previous owner of the building was Brendan Kilty, a Joyce-loving barrister who restored the ground floor and created a literary venue. But he filed for bankruptcy in 2017 and sold the house to the current co-owners Fergus McCabe and Brian Stynes (the former All-Ireland Gaelic footballer), who insist that the hostel plan is the only financially viable option.

The banality of the proposal and the arrogance of the An Bord Pleanála planners who approved such a project in the face of consistent and widespread public opposition should come as no surprise, given the architectural havoc wreaked on the city (and on the rest of Ireland) over the past few decades of economic boom and bust. Dublin was once a far more habitable place, scruffy and accommodating, with cheap digs, and convivial bars, but recent years have seen the loss of many pubs, theatres, venues and gallery spaces, all razed to the ground and replaced by plug-ugly hotels and offices and penthouses. Creative folk, and others with ordinary and essential jobs, have been priced out of a city which increasingly caters only for tourists and wealthy suburban visitors, with rapacious landlords charging astronomical rents and a horrifying spike in homelessness. As the novelist Paula McGrath tweeted pithily:

> These endless hostels and hotels are symptoms of a whiskey and leprechaun version of Ireland . . . which ignores climate change and the need to appeal to locals as well as those arriving, shamrock-eyed, via long-haul flights.

On Bloomsday 2021 the Irish *Independent* reported that a letter addressed to Culture Minister Catherine Martin from Hollywood actress Anjelica Huston, star of the 1987 film, had been read out on the steps of the Usher's Island house, calling on the Irish Government to preserve the building:

> For a site of such major cultural significance to be at the mercy of private owners is heartbreaking. I am writing to implore you to take all measures possible as Minister for Arts and Culture to preserve this site.

I look again at that open letter from Tóibín et al, which says:

> In the decades since Joyce's death, too many of the places that are rendered immortal in his writing have been lost to the city.

This is completely true, yet it also strikes me as a contradiction. Joyce's claim that in the aftermath of some catastrophe Dublin could be re-built brick-by-brick by referring to his writing was never meant to be taken literally, or even seriously. But if buildings and places can be rendered immortal by writing, then the built environment itself, relatively mutable, can perhaps be left to fend for itself. The text endures, the buildings come and go.

But it can be a bit trickier than that. When Bloom nips out to Dlugacz the butcher in Dorset Street for his breakfast kidney, he passes a corner pub a short distance from his house, which is briefly and beautifully evoked:

> He approached Larry O'Rourke's. From the cellar grating floated up the flabby gush of porter. Through the open doorway the bar squirted out whiffs of ginger, teadust, biscuitmush. Good house, however: just the end of the city traffic.

This reminds me of a digression in *dark and true and tender*, a monograph about the pubs of Hull by Irish writer David Wheatley:

> There is a pub on Dublin's north side called Larry O' Rourke's, which is mentioned in *Ulysses*. Mr Bloom pauses to discuss the Russo-Japanese war of 1904 with Larry himself on Dorset Street. A few years ago the pub's name was changed to the James Joyce. In Joyce's name, a piece of genuine Joycean history is abolished. That's postmodernism, I tell them.*

*First printed in the *Dublin Review* 44 (Autumn 2011) and later published by CB editions as a pamphlet in 2012.

15. Clongowes Wood College—a Mission Statement

It was St Ignatius of Loyola, founder of the Society of Jesus (better known as the Jesuits), who said, although he's often misquoted: 'Give me a child till he is seven years old, and I will show you the man.'

Young James Joyce was, you might say, a late adoptee. At the age of six and a half he was despatched to the Jesuit institution of Clongowes Wood College where, for a while, he was nicknamed 'Half Past Six.'

Clongowes, a secondary boarding school twenty miles from Dublin in County Kildare, was (and is) run by the Jesuits. Around 450 boys study at there, and the annual fee is just over €20,000 a year. What's on offer is not just an education, but what we used to call a *schooling*.

Their website used to describe the aims and outcomes of a Jesuit education, and what kind of graduate the world can expect to encounter. I had the good sense to cut and paste the content some years ago, before it was entirely revised. Despite close scrutiny I could find no reference back then to their most celebrated old boy, and there's certainly none today—it appears to be the only place on the planet where Joyce has left no trace. I suspect it's what he would have wanted.

Here's what they used to say on their website:

The Aim of a Jesuit Education

We aim to form leaders in service in imitation of Christ Jesus, men and women of Competence, Conscience and Compassionate Commitment. [all upper case *sic*]

Competence embraces a broad spectrum of abilities—academic proficiency (including the ability to reason reflectively, logically and critically), technological and vocational skills, an appreciation of creative arts, sport and leisure, and effective communication skills.

A person of conscience discerns what is right, good and true, and has the courage to do it, takes a stand when necessary, has a passion for social justice and is an influential leader in the community.

A compassionate person responds to those in greatest need and walks with others to empower them, in solidarity and empathy; such a person manifests a preferential love of the poor, which 'ought to manifest itself in deeds rather than words.'

Competence in skills (intellectual and practical), allied to an informed conscience, which knows what is good, true and just and moves one to act according to those values, both involve the heart. A compassionate heart, which recognises the Lord presenting the faces of those in greatest need and which impels a response will be manifest in the profile of a Clongowes graduate.

Profile of a Graduate

If Clongowes Wood College is successful in its mission a Graduate will tend to be:

A grateful, honest and forgiving person
Committed to a Christian faith in a secular society, open to growth
Intellectually competent
Socially able
Culturally aware
Physically and emotionally developed
Committed to strive for excellence
Willing and able to exercise leadership

Joyce would score at best 3 out of 8 by this reckoning. As Flann O'Brien pointed out in his essay in *A Bash in the Tunnel* (see essay 85) our man confidently replaced the intellectual legacy of Jesuit casuistry with his own 'home-made chaosistry'.

16. WHAT REALLY HAPPENED ON 16TH JUNE

Nora Barnacle from Galway was working as a chambermaid at Finn's Hotel in Dublin, at the east end of South Leinster Street and the junction with Lincoln Place. She was twenty years old.

On 10th June 1904 Joyce saw her 'sauntering' (as he later said) along Nassau Street and was immediately attracted. He approached her and asked her for a date. She agreed but didn't turn up so he sent her an ardent note, care of Finn's: 'I hope you will be kind enough to make one with me—if you have not forgotten me!'. They met again on 16th June 1904—a Thursday—and walked together along the south bank of the Liffey to the suburb of Ringsend, where Nora slipped her hand inside his trousers and tugged him off. It's a moment rarely commemorated in the annual Bloomsday festivities, and that's a pity.

Joyce helpfully provided a vivid description in a letter to Nora, dated 3rd December 1909:

> It was you who slid your hand down inside my trousers and pulled my shirt softly aside and touched my prick with your long tickling fingers, and gradually took it all, fat and stiff as it was, into your hand and frigged me slowly until I came off through your fingers, all the time bending over me and gazing at me out of your quiet saintlike eyes. It was your lips too which first uttered an obscene word.

A prurient afterthought. While biographers are very keen to establish the earliest sexual experiences of their subject, they seldom trouble to uncover what may be the last. There are obvious reason for this, but still . . .

Joyce is a very sexy writer and as for the sex in *Finnegans Wake*—how long have you got? It's a book crammed with the most wonderful filth, a 'cathedral of lovejelly' to quote a favourite phrase. Characters are gender fluid, appearing in various non-binary incarnations such as 'the hemale' and there's an undertow of carnality throughout, much of it illicit, with a shadowy suggestion of incest between the protean Humphrey Chimpden Earwicker (whose initials HCE stand variously for 'Here Comes Everybody', 'Haveth Childers Everywhere', 'He'll Cheat Everyone' and 'Our Human Conger Eel') and his daughter. Sex in *Finnegans Wake* is messy, noisy, aromatic and hilarious, constantly implied but never quite achieved. In that respect, if no other, the novel resembles a 'Carry On' film. I leave the casting to others, but Sid James is clearly Earwicker and Hattie Jacques Anna Livia.

17. Annoying Noyes

Of all the vituperative critical assaults on *Ulysses* in the year of its publication the following review, by the poet Alfred Noyes in the *Sunday Chronicle* (29th October 1922), takes some beating. Here it is in full:

> I have picked on *Ulysses* because it brings to a head all the different questions that have been perplexing literary criticism for some time. There was no answer possible in this case. It is simply the foulest book that has ever found its way into print. Yet it has received columns of attention from many of the leading journals, and its author has been proclaimed a slightly mad genius, but still a genius.
>
> The writing in this book is simply bad as writing, and much of it is as obscure through sheer disorder of the syntax. But—there is no foulness conceivable to the mind of madman or ape that has not been poured into its imbecile pages.
>
> Yet some of our 'intellectuals', including one of our leading novelists, have been stating that its author comes within measurable distance of having written the best book in the world.
>
> No word or thought conceivable in Dublin or the New York Bowery is omitted, and the foulest references to real persons in this country, attributing vile diseases to them, amongst other equally disgusting suggestions.
>
> I have recited the case of this book because it is the extreme case of complete reduction of absurdity of what I have called the "literary Bolshevism of the hour." It can do little harm because the police are, on the whole, circumventing our pseudo-intellectuals.
>
> But what concerns all of us, and most urgently requires consideration, is that our Metropolitan criticism should be treating works such as those by Mr. Joyce seriously as a work of genius at the very moment when journal after journal is helping depreciate the value of some of the noblest pages in our literature.
>
> The battle that is being waged over the works of Tennyson, for instance, the assault that has been made on all the Victorian writers—and it is interesting to note that Bolshevik Russia has recently been declaring that Dickens is more dangerous than Denikin—are indications of the destructive spirit which may lead us on the road to barbarianism.

Noyes (1880–1958), a popular poet and writer in his day, was the author of, among many other titles, *Forty Singing Seamen and Other Poems*. He is today remembered (just about) as the author of a jolly ballad, very popular with English folk singers, called *The Highwayman*:

> The wind was a torrent of darkness among the gusty trees.
> The moon was a ghostly galleon tossed upon cloudy seas.
> The road was a ribbon of moonlight over the purple moor,
> And the highwayman came riding—
> Riding—riding—
> The highwayman came riding, up to the old inn-door.

He was only two years older than Joyce when his blimpish review appeared. With minor alterations it could be reprinted in the pages of the *Daily Mail* today, because the philistine position and the rhetorical armoury at their disposal never varies in tone or content, and never develops. Their lexicon of disparagement remains stuck in the early 20th century, along with their knowledge, taste and judgement. Noyes, querulous, confused and angry, cannot understand how a work of art that he condemns as foul can be acclaimed by other people whom he suspects (quite rightly) are much smarter than he is, people in a far better position to judge. He speaks, of course, for the majority of his philistine readers and his paymasters know this, which is why he gets the gig. The philistine is always confident, always indignant, always confused, seldom interesting, usually on the right politically and always, *always* wrong.

18. Eccles Street Revisited

On entering the Bloom residence at 7, Eccles Street early in the morning on a June day in 1904, you find yourself in a cluttered hallway with a crowded hallstand. To your left there's a door to the ground floor living-room and, further down the hall, another door to the back parlour which serves as the dining-room. From the rear window there's a view of a sizeable, untidy garden. Straight ahead a staircase leads down to the basement kitchen and up to the first floor bedroom where Molly and her Poldy are still asleep in their bedstead with the loose brass quoits; next to that their daughter Milly's room, no doubt kept 'just so' against her return from her job at the photographer's shop in Mullingar.

The top floor rooms, once occupied by live-in servants—a cook and a house-maid—are currently empty, a sign that the neighbourhood has come down in the world. The Blooms do have domestic help in the shape of a Mrs Fleming, who lives out. Molly has a low opinion of her.[*]

So it's a four-storey building with at least eight rooms, which seems rather large for their needs, although given the dilapidated outside jakes it's hardly a grand place. In 1967 the building was reduced to a single-storey facade and by the time I first visited the site in 1982 the remains were in the final stages of dilapidation, with the front doorway and window both bricked up, although the railings around the basement area were still in place.

There are other Eccles streets—in Belfast, Preston, Glasgow, Sheffield and Ramsbottom, near Bury—and there are three English towns called Eccles, the most famous in Lancashire (home of the eponymous cake) and the others in Norfolk and in Kent. As a surname Eccles first appears in Scotland in the second half of the 12th Century and today suggests, at least to an older generation of radio listeners, the serenely witless character in *The Goon Show* created

---

[*] An arrangement possibly shared with the best-known address in all of literature: the home of the world's only consulting detective at 221 Baker Street. In the canonical Conan Doyle stories and novels the address is always given thus—the more familiar '221B' derives from the later films. Much speculation surrounds the arrangements in the rest of the building. Where did Mrs Hudson, the housekeeper, live?

and played by Spike Milligan (or 'stately, plump Spike Milligan' as I like to think of him).

More fancifully, 'Eccles' is also the standard abbreviation for the Old Testament Book of Ecclesiastes, and this opens up a fresh line of wonky speculation. In *A Portrait of the Artist as a Young Man* Father Arnall, the Latin teacher at Clongowes Wood College, preaches a sermon during a three-day spiritual retreat dedicated to St Francis Xavier and begins by reflecting on the Four Last Things: death, judgment, hell and heaven. He chooses as his text 'In all thy works remember thy last end, and thou shalt never sin' which, he tells the boys, comes from the Old Testament Book of Ecclesiastes 7:40.

Oh no it doesn't. Chapter 7 of Ecclesiastes has only 29 verses; it doesn't go up to 40. Father Arnell's text is actually taken from *Ecclesiasticus* 7:40.

Ecclesiasticus, as any clued-up Jesuit should know, has nothing at all to do with Ecclesiastes. The former, also known as the Book of Sirach, is a Hebrew work of ethical teachings dating from around 200 BC and written by the Jewish scribe Ben Sira of Jerusalem; the latter is the more familiar Old Testament Book, the one that opens thus, in the King James Version:

> A good name is better than precious ointment; and the day of death than the day of one's birth.

Is the error Joyce's? Or Father Arnell's? Without a moment's hesitation I can tell you that I have no idea.

19. What I know about Mr Bloom

In the 'Nestor' episode of *Ulysses* Stephen's anti-Semitic employer Mr Deasy tells him that Ireland 'has the honour of being the only country that never persecuted the jews' then adding, with a banal flourish, 'And do you know why? Because she never let them in.'

He's not even wrong, as they say. In 1746 a bill had been introduced in the Irish House of Commons 'for naturalising persons professing the Jewish religion in Ireland', the first reference to Jews in the House up to this time.

In 1866, the year of Leopold Bloom's birth, only nine children were born to Jewish parents in Dublin and the city's Jewish community was in steep decline, numbering just a few hundred. It was only in the 1870s, with the arrival of Jewish immigrants from towns in north-western Lithuania, that the community revived. It grew to more than 2,000 by the end of the century and 3,000 by the outbreak of the Great War.

So Ireland did indeed 'let them in' and the Jewish population doubled in twenty years, with around 70% living in Dublin. It peaked at around 5,000 in the 1940s but has since undergone a second long-term decline, the result of assimilation and emigration. By the time of the 2011 census it had fallen to 1,984 and at the time of writing is closer to 1,000, in a country with a population of 4.6 million. There are now only four synagogues in the Republic—three in Dublin, one in Cork.*

Deasy's crass perspective is prompted by enduring anti-Semitic myths: Jews have 'sinned against the light', they covertly control the financial institutions and the press and have brought about the death of England. His unawareness of Ireland's (relatively) tolerant history is simply an aspect of his ignorance.

That Joyce made the main character of *Ulysses* a Dublin Jew with Hungarian roots is, on the face of it, paradoxical—that an Everyman should also be a member of a tiny minority. Joyce was certainly a philo-Semite, although this was part of a complex set of attitudes that

---

Lost in Little Jerusalem: Leopold Bloom and Irish Jewry by Cormac Ó Gráda of University College Dublin is published online as part of UCD's Project Muse, and recommended. The Irish theatre director and film maker Louis Lentin (1933–2014) made *No More Blooms*, an RTÉ documentary examining Ireland's attitude to the Jewish Refugee Problem, 1933–46.

deserve closer examination and I recommend David Pierce's *James Joyce's Ireland* (Yale University Press, 1992) for a lucid consideration of the subject.

Joyce consistently uses the lower case for jew/jewish, unlike T.S. Eliot whose notorious 'Gerontion' line 'The jew is underneath the lot' was not made any more tolerable by his later quietly changing 'jew' to 'Jew'. While his Dublin acquaintances invariably call him 'Bloom' (chummily or disparagingly), to his creator he's always a Mister. Mr Bloom.

Commentators tend to refer to him as Bloom, dropping the honorific. Joyce does too, come to think of it, throughout the 'Ithaca' episode (the one with the interminable questions and answers, e.g. 'What act did Bloom make on their arrival at their destination?'). But elsewhere it's always Mr Bloom and I like that—the formality, the detachment, the respect.

It strikes me that I know far more about the fictional Leopold Bloom than I know, or ever will know, about my own father. Not just the private stuff in either case—I mean the most basic information. I don't know the date of my father's birth, for instance, or even the year, for reasons I explain later in this book. I don't know anything much about what he thinks, or feels, or what matters to him. I really don't know him at all, and he doesn't know much about me, which is a loss to us both.

So what do I know about Mr Bloom?

I should begin by pointing out that, strictly speaking, Mr Bloom is not really a Jew but simply Jew-*ish*, because Jewishness is matrilineal and Bloom's mother Ellen wasn't a Jew. She was probably a Catholic, since she appears in the 'Circe' episode of *Ulysses* holding an Agnus Dei and swearing by the blessed Redeemer and Sacred Heart of Mary.

In the 'Ithaca' episode of *Ulysses* we also learn that Bloom's father Rudolf Virág (later Rudolph Bloom) 'had been converted from the Israelitic faith and communion in 1865 by the Society for promoting Christianity among the jews subsequently abjured by him in favour of Roman catholicism at the epoch of and with a view to his matrimony in 1888.' So Leopold, an only child, is the result of a mixed marriage.

In Ireland boys would traditionally follow their father's religion and girls their mother's, so Bloom was raised as a Protestant by his Jewish father but converted to Catholicism when he married Molly. His fellow Dubliners tend to see him as a Jew, and he sometimes chooses to identify as one.

What else do I know about Mr Bloom?

Let me count the ways, and I'll stop my list at 38, which is Mr Bloom's age in the novel. I should point out that what follows is ALL DONE FROM MEMORY in about half an hour, although I later checked some of the dates (correcting two of them) and amended my very approximate spelling of 'Szombathely'.

1. Mr Bloom was born in 1866.

2. Mr Bloom is the only child of Rudolf Virág, a Hungarian Jew from Szombathely and Ellen Higgins, an Irish Protestant. His father committed suicide by drinking poison. His mother is also dead, but I'm unsure of the details.

3. Mr Bloom married Marion Tweedy on 8th October 1888, converting from Judaism to Catholicism to do so.

4. Mr Bloom has a daughter, Millicent (born on 15th June the following year) who works in a photographic shop in Mullingar. His son Rudolph (Rudy) was born in late 1893 but died after 11 days.

5. Mr Bloom's mother-in-law was called Lunita Laredo, but Molly knows nothing much about her.

6. Mr and Mrs Bloom live in a four-storey terraced house at 7, Eccles Street, Dublin.

7. Mr Bloom's wife Molly is a singer who is having an affair with her manager, Hugh 'Blazes' Boylan. Mr Bloom knows this.

8. Mr Bloom carries a 'lucky potato' in his pocket, a custom widely regarded at the time as a cure for arthritis.

9. Mr Bloom works as a canvasser, organising advertising space in Dublin newspapers.

10. Mr Bloom is calm, thoughtful, humane and tolerant. He has a speculative nature, and hates violence. If there's a phrase in the novel to sum him up it's his 'unhasty friendliness'.

11. Mr Bloom is erratically well-read (see the catalogue of books in his modest library).

12. Mr Bloom likes the taste of offal.

13. Mr Bloom masturbates discreetly while watching a young girl playing on the beach.

14. Mr Bloom looks at his cat 'curiously, kindly'. Defining qualities.

15. Mr Bloom has plans for improving the city's tram system.

16. Mr Bloom is fastidious, revolted by the sight of a lunchtime crowd noisily wolfing down their grub.

17. Mr Bloom sleeps head-to-toe with his wife.

18. Mr Bloom is subject to low spirits (on the way home after buying his pork kidney, for instance).

19. Mr Bloom reads while at stool in the dilapidated jakes, the copy of *Reveille* also serving as his arse wipe.

20. Mr Bloom has modest poetic leanings, and is capable of drafting a decent acrostic.

21. Mr Bloom is a peaceful man but prepared to stand up to bullies.

22. Mr Bloom buys lemon-scented soap from Sweny's the chemist before heading to the public baths.

23. Mr Bloom corresponds with a woman named Martha Clifford of Dolphin's Barn, using the pseudonym Henry Flower. Mrs Bloom knows this.

24. Mr Bloom is generous, but keeps careful accounts.

25. Mr Bloom knows the meaning of the word 'metempsychosis'.

26. Mr Bloom is pale, pasty-faced, and not robust-looking.

27. Mr Bloom has an an eye for the ladies.

28. Mr Bloom has masochistic tendencies.

29. Mr Bloom is prone to delusions of grandeur (his meteoric social elevation in the 'Circe' episode for instance).

30. Mr Bloom enjoys puns and riddles, and word play: 'House of Key(e)s' for example.

31. Mr Bloom has many acquaintances, but no close friends.

32. Mr Bloom can be absent-minded (letting the breakfast kidney burn, forgetting to return his copy of Conan Doyle's *The Stark-Munro Letters* to his local library).

33. Mr Bloom was stung on the chest by a bee while sleeping in the Eccles Street garden on Easter Monday.

34. Mr Bloom is an attentive, loving husband, no longer in his prime.

35. Mr Bloom's peregrinations around Dublin after leaving his home take the form of an erratic question mark (and I think Frank Delaney was the first to point this out).

36. Mr Bloom wears a dark funeral suit throughout the day.

37. Mr Bloom is superstitious (see that lucky potato).

38. Mr Bloom is uncircumcised.

Of course the aforementioned 'Ithaca' episode in *Ulysses*—the extended catechism that comes before Molly Bloom's soliloquy—provides a vast amount of detailed information about Bloom's circumstances, memories, possessions, social contacts and so on, but none of these came to mind when I made the above list, and if I made another list tomorrow it might be completely different. My point, such as it is, is that I know far more about Mr Bloom, who doesn't even exist, than I do about my closest friends and members of my family. Make of that what you will.

20. The Buck stopped there

The academic Dr. David McCallister shared with me the following exchange between his undergraduate self and Professor John Sutherland when he (David) was a student at University College London in the late 1990s. Before I share it with you I should point out that he (David again) added that Professor Sutherland was a very helpful and supportive tutor at the time and is fondly remembered now. Here's the exchange:

> SUTHERLAND: So what are you tackling for our next tutorial?
>
> McCALLISTER: *Ulysses*, but not sure what topic yet.
>
> SUTHERLAND: I'll set a question. Write on 'the stately and the plump'.
>
> McCALLISTER: So just the first two words of a long and complex novel?
>
> SUTHERLAND: Yes, stately and plump. See you next week!

John Sutherland is a distinguished critic, prolific author and Emeritus Lord Northcliffe Professor of Modern English Literature at University College London. Inviting an undergraduate to write about the two first words of *Ulysses* is a neat tutorial trick which lets the tutor off the hook when it comes to reading the novel again, although I'm struck by Sutherland's use, twice, of the definite article; it's like saying *The Pride and the Prejudice* (which in turn sounds like a mid-century Hollywood blockbuster).

McCallister, then a third year student, turned in a decent piece of work and went on to greater things—he is now Senior Lecturer in Victorian Literature at Birkbeck College, University of London. But the nagging question remains, and I'm sorry to be so blunt: has Professor Sutherland ever read *Ulysses*?

In *How to Be Well Read: A Guide to 500 Great Novels* (2014) Sutherland made the surprising claim that Leopold Bloom is childless, although as anyone who has read the novel will know he has a daughter (the aforementioned Milly) and a son (Rudi), who died in infancy and whose spectral appearance is arguably the climax of the novel. The previous year Sutherland had stated, in *A Little History of Literature* (2013), that Bloom is a 'clerk' or 'desk-slave'. He is neither, and to claim so is like insisting that Yossarian in *Catch-22* is a New Orleans cop. This led to a flurry of online speculation that he hadn't read the entire novel and the Buck, you might say, stopped there.

Sutherland has elsewhere made some strikingly off-kilter statements about *Ulysses*, claiming in a newspaper interview that it is 'a novel without a single working-class character' (there are many) and that 'most of it is about sex and crapping' (if only). His bizarre comments were prompted by Jeremy Corbyn, the Labour Party leader at the time, expressing an interest in the novel, a preference that Sutherland found objectionable for reasons that probably made sense to him at the time.*

John Sutherland came to public attention thanks to the best-selling books *Is Heathcliff a murderer?* and *Can Jane Eyre be Happy?*, two entertaining collections of essays about Victorian fiction in which he applies close reading techniques to highlight anachronisms and inconsistencies, slips and gaffes. He appears on this occasion to have been hoist by his own petard, whatever that means.

---

*Speaking to Peter Carey of the *Guardian* (14th June 2019) Corbyn said he recalled first reading the novel in the early 1980s, while travelling round Europe and north Africa by train. An Irish friend had told him to take a copy on a journey that proved endless. He didn't tackle it from start to finish, and apparently has never done so, instead regularly dipping into favourite passages. It's an approach he recommends to first time readers today:

> Read a little bit at a time and think about it and then move on, but don't beat yourself up if you don't understand it.

It's an approach I've adopted for *Finnegans Wake* but I'm not convinced that it works so well with *Ulysses*, which is a scrupulously-constructed circadian novel rather than the linguistic equivalent of an all-you-can-eat buffet.

21. CRAYONING ACHIEVEMENT

In *Iron Man 2*, the 2010 superhero movie directed by Jon Favreau, the corporate arms dealer Justin Hammer (played by Sam Rockwell) describes to his clients, with eloquent relish, some high-tech armour-piercing missiles:

> These are the Cubans, baby. This is the Cohibas, the Montecristos. (*He takes a small missile out of a box.*) This is a kinetic-kill, side-winder vehicle with a secondary cyclotrimethylene-trinitramine RDX burst. It's capable of busting a bunker under the bunker you just busted. If it were any smarter, it'd write a book, a book that would make *Ulysses* look like it was written in crayon. It would read it to you. This is my Eiffel Tower. This is my Rachmaninoff's Third. My *Pietà*. It's completely elegant, it's bafflingly beautiful, and it's capable of reducing the population of any standing structure to zero.

Hammer's monologue is an example of *radiant particularisation*, a useful linguistic term coined by the writer Jonathan Meades.[*] It's a form of competitive rhetorical one-upmanship employed here by Shakespeare in *Timon of Athens*:

> Painter: Y'are a dog.
>
> Apemantus: Thy mother's of my generation. What's she, if I be a dog?

Apemantus ('philosopher and churl') slices the Painter's crude serve back across the net and, in so doing, raises the game in an escalating exchange that would ideally continue until one or the other admits defeat. In the *Iron Man* monologue Hammer battles energetically with himself for verbal supremacy in a giddy succession of superlatives ending, appropriately enough, in a depopulated void, a zero. It's a performance reminiscent of something John Keats said in a letter to his close friend, the painter Benjamin Robert Haydon, on 8th March 1819:

> Conversation is not a search after knowledge, but an endeavour at effect.

---

[*]1. See 'Spode' in his debut short story collection *Filthy English*, published by Jonathan Cape in 1984.

Cuban cigars aside, Hammer's cultural references are all European and therefore, in Hollywood terms, exotic, decadent and potentially treacherous. Such highbrow foreign achievements—all *non*-American and therefore *un*-American—are a scriptwriter's indulgence but, as the screenwriter Justin Theroux may be surprised to learn, *Ulysses* was indeed written in something close to crayon, as Joyce's publisher Sylvia Beach recalled:

> *Ulysses*, like everything else of Joyce's, was written entirely by hand. He used blunt black pencils—he found the ones he wanted at [W.H.] Smith's in Paris—and pencils of different colours to distinguish the parts he was working on. Fountain pens he didn't understand at all. They bewildered him. Once I found him struggling to fill one, covering himself with ink as he did so.

22. Tramways and sigla

The 'Aeolus' episode of *Ulysses* (the one set mostly in the offices of *The Freeman's Journal*) opens with an evocative description of the Dublin United Tramways Company terminus on O'Connell Bridge, the hub of what was then the most modern and complex system in Europe, extending for 54 route miles:

IN THE HEART OF THE HIBERNIAN METROPOLIS

Before Nelson's pillar trams slowed, shunted, changed trolley, started for Blackrock, Kingstown and Dalkey, Clonskea, Rathgar and Terenure, Palmerston Park and upper Rathmines, Sandymount Green, Rathmines, Ringsend and Sandymount Tower, Harold's Cross. The hoarse Dublin United Tramway Company's timekeeper bawled them off:

—Rathgar and Terenure!

—Come on, Sandymount Green!

Right and left parallel clanging ringing a doubledecker and a singledeck moved from their railheads, swerved to the down line, glided parallel.

—Start, Palmerston Park!

Elsewhere in *Ulysses* Mr Bloom speculates in his mild commonsensical way about how Dublin might improve its transport infrastructure:

I can't make out why the corporation doesn't run a tramline from the Parkgate to the quays.

And later his voyeuristic gaze, directed intently at a woman climbing into a carriage ('Watch! Watch! Silk flash rich stockings white. Watch!'), is rudely interrupted when a tramcar suddenly slews in between them.

At the end of the 'Sirens' episode Mr Bloom has a flatulent feeling which he blames on his lunchtime burgundy. He exercises restraint until the noise of a passing tram offers him the chance to let rip in public.

Prrprr.

Must be the bur.

Fff. Oo. Rrpr.

Nations of the earth. No-one behind. She's passed. Then and not till then. Tram. Kran, kran, kran. Good oppor. Coming. Krandlkrankran. I'm sure it's the burgund. Yes. One, two. Let my epitaph be. Karaaaaaaa. Written. I have.

Pprrpffrrppfff.

Done.

There are two penny tram fares listed when Mr Bloom tots up his accounts at the end of the day. One took him to Newbridge Avenue, a short walk from the Dignam house, the second took him back from Sandymount in the evening to the maternity hospital.

Mr Bloom would, I'm sure, enjoy *The Bloomsday Trams: Dublin's Tramway Fleet of James Joyce's Ulysses* by David Foley M.A. (Book-Surge, 2009), the most engagingly niche perspective on the novel I've ever read. The author admits in his introduction that he 'was unprepared for how difficult this task was to become' although he is commendably undaunted by any slight claim Joyce may have to being a great novelist. The first chapter lists 'those tramway references that need explanation and in some cases correction from Joyce.' The most startling fact among many startling facts is that between 1903 and 1918 most Dublin trams carried symbols instead of numbers to show their route and destination.

Frank Delaney (see essay 89, 'De minimis non shabby curate lex') shared some typically lucid thoughts on the subject in *James Joyce's Odyssey. A Guide to the Dublin of Ulysses* (Paladin, 1987):

> The tram which went from Glasnevin to Rialto bore a brown lozenge badge to indicate its route. From Nelson's Pillar to Sandymount was indicated by a green crescent. A green shamrocked tram bore you to Dalkey, a green Maltese Cross from Rathfarnham to Drumcondra. Two blue diamonds decorated the tram which linked Donnybrook to the Phoenix Park and a white circle tram reached the quiet pools of Palmerston Park. It didn't, therefore, matter whether you could read. All that mattered was whether you walked. The tram conductor's manual urged: "Keep a sharp lookout for passengers and by signalling, induce persons to travel who would otherwise walk".

The chart reproduced overleaf gives the 17 routes and their associated symbols, which were supplemented by name boards on each

The Cars on the Several Routes are distinguished, in addition to the Name Boards on each side and the Destination Indicators at either end, by the following Signs above the destination Indicators:-

NELSON'S PILLAR AND TERENURE *(VIA RATHMINES)*	△	RATHFARNHAM AND DRUMCONDRA *(VIA HAROLD'S CROSS)*	⊠
NELSON'S PILLAR AND DARTRY ROAD *(VIA UPPER RATHMINES)*	◭	RIALTO AND GLASNEVIN *(VIA DOLPHIN'S BARN)*	◆
DONNYBROOK AND PHŒNIX PARK *(VIA MERRION SQUARE)*	◇◇	NELSON'S PILLAR AND DALKEY	✤
DONNYBROOK AND PHŒNIX PARK *(VIA STEPHEN'S GREEN)*	⩗⩗	NELSON'S PILLAR AND CLONSKEA *(VIA LEESON STREET)*	◠◠
KINGSBRIDGE AND HATCH STREET *(VIA SOUTHERN QUAYS & WESTLAND ROW)*	□	NELSON'S PILLAR & SANDYMOUNT *(VIA RINGSEND)*	◡
PARK GATE AND BALLYBOUGH	◈	NELSON'S PILLAR & DOLLYMOUNT	▽
INCHICORE AND WESTLAND ROW	⬮	COLLEGE GREEN & WHITEHALL *(VIA CAPEL ST. & DRUMCONDRA)*	♡
O'CONNELL BRIDGE & PARK GATE *(VIA NORTHERN QUAYS)*	□	KENILWORTH ROAD AND LANSDOWNE ROAD	◻
NELSON'S PILLAR & PALMERSTON PARK	○		

Dublin tramway route symbols

side of the tram and destination boards at either end. How these seemingly random symbols were chosen is anyone's guess, but they served to make the tram services originating and terminating at Nelson's Pillar more intelligible for passengers.

At night, trams carrying these symbols would also have an array of different coloured lights to aid identification, described in the 'Circe' episode, which opens at 'the Mabbot street entrance of nighttown, before which stretches an uncobbled tramsiding set with skeleton tracks, red and green will-o'-the-wisps and danger signals.' *

Two of the capital's tram services never carried any symbols, however. One was the route to Sandymount (operated by unique single-decker trams because of a low overhead railway bridge in Bath Avenue, so no further identification was necessary); the other was to Howth, which was operated by another company and which had a fleet of very distinctive bogie cars that needed no additional decoration. It's a coincidence that Howth and Sandycove, both places with a particular Joycean connection, should share this distinction.

---

*In the 'Eumaeus' episode 'a Dublin United Tramways Company's sandstrewer' passes Bloom and Stephen, prompting the former to mention his close encounter with one of these machines at the beginning of the 'Circe' episode.

Can there—and this is a wild speculation—can there be a remote connection between these tram symbols and the sigla (i.e. signs, from the singular *siglum*, a diminutive of the Latin word *signum* meaning 'sign' or 'mark') employed by Joyce during the creation of *Finnegans Wake*, marks which helped the author to navigate the dense thickets of accumulating prose, each sign referring to a particular character?

I expect that if there's anything at all to to this speculation it will already have been exhaustively explored by proper scholars. It strikes me that the *Wake*, along with a handful of sacred books, must be among the most closely-scrutinised texts ever published, with every word analysed, annotated and subject, much of the time, to a consensus. Admittedly that's a consensus involving a relatively small community of dedicated admirers, but this still prompts the question: is there anything left to find out about the *Wake*? Any undiscovered seam yet to be mined? Or has it by now been collectively exhausted?

The answer to the last question is no, because the jury is still out on some very fundamental equations—such as whether the *Wake* is a dream at all and, if so, whose. There's still work to be done.

Between 1938 and 1940 Dublin's trams—all 330 of them—were decommissioned and replaced with 220 double-decker buses built by the Leyland Company in England. Their promotional slogan could have come from the pages of *Finnegans Wake*: 'When you bury a tram, mark the spot with a Titan'.

23. HEAVEN SCENT

the nice perfumios that came cunvy peeling off him (nice!) which
was angelic simply, savouring of wild thyme and parsley jumbled
with breadcrumbs (O nice!)

—Finnegans Wake

One bright warm June afternoon in the last century I was walking
alone along the rue de la Trinité in Paris when I suddenly became
aware of a fragrance which set my nerves jangling, my head spinning,
my heart thumping, my pulse racing. Looking around, I saw an in-
timidatingly chic dark-haired woman in a fur coat walking towards
Odéon. I was 19 and she may have been in her thirties, or forties, or
sixties. In a moment of uncharacteristic bravado I trotted after her
and, in my stammering schoolboy French (it's got far worse since
then), asked her what it was that made her smell like that (a pretty
accurate translation of my gauche interrogation). She shrugged and
smiled and said 'Mais . . . c'est *Vol de nuit*, monsieur,' and continued
on her way. I doubt that the encounter made her day, but it certainly
made mine. I continued along the street in the cool shade of the great
church, rendered light-headed by the gorgeous aftermath of her passing.

Later that week in the department store Samaritaine I tracked
down the perfume and, faced with an aloof, enamelled and sceptical assistant, I managed to blag a sample, dabbing it self-consciously
on my left wrist. Leaving the building I crossed the river and headed
eastwards along the Quai de l'Horloge in the company of a vaporous
spirit guide. I could still detect a faint trace of the fragrance in my
hotel room the following morning.

The creation of Jacques Guerlain, it was launched in 1933 and
named after Antoine de Saint Saint-Exupéry's 1931 novel *Night Flight*
(a marvellous account of the early days of aviation from the author
of *Le petit prince*). The top notes are bergamot, galbanum and petit grain; below that jasmine, daffodil and spices; the base combines
earthy woodsy notes of iris and vanilla—together combining into
the most alluring and complex aroma, or succession of aromas, you
can possibly imagine. The gorgeous chunky glass bottle represents a
rapidly spinning aircraft propeller and legend has it that the perfume
was concocted for, or at least worn by, professional courtesans flying

overnight from Paris to North Africa between the wars. Imagine that. It has a fabulous *sillage* which lasts for hours.

Sillage—pronounced 'see-yage'—is a wonderful word for an absolutely wonderful thing: the scented trail left by the wearer of a fragrance. It translates more or less as 'wake' in English—as in the trace left in the sky by an aeroplane, or the white water behind a speedboat, and nothing at all to do with funerals.* Perfumes are activated by body heat, which is why they're applied to the wearer's pulse points, those places where the blood pumps near the skin's surface: the wrists, the neck, behind the ears.

Joyce was not boasting when he said that he had discovered he could do anything with language. In his fine book *James Joyce and the Making of Ulysses* (1934), Frank Budgen recalled the following conversation:

> I enquired about Ulysses. Was it progressing?
>
> "I have been working hard on it all day," said Joyce.
>
> "Does that mean that you have written a great deal?" I said.
>
> "Two sentences," said Joyce.
>
> I looked sideways but Joyce was not smiling. I thought of Flaubert.
>
> "You have been seeking the *mot juste*?" I said.
>
> "No," said Joyce. "I have the words already. What I am seeking is the perfect order of words in the sentence. There is an order in every way appropriate. I think I have it."
>
> "What are the words?" I asked.
>
> "I believe I told you," said Joyce, "that my book is a modern Odyssey. Every episode in it corresponds to an adventure of Ulysses. I am now writing the Lestrygonians episode, which corresponds to the adventure of Ulysses with the cannibals. My hero is going to lunch. But there is a seduction motive in the Odyssey, the cannibal king's daughter. Seduction appears in my book as women's silk petticoats hanging in a shop window. The words through which I express the

---

*Samuel Beckett had another take on the literary *sillage* of his friend and mentor. Writing in August 1931 to Charles Prentice (who worked for the publisher Chatto & Windus) about his novel *Echo's Bones*, he said 'Of course it stinks of Joyce, in spite of my most earnest endeavours to endow it with my own odours.' I once asked Beckett's god-daughter, the musician and author Alba Arikha, what her godfather smelled like. Cigars, she said, though not unpleasantly so.

effect of it on my hungry hero are: 'Perfume of embraces all him assailed. With hungered flesh obscurely, he mutely craved to adore.' You can see for yourself in how many different ways they might be arranged."

The whole passage from which this is taken is one of matchless sensuality and worth typing out in full:

A warm human plumpness settled down on his brain. His brain yielded. Perfume of embraces all him assailed. With hungered flesh obscurely, he mutely craved to adore.

There's another moment in *Ulysses*, in the 'Nausicaa' episode, when Mr Bloom smells Gerty McDowell's scent and thinks of Molly, his wife:

Wait. Hm. Hm. Yes. That's her perfume. Why she waved her hand. I leave you this to think of me when I'm far away on the pillow. What is it? Heliotrope? No, Hyacinth? Hm. Roses, I think. She'd like scent of that kind. Sweet and cheap: soon sour. Why Molly likes opoponax. Suits her with a little jessamine mixed. Her high notes and her low notes. At the dance night she met him, dance of the hours. Heat brought it out. She was wearing her black and it had the perfume of the time before.'*

Opoponax is, according to perfumesociety.org, 'a wonderful name for a glorious gum resin ingredient that's smokey and soft, luminous and sensual all at once.' It reportedly smells like crushed ivy leaves, or of angelica, frankincense and celery. The resin is extracted from the bark of the *Commiphora eyrthraea* tree (mostly from Somalia), and is also known as 'sweet myrrh'.

I was delighted to discover a range of 'highbrow lotions' inspired by *Finnegans Wake*, available from the Italian perfumer Mirko Buffini. Here, verbatim, is an extract from the company website[†]:

I belong to you and you belong to me

"H.C.E." collection is made up of 10 fragrances marked by special words coming from the novel "finnegans wake" written by James Joyce.

---

*Cited in Laura Frost's 'James Joyce and the Scent of Modernity', a chapter in her book *The Problem with Pleasure: Modernism and its Discontents*, p 55

[†]www.mirkobiffinifirenze.com

The main character of "finnegans wake" is a middle-aged man owner of a tavern, named Humphrey Chimpden Earwicker, often shortened to "H.C.E.", which means also "here comes everybody", the expression that identifies the "everyman" of Joyce.

He is both an ordinary man and Father at the same time.*

---

*The ten fragrances are: Finnegan, From, Gigot, Herma, Mr. Fry, NNN, Wake, Woid, Youth and Zeit, all priced between €29.00 and €160.00. The first named fragrance is part of the 'woody, spicy' olfactory family. The website strapline for the Finnegan fragrance is: 'Catchy chours of evey day' [*sic*], which isn't a line from the novel. The website also gives details of the company's founder:

> Founded in 2012 by the namesake designer, Mirko Buffini Firenze plunge its roots in the tradition of Florentine perfumery school. The olfactory experience of Mirko Buffini starts with a gift received from a friend: a fragrance that inspires his tireless research of the perfect perfume. Mirko Buffini Firenze's fragrances keep all the olfactory notes gathered during different journeys beyond the traditional geographic borderds, [*sic*] in which the excellence of Made in Italy is seen as the starting and ending point, emphasizing the quality of row [*sic*] materials and the artisan process.

24. Mrkgnao!

Ulysses has been translated into French twice. The first translation was by Auguste Morel in 1929, a version approved by Joyce himself and published by the bookseller and writer Adrienne Monnier (1892–1955) under her imprint La Maison des Amis des Livres.

Monnier was among the first women in France to found and run a bookshop, thanks to her father Clovis, a postal sorter (*postier ambulant*) who was employed on the French equivalent of Britain's night mail service. He was seriously injured in a train crash in 1913 and passed on to his daughter the entire sum he received in compensation—10,000 Francs. This she used to set up her business.

Adrienne Monnier was also the founder of the magazine *Le Navire d'Argent*, a vital part of the literary scene of 1920s Paris, the first edition of which, in May 1925, contained a French-language translation prepared jointly by Monnier and Sylvia Beach of 'The Love Song of J. Alfred Prufrock'. Monnier offered Beach advice and support when the latter set up Shakespeare and Company in rue de l'Odéon, opposite Monnier's shop in the Latin Quarter. The two women were partners both in business and in life.

The second translation of *Ulysses* appeared in 2004 and involved a team of eight, led by Jacques Aubert (1932–2020) as technical director.* One of the translators, Bernard Hœpffner, wrote a fascinating account of this collaboration for *The Paris Review* (25th July 2017) with examples of the ingenious solutions negotiated en route:

> The problem posed by 'throwaway', which appears nineteen times in *Ulysses*, is that sometimes it's the name of a racehorse, sometimes it has to do with a leaflet, sometimes it's a verb, and it seems to be irresoluble. Pascal proposes translating the name with 'Jetsam', which would let us play off 'jette ça', while the object would be a 'prospectus'. The echo split in two. Proposition accepted by all.

---

*The translators of the 2004 edition were Tiphaine Samoyault (*Les Lestrygons, Les Sirènes, Le Cyclope, Pénélope*), Patrick Drevet (*Hadès, Nausicaa*), Sylvie Doizelet (*Charybde et Scylla*), Bernard Hœpffner (*Éole, Circé,* Itahque), Marie-Danièle Vors (*Calypso*), Jacques Aubert (*Télémaque, Les Rochers Errants*), Pascal Bataillard (*Protée, Les Lotophages, Eumée*) and Michel Cusin (*Nestor*). This edition retained the 1929 translation of *Les Bœufs du Soleil* (*Oxen of the Sun*) by Auguste Morel, Stuart Gilbert and Valery Larbaud.

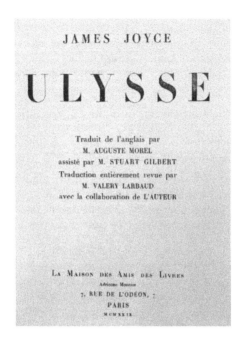

JAMES JOYCE

U L Y S S E

Traduit de l'anglais par
M. AUGUSTE MOREL
assisté par M. STUART GILBERT
Traduction entièrement revue par
M. VALERY LARBAUD
avec la collaboration de L'AUTEUR

LA MAISON DES AMIS DES LIVRES
Adrienne Monnier
7, RUE DE L'ODÉON, 7
PARIS
MCMXXIX

Title page of Morel's *Ulysse*

How to choose between the two French translations? We might compare two versions of the passage in which Bloom speculates about his cat (and I've tweaked the length of lines for easier comparison). Here's the original:

— Milk for the pussens, he said.

— Mrkgnao! the cat cried.

They call them stupid. They understand what we say better than we understand them.

She understands all she wants to. Vindictive too. Wonder what I look like to her.

Height of a tower? No, she can jump me.

Now here's the Morel translation from 1929:

— Du lait pour la minouche!

— Mrkrgnaô!

On prétend qu'ils ne sont pas intelligents. Ils nous comprennent mieux que nous ne les comprenons. Elle comprend tout ce qui concerne ses besoins. Et la mémoire des offenses. Me demande comment je lui apparais. Haut comme une tour? Non, elle me saute sur le dos.

And here's the same passage from the Aubert edition of 2004:

— Du lait pour la minette ! dit-il.

— Mrkrgnao ! se plaignit la chatte.

On dit qu'ils sont stupides. Ils comprennent ce que nous disons mieux que nous ne les comprenons. Elle comprend tout ce qu'elle veut. Et rancunière avec ça. Me demande de quoi j'ai l'air pour elle. Aussi haut qu'une tour ? Non, elle peut sauter plus haut que ma tête.

I'm charmed by the change from the English 'Mrkgnao!' to the Gallic 'Mrkrgnaô!' in the 1929 translation, and by the later reversion to 'Mrkrgnao!', a decision that must have been the subject of much heated discussion. It would be a Herculean task to compare the two versions (which should surely be published as a single volume, interleaved) and, without having the expertise to judge, I'm drawn to the original simply because it comes with Joyce's approval. But a translator friend who knows far more about the French language than I do reckons that the Aubert version is by far the better of the two. Of the Morel she singles out 'Elle comprend tout ce qui concerne ses besoins' as a 'simply awful' translation of 'She understands all she wants to.' Fair enough, although I'm in two minds about the exclamation marks imposed on Bloom in both versions—too frisky?[*]

To celebrate the publication of the original French translation Adrienne Monnier organised a luncheon at the Léopold Restaurant in Les Vaux de Cernay, a small village near Versailles, on Tuesday 27th June 1929. The guests included Léon-Paul Fargue, Eduard Dujardin, Paul Valéry, Jules Romains, and Philippe Soupault, although oddly enough none of the translators was invited.

---

[*] *Ulysses* is not the most frequently translated book by an Irish writer. That honour goes to John Boyne's *The Boy in the Striped Pyjamas* (2006), a Holocaust fiction described by the Auschwitz-Birkenau State Museum as one that 'should be avoided by anyone who studies or teaches about the Holocaust.' Boyne claims he wrote the entire first draft in two and a half days, 'without sleeping much'. It has to date appeared in 47 languages.

Here's the menu in full:

Le Paté Léopold

Les quenelles de veau Toulouse

Le poulet de Bresserôti

Les pommes nouvelles au beurre

La salade de laitue mimosa

Les fromages variés

La tarte aux fraises du jardin

Vin blanc, vin rose, vin rouge

Passe-tout-grain de nuits (a red or rosé wine produced within Bourgogne appellation)

Moulin-à-Vent (the highest rated of all the Beaujolais Crus)

Cafe filtre

Liqueurs

Also in attendance was Samuel Beckett, who doesn't appear in the group photograph, reportedly because he was too pissed to stand up straight.

This was among the first public celebrations of the book and I wonder if there's ever been any attempt since then to recreate this modest menu. Today's Bloomsday celebrants tend to go for the kidney-fried-in-butter breakfast or the gorgonzola-sandwich-and-burgundy lunch. Dinner doesn't get a look-in.

The restaurant is still trading as Les Salons Léopold at route des Cascades, 78720 Cernay-la-Ville, France.

25. WHAT ARE THE ODDS?

Here's a well-known photograph of Joyce and his publisher Sylvia Beach sitting together in her office at Shakespeare and Company (12, rue de l'Odéon) and, behind them, two newspaper placards, no doubt obtained locally, and surreptitiously.

Bookmakers: publisher and author (photographer unknown)

The top one, advertising *Sporting Life* (known colloquially as 'The Pink 'Un') screams *THE SCANDAL OF "ULYSSES"*, below which are some horse racing odds:

SARGON (5–1)
SQUARE DANCE (9–2)
KILLEEN (7–2)
KILVEMNON (7–2)

Sargon and Kilvemnon had, according to the *Pall Mall Gazette* (27th March 1922), both won their respective races at Warwick and *Sporting Life* had tipped them both, which explains the placard. 'The Pink 'Un's' literary critic was an anonymous hack named 'Aramis', whose view was that

> [*Ulysses*] appears to have been written by a perverted lunatic who has made a speciality of the literature of the latrine ... I have no stomach for *Ulysses*. [. . .] James Joyce is a writer of talent, but in

Ulysses he has ruled out all the elementary decencies of life and dwells appreciatively on things that sniggering louts of schoolboys guffaw about. In addition to this stupid glorification of mere filth, the book suffers from being written in the manner of a demented George Meredith. There are whole chapters of it without any punctuation or other guide to what the writer is really getting at. Two-thirds of it is incoherent, and the passages that are plainly written are devoid of wit, displaying only a coarse salacrity [*sic*] intended for humour.

Later in the review 'Aramis' says, memorably, that *Ulysses* would 'make a Hottentot sick'.

There's a second placard in the photograph announcing the author Arnold Bennett's review of the novel, which appeared in *The Bookman* (August 1922). 'I see nothing very wonderful in this' he harrumphed.

Has there ever been an anthology of authors writing about *Ulysses*? By which I mean a collection of writings for and against by other novelists, contemporaries of Joyce, whether in reviews or essays or letters or diary entries? And has there ever been a collection of the countless *negative* reviews published over the past century, of the greatest novel ever written? That could be interesting, and form the basis for a chapter in my long-planned *Short History of Philistinism*.

My take on the subject—hardly original—is that throughout the 19th and 20th centuries and in our time, any innovation in the arts, from *The Rite of Spring* to *Anarchy in the UK*, from the Fauves to the *Entartete Kunst*, from Alfred Jarry's *Ubu Roi* to Beckett's *En attendant Godot*, from Duchamp's 'Fountain' to Carl Andre's 'Equivalent VIII', has been met with precisely the same incomprehension, hostility, derision and mockery, the artists invariably depicted as cynical conmen trying to pull a fast one on the public in order to make a dishonest living.

If I can persuade a publisher to back the project I'd start start my researches at the James Joyce Collection in the University of Buffalo, the source of the photograph that prompted this essay. Looking at the website page that summarises the unrivalled contents of the collection and then at the magnificent catalogue I found myself reflecting glumly on the lack of a paper trail left by most writers these days:

> Covering the entire span of his artistic life, the James Joyce Collection is the largest Joyce collection in the world and contains his

private library; holograph drafts, typescript pages and corrected galleys and page proofs for *Ulysses*; 66 notebooks, transcriptions, typescripts, galleys, page proofs and the author's copy with corrections of *Finnegans Wake*; documents for *A Portrait of the Artist as a Young Man* and Joyce's lecture on Daniel Defoe; the notebook for *Exiles*; hundreds of letters between Sylvia Beach and Joyce; Beach's printing records for the publication of *Ulysses*; John Quinn's letters to Beach and Joyce regarding the trial over *Ulysses* and *The Little Review* as well as other Joyce and Beach correspondence; Joyce's presentation copies to Beach; portraits and over 150 photographs of Joyce and his family; numerous personal artifacts [*sic*] owned by Joyce; thousands of his newspaper clippings; and notebooks, sketchbooks and letters by Joyce's daughter Lucia Joyce. Supplementing the archive is a complete set of first editions, including all issues and states of every book published by Joyce, translations, a large number of his magazine appearances and virtually all the literary criticism in book form on Joyce.

The founding donation, known as The Wickser Gift after its donor, consisted of the contents of the Librairie La Hune's Joyce exposition, held in Paris in 1949 to raise funds for the Joyce family. It included manuscripts, Patrick Tuohy's portraits of Joyce and his father and other items of memorabilia. Perhaps the most extraordinary part of this gift was Joyce's private library, which arrived in Buffalo in the same condition as it was when packed for storage after Joyce left Paris to flee the Nazi occupation. Further acquisitions came over the years from, among others, Marie Jolas and Sylvia Beach. It's fully catalogued and available to inspect online.

But back to the Turf. A racehorse features in one of the few conventional plot points in *Ulysses*, one worthy of a modern-day situation comedy. Bloom bumps into a Dublin loafer named Bantam Lyons outside Sweny's chemist shop and offers him his newspaper ('—I say you can keep it, Mr Bloom answered. I was going to throw it away.'). Lyons thinks this is a tip for a horse named Throwaway, an outsider running in that day's Epsom Gold Cup. The tip is passed around Dublin and Lenehan later claims that Bloom had himself placed a big wager on Throwaway at odds of five to one. The horse comes from behind to win (as happened in real life) and there follow some predictably anti-Semitic speculations about the Jews having a hand in everything. (The problem 'Throwaway' posed for the French translators is touched upon in the previous essay.)

Still on the Turf, one of many revelations in Vivien Igoe's book *The Real People of Joyce's Ulysses: A Biographical Guide* (University College Dublin Press, 2016) is about the jockey Herbert 'Morny' Cannon, who appears in the novel. Here's Bloom, musing about the Epsom Gold Cup: 'Zinfandel's the favourite, Lord Howard de Walden's, won at Epsom. Morny Cannon is riding him[.]' What I didn't know is that Cannon was great-uncle of the legendary jockey Lester Piggott (b. 1935). Cannon rode his first winner at the age of 13 and was, like his great-nephew, a phenomenal jockey. It must run in the family.

26. AUTOLYCUS AT BLETCHLEY PARK

In 2015 the American entertainer Cher (b. 1946) shared her thoughts on Twitter about immigration and what she saw as the threat from radical Islamist militants. Her tweet was accompanied by an elaborate series of emojis (all the rage back then), which prompted a pithy response from one Bandon Stosuy, Editor in Chief of *The Creative Independent*. He tweeted (at 1:09am on 1st Dec 2015) 'Cher is the James Joyce of emojis', attracting 55 likes.

If Cher is the James Joyce of emojis, does that make James Joyce the Cher of literature? Does it work like that? Joyce, who had a keen interest in cryptology, in codes and ciphers, would surely have seen the potential of emoticons and emojis. He would have felt at home among the polyglot wartime code-breakers of Bletchley Park.

In *Ulysses* Leopold Bloom keeps tucked away in an unlocked bedroom drawer '3 letters in reserved alphabetic boustrephodontic punctated quadrilinear cryptogram (vowels suppressed) N.IGS./WI.UU.OX /W.OKS.MH/Y.IM'.

In case that's not immediately clear, David Kahn's fascinating book *The Code-Breakers* (1967) offers a helpful gloss.[*] 'Quadrilinear' means 'in four lines'; 'reversed alphabetic' means 'a = z, b = y, c = x etc'; 'boustrephodontic' is derived from a paleographic term describing a text that runs left and right on alternate lines (a pattern used incorrectly by Bloom in the coded *aide-mémoire* of his correspondent's address in Dolphin's Barn).

Here's the solution:

```
N.IGS.
martha
WI.UU.OX
droffilc
W.OKS.MH
dolphins
Y.IM
barn
```

Joyce's friend John F. Byrne, (a former real-life resident at 7, Eccles Street) was the inventor, in 1918, of an unbreakable encryption sys-

---

[*] *The Codebreakers: The Comprehensive History of Secret Communication from Ancient Times to the Internet* by David Khan (Scribner, 2nd revised edition, 1997).

tem he called the Chaocipher. This homespun version of the Enigma machine consisted of some bits of string and other odds and ends and could fit in a cigar box, but was enough to make his sister declare that he deserved a Nobel Prize.[*]

Byrne's simple and ingenious cipher is based on two rotatable rings, each inscribed with the 26 letters of the alphabet. On Byrne's version these rings were adjacent to each another and engaged at a point on their respective circumferences, but most descriptions of the system use concentric rings for clarity and simplicity. The inner ring is known as the plain-text ring and the outer as the cipher-text ring. To encipher a letter you choose the plain-text on the inner ring and record the corresponding symbol on the outer ring. After each encipherment the rings are 'permuted', i.e. revolved, and this 'chaoticises' the process, rendering the encryption unbreakable, because any correspondence between the two alphabets changes slightly at each step, and entirely after many steps.[†]

Byrne's Chaocipher archive is now held in the US National Cryptologic Museum, which is located in a former motel in Maryland. The Museum's Wikipedia entry has this oddly pedantic note about opening times:

> The NCM includes a gift store whose operational hours coordinate with the museum's operational schedule (i.e., if the museum is closed altogether, opens late, or closes early, the gift shop does likewise) and an unclassified library with weekday-only operating hours that also represent the museum's weekday operational schedule.

Could this information be expressed less cryptically? There's more, if you're planning a visit:

> The library includes over a dozen boxes of the files of Herbert Yardley, declassified Enigma messages, technical reports, and books in-

---

[*]John F. Byrne *Silent Years: An Autobiography with Memoirs of James Joyce and Our Ireland* Published by Farrar, Straus and Young, New York (1953). Byrne, Joyce's closest university friend, was the model for Cranly in *A Portrait*. Byrne encouraged Joyce's elopement to Europe with Nora. When Joyce returned to Dublin in 1909 Byrne restored Joyce's trust in her, dismissing claims that she had had other relationships. It was an intensely emotional exchange and Joyce commemorated that moment by adopting by Byrne's Eccles Street address.

[†]I'm making a hash of explaining this and refer you to the website interference.org run by Carl Scheffler.

cluding how to crack the Data Encryption Standard using Deep Crack.

'Deep Crack' is the name of a machine built by the Electronic Frontier Foundation (EFF) in 1998, designed to mount a 'brute force' attack in which all possible passwords and phrases are used until the correct one is found (a variant on the 'monkeys with typewriters' approach to Shakespeare). It employs a 56-bit key, which means there are two-to-the-power-of-fifty-six possible keys under which a message can be encrypted, which means exactly 72,057,594,037,927,936, or approximately 72 *quadrillion* possible keys.

Will *Finnegans Wake* ever be subjected to brute force cryptographic analysis as a way to root out any hidden meanings? Joyce famously said he expected readers to spend their entire lives navigating his work—could there be the equivalent of an unopened chamber deep in the structure of the *Wake*?

One Joyce scholar had a particular theory, or obsession. Grace Eckley believed that the overwhelmingly dominant influence on Joyce in *Finnegans Wake* was the Victorian journalist, editor and father of the British tabloid W.T. Stead (1849–1912), who died in the Titanic disaster and was hailed as the greatest newspaperman of his age. His biographer W. Sydney Robinson wrote that 'He twisted facts, invented stories, lied, betrayed confidences, but always with a genuine desire to reform the world—and himself.' Eckley explored her theory with relentless single-mindedness in three books: *Children's Lore in Finnegans Wake* (1985), *The Steadfast "Finnegans Wake"* (1994), and *The Steadfast James Joyce* (1997). For Eckley, Stead's journalism, fiction, life and messages from beyond the grave provided the key to the *Wake*.

Reviewing *The Steadfast "Finnegans Wake"*,* Martha Fodaski Black calls out Eckley for her 'mind-boggling non sequiturs' and for being 'relentless in her logocentric insistence on the equation that HCE equals Stead', comparing the author memorably to 'the blind man who felt the elephant's tail and concluded that the earth's largest mammal was a reptile.'

Just as mind-boggling (and bringing us back to Cher) there exists an edition of *Ulysses* re-told in emojis by Malarie Piercy (Illus-

---

*James Joyce Quarterly Vol. 32, No. 2 (Winter, 1995), pp. 441–446.

trator) and Jon Klopfer (Editor), published on Kindle in 2014 by an outfit called Jonki Monkey Networks. This is how they pitch their approach:

> The unique Emoji Assist Edition adds graphics of emotional states Books next to paragraphs and dialogue. This derivative work of the classical novel uses using several linguistic metrics to enhance the reader's experience. It also provides a new and unique experience when reading or re-reading this beloved classic. While we preserve the original text—we strive to provide you with the highest quality linguistic analysis of emotional states implied by this classical work. Thousands of hours have been put in to research and development of the software required to create this edition. Jonki Monkey Networks hope you find our annotative illustrations entertaining and enlightening.

In fact, and disappointingly, 'the highest quality linguistic analysis' results in nothing more than a narrow range of facial emoticons at the start of each paragraph or utterance, suggesting (erratically and innaccurately) the emotional tone of what follows. Something like this:

> ☺ Stately, plump Buck Mulligan came from the stairhead, bearing a bowl of lather on which a mirror and a razor lay crossed. A yellow dressinggown, ungirdled, was sustained gently behind him on the mild morning air. He held the bowl aloft and intoned:
>
> ☺ —*Introibo ad altare Dei.*
>
> Halted, he peered down the dark winding stairs and called out coarsely:
>
> ☺ —Come up, Kinch! Come up, you fearful jesuit!
>
> ☹ Solemnly he came forward and mounted the round gunrest. He faced about and blessed gravely thrice the tower, the surrounding land and the awaking mountains.

The publishers have applied the same treatment to other novels, also available on Kindle, including *Little Women, Pride and Prejudice, Wuthering Heights* and *Great Expectations.*

27. SIX HUNDRED CHARACTERS WITHIN REACH OF AN AUTHOR

Apart from Stephen Dedalus and the Blooms there are more than six hundred individual characters in *Ulysses*. I've kept erratic notes over the years but always manage to lose count, and still can't offer a comprehensive list. What follows, lifted from several online sources, is a list of the more significant, alphabetically arranged. It comes with a challenge for those of you who know the novel reasonably well: which of the following can you identify?

Mrs Yelverton Barry	John Eglinton
Mrs Bellingham	Lieutenant Gardner
Richard Best	Richie, Sara & Walter Goulding
Milly Bloom	Haines
Edy Boardman	Zoe Higgins
Blazes Boylan	John Hooper
Josie Breen	Joe Hynes
Denis Breen	Corny Kelleher
Cissy, Jacky & Tommy Caffrey	Mina Kennedy
Nurse Callan	Barney Kiernan
Private Carr	Ned Lambert
The Citizen	Lenehan
Martha Clifford	Vincent Lynch
Bella Cohen	Bantam Lyons
Private Compton	Thomas W. Lyster
Father John Conmee	Gerty MacDowell
Punch Costello	Dr. Madden
Martin Cunningham	Denis J. Maginni
Garrett Deasy	John Henry Menton
May Golding	Buck Mulligan
Dilly Dedalus	City Councillor Nannetti
Katey, Boody & Maggy Dedalus	J.J. O'Molloy
Simon Dedalus	Jack Power
Patrick "Paddy" Dignam	Mina Purefoy
Mrs Dignam	Kitty Ricketts
Patrick Dignam, Jr.	George William Russell (A.E.)
Dr Dixon	Cyril Sargent
Ben Dollard	Staggering Bob
Bob Doran	Florry Talbot
Lydia Douce	Mrs Mervyn Talboys
Mary Driscoll	

Writing in 1997, the Joyce critic Joseph Kelly observed that, while Joyce himself is very much present in our culture, his characters are not:

> There are plenty of allusions in popular culture to James Joyce. Why are there no allusions to Stephen and Leopold and Molly? Why hasn't *Ulysses* inspired a sitcom or at least a miniseries? Why don't college kids call certain rakes 'boylans'?*

For starters college slang has a more robust contemporary lexicon at its disposal, and from livelier sources, than a century-old novel. Kelly's observation might apply equally to Holden Caulfield, or Yossarian, or Billy Pilgrim, or Humbert Humbert or any number of 20th century literary characters. Earlier characters such as Robinson Crusoe, Jane Eyre, Frankenstein's Creature and Count Dracula did not have to compete with cinema, radio, television and the internet when making their secure and enduring claim on popular culture.

Despite the enormous presence of Joyce online today, and the haphazard annual tribute of Bloomsday, and all the films and the graphic novels and the theatre adaptations and the merchandise and so on, it's true that Joyce's characters do not have the broad popular appeal and recognition of, say, Crusoe, Finn or Dracula. The reasons for this are not hard to pin down—policing by the Estate restricted the novel's presence in the public domain; the characters and situations portrayed are less open to reduction and pastiche, and the book's readership has always been, will always be, limited in number. That's never going to change.

---

*'A Defense of Danis Rose' by Joseph Kelly, *James Joyce Quarterly* Vol. 35/36, Vol. 35, no. 4—Vol. 36, no. 1 (Summer—Fall, 1998), p. 822.

28. THE FAMILY FIRM

There's a Collard & Collard piano in *Ulysses*. It appears in the 'Sirens' episode, the one that begins 'Bronze by gold heard the hoofirons, steelyringing Imperthnthn thnthnthn' and in which the two Ormond Hotel barmaids, Lydia Douce and Mina Kennedy, strain to see the viceregal cavalcade passing by:

> Miss Douce's brave eyes, unregarded, turned from the crossblind, smitten by sunlight. Gone. Pensive (who knows?), smitten (the smiting light), she lowered the dropblind with a sliding cord. She drew down pensive (why did he go so quick when I?) about her bronze, over the bar where bald stood by sister gold, inexquisite contrast, contrast inexquisite nonexquisite, slow cool dim seagreen sliding depth of shadow, *eau de Nil*.

> — Poor old Goodwin was the pianist that night, Father Cowley reminded them. There was a slight difference of opinion between himself and the Collard grand.

> There was.

> — A symposium all his own, Mr Dedalus said. The devil wouldn't stop him. He was a crotchety old fellow in the primary stage of drink.

> — God, do you remember? Ben bulky Dollard said, turning from the punished keyboard. And by Japers I had no wedding garment.

Father Cowley is recalling a formal concert back in 1895, one which Molly Bloom also remembers in her soliloquy:

> Ben Dollard base barreltone the night he borrowed the swallowtail to sing out of in Holles street squeezed and squashed into them and grinning all over his big Dolly face like a wellwhipped childs botty didnt he look a balmy ballocks sure enough that must have been a spectacle on the stage imagine paying 5/- in the preserved seats for that to see him and Simon Dedalus too he was always turning up half screwed

Ulysses doesn't say where the concert took place, but it could have been in the Antient Concert Rooms or the Mansion House, where Goodwin accompanied Molly in another concert.

Now, and with a faint stink of the lamp, here's the history bit. F.W. Collard was a director of the company Clementi & Co., a well-respected piano manufacturer founded by the pianist, composer and

Collard & Collard upright piano

music publisher Muzio Clementi around 1800. When Clementi died in 1832 the firm was renamed Collard & Collard and soon became one of the great British piano makers of the 19th century. The modest 'cottage style' of the kind acquired by the Pooters in *The Diary of a Nobody* (1892) by George and Weedon Grossmith were small uprights, although the company also made concert grands.* The make of piano in *Ulysses* not only seems right for the context but also offers, in this most musical episode of the novel, a satisfying echo of 'Dollard'. In 1929, the firm was sold to the Chappell Piano Company of London, but instruments bearing the Collard & Collard name remained in production until about 1960. These pianos—rather baroque objects by today's standards—can be picked up today for next to nothing. The former Collard & Collard piano factory and showroom in Camden Town can still be seen—it's the distinctive circular building in Oval Road. Camden was home in the 19th century to many piano-makers because easy access to the canal network, and later on the

---

*In this comic masterpiece Mr Pooter notes with quiet pride the arrival in his Holloway home of 'our new cottage piano (on the three years' system), manufactured by W. Bilkson (in small letters), from Collard and Collard (in very large letters).'

railway terminals at Euston, St Pancras and King's Cross, meant that materials could be brought in and the finished instruments shipped out around the country. The piano in the Ormond Hotel would have travelled by train from Euston to Holyhead and across the Irish Sea to Kingstown (later Dunleary, now Dún Laoghaire).

29. Father Jack Hackett and some thoughts on editions

The word 'yes' occurs 359 times in *Ulysses*, while 'no' appears 680 times and you can make of that what you will. I get these two figures from the *Ulysses* concordance, a website where one can fritter away many happy hours.* By way of tribute to the late Frank Kelly, the actor who played the scrofulous Father Jack Hackett in *Father Ted*, here are four more word counts from the same novel:

drink	62	
girls	45	
arse	10	
feck	0	(although there's the odd variant on 'fuck')

Which is all by way of throat-clearing, because the real subject of this essay is: what's the best edition of *Ulysses* to read?

I have four copies of the novel: the facsimile first edition (published by Dover Publications), the alphabetised Popper version (see essay 72 'Artists of the Portrait'), a Penguin paperback I bought in Dublin on Bloomsday 1982 and (my favourite) the 1960 Bodley Head edition, the dust wrapper of which features the Homeric bow design by Eric Gill. Another Penguin edition, the one I bought on my 16th birthday, has long since disintegrated. Many of the loose pages were pasted up on the walls of the lavatory in a flat I rented in Hackney in the 1990s.

There are multiple editions of *Ulysses* available on the market and your choice will depend on what you expect of the novel and, of course, your budget. Many readers will be attracted to any version that claims to be 'definitive', a description that would seem to apply to the so-called 'Corrected Text', edited by Hans Walter Gabler and published to initial acclaim on Bloomsday in 1984. But beware—we are entering a minefield.

Gabler, a professor in the Institute for English Philology at the University of Munich, led a ten-strong team for ten years, working together to correct, it was announced, 'more than 5,000 errors' that had crept into the first edition, many of them the result of the typesetters at l'imprimerie Darantière working in a language they did not understand.

*joyceconcordance.andreamoro.net

A cynical observer might suspect that this corrected text was commissioned because the Estate wanted to create a version sufficiently different from prior editions to justify a renewed copyright, and that cynical observer would be right.

In an approach that would prove controversial, Gabler assembled a hypothetical 'original' text by collating all the surviving manuscripts, typescripts, corrected proofs and previously-published editions, a method justified by his belief that Joyce's glaucoma was the cause of textual variations that the author himself was unaware of, and would not have endorsed. That the process of collation involved state-of-the-art computers gave the entire project a certain high-tech prestige and Gabler's innovative use of what he termed a 'copytext' was heralded as ground-breaking.

Now when it came to editing *Ulysses* in the past, editors had traditionally worked with existing manuscripts, typescripts and previous editions, the advantage being that whatever previous version was employed as a copytext would be unified and continuous, a coherent whole. You might think—I would—that the 1922 first edition, the one published on Joyce's 40th birthday, would be the starting point, perhaps followed by the widely-admired 1960 Bodley Head edition. Gabler, however, saw both of these versions as corrupt and unreliable and proceeded to reconstruct the novel line by line, collating all the various stages of Joyce's actual composition, starting with what is known as the Rosenbach Manuscript, the handwritten copy Joyce produced between 1917 and 1921 for the American collector John Quinn. This manuscript oddly took precedence over the typescript Joyce supervised prior to publication.

The result was what textual critics call a 'genetic' or 'conflated' version, something entirely new and (this strikes me as important) not a version that the author himself ever wrote or saw or approved of. Supported by the Joyce Estate and many leading Joyce scholars, the 'critical and synoptic edition' prepared by Gabler, with Wolfhard Steppe and Claus Melchior, was published in three volumes in 1984.

Gabler's approach drew criticism from many quarters and most notably from the Joyce scholar John Kidd who, in April 1985, delivered his paper 'Errors of Execution in the 1984 *Ulysses*' to the Society for Textual Scholarship in New York, the first sustained public criticism of Gabler's methods. In it, Kidd levelled three charges against Gabler's editorial approach:

1. that Gabler included a number of hypothetical documents that have been lost, but the existence of which is inferred from other documents, and had treated them as authoritative in developing his copytext;
2. that when working with the new copytext, Gabler corrected Joyce's spelling of English and foreign words and revised Joyce's own punctuation, use of compound words and certain details such as dates and sums of money (in Bloom's end-of-day bookkeeping);
3. that Gabler ignored Joyce's continued involvement with the text after completing the manuscript, such as his directions to professional typists, his corrections to printed editions published during his lifetime and his agreement to changes made by others.

None of this percolated into the wider world at the time because it was a matter of interest only to specialists. But that would change with the appearance in 1986 of the single-volume reading edition, aimed at the mass market and entitled *Ulysses: The Corrected Text*. This was produced, with the Estate's blessing, under a fresh copyright and was for some time the only version of the novel available in American bookstores.

Reviewing the Gabler edition in *The Guardian* newspaper (19th June 1986), Anthony Burgess admitted that 'the gain to the average non-Joycean reader will seem trivial' while concluding enthusiastically that 'this brilliant job of editing, matched by a brilliant introduction, has polished the greatness to a high shine.'

In the summer of 1988 John Kidd published an essay on the Gabler text in *The New York Review of Books*, a well-argued critique entitled 'The Scandal of *Ulysses*'. Kidd again pointed out the flaws in Gabler's methodology, and the 400 places where Joyce's style had been lost or compromised in favour of what he called 'inauthentic' changes, making a strong case that *Ulysses: The Corrected Text* was, to put it politely, a dog's breakfast. Issues that had been in circulation for years among textual scholars suddenly became a matter for public attention and debate. The literary world reached for a big tub of popcorn and settled down to enjoy an epic clash.

Borges observed that literary spats are always ferocious because the stakes are so low, but that wasn't the case here because *Ulysses* was and remains a valuable commercial property, with around

100,000 copies sold in the United States each year. There were also reputations at stake, not only those of Gabler and Kidd, but of hundreds, perhaps thousands of academics around the world with a professional interest in Joyce.

Gabler's response appeared in the NYRB on 18th August 1988, starting with an oddly-worded blanket rebuttal:

> The article is couched in the allegation, continuously reemphasized, that the editors did not compare all their work against the original documents.

But he and his fellow editors did just that, he insists, before going on to reject what he calls Kidd's 'rhetoric of allegations, insinuations and sweepingly generalising assertions.' He summarily dismisses three issues raised by Kidd regarding 'name forms' (i.e. spelling) as they appear in *The Corrected Text*, then continues:

> This leaves us with twelve examples. For ten of these, the complaint goes against two commas, two colons, one capital letter, one case of the author's underlining in one manuscript against his not underlining (for italics) in another, one instance of a row of dots for an ellipsis, and three recording problems that affect not the text, but the apparatus in the critical and synoptic edition only.

Gabler expects us to strain at gnats while swallowing camels because the single most contentious change in his edition is not a comma or colon or ellipsis, or even the wrong spelling of a surname, but the so-called 'love passage' in the 'Scylla and Charybdis' episode. To understand the impact of Gabler's intervention we have to go back to the end of 'Proteus' (the second episode in the novel), when Stephen asks himself:

> What is that word known to all men?

Much later. in the novel's phantasmagoric 'Circe' episode, Stephen addresses the same question to his dead mother:

> Tell me the word, mother, if you know now. The word known to all men.

The same unanswered question is posed during Stephen's interior monologue in the 'Scylla and Charybdis' episode but, in a bold editorial move, Gabler confidently took it upon himself to supply the answer:

> Do you know what you are talking about? Love, yes. Word known
> to all men.

Gabler found this version in the Rosenbach manuscript and assumed that a tired or distracted typist had mistakenly omitted the
words 'Love, yes' when working from what he calls 'a collateral
manuscript' for the first Shakespeare edition, although the omission
had gone unnoticed by Joyce at the time and by everyone else ever
since. The answer to the question did not appear in the first or second editions of the novel published during Joyce's lifetime so we can
safely assume that he approved of the omission, if that's what it was,
and that Gabler's decision to restore the word (a spoiler comparable
to yelling '*Rosebud* is a sledge!' during the first reel of *Citizen Kane*)
is at least open to question.

The novelist John Updike delivered a stylish *coup de grâce* on the
Gabler edition with a letter to the *NYRB* in which he described
what he regarded as the most scandalous of the many controversial
changes in Gabler's text, namely:

> the setting of all dialogue, prefaced with a dash in the French
> manner, flush left. This typographical eccentricity is so unusual
> as to be disfiguring, and it does not appear in the text of which
> Joyce repeatedly read proofs, which is conventionally indented.
> His manuscripts do show the dash without indentation, but what
> we have here, as in the almost unreadable Thomas H. Johnson tran-
> scriptions of Emily Dickinson's manuscript poems, is a mistaken
> scholarly fidelity to holograph mannerisms that were never meant
> by the author to be translated into type.*

I remember my first reading, aged fifteen, of *A Portrait of the Artist
as a Young Man* and can recall how very strange I found the 'continental' method of indicating direct speech with an indented dash
rather than the familiar '66' and '99' speech marks I was used to.
There was a liberating sense of being part of something new, of being granted a kind of cultural promotion—like hearing Philip Glass
for the first time. The lack of fiddly punctuation marks in *A Portrait*
added to the book's aura, its freshness, its invigorating modernism.
This, one thought, one felt, *this* is the way to do it, and I cannot begin
to imagine what editorial whim led Gabler and his team to adopt a

---

* *The New York Review of Books*, 18th August 1988.

'flush left' setting, thus dispensing with such a distinctive visual aspect of Joyce's writing. As Kidd himself said in his punchy response to Gabler's *NYRB* letter, when it came to punctuation the Corrected Text fell outside the very tradition Joyce inaugurated.

While the Gabler project had initially enjoyed the support of many distinguished Joyce scholars, a rift developed over the years between the editor and the Academic Advisory Committee, which included Joyce's biographer Richard Ellmann.

A letter from Ellmann to Gabler following a meeting in Oxford in June 1983 refers bluntly to the latter's 'doctrinaire inflexibility' and 'rigid stance' and hints (this must have gone down well) that Gabler's command of idiomatic English may not be up to scratch. Ellmann's exasperation with the editor is clear: 'much of what you have been describing as logical or systematic is in fact capricious, based upon aesthetic, linguistic, or psychological inferences that are open to question.'

There seems to have been some inexcusable pilfering by Gabler of Kidd's own researches, to the extent that Kidd claimed that most of the changes made by Gabler between the 1984 three-volume edition and the 1986 Corrected Text were taken without acknowledgement from Kidd's own papers, articles and interviews. Kidd's casual remark, for instance, to a reporter from *The Washington Post* (2nd April 1985) prompted Gabler to add a full stop after 'bottom of the ashpit' on page 264, right in the middle of Molly Bloom's soliloquy which is otherwise, famously, barely punctuated at all.

Such egregious changes aside, it struck me then, and strikes me now, that any claim by any editor that a scrupulously corrected text will make *Ulysses* more approachable for 'the common reader' is all absolute bollocks, because *Ulysses* isn't aimed at the common reader, whoever he or she or they may be. It's a novel that demands commitment, perseverance, patience and access to commentaries, of which there are many, in print and online. What I said about poetry earlier in this book applies equally to this novel—it's not for everyone, but it can be, and should be, for *anyone*. But anyone who is put off reading *Ulysses* by the inclusion or exclusion of a comma, or accent, or umlaut, or by a double 'n' in Connolly (one of the Gabler gaffes pounced on by Kidd), or any of the myriad typographical minutiae at the heart of the dispute, needs their head seeing to.

In 1990 the American publisher Random House quietly dropped the Gabler edition, replacing it with the 1961 version, and the collapse of Gabler's credibility accelerated. In the same year in the United Kingdom the Bodley Head revived its 1960 version, the one on which the Random House version was based. In both countries Everyman's Library followed suit and, two years later, Penguin also dropped Gabler in favour of the 1960 text.

On the strength of his critique Kidd was rewarded a position at Boston University, where he set up the James Joyce Research Center and the firm of W.W. Norton commissioned a seven-volume edition of Joyce's complete works for $350,000.

But this so-called Dublin Edition suffered the first in a series of setbacks when Kidd's original editor at Norton, Barry Wade, died in 1993 aged 41. Wade's successor left soon after, and the company went on to lose a set of page proofs. When the Joyce Estate raised objections the entire project was abandoned.*

In 2018 a *New York Times* article inaccurately described Kidd as 'missing'.† Following the closure of the James Joyce Research Center the unemployed Kidd had become somewhat eccentric, reportedly spending his days feeding the pigeons in Marsh Plaza at the centre of the Boston University campus. Tracked down by the journalist Jack Hitt to his home in Rio de Janeiro, he cut rather a forlorn and marginal figure.

If the Kidd/Gabler dispute had any positive outcome it was the re-appearance in print of the 1960 edition which, among other virtues, features the indented dash mentioned by Updike and the bold newspaper headlines in the 'Aeolus' episode. The Gabler version remained available from Vintage International but, thanks to the interventions of Gabler, Kidd and many other textual scholars and theorists, it's now clear that there can never be a definitive edition of *Ulysses*, only competing critical editions each with different degrees of legitimacy. My advice is to get your hands on the cheap Dover facsimile, the version Joyce knew and handled. It's like a painting stripped of dull layers of varnish and, with the contentious in-

---

*No further editions of *Ulysses* would appear until 2010, when the Estate gave permission to Wordsworth Editions in Britain to publish a cheap paperback reprint of the 1932 Odyssey Press edition. This edition, unattractive but serviceable, costs less than a Starbucks Americano.

†'The Strange Case of the Missing Joyce Scholar' by Jack Hitt (*New York Times*, 12th June 2018).

terventions of later editors removed, the multiple typos make it feel fresh and urgent.

I'd also give a wide berth to the so-called 'Readers Edition' of 1997, published in London by Picador. It was edited by Danis Rose, 'one of the most distinguished scholars of James Joyce's compositional methods and practice' who waxed lyrical over his own achievement in *The New York Times* (23rd June 1997):

> If you think of 'Ulysses' as Joyce's mansion and each of the rooms as each of the episodes [,] I went in and opened the windows, let in the light and air, cleaned out the cobwebs so we could view with awe and admiration the beauty of the architecture and the exquisite craftsmanship of the furniture.'

This sounds more like a makeover show on the telly, with the emphasis on dusting. Rose's view was that, while a scholarly edition might be expected to attain and retain a degree of textual stability, a reader's edition should reflect the needs, expectations, competences and perspectives of successive generations of readers, or at least the needs, expectations, competences and perspectives as decided by Rose himself. His text was, in the words of *The New York Times* 'substantially tinkered with' in a democratising crusade that involved changing Joyce's 'snotgreen scrotumtightening sea' into 'snot-green scrotum-tightening sea' (because clearly no ordinary reader can be expected to manage such long words without the crutch of a hyphen). In all Rose, made between eight and ten thousand changes in spelling and punctuation (which included adding apostrophes to Molly Bloom's soliloquy, as well as hyphens and capitals, and italics) and breaking up Joyce's distinctive compound words (changing, for example, 'lookingglass' to 'looking glass').

If the Rose edition had any positive impact it was to unite the Gabler/Kidd factions into one, along with the majority of Joyce scholars and admirers. Speaking for myself (and what else can I do?) I don't buy the idea that Rose is championing the common reader by smuggling the book out of academe's ivory tower and into the popular forum. Rose's advocates argue that his critics have 'an exaggerated respect for Joyce's abilities as a writer'* which is a very silly thing to say.

---

* 'A Defense of Danis Rose' by Joseph Kelly, *James Joyce Quarterly* Vol. 35/36, Vol. 35, no. 4—Vol. 36, no. 1 (Summer—Fall, 1998), p. 816.

30. BECKETT'S GROUNDHOG DAY

Here's something very special: an insanely covetable association copy of *Ulysses*, advertised on abe.com by a dealer in Montreal:

> **Joyce, James.**
>
> Published by Random House, New York (1948)
>
> **Used · Hardcover · First Edition · Signed**
>
> Quantity Available: 1
>
> **Item Description:** Random House, New York, 1948. Modern Library Reprint. Joyce, James. ULYSSES. Samuel Beckett Presentation Copy. Joyce Signature. New York. Random House, 1948. The Modern Library Edition, later printing. 8vo., 768pp. Sea-green cloth. A near fine copy in a very good modestly restored black dustwrapper. This copy of James Joyce's Ulysses from the library of Ray DaBoll, considered one of the most talented calligraphers & designers in America, inscribed by Beckett on the title-page in black ink: "On his birthday and yours / Sam Beckett / Feb 2 (Groundhog Day)"—Making reference to James Joyce's birthday (February 2nd—Groundhog Day). There are Beckett inscriptions & then there are Beckett inscriptions—This elegant display of Beckett Brain Works, the latter, with Ray DaBoll's bookplate on the front pastedown. In addition, a fine example of Joyce's signature tipped to the front free endpaper. A Clever Beckett Presentation—Superb Association Copy— Fine Joyce Signature. In a custom TBCL Modern Clamshell Case. Punxsutawney Phil says. "It's our Birthday—This is a nifty gift". Signed by Author(s). Bookseller Inventory # 3255

A nifty gift indeed, like owning a photograph of Sean Connery signed by Roger Moore. The price? $17,750 (around £13,500), plus 15 bucks postage to the US.

When, one wonders, did Beckett sign this copy? How did he learn about Groundhog Day, by which I mean the annual meteorological prognostication held in the Pennsylvanian town of Punxsutawney? I'd never heard of the ceremony until the eponymous movie was released in 1993, and Beckett died in 1989, so did he catch wind of it during trips to the United States, where the event is widely broadcast?

Beckett would, I reckon, have enjoyed the film, with Bill Murray (surely to be cast one day in *Krapp's Last Tape*) as the sardonic television weatherman Phil Connors who finds himself trapped in a never-ending purgatorial loop, a very Beckettian situation, forever failing better in a permanently cyclical *temps mort*. The film explores the same redundancies and permutations and repetitions that Beckett explored, and just as fruitfully.

This prompts some further thoughts on Beckett and Joyce, two writers who are forever yoked.

When working with Joyce on the *Wake*, Beckett took to wearing the same size of tight-fitting shoe favoured by his mentor, which was an excruciating form of tribute because Beckett's feet were bigger than Joyce's. That, at least, was the view of Beckett's friend Georges Pelorson:

> I noticed Sam was walking almost like a duck. I said to him 'What's the matter with you, are your feet hurting?' and he said 'yes.' 'Why, are you tired?' and he answered 'No it's my shoes. They're too tight.' 'Well, why don't you change them?' I got no answer or rather I got it years later . . . Sam was sitting nearby and as I was looking at him all of a sudden I realized that his shoes were exactly the same size as Joyce's, though evidently his feet were not . . . Of course, at the time he was really haunted by Joyce, imitating him in all his most characteristic attitudes, dressing like him, eating the same food as him, holding himself like him.*

The opening business about ill-fitting boots in *Waiting for Godot* may be a reference to this, and so too the moment later in the play when Vladimir berates Estragon:

> 'There's man all over for you, blaming on his boots the faults of his feet.'

The original French text of *Waiting for Godot* was written between 9th October 1948 and 29th January 1949, but the play would not be performed until 5th January 1953, when it opened at the tiny Théâtre de Babylone in Paris. In Beckett's English translation (or to be more accurate his *Hiberno*-English translation) both tramps, in common with most of the author's eloquent derelicts, speak like Trinity College graduates come down in the world, a pair of articulate, deracinated scholars. Has there ever been a *Godot* production in which Vladimir and Estragon are explicitly played as Joyce and Beckett, in physical appearance and dress and speech and manner? I'd like to see that.

---

*From a review of Beckett's *Echo's Bones* by Fintan O'Toole, The New York Review of Books (19th March 2015)

In *The Books at the Wake: A Study of Literary Allusions in James Joyce's Finnegans Wake* by James A. Atherton (Faber and Faber, 1959) the author quotes a well-known story, which Richard Ellmann originally heard from Beckett himself:

> Beckett was taking dictation from Joyce for *Finnegans Wake*; there was a knock on the door and Joyce said "Come in". Beckett, who hadn't heard the knock, by mistake wrote down "Come in" as part of the dictated text. Afterwards he read it back to Joyce who said: "What's that 'Come in'?"
>
> "That's what you dictated," Beckett replied. Joyce thought for a moment, realizing that Beckett hadn't heard the knock, then he said, "Let it stand".

Who was it that knocked on the door so softly that Beckett couldn't hear it? Was it Lucia? Nora? Would either of them be inclined to knock on the door in their own home? Or are we invited to infer the Parisian equivalent of the person from Porlock interrupting Coleridge's opium reverie?

More importantly, where exactly in the published version of *Finnegans Wake* does that rogue 'Come in' crop up? The internet is uncharacteristically mute on the subject and the *Wake* scholar Finn Fordham assured me that the phrase doesn't appear in the novel and that the Beckett/Joyce exchange never happened. He should know.

In fact the phrase *does* occur three times in the *Wake*, although never as the random interjection of the anecdote. You can look them up on the online concordance fweet.org,* where you'll find this, the nearest candidate:

> come in, come on, you lazy loafs! (p 393, line 27)

But that line (as Peter Chrisp has pointed out in his *Wake* blog) occurs in the so-called 'Mamalujo' episode, which was first published in the *Transatlantic Review* in 1924, three years before Beckett met Joyce for the first time. It's possible, of course, that the incident did occur as recorded by Ellmann but that Joyce changed the phrase in a later draft.

---

*FWEET stands for 'Finnegans Wake Extensible Elucidation Treasury'. It is, at the time of writing, the depository of nearly 90,000 notes on the novel, submitted by readers from all over the world.

31. The first Bloomsday

The earliest *Ulysses* celebrations go as far back as 1924 when Sylvia Beach, Joyce's publisher, noted in a letter that 'There is a group of people who observe what they call Bloom's day– 16 June,' although no further details were given.

The first Bloomsday proper was organised in 1954 when, to mark 50 years since the day on which the novel is set, the Dublin artist, writer and publican John Ryan and the novelist Brian O'Nolan (aka Flann O'Brien) hatched up the idea for a day-long pilgrimage around the city, visiting locations that feature in the novel. They were joined by the writers Anthony Cronin and Patrick Kavanagh, James Joyce's cousin Tom (a dentist) and A.J. 'Con' Leventhal, Registrar of Trinity College Dublin. Two horse-drawn cabs were hired, the better to recreate the long ride to Paddy Dignam's funeral, and each member of the group—in a gesture that anticipates today's world of cosplay—took on a role in the novel. Cronin was Stephen, O'Nolan his father, John Ryan was the journalist Martin Cunningham and 'Con' Leventhal, being Jewish, was Bloom. (Leventhal, incidentally, had interviewed Joyce in Paris in February 1922 on the day *Ulysses* was published.)

The pilgrims foregathered as planned at the modernist Sandycove home of Michael Scott, near the Martello tower (see essay 76 'The Ondt and the Gripes'). It wasn't yet mid-morning but O'Nolan was already plastered because he'd been drinking in the pubs around the city's cattle market, which were licensed to open at 7:30am. He and Kavanagh decided to climb the steep slope from the Scott house to the Tower and at one point O'Brien grabbed the latter's ankle, which led to an unseemly squabble between the two writers as they scrambled upward.

John Ryan made a short film of the day, a fragment of which can be found online. It's a wonderfully disreputable home movie, showing a group of unhealthy-looking literary men in long raincoats pissing up against the sea wall on Sandymount Strand and weaving unsteadily around in front of the camera. When they reached central Dublin and the Bailey pub in Duke Street (owned by Ryan) another row broke out and the celebration descended into inebriated chaos.

From left: John Ryan, Anthony Cronin, Brian O'Nolan (Flann O'Brien), Patrick Kavanagh and Tom Joyce.

This seems to me *exactly* how Bloomsday should be commemorated—a poorly planned, disorganised, uncommercial affair, soon abandoned, with plenty to drink and no solemnity. But what do we get, most of the time? *Readings.* The Rosenbach Museum & Library in Philadelphia (see essay 60 'Who was that masked man?') closes down nearby Delancey Street on Bloomsday and 'in addition to dozens of readers, often including Philadelphia's mayor, singers from the Academy of Vocal Arts perform songs that are integral to the novel's plot'. Some fans wear bowler hats or straw boaters 'in honor of certain characters from the novel' and traditional Irish cuisine is provided by local Irish-themed pubs. The whole event is billed as 'family friendly' but, as the Rosenbach website is at pains to point out, the day is 'a celebration of *Ulysses*, a novel which includes mature content. Consider our Bloomsday readings PG-13 rated: parental discretion is advised.'

'Mature content'? 'Parental discretion'? It all sounds bloody *awful*. Would the shambolic literary drunks in Ryan's home movie be welcome there? And even if so, would they wish to stay?

In April 1967 it was John Ryan who, following 'negotiations of be-wildering complexity', rescued the front door to the Blooms' house at 7, Eccles Street shortly before the derelict building (which was owned at the time by one Denis Spierin, who ran a butcher's shop on nearby Dorset Street) was largely demolished. Ryan installed the door in the vestibule of his pub, the Bailey, and there it remained for many years before being moved to the James Joyce Centre at 35, North Great George's Street, where it is now displayed.

32. READING *ULYSSES*

In June 2021 the Músaem Litríochta na hÉireann/The Museum of Literature Ireland (with the English acronym MoLI being a nod towards Mrs Bloom's surname) announced a series of fortnightly online *Ulysses* readings.* Here's the press release:

Ulysses—for the Rest of Us!

Always wanted to read *Ulysses* but were too afraid to start? *Ulysses* may be one of the most famous and influential novels ever published, but how many have actually read it? *Ulysses—for the Rest of Us!* is a new free public book club at MoLI that will demystify this extraordinary 100-year-old novel, and offer fresh and easy routes into James Joyce's vast, elaborate and often hilarious masterpiece for every reader. This summer, join your guide—author, activist and podcast host Conner Habib—as he unlocks *Ulysses*, episode by episode, from Stephen Dedalus's breakfast in Sandycove through to Molly Bloom's famous closing monologue.

These readings would take place on Thursday evenings until September and offer newcomers to the novel 'fun and accessible introductions to each episode.'

Conner Habib's name was new to me so I looked him up and discovered that he's an amiable American who 'presents complex philosophical, spiritual, and political ideas in an engaging and accessible way,' mainly through a long series of podcasts with (mostly) countercultural figures, navigating off-trail subjects. So far so good.

He is also, in his own words, 'a porn performer, occultist and academic' (and in that order, one hopes, because academics aren't what's needed here). As a porn performer he's appeared in such titles as *One Thing Leads to Another*, *Night Maneuvers*, *Caught in the Act*, *The Mix*, *Devious, Inc.*, and *Locker Room Spy Guy*.

I signed up like a shot, as did hundreds of others, because we need new voices and fresh takes and I'd far rather hear what Conner Hanib has to say about *Ulysses* than practically any other Joycean on the planet. I was, I'll admit, in 'twosome twiminds' (as Joyce would say)

---

*To mark Bloomsday 2021 MoLI offered 'a lovely set of James Joyce merchandise' for 10 euros. This 'exclusive bundle' featured 'a postcard, keyring, lapel pin and magnet so that you can really show off your love for one of Ireland's greatest writers!' Imagine writing that.

about that capitalised 'Rest of Us', implying that readers of *Ulysses* are a cranky elite rather than a diligent minority, but let's not quibble.

Before the first group session on 16th June we were invited to something called a 'tailored walkthrough' of the first three episodes of the novel. These were unpretentious, off-the-cuff and *very* brief.

A faint alarm bell began to ring when, in his opening address, Habib referred repeatedly to the 'chapters' of *Ulysses*. Joyce, who certainly knew what he was doing, organised his novel in three parts (I, II and III), with each part containing separate *episodes*, 18 in all and none of them numbered or titled, none of them presented as 'chapters'. It was Hans Walter Gabler (see essay 29) who introduced numbered chapters in his controversial and widely-discredited synoptic version of the text, and to my surprise it was the very edition that Habib recommended to his readers, a choice endorsed by MoLI. He admitted that his choice of text would annoy academics (without giving any of the back story) and I liked him for that, and formed the impression that he chose it because this is the edition he knows best, and because the Gabler pagination tallies with Don Gifford's *Ulysses Annotated* (University of California Press, 2008), which he also recommended. Fair enough—but why not recommend the cheap and cheerful Wordsworth edition, widely available in Britain? Two weeks into the readings the MoLI website added a belated remedial note:

> [I]n some editions of *Ulysses*, the episodes—or chapters—are not clearly demarcated. To make things easier to navigate, we've created an index of first lines for each episode, which you can compare to your edition.

For 'some editions' read 'most'. It's a shame this wasn't addressed before the series began, but again I'm not going to quibble. I'll come back to Habib in just a moment, but here's a beneficial digression prompted by his thoughts on 'chapters' and the MoLI note that followed.

Joyce's schema, taken from Homer's *Odyssey*, makes up for the lack of chapter numbers or titles but, since none of the Greek names appears anywhere in the novel, readers who are aware of the underlying structure but unfamiliar with the Homeric original may feel at a disadvantage. I know I did, on my first reading, and I wish I'd known then what I know now, and want to share with you. It's a simple and sensible proposal for a new naming convention for the 18 episodes of

Ulysses which combines the Homeric title with, as an *aide-mémoire*, the first few words of each episode. This suggestion was posted on 29 January 2012 by '11yses' on the website 11ysses.wordpress.com, and here it is:

Book I—The Telemachiad—episodes 1–3

1. Telemachus—'Stately, plump Buck Mulligan'
2. Nestor—'You, Cochrane'
3. Proteus—'Ineluctable modality of the visible'

Book II—The Odyssey—episodes 4–15

4. Calypso—'Mr. Leopold Bloom ate'
5. Lotus Eaters—'By lorries along Sir John Rogerson's'
6. Hades—'Martin Cunningham, first'
7. Aeolus—'IN THE HEART OF THE HIBERNIAN'
8. Lestrygonians—'Pineapple rock. Lemon platt, butter scotch'
9. Scylla and Charybdis—'Urbane, to comfort them'
10. Wandering Rocks—'The Superior, the Very Reverend'
11. Sirens—'Bronze by gold heard the hoofirons'
12. Cyclops—'I was just passing the time of day'
13. Nausicaa—'The summer evening had begun to fold'
14. Oxen of the Sun—'Deshil Holles Eamus'
15. Circe—'The Mabbot street entrance of nighttown'

Book III—The Nostos—episodes 16–18

16. Eumaeus—'Preparatory to anything else Mr Bloom brushed'
17. Ithaca—'What parallel courses did Bloom and Stephen'
18. Penelope—'Yes because he never did a thing like that before'

Now you may not find this handy but I have to admit I certainly do, not least because there are times in my life when I forget whether, say, the 'Sirens' episode comes before or after 'Cyclops' and other times when I forget the opening words of 'Eumaeus' or 'Ithaca'. Call them senior moments.

Back to the MoLI readings with Conor Habib. Alarm bells rang a little louder when he insisted that Joyce's painstaking Homeric substructure, outlined above, is 'overemphasised', thereby brushing aside a central and defining feature of the novel.* Then he added, to my surprise 'I love *Ulysses* because of the plot.' Plot? *What*

---

*The writer Katherine Mansfield and her husband, the critic Middleton Murry, met Joyce in London on 27th April 1922 and she later wrote to her friend Violet Schiff:

plot? There *is* no plot in *Ulysses*, only consecutive situations (break-fast/funeral/lunch/brothel/night), each enriched by Joyce's extraor-dinary range of virtuosic prose styles and the underlying (allegedly 'overemphasised') Homeric schema. Much of what occurs happens inside Bloom's head, and there's no plot to be found there, only his thoughts and memories and speculations.

Habib repeatedly reminded us in his tailored walkthroughs that the novel is 'difficult' and that lots of readers simply give up. I wish he hadn't pre-empted any such reaction because that's precisely the issue he was signed up to address, not to re-enforce or, come to that, even mention. If prospective readers are repeatedly told in advance that something is difficult and that most other readers give up, they will surely be more predisposed to side with the majority when the time comes, and to give up themselves. Habib said more than once that this critical point occurs in 'chapter 3' (i.e. what Joyce presents as the third episode, 'Proteus'). The fact that Stephen, the main subject of the episode, has a rather pretentious vocabulary at his disposal and likes to flourish his intellectual chops is not really much of a problem—you can look up 'agenbyte of inwit' online if the medieval phrase for remorse is new to you (as it was to me and always has been to every reader of *Ulysses*, ever). It takes a few seconds and then you're back on the beach with the dead dog and the live dog and the snot on the rock and the heart-stopping moment with the ship.

The first formal reading group was on Thursday 24th June and I logged on with high hopes, having scrupulously re-read the first three episodes—'Telemachus', 'Nestor' and 'Proteus'—and hell yes, I was even prepared to call them chapters. With a large international audience in attendance—many from the United States—Conner jogged through the opening chapters with an impressively detailed and sensitive attention to the text. His opening comments were thoughtful, illuminating, expert and, a slightly distracting nervous

> Joyce was rather . . . difficile. I had no idea until then of his view of Ulysses—no idea how closely it was modelled on the Greek story, how absolutely necessary it was to know the one through and through to be able to discuss the other. I've read the Odyssey and am more or less familiar with it but Murry and Joyce simply sailed out of my depth. I felt almost stupefied.

Joyce had a different take on the meeting and would later tell a friend that 'Mrs Murry understood the book better than her husband.'

laugh aside, serious without being solemn. Any doubts I had were dispelled; I was soon hooked, and making notes, and learning things. He did a great job and it was time well spent.

But after that first reading, promptly, explicably, with amicability, gratefully, I dropped out. This was no reflection at all on Conner Habib but on the night of the following reading I'd signed up for the online launch of Isabel Waidner's third novel *Sterling Karat Gold*. One of the frustrations of cultural life during lockdown was the frequent clashes of online events but Waidner is a favourite author, and any new book from them is an event, and I didn't want to miss the launch. Also, I hate to fall even further behind than I am already when it comes to reading contemporary writers, especially now, when the stakes are so high.

What do I mean by that?

It's to do with time passing, and a sense of my own mortality as I reach the Saturday afternoon of life's week, and the deplorable state of, you know, *everything*, and the need to continue to make an effort not to fall back on old habits and established preferences. And it's to do with my personal history and situation, which I'll try and get around to later in the book, in essay 50. I do hope Conner Habib's audience stuck with it and finished the novel under his thoughtful and expert guidance. The MoLI website has (at the time of writing) uploaded all the sessions, so you may be able to catch up.

33. HOBBY HORSE

Here, gentle reader, is a list of ten novels by ten different authors. My question is this: apart from being out of print (with one exception) and more or less completely forgotten, what do all ten novels have in common?

> *If Winter Comes* by A.S.M. Hutchinson
> *The Sheik by* Ethel M. Dell
> *Gentle Julia by* Booth Tarkington
> *The Head of the House of Coombe* by Frances Hodgson Burnett
> *Simon Called Peter* by Robert Keable
> *The Breaking Point* by Mary Roberts Rinehart
> *This Freedom* by A.S.M. Hutchinson
> *Maria Chapdelaine* by Louis Hémon
> *To the Last Man* by Zane Grey
> *Babbitt* by Sinclair Lewis

We'll come to the answer in a moment.

The Western writer Zane Grey is, my American publisher assures me, still well known in the States, but his name rings only a very faint bell on my side of the Atlantic and (in my case, at least) it's because he's cited as an influence by the hapless Holly Martins during a disastrous British Council lecture in Carol Reed's film version of *The Third Man* (see essay 66 'A Night in Vienna'). Ethel M. Dell rings another, equally faint bell because it's her syrupy romantic prose style that Joyce adopted in the 'Nausicaa' episode of *Ulysses*—the one in which Bloom has a hand shandy on Sandymount Strand. Booth Tarkington wrote *The Magnificent Ambersons*, which was filmed by Orson Welles. *Babbitt*, the most literary book on this list, is still in print but I haven't read it because you can't read *everything*, and the title makes me think of Elmer Fudd. The other writers are all now pretty much forgotten, as are their books.

Which brings us to the answer.

According to the trade magazine *Publishers Weekly*, these were the ten top-selling works of fiction in the United States in 1922, the year *Ulysses* was published.

Of the one hundred top sellers of that decade listed in the same magazine I've read only *All Quiet on the Western Front*, *Gentlemen Prefer Blondes* (a favourite of Joyce's) and P.C. Wren's once hugely popular *Beau Geste*. All of these were made into films, which may account for their durable cultural presence. Of the remainder there's a handful of worthy middlebrow authors: Thornton Wilder, Sinclair Lewis and John Galsworthy (who was quite incredibly awarded the Nobel Prize in Literature in 1932), but I haven't read any of their 1920s works. The rest of the titles are genre potboilers—romances, westerns, whodunnits and that sort of thing.

Now here are ten other novels, none of them huge best-sellers at the time, all published after *Ulysses* but within the same decade:

A Passage to India (1924)
Mrs Dalloway (1925)
The Trial (1925)
The Great Gatsby (1925)
The Sun Also Rises (1926)
To the Lighthouse (1927)
Lady Chatterley's Lover (1928)
Decline and Fall (1928)
A Farewell to Arms (1929)
A Room of One's Own (1929)

None of these has ever been out of print and they're all so well known that there's no need to name the authors. Seven of these ten novels appear on the Connolly 100 list (he did not include *The Trial*, *Mrs Dalloway* or *A Room of One's Own*), but they all deserve a place. If you're reading this essay the chances are you've read most, or all, of these novels.

What they have in common, to a greater or lesser extent, is a commitment to complexity and to fresh ways of thinking and writing. The authors—E.M. Forster, Virginia Woolf, Franz Kafka, F. Scott Fitzgerald, Ernest Hemingway, Woolf again, D.H. Lawrence, Evelyn Waugh, Hemingway again and Woolf for the third time—all wrote 'difficult' books which were read at the time by a small and highly educated contemporary audience; *To the Lighthouse*, for instance, sold around 4,000 copies in the year following its publication. It's my guess that the accumulated readership for each of these novels by now outnumbers the combined readership of the ten best-sellers at the start of this introduction. Or nearly.

This second list is incomplete. I have omitted *À la recherche du temps perdu* as only five of its seven volumes were published in the

1920s; and there's no poetry, so no Eliot or Pound. I could add another dozen books from the decade of equal quality and most of them by P.G. Wodehouse, but I think I've made my point—that great books last but bad ones, however popular they may be at the time, don't. For Peter B. Kyne, Harold Bell Wright and Joseph C. Lincoln read Dan Brown, Jeffrey Archer and John Grisham; for Ethel M. Dell read E.L. James.

Was there ever a more productive decade for serious anglophone literature than the 1920s? I don't think so. But when it comes to backing the innovative and the unfamiliar, when it comes to playing the long game—have today's big publishers learnt any lessons from history? Have they hell. Thank the stars for the indies.

34. WHAT CAUSES PIP IN POULTRY?

Neal Kosaly-Meyer is a Canadian composer and pianist who, prompted by John Cage's *Wake*-inspired composition *Roaratorio* (1979), first read *Finnegans Wake* at the age of 25. He was stopped in his tracks when he came across the first of the novel's hundred-letter thunder words, which you'll recall goes like this:

bababadalgharaghtakamminarronnkonnbronntonnerronntuonn-
thunntrovarrhounawnskawntoohoohoordenenthurnuk.

He decided to learn the word by heart and, having done so, began to approach the book as a whole, not (as he puts it) as a reader, but as a musician. He went on to commit the first chapter to memory, performing it as a kind of party trick for friends at his apartment, but he didn't stop there. In 2012 he committed himself to the colossal challenge of memorising the entire text and set about it systematically, learning 37 pages a year at the rate of a page a week, with the odd break. It almost seems reasonable. He would, at this rate, take 17 years to memorise *Finnegans Wake* (the same length of time it took Joyce to write it) and he was 54 when he started so he's now in his mid-sixties and, I hope, still going strong with nine years to complete the job.

This prompts thoughts on what I might call my own literary memory.

If we're ever chained to a radiator together and you'd like me to distract you I can reel off 'The Walrus and the Carpenter', or Masefield's 'Cargoes', or Tennyson's 'The Splendour Falls' and chunks of Pope and Dryden and Marvel and Milton as well as plenty of Eliot and Auden and Larkin and other dead white guys. It's part of my cultural baggage because I'm a product—or a victim—of my education, part of which involved committing poetry to memory and being tested on it, the better to equip my generation of tail-end New Elizabethan grammar school boys to fill middle-ranking management roles in the Civil Service. I also have some Stevie Smith and Alice Oswald by heart, but I'm afraid it's mainly the aforementioned dead white guys who make up my radiator repertoire.

What about prose? I glumly reflect that I've forgotten most of the books I've ever read, whether fiction or non-fiction, apart from the odd fact, or character, or plot point, or figure of speech. Aphorisms tend to stick, if inaccurately recalled.

I know a fair bit of the Bible because I had that kind of upbringing, but I'm not in the same league as those diligent scholars who commit to memory the entire Quran (77,430 words), or the Bible (783,137 words in the King James Version), or even, dauntingly, the Talmud (around 2 million words). In the latter case let's take a moment to boggle at the Shas Pollak, a small group of Jewish mnemonists who, according to a report by George Stratton in the *Psychological Review* (1917), together memorised the exact layout of words in more than 5,000 pages of the 12 books of the standard edition of the Babylonian Talmud.

In his report Stratton quoted a letter from a Reverend Dr. David Phillipson of Cincinnati who described the so-called 'pin test':

> A pin would be placed on a word, let us say, the fourth word in line eight; the memory sharp would then be asked what word is in the same spot on page thirty-eight or fifty or any other page; the pin would be pressed through the volume until it reached page thirty-eight or page fifty or any other page designated; the memory sharp would then mention the word and it was found invariably correct. He had visualized in his brain the whole Talmud; in other words, the pages of the Talmud were photographed on his brain. It was one of the most stupendous feats of memory I have ever witnessed and there was no fake about it.

This sounds like a collective example of an Autistic Spectrum Disorder, like naming the day of the week for any date over hundreds of thousands of years, past or future. A stupendous feat to be sure, but one without utility. And what are we to make of the extraordinary Canadian mnemonist Dave Farrow who, in 1996, at the age of 21, and under intense scrutiny by observers from the Guinness Book of Records, memorised the order of 52 decks of playing cards, randomly shuffled together. That's a total of 2,704 cards in a single sighting, each one recalled with complete accuracy. Years later, defending his title, he committed to memory, on a single sighting, a random sequence of 59 separate packs of cards (3,068 in total), which took around 14 hours to memorise and a further nine hours to recount. On this occasion he made a single mistake, which he immediately corrected without any help. His record remains unbroken to this day.

When it comes to other fictions, and even books I have read many times and love, I can recall only odd lines, with haphazard accuracy. Many of them from Joyce, as it happens.

After several false starts I've been re-reading *Ulysses* off and on since I was sixteen—younger than Stephen Dedalus—and am now old enough to be Leopold Bloom's late father. I will, I hope, read it again at least twice more from cover to cover before I give up the ghost.

Whenever I re-read *Ulysses* I recall earlier engagements with the novel in other cities at other times in my life: Paris in my twenties, Moscow and Beijing in my thirties, Ljubljana and Zagreb in my forties. Future re-readings connect me to an as-yet unknown older self.

I have forgotten—sometimes completely—many of the novels I first read forty years ago. Twenty pages into *Barnaby Rudge* recently—the one Dickens work I was quite sure I'd never read—I came across some pencilled marginal notes in my own handwriting and felt like a spectre re-visiting my own life. And this sensation prompted some gloomy thoughts on time's passing, of life's unrecoverable moments, of mutability. Did I really waste precious hours of my irrecoverable youth reading *Barnaby Rudge*, only to forget all about it forty years later? How much of my life have I frittered away on reading?

My bedside table has within easy reach a few childhood favourites: *The Otterbury Incident*, *The Land of Green Ginger* and *Through the Looking-glass*, books that were read to me as a child, that I've read to our own children and which I now, in the dead of night and unable to sleep, sometimes re-read to myself. Also to hand is Auden's commonplace book *A Certain World*, a Wodehouse or two and some Raymond Chandlers. And there's a copy of *Finnegans Wake*. For reasons I'll explain in a later essay, I shall never get around to reading this properly, but a page or two acts as an erratically reliable soporific.

35. CATASTRAPOSTROPHE

The highbrow literary magazine *The Criterion* first appeared in 1922, was acquired by the publishers Faber and Gwyer in 1927 and relaunched in April that year as *The Monthly Criterion*. Its newly-appointed editor, T.S. Eliot, celebrated by attending a boxing-match at the Royal Albert Hall. An agreement that the new magazine 'shall bear the name of the editor prominently on the cover' didn't prove much of a crowd-puller and sales peaked at around 800 copies per issue. Publication was temporarily suspended when the co-proprietor Lady Rothermere withdrew her financial support and Eliot, one suspects, was secretly glad to see the back of her. She had earlier tried to interest him in a book by her sister, which tested his courtesy to breaking point:

> I wish she might know that I spell my name with one L, that my poem is not *WasteLands*, and that Joyce's book is *Ulysses*, not *Odyssey*!

Penguin *Dubliners*

It could have been worse—according to Gavin Ewart the Queen Mother on meeting Eliot referred to *The Waste Land* as *The Desert Song*. Joyce, no doubt for mischievous reasons of his own, made a habit of writing his publisher's name as *Elliot*. And, incidentally, he pronounced both Ulysses and *Ulysses* as 'Olyssays'.

While we're on the subject of titles—it was Flann O'Brien who claimed that Joyce's early death at 59 was hastened by his intense irritation at the frequent and erroneous inclusion of an apostrophe in the title of *Finnegans Wake*. Happily our author was not alive to see the cover of this edition of *Dubliners*, published by Penguin. It would have been the death of him.

That intrusive apostrophe is commonplace, and seems to be especially popular with those who like to disparage the novel. We can safely assume it's down to the apostrophised title of the original ballad repurposed by Joyce, although it wasn't until 1976 that the Joyce scholar Jane S. Meehan revealed the likely origin in a short essay appearing in an issue of *A Wake Newslitter* entitled 'Tim Finigan's Wake', her title coming from the Irish-American ballad composed by the Dublin-born theatre manager John F. Poole who had arrived in New York from Ireland as a 12-year-old.[*]

By his early thirties he was the manager of several New York theatres and a well-known writer of songs and comic skits, not least for the singer/entrepreneur Tony Pastor, known as 'the Father of Vaudeville'. 'Tim Finigan's Wake', a song about a drunken builder's death following a fall from a ladder and his subsequent resurrection, seemed to Meehan the likely source for Joyce's choice of title. This is on the face of it a reasonable assumption, but it turns out she was wrong because Poole was born in either 1833 or 1835 and was therefore only nineteen or twenty-one and not yet in any way involved in the theatre when, in 1854, an earlier piano arrangement of the 'popular comic song' called 'Finigans Wake' by one John Durnal was published. (You'll note the lack of an apostrophe on the cover of the piano score.)

Durnal's 'Finigans Wake'

[*]Meehan's article, and much else besides, can be found on a wonderful website called JoyceTools: hwww.riverrun.org.uk/joycetools.html, run by Ian Gunn in honour of the Joyce scholar Clive Hart. It's a treasure trove, and includes a complete run of *A Wake Newslitter* and its successor *A Finnegans Wake Circular*.

When *Tony Pastor's Complete Budget of Comic Songs* eventually appeared in 1864 it did not include Poole's 'Tim Finigan's Wake', in spite of being edited by Poole himself. The song did feature in *Tony Pastor's Book of 600 Comic Songs* published three years later, and this was thirteen years after the original publication of Durnal's 'Finigans Wake'. So was the latter the true inspiration for Joyce's title?

John F. Poole died in Brooklyn in 1863. The cause of death was dropsy, brought on by—and you couldn't make this up—*a fall from a ladder*.

TIM FINIGAN'S WAKE.

By John F. Poole.

As sung by Tony Pastor.

Air—" The French Musician."

Tim Finigan lived in Walker street,
  A gentleman Irishman—mighty odd—
He'd a beautiful brogue, so rich and sweet,
  And to rise in the world he carried the hod.
But, you see, he'd a sort of a tippling way—
  With a love for the liquor poor Tim was born,
And to help him through his work each day,
  He'd a drop of the craythur' every morn.

          Chorus.
    Whack, hurrah! blood and 'ounds, ye sowl ye!
      Welt the flure, yer trotters shake;
    Isn't it the truth I've tould ye,
      Lots of fun at Finigan's wake!

One morning Tim was rather full,
  His head felt heavy, which made him shake;
He fell from the ladder and broke his skull,
  So they carried him home his corpse to wake.
They rolled him up in a nice clean sheet,
  And laid him out upon the bed,
With fourteen candles round his feet,
  And a couple of dozen around his head!
                          Whack, hurrah, etc.

John F. Poole's 'Tim Finigan's Wake'

36. TIME MANAGEMENT

For those of you who lead busy lives, are 'time poor' and therefore need to quantify the opportunity cost of becoming and remaining literate, here's a handy guide to reading Joyce, with data provided by howlongtoread.com:

Title	Word Count	Est. reading time
Dubliners	67,565	about 5 hours
A Portrait of the Artist as a Young Man	84,810	about 6 hours
Ulysses	264,861	about 18 hours

The website, which is 'an Amazon Associate', reduces reading to a rigid formula based on the number of pages and an average reading speed, without taking into account the kind of text. There are 12 million books on the site with reading times ranging from *The Cat in the Hat* (1 hour 11 minutes) to the *Tractatus Logico-Philosophicus* (1 hour 51 minutes). These two examples alone might lead you to question its reliability.

Finnegans Wake is problematic not because of the word count (which is lower than *Ulysses* at around 225,000) but because of the words, and the syntax, and everything else. Yet howlongtoread.com confidently asserts that the average reader (barrelling along at 300 words per minute) will take just 42 minutes to read it from cover to cover, so somebody has clearly screwed up. Come to that, they insist that the same average reader will need no more than 21 minutes to read all of Ezra Pound's *Cantos*.

Of course it takes weeks, or months, or *years* to read. I've been slogging through it doggedly for more than four decades and expect I'll never reach the end, and if I ever do so I know I'll then have to start all over again. Sisyphus had it easy.

But, as I was surprised to discover, it can take even longer to plough through the *Wake* in the company of like-minded others. I spent a memorable autumn evening a few years ago with a *Wake* reading group run by the Joyce scholar Professor Finn Fordham (and there's a dazzling example of nominative determinism for you). Ten of us sat around a large table in an upper floor room of the University College London Senate Building in Bloomsbury and together, in the course of two hours, we worked conscientiously and very enjoyably through three consecutive sentences. I enjoyed every minute spent with this engaged and engaging polyglot group of readers, all of whom brought different kinds of knowledge and expertise to the gathering. I realised that night, with a combination of dismay and relief, that an exhaustive reading of the *Wake* is not something any single reader can ever hope to accomplish, and that I should therefore, and with a clear conscience, continue not to persevere (if you see what I mean), secure in the knowledge that similar groups all over the world were doing so on my behalf. More relief than dismay, if I'm honest.

But what of those who are, or claim to be, simply too busy to be doing with *Ulysses*, let alone the *Wake*? To mark Bloomsday in 2004 BBC News online offered a chortling take on 'a book that few have read and even fewer comprehend'. The impeccably philistine perspective featured 'an irreverent simple chapter-by-chapter guide' by one Neil Smith, a relentlessly jocular debunking of the masterpiece in which each chapter was jauntily summarised. Here, for instance, is his take on the 'Circe' episode in its entirety:

> READER *(horrorstruck)* Blimey, this looks like heavy going.
>
> STEPHEN'S DEAD MOTHER No kidding! There's over 100 pages of this stuff, all written in the style of a play script. But all you need to know is that Bloom follows Stephen to a brothel where they have lots of freaky hallucinations.

At which point this effort to popularise a complex highbrow work of art disappears up its own snickering backside. 'All you need to know' FFS. I'll never understand why popularisation can't be accompanied by a degree of reverence, and why 'debunking' is seen as a worthwhile way to spend one's allocation of years on earth, but there it is and here we are.

The BBC invited readers to submit their own summaries, most of which were even less engaging than Smith's, but there was a good effort from Roger Moss of Brighton, England, who nailed each of the 18 episodes with admirable concision:

> Boy refuses to meet dying mum's maker. Man meets butcher. Boy's dad meets man. Man meets editor. Editor meets boy. Boy meets cronies. Man meets classical statue's bottoms. Everybody meets everybody in the streets. Man meets barmaids. Wife meets lover. Man meets bigot. Gerty meets man's eyes. Boy meets drunken soldier. Man meets boy (at last). Boy and man meet lying sailor. Boy's

lips meet man's cocoa. Man meets wife's bottom in the bed. Wife meets boy (in her dreams).

That's pretty much it, if you need to know the plot, such as it is. Moss hits on something central to *Ulysses*—it's all about chance encounters in an urban setting, and the randomness of human interaction.

For those unable or unwilling to put in the 18 hours allegedly required to tackle *Ulysses* it may be worth waiting for an English translation of a German language novel by the Swiss writer Reto Hänny, (born 1947) entitled *Blooms Schatten* ('Bloom's Shadow'). Published in 2014, it's a retelling of *Ulysses* in a single sentence of 145 pages.

37. LOTS OF FUN ON FINNEGANS WEB

This essay would be by far the longest if presented simply as a catalogue of the multitudinous *Wake*-related websites and creative projects currently available online, because the *Wake* seems to have adopted the internet as its natural medium. As David Rose has pointed out:

> the operant structure of the *Wake* is reminiscent of the internet and of fungal mycelium—vast networks of threadlike process lacking a center and leading everywhere. In fact, when the internet first reached a critical mass of popularity in the mid-1990s, Joyceans were quick to realize the potential for hyperlinking the text of *Finnegans Wake* in ways that would streamline our probing its interconnectivity. Why? Because *Finnegans Wake* was already hyperlinked! Rhizomatic Joyce had anticipated hypertext by seven decades.[*]

The botanical term 'rhizomatic' was employed in a philosophical sense by the French post-structuralists Gilles Deleuze and Félix Guattari in their *Capitalism and Schizophrenia* project (1972–1980). They used it to describe a theoretical approach to research that allowed for multiple perspectives when, for instance, representing and interpreting data, just as the rhizome in nature, the fungal mycelium, sends out roots in all directions, spreading and replicating. They contrasted this rhizomatic model with a traditional 'arbolic' or 'arborescent' (tree-like) concept of knowledge, one which involves hierarchies, dualist categories and binary choices. Deleuze and Guattari's model challenges established systems and power structures, proposing a non-hierarchical and less discriminatory mode of interpreting the world, one that was anticipated by Cyril Connolly in his expansive aphorism: 'I believe in God the Either, God the Or, and God the Holy Both.'

Joyce's widening presence in the digital realm means he is increasingly dematerialised, dispersed and elusive, becoming ever harder to fix and to formulate. The works remain as relatively stable texts, both in print and online, but the aura surrounding them is less stable, less predictable, less navigable and more bewildering.

---

[*] 'Cryptogrammic Cryptograms: Fungi in *Finnegans Wake*' by David Rose in 'Notes from Underground'. Appearing online in fungimag.com (Winter 2011).

David Rose's take on the *Wake* as a hypertext-in-waiting is supported by the Twitter account @finnegansreader, which is dedicated to tweeting the entire text of *Finnegans Wake*, originally in fragments up to 140 characters, later raised to 280. With around 4,000 followers, it complements @Ulyssesreader, which offers much the same service to more than 7,000 followers.

I signed up to @finnegansreader but was soon overwhelmed with so many tweets (which arrived in huge batches overnight) that I unsubscribed after a few days. It struck me, however, that the *Wake* was far more assimilable in tiny fragments, with each tweeted group of words isolated from the distractions of a surrounding text making a greater impression as a free-standing entity. Although a flurry of *Wake* quotes at odd times of the day and night would be distracting, if I ever find myself working in an office again I'd sign up again like a shot, seeing such tweets as a vital connection with the real world.

Another Twitter account is @FW_WOTD 'deciphering *Finnegans Wake* a word at a time'. This tweets daily definitions of *Wake* words and is even less popular than the other two, which I hope is some sort of a recommendation. A quick check on the latest tweet threw up the zeitgeisty:

> 'nuder' (FW 268.18 & 493.19) adj. Neither masculine nor feminine but neuter when without clothes or nude.

A favourite *Wake*-related website is something simply inconceivable before the availability of digital technology. Co-founded in 2014 by Derek Pyle and Kelley Kipperman, *Waywords and Meansigns* is a project involving 'a host of musicians and writers, artists and scholars, weirdos and generally adventurous people'. There are currently seventeen musicians from around the world working together to produce a musical version of the whole book, unabridged. They've done this three times now, with different casts of musicians and readers.

The first complete setting, which lasted for more than 24 hours, was made available free of charge on 4th May 2015 to mark the 76th anniversary of the *Wake*'s publication. Mariana Lanari and Soerd Leitjan, who are based in the Netherlands, perform the first part of the first version—around 90 minutes of readings and music—and it's a particular pleasure to hear their non-Irish voices getting to grips with the text, giving the original an extra vibrancy. The second setting was released on February 2nd 2016, Joyce's 134th birthday. In both versions the book was broken down into its seventeen chapters with different contributors assigned to each. The only stipulations were that the spoken words should be audible and the text unabridged.

The third version, bringing the running total to around 70 hours, debuted on May 4th 2017 and was the final group release. The plan is to continue releasing short individual contributions. It's worth a close look, and listen.[*]

The James Joyce Digital Archive has all the drafts of *Finnegans Wake* and a 'chicken guide' by the scholar Danis Rose.[†] You can download many essential resources from Joyce Tools, including the aforementioned *A Wake Newslitter* and *A Finnegans Wake Circular*.[‡]

Mentioned elsewhere in *Multiple Joyce*, fweet.org is 'an international bureau for the decoding' of *Finnegans Wake*. The site had its analogue origins in *A Wake Newslitter*, first produced by Fritz Zenn and Clive Hart in the University of Sydney in 1962, material from which later appeared in book form as *Annotations to Finnegans Wake* (1980) by Roland McHugh 1980. It's all now available online in Raphael Slepon's fweet website, which has attracted well over 3 million searches since it opened 'on Yom Kippur eve, October 12, 2005'.

Finally, at finwake.com you'll find a fully annotated text navigating the multiple and simultaneous layers of the novel, excavating each stratum of meaning beneath each word. This will slow your reading speed down to a snail's pace but it addresses a concern expressed by Jay David Bolter, that both *Ulysses* and *Finnegans Wake* are 'texts that have been flattened out to fit on the printed page'. It's yet another way into the text and, like the book itself, is best taken in small doses.[§]

While the internet has certainly enriched our understanding of *Finnegans Wake*, *Finnegans Wake* has in turn immeasurably enriched the internet. In what we might see as the book's apotheosis, its online presence seems to be, like the universe itself, finite but without limit.

---

[*] waywordsandmeansigns.com
[†] https://www.jjda.ie/main/JJDA/F/FF/app/chka.htm
[‡] http://www.riverrun.org.uk/joycetools.html
[§] *Writing Space Computers, Hypertext, and the Remediation of Print* by Jay David Bolter (2nd edition, Routledge 2001).

And, also like the universe itself, there are vast regions beyond our current understanding. Late in my online researches, I stumbled across one of those online 'unwrapping' reviews, a straight-to-camera short film in which a member of the public talks us through the features of some newly-acquired product, offering an appraisal and final judgement. In this case, a fan of *Monster High* unboxed his very own Finnegan Wake™ and, in the course of an 8-minute monologue, listed its features before announcing that it was 'super cool et très originale'.* That the review was delivered in French made the exercise seem more intellectually respectable than if it had been in (say) an affectless LA drawl, but that's just me being unforgivably snobbish. The young presenter had a sharp haircut and was eloquent in his praise of the kind of toy anathematised by Roland Barthes in *Mythologies*.

Despite all this there's still a long way to go when it comes to exhausting the *Wake* as a text. Joyce once declared that he expected *Ulysses* 'to keep the critics busy for three hundred years', which, given its publication in 1939, would take us to the year 2239, by which time it's quite possible that life as we know it on our planet will be lived in conditions currently inconceivable to us, and I expect the heat death of the universe will come sooner than we we run out of critical approaches to *Finnegans Wake*. Following Barthes' lead, the Death of the Reader is now a distinct possibility.

*https://www.youtube.com/watch?v=aMfzKOhs7Fw Posted 10 September 2015.

38. CAUGHT GESTURE

In 1983 an Oxford academic called Ronald Bush published a book about T.S. Eliot, at one point casually using an off-hand phrase referring to Joyce. The late Clive James, who knew a thing or two about poetry and had a hair-trigger bullshit detector, pounced:

A Gesture Towards James Joyce by Clive James

> My gesture towards *Finnegans Wake* is deliberate.
> —Ronald Bush, *T.S. Eliot: A Study in Character and Style*

The gesture towards *Finnegans Wake* was deliberate.
It was not accidental.
Years of training went into the gesture,
As W.C. Fields would practise a juggling routine
Until his eczema-prone hands bled in their kid gloves;
As Douglas Fairbanks Sr trimmed the legs of a table
Until, without apparent effort and from a standing start,
He could jump up on to it backwards;
Or as Gene Kelly danced an entire tracking shot over and over
Until the final knee-slide ended exactly in focus,
Loafers tucked pigeon-toed behind him,
Perfect smile exultant,
Hands thrown open saying 'How *about* that?'

The gesture towards *Finnegans Wake* was deliberate.
Something so elaborate could not have been otherwise.
Though an academic gesture, it partook in its final form
Of the balletic arabesque,
With one leg held out extended to the rear
And the equiponderant forefinger pointing demonstratively
Like the statue of Eros in Piccadilly Circus,
Or, more correctly, the Mercury of Giambologna,
Although fully, needless to say, clad.

The gesture towards *Finnegans Wake* was deliberate,
Its aim assisted by the position of the volume,
A 1957 printing in the yellow and orange wrapper
Propped on a sideboard and opened at page 164
So that the gesture might indicate a food-based conceit
About *pudding the carp before doeuvre hors—*
The Joycean amalgam in its lucidic essence,
Accessible to students and yet also evincing

The virtue of requiring a good deal of commentary
Before what looked simple even if capricious
Emerged as precise even if complex
And ultimately unfathomable.

The gesture towards *Finnegans Wake* was deliberate,
Being preceded by an 'It is no accident, then',
An exuberant 'It is neither accidental nor surprising'
And at least two cases of 'It is not for nothing that',
These to adumbrate the eventual paroxysm
In the same way that a bouncer from Dennis Lillee
Has its overture of giant strides galumphing towards you
With the face both above and below the ridiculous moustache
Announcing by means of unmistakable grimaces
That what comes next is no mere spasm
But a premeditated attempt to knock your block off.

The gesture towards *Finnegans Wake* was deliberate
And so was my gesture with two fingers.
In America it would have been one finger only
But in Italy I might have employed both arms,
The left hand crossing to the tense right bicep
As my clenched fist jerked swiftly upwards—
The most deliberate of all gestures because most futile,
Defiantly conceding the lost battle.

The gesture towards *Finnegans Wake* was deliberate:
So much so that Joyce should have seen it coming.
Even through the eyepatch of his last years.
He wrote a book full of nothing except writing
For people who can't do anything but read,
And now their gestures clog the air around us.
He asked for it, and we got it.

'A book full of nothing except writing'. Oof! Clive James had clearly read the *Wake*, or at least knew it well enough to lift 'pudding the carp before doeuvre hors' from its pages, where it appears parenthetically thus:

> (the appetising entry of this subject on a fool chest of vialds is plumply pudding the carp before doevre hors)

For reasons I'll explain in essay 50 there are times when I lean towards Clive James's take on the *Wake* and, come to that, side with Beckett's Molloy in *Molloy* (1951):

> A mug's game in my opinion and tiring on top of that, in the long run.

Admittedly he was talking about sex. There are other times, though, when I come across a line or two of the *Wake* and I briefly resemble the character Moran, in the same novel:

> And I said, with rapture, Here is something I can study all my life, and never understand.

39. May the Wake be with You

The first serious study of Joyce's last novel was *A Skeleton Key to Finnegans Wake* by Joseph Campbell and Henry Morton, published in 1944. It saw the first critical application of the Joycean coinage 'monomyth', a word that appears just once in the *Wake** but which would later be recycled in another book by Campbell, one that would turn out to have an absolutely astonishing impact on popular culture.

In *The Hero with a Thousand Faces* (1949), Campbell recycled Joyce's term 'monomyth' to describe a narrative archetype, or story structure, that underlies (for instance) the lives of the Buddha, Moses, Jesus and Mohammed. A template, if you like. The skeleton key to the *Wake* became, in Campbell's hands, a swipe card pass to all mythology.

Campbell also dubbed the monomyth 'The Hero's Journey' and offered the following brisk description, one which could today form the basis of a Hollywood blockbuster pitch:

> A hero ventures forth from the world of common day into a region of supernatural wonder: fabulous forces are there encountered and a decisive victory is won: the hero comes back from this mysterious adventure with the power to bestow boons on his fellow man.

The gender bias in Campbell's approach reflects the priorities of mid-century scholarship and also, to be fair, the predominance of male characters in narratives from the Odyssey onwards. Yet arguably the best cinematic realisation of the Hero's Journey, released ten years before Campbell's book appeared, actually features a female lead. Here's Rick Polito's celebrated synopsis of the movie in question:

> Transported to a surreal landscape, a young girl kills the first person she meets and then teams up with three strangers to kill again.

It's *The Wizard of Oz* (1939), although not as most of us recall it. Young Dorothy Gale leaves her home in Kansas, makes new friends on the road to the Emerald City, endures a series of trials, overcomes

---

*'At the carryfour with awlus plawshus, their happy-ass cloudious! And then and too the trivials! And their bivouac! And his monomyth! Ah ho! Say no more about it! I'm sorry!'

adversity and eventually arrives back home, a little older and much wiser. The film uncannily anticipates Campbell's later take on the monomyth and the links between Oz and *Ulysses* are certainly worth a digression.

The author L. Frank Baum (1856–1919) published the first of his many *Oz* books in 1900, working the idea into the ground over the following twenty years with diminishing returns. Joyce may have been aware of these books, as some commentators claim (although since the family spoke only Italian at home I can't picture him reading them to Giorgio and Lucia). There appear to be two references to Baum's books in the 'Circe' episode of *Ulysses*: the first when the prostitute Zoe fans herself and exclaims 'I'm melting!' (conceivably a reference to the liquidation of the Wicked Witch of the West) and the second is this:

> Laughing witches in red cutty sarks ride through the air on broomsticks.

I'm unconvinced. Surely 'I'm melting' was a commonplace way of telling the world how hot one felt, cognate with 'I'm freezing' or 'I'm starving.' And broomstick-riding witches are part of a tradition long pre-dating Baum's stories. 'Cutty Sark' was 18th century Scots for 'short chemise' and a nickname of the witch Nannie Dee, a sorceress created by Robert Burns, who uses the name in his 1791 poem 'Tam o' Shanter'. It's a powerfully erotic image—the witch astride her broomstick with knickers on display—and certainly appropriate for the brothel setting in *Ulysses*. But Joyce didn't need Baum as a source, and perhaps this is a rare case in which the Joycean aura doesn't overlap persuasively with some other cultural manifestation.

But to return to the monomyth: the most startling connection between *Finnegans Wake* and popular culture is *Star Wars*. One might argue—and I will—that without the *Wake* we would have no Luke Skywalker, no bleeping androids, no Obi-Wan Kenobi, no Death Star and no Darth Vader.

In 1999 George Lucas, creator of *Star Wars*, confessed his debt to Campbell in a televised interview explaining how the concept of the monomyth shaped the *Star Wars* saga from the start. The young hero Luke sets out on a journey (which soon becomes his 'destiny') from his humble origins on a Tatooine farmstead (compare Dorothy's

Kansas). He is accompanied by his android pals (one of which resembles the Tin Man in *Oz*, and don't get me started on the self-evident kinship of the Cowardly Lion and Chewbacca), he overcomes challenges, then commits to and fights bravely for a cause before confronting his nemesis, the wizard-like Darth Vader.

That *Star Wars* resembles *The Wizard of Oz* structurally is all down to the idea of the Joycean monomyth as outlined by Campbell and studied by Lucas.*

Finnegans Wake was first published in book form by Faber and Faber on Thursday 4th May 1939, a date that has since become celebrated as Star Wars Day. Why? For a punning reason that would doubtless meet with Joyce's approval. May the Fourth be with you.

---

*The television writer, director, and producer D.B. Weiss is co-creator and show runner of *Game of Thrones*, the television adaptation of George R.R. Martin's *A Song of Ice and Fire*. Weiss was awarded an MPhil in Irish Literature from Trinity College Dublin, where he wrote his thesis on *Finnegans Wake*. It was there that he met his long-term writing collaborator David Benioff, who was researching Beckett. In 2018, Disney studios announced that the two men would write and produce a series of new *Star Wars* films.

40. Silence, Exile and Punning

> The Good and Great must ever shun
> That reckless and abandoned one
> Who stoops to perpetrate a pun.

So wrote that inveterate punpertrator Lewis Carroll, and he was right—puns are not admired or even tolerated by 'the Good and Great' i.e. grown-ups, for whom puns rank precariously above sarcasm as the second-lowest form of wit.[*]

Other views are available. 'There is nothing quite so enjoyable as the much-maligned Joycean pun,' according to Eimear McBride[†], and I completely agree with her. But punning, even at Joyce's level of virtuosity, tends to elicit groans from the sceptical, and the more elaborate the pun the more excruciating the effect. It's possible that a compulsion to make puns is down to a neurological abnormality. This is worth a closer look.

Foerster's syndrome is a very rare and utterly bizarre neurological condition first described by the German neurosurgeon Ottfrid Foerster. In 1929 he was carrying out brain surgery on a patient suffering from a tumour in the third ventricle, a small cavity deep down in the mid brain and immediately adjacent to those structures associated with the arousal of emotions. When Foerster began to manipulate the tumour, the patient, who was conscious, suddenly erupted into a fluent and relentless stream of puns, all of them related (unsurprisingly) to thoughts of knives and butchery.

---

[*]'When is a Pun not a Pun?' says a line in the Wake, a text absolutely supersaturated with polyglot puns. The Messiah, one could argue, made a mild ecclesiastical pun when he appointed Saint Peter as the foundation of the Christian religion (at least in the Latin version): '*Tu es Petrus, et super hanc petram aedificabo ecclesiam meam*' ('You are Peter, and on this rock shall I build my church'). This makes more sense, but loses all dignity, if we translate Peter as 'Rocky'. ('You are Rocky, and on this rock . . .' etc), because in Latin *petrus* means 'rock', geddit? It's a pun in Matthew's original Greek, where the name is 'Petros', and also in the original Aramaic spoken by Jesus, who called Simon 'Cephas', which means rock in Aramaic. Saint Peter was known by both names in his lifetime—the Apostle Paul calls him both Peter and Cephas. Frank Budgen wrote in his obituary of Joyce (*Horizon* magazine, February 1941): 'Rebutting the charge of vulgarity against the use of the pun, he said: 'The Holy Roman Catholic Apostolic Church was built on a pun. It ought to be good enough for me.'

[†]In *gorse* journal, 9th June 2014.

In that same year a German psychiatrist called Dr. A.A. Brill reported what he believed was the first case of *Witzelsucht* in the *International Journal of Psychoanalysis*.

Witzelsucht (from *witzeln*, meaning to joke and *sucht*, meaning an addiction, or yearning) is a very odd set of neurological symptoms characterised by a tendency to make puns and to tell jokes or pointless stories in socially inappropriate situations. This 'pun mania' is sometimes associated, although very rarely, with the condition of hypersexuality, a Tourettish tendency to make explicit and sexual comments. This disorder is most commonly observed in patients with damage to their right frontal lobe, the part of the brain most involved in the cognitive processing of decision-making, and elderly people are particularly prone to *Witzelsucht* because of the decreasing amount of grey matter. *Dorland's Illustrated Medical Dictionary* defines *Witzelsucht* as 'a mental condition characteristic of frontal lesions and marked by the making of poor jokes and puns [. . .] at which the patient himself is intensely amused'.

Relentless punning? Inappropriate sexual references? It would take a stronger character than mine to resist the compulsion to call it 'punnilingus'. You can find some unsettling accounts of the condition online, and be warned they're not for the faint-hearted.

Has anyone yet made a connection between Joyce's relentlessly compacted multilingual punning in the *Wake*, the sexual content (not least Earwicker's incestuous feelings for his daughter) and *Witzelsucht*? I can find nothing at all linking Joyce's last book to this neurological anomaly, and I am not for a moment implying that he suffered from such a condition, or anything like it. Nor, come to that, do those readers who relish the epic punorama of the *Wake*. I'm afraid that I may appear smug in sharing this minor discovery—but there's no smirk without fear.

41. WUGS AND GUTCHES

Here's the novelist Jenny Turner, writing in the *London Review of Books* (15th November 2001):

> A writer, born around 1890, is famous for three novels. The first is short, elegant, and an instant classic. The second, the masterpiece, has the same characters in it, is much longer and more complicated, and increasingly interested in myth and language games. The third is enormous, mad, unreadable.

Joyce, you say? Wrong. The title of her article is 'Reasons for Liking Tolkien' and the three novels she has in mind are *The Hobbit* (1937), *The Lord of the Rings* (1955) and *The Silmarillion* (1977).

It's not easy to think of two writers more dissimilar than Joyce and Tolkien, yet they have at least one thing in common. Both *Ulysses* and *The Lord of the Rings* have been voted the greatest novels of the twentieth century by, respectively, the BBC programme *Bookchoice* and Waterstone's bookstore (in 1997), and by The Modern Library (in 1998). The fact that these votes happened nearly a quarter of a century ago makes me wonder about the reputations of the novels and their authors today and, come to that, why we continue to conduct these annoying and pointless polls.

There are other similarities. Tolkien's Middle Earth topography is as meticulously rendered as that of Joyce's Dublin, its elaborate invented languages comparable to the nocturnal lexicon of the *Wake*, and the epic undertow of *The Lord of the Rings* bears comparison with Joyce's greatest novels. Both authors share an interest in an underlying or embedded mythology, both have a gift for linguistic innovation and both attract fiercely committed admirers, and detractors. None of Tolkien's major works appeared during Joyce's lifetime, but Tolkien was certainly aware of Joyce and the Tolkien scholar Margaret Hiley has found extensive evidence of the former's engagement with the latter. *

According to the website tolkiengateway.net there are three references to Joyce in Tolkien's writing, two of which are vanishingly

---

* 'Bizarre or dream-like': J.R.R. Tolkien on Finnegans Wake' by Margaret Hiley, published in *Joycean Legacies* edited by Martha C. Carpentier (Palgrave Macmillan, 2015).

slight—a brief note on the back of a manuscript page of *The Lord of the Rings* and the line 'Anna Livia Plurabelle' scribbled down and then struck out in a diary entry for 1931.

The third is more intriguing. References to Joyce and to Gertrude Stein occur in a draft of a lecture entitled 'A Secret Vice' given by Tolkien at the Oxford Esperanto Congress in August 1930 in which he contrasts 'auxiliary' languages (such as Esperanto) with languages constructed purely to give aesthetic pleasure, of which there are plenty in the Tolkien canon.

Tolkien's thoughts, prompted by a reading of Joyce, concern the connection between sound, script and meaning when it comes to fictional languages. He admits to a 'fascination with pure sound,' with a particular focus on harmony, and he appears to criticise Joyce for not going far enough in the *Wake*. Margaret Hiley suggests that *The Lord of the Rings* (1954–55), like *Finnegans Wake*, works towards 'a narrative strategy [that] illuminates the process of interpretation on the part of the reader and writer.'

In the lecture Tolkien is particularly interested in what he calls 'secret' languages, recalling two from his own childhood: Animalic and Nevbosh.

The first of these was invented by Tolkien's young cousins Mary and Marjorie Incledon in around 1905. The teenage Tolkien, already immersed in Anglo-Saxon and Latin, found this a congenial activity despite it being linguistically very crude and based on nothing more creative than random substitution. The only surviving Animalic fragment is '*Dog nightingale woodpecker forty*', which means 'you're a donkey' because 'donkey' was the Animalic word for 'forty', and 'forty' for 'donkey'. High frequency lexical items such as articles and auxiliary verbs were replaced by longer and more cumbersome nouns such as 'woodpecker' for 'a' and the process was essentially ludic—a secret language *game*. The significance of it is that this was likely to have been Tolkien's earliest engagement with a form of invented language.

When Marjorie lost interest, her sister Mary and some other children began to construct a more sophisticated new language called Nevbosh, which is itself the Nevbosh word for 'New Nonsense'. If Animalic had been simply a game then Nevbosh was more like a code, and marked Tolkien's first true involvement with the creation of a significant word-horde in an imaginary tongue. 'I was a member of the Nevbosh-speaking world,' he later recalled, and what especially interested him at this stage were Nevbosh words that were not just distorted versions of standard English but entirely original, a phonoaesthetic combination of sound and meaning that was purely delightful. This was the approach he adopted when creating the languages of Middle Earth.

The only surviving Nevbosh text is a limerick given in Humphrey Carpenter's authorised biography of Tolkien, published in 1977:

> *Dar fys ma vel gom co palt 'hoc*
> *pys go iskili far maino woc?*
> > *Pro si go fys do roc de*
> > *Do cat ym maino bocte*
> *De volt fac soc ma taimful gyróc!'*

> There was an old man who said 'how
> can I possibly carry my cow?
> > For if I was to ask it
> > To get in my pocket
> It would make such a fearful row!'*

In his 1930 lecture Tolkien observed that children, when 'distorting' words already known to them, demonstrated an intuitive understanding of elementary phonetics, a view that anticipated the ground-breaking work undertaken in the late 1950s by the psycholinguist Jean Berko Gleason (born 1931), whose main interest was in childhood language acquisition. In 1958 she developed the celebrated 'Wug test' (you can find it quite easily on the internet) in which young children were presented with a picture of an imaginary creature called a Wug and, prompted by a second picture showing a pair of such creatures, invited to say what the plural form might be. The answer was the monosyllabic 'Wugs' of course, and with the plural 's' invariably pronounced as the voiced phoneme /z/, as in /wʌgz/. When a second solitary creature—a 'Gutch'—was shown, the plural form (the children all agreed) could only be the two-syllable 'Gutches', with the 's' pronounced as an unvoiced /s/, as in 'crutches'.

Now this simple test demonstrates that even very young children have an innate and remarkably sophisticated knowledge and under-

---

*Wouldn't 'terrible' or 'horrible' scan far better than 'fearful' in the last line?

standing of linguistic morphology—how words are formed, and how they relate to other words. They have an internalised linguistic system which enables them to produce the correct form of plurals, past tenses, possessives, and other words from scratch, using words they have never heard before, and this proves that they have developed and can apply general rules from the language they have already heard.

Finnegans Wake is the mother of all Wug tests, one in which adult readers are invited—or compelled—to intuit correlative meanings from the jostling multitude of Wugs and Gutches that constitute the novel's nocturnal Esperanto.

42. JABBERWAKEY

In May 2021, during a lull in the pandemic, the Victoria and Albert Museum in London launched 'Alice: Curiouser and Curiouser', an exhibition devoted to the cultural legacy of Lewis Carroll's two most celebrated books. Reviewing the show the art critic Jonathan James invoked Joyce, 'whose nonsense masterpiece *Finnegan Wake* is a Carroll homage' (*Guardian* website 19th May 2021).

Lewis Carroll and Alice feature significantly in the *Wake*, although Joyce said in 1927 (when he was already five years into the composition of the novel) that he had never read anything by the author until a certain Mrs Nutting 'gave me a book, not Alice, a few weeks ago—though, of course, I heard bits and scraps.' James Atherton (author of *The Books at the Wake*) reckons that Joyce was probably referring to Carroll's now all-but-forgotten and virtually unreadable *Sylvie and Bruno* (1889), and that Joyce's reading of it prompted his subsequent close interest in both Carroll (born Charles Lutwidge Dodgson) and Alice Liddell. Together and separately they haunt the pages of the *Wake*, as Atherton makes clear: 'old Dadgerson's dodges', 'Dodgfather, Dodgson and Coo', 'wonderland's wanderlad', 'liddel oud oddity', 'loose carollaries', 'Lewd's carol' and so on, including this extended riff:

> Though Wonderlawn's lost us for ever. Alis, alas, she broke the glass! Liddell looker through the leafery, ours is mistery of pain.

There are also many other Carrollian moments in the *Wake*, including anagrams and reversed spellings. Perhaps Joyce was also thinking of Alice as a subject for psychoanalysis when he wrote about girls 'when they were yung and easily freudened.'

Atherton's view was that *Sylvie and Bruno* was Carroll's *Finnegans Wake*, and he noted sardonically that

> James Joyce worked for seventeen years on *Finnegans Wake*, a book quite as original as *Sylvie and Bruno*; indeed one which will probably remain for ever the standard example of the danger of being too original.

Sylvie and Bruno is certainly original, and relentlessly so. But there's no joy in it, no laughter.

'Impenetrability! That's what I say!'

For my money the *Looking-glass* poem 'Jabberwocky' is the moment at which Carroll most directly anticipates the Joyce of *Finnegans Wake*. The earliest version of this poem appeared in *Mischmasch*—a periodical that Dodgson wrote and illustrated for the amusement of his family from 1855 to 1862. In German 'mischmasch' means a disorderly arrangement of things and the word appears several times in *Finnegans Wake*: 'mitsch for matsch', 'mishmash mastufractured on europe you can read off the tail of his' and '(mschlmsch!) with nurse Madge, my linking class girl.'

The 'Jabberwocky' lexicon is partly explained to Alice by Humpty Dumpty, who introduces her to 'portmanteau words' such as 'slithy' (combining, or packing together, 'lithe and slimy'), although such words consist of just two elements whereas Joyce packs his linguistic baggage to bursting point.

Humpty Dumpty makes his presence felt early on in the *Wake*, in the opening verse of *The Ballad of Persse O'Reilly*:

> Have you heard of one Humpty Dumpty
> How he fell with a roll and a rumble
> And curled up like Lord Olofa Crumple
> By the butt of the Magazine Wall,
> (Chorus) Of the Magazine Wall,
> Hump, helmet and all?

He thereafter features repeatedly, but as the traditional nursery rhyme figure who sat on a wall and had a great fall, rather than the *Looking-glass* character. I find it hard to believe that Joyce could have slogged his way through *Sylvie and Bruno* without reading either of Carroll's two Alice books, given their cultural ubiquity and astonishing quality. The spectral presence of Humpty Dumpty throughout *Finnegans Wake* is also harder to explain if Joyce never read *Through the Looking-glass*. But apparently he didn't, so there we are.

Joyce co-opts Humpty Dumpty as one of many mythological versions of the Fall of Man, although typing that phrase reminds me of Finn Fordham's droll observation that 'one of the most enduring universal myths about *Finnegans Wake* [is] that it is about enduring universal myths'.*

I recommend Fordham's book to anyone with an interest in the *Wake*. It's full of incisive observations, among which a favourite is that 'the first impression of a mix of recognisable sense and incomprehensible nonsense will always return, however deeply immersed you get in the book'. This is so true—no matter how much one is exposed to *Finnegans Wake*, no matter how many times you read and re-read a page or two, or a line or two, you never fully overcome the sense that it is essentially incomprehensible, and inexhaustibly so. There's glory for you!

---

* *Lots of Fun at Finnegans Wake: Unravelling Universals* by Finn Fordham (Oxford University Press, 2013)

43. PASSING MUSTER

The Joyce family spent a few weeks in July and August 1923 on holiday in the Sussex seaside resort of Bognor Regis, staying at the Alexandra Guest House on Clarence Road. Joyce grumbled, in a letter to his American patron Harriet Shaw Weaver, about the over-enthusiastic service and the 11pm curfew.

They were joined in Bognor by Kathleen Barnacle, Nora's youngest sister, who bought a pair of shoes locally which promptly split. Nora went back to the shop to complain and told the manager: 'My husband is a writer and if you don't change them I'll have it published in the paper.' This was, according to Richard Ellmann, 'the only recorded occasion on which Nora spoke of her husband's occupation with any approval.'

Ellmann claims it was the raucous sound of seagulls on the beach that prompted Joyce to compose the 13-line song in *Finnegans Wake* which begins:

> Three quarks for Muster Mark!
> Sure he hasn't got much of a bark
> And sure any he has it's all beside the mark.

Forty years later, in 1964, the American physicist Murray Gell-Mann (1929–2019) postulated the existence of fast-moving sub-atomic particles but couldn't think of what to call them. Although many sources insist that he took the name from *Finnegans Wake* the fact is that he'd already settled on the word before finding it in the *Wake*, as he explained in *The Quark and the Jaguar* (1994):

In 1963, when I assigned the name 'quark' to the fundamental constituents of the nucleon, I had the sound first, without the spelling, which could have been 'kwork'. Then, in one of my occasional perusals of *Finnegans Wake*, by James Joyce, I came across the word 'quark' in the phrase 'Three quarks for Muster Mark'. Since 'quark' (meaning, for one thing, the cry of the gull) was clearly intended to rhyme with ''Mark', as well as 'bark' and other such words, I had to find an excuse to pronounce it as 'kwork'. But the book represents the dream of a publican named Humphrey Chimpden Earwicker. Words in the text are typically drawn from several sources at once, like the 'portmanteau' words in *Through the Looking-glass*. From time to time, phrases occur in the book that are partially determined by calls for drinks at the bar. I argued, therefore, that perhaps one of the multiple sources of the cry 'Three quarks for Muster Mark' might be 'Three quarts for Mister Mark,' in which case the pronunciation 'kwork' would not be totally unjustified. In any case, the number three fitted perfectly the way quarks occur in nature.

There are three quarks in every proton and every neutron, and they form a cornerstone for particle physics. Working independently from Gell-Mann, the Russian-American physicist George Zweig came up with an identical quark model, although he named it 'aces'. This never caught on and it was Gell-Man who went on to win the Nobel Prize in Physics in 1969.

Along with antiquarks and gluons, quarks form the underlying elementary particles in the structure of hadrons, and of course we all know what they are, although I'll admit to having no clear idea what a Large Hadron Collider really does and, come to that, whether the adjective 'large' refers to the Hadrons under investigation, or to the Collider itself. Are there smaller Hadrons, smaller colliders?

Bognor, meanwhile, has another significant connection with the *Wake* because it was here that Joyce found the name for its main character, the publican Humphrey Chimpden Earwicker. Writing in *A Wake Newslitter* in 1979 the Joyce scholar Peter Timmerman reported his discovery of a description in a 1923 guidebook of Sidlesham Church in a district near Bognor known as the Hundred of Manhood. Among the names engraved on tombstones in the churchyard are Glue, Gravy, Boniface, Anker, Northeast . . . and Earwicker.* Early in the *Wake* Joyce explains the origins of Earwicker thus:

> Now . . . concerning the genesis of Harold or Humphrey Chimpden's occupational agnomen . . . and discarding once for all those theories from older sources which would link him back with such pivotal ancestors as the Glues, the Gravys, the Northeasts, the Ankers and the Earwickers of Sidlesham . . .

---

*Peter Chrisp, author, performer and Joyce scholar *non pareil*, writes a very fine *Finnegans Wake* blog called *From Swerve of Shore to Bend of Bay* (peter-chrisp.blogspot.co.uk) which includes many photographs of the Sidlesham gravestones (see his blog for Monday 13th January 2014).

44. YA, DA, TRA, GATHERY, PIMP, SHESSES, SHOSSAFAT, OKODEBOKO, NINE!

The American author Robert Anton Wilson (co-author with Robert Shea of the cultish *Illuminatus!* trilogy) observed that the first sentence of *Ulysses* contains 22 words, that it was published on Joyce's 40th birthday, 2nd February 1922 (or, numero-palindromically, 2/2/22), and that the number 22 recurs throughout the book.

The 18 episodes making up *Ulysses* are in all likelihood prompted by Jewish mysticism, in which 18 corresponds to the value of the letters in the Hebrew word for life (chet + yud = chai), and Bloom's Dublin perambulations correspond not only to Odysseus but to the legend of the Wandering Jew.* More locally, as it were, on page 360 of the original Shakespeare and Company edition of *Ulysses*, Joyce references the number of degrees in a circle by having Bloom think of a circus horse walking in a ring; while on page—but this sort of thing can quickly drive you nuts.

As a callow undergraduate I pointed out to my unimpressed tutor that the 23rd line of Milton's *Paradise Lost* begins with the word 'Illumine' and this, I insisted, confirmed the poet's awareness of the Ancient Bavarian Order of Illuminati, 23 being a number of particular significance in that secret society. I'd just read the Shea-Wilson trilogy and was much in thrall to crackpot numerological exegesis.†

But some numbers *are* suggestive.

Take, for instance, the commonplace and usually unchallenged assertion that Shakespeare has the largest vocabulary of any writer in English. This is usually estimated at 34,000 words, a figure which is further asserted to be around double what an educated person uses in their lifetime. But the linguist David Crystal says that this much-quoted tally is misleading, not least because the figure is inflated by including all the variants of dictionary 'head words'. So the verb 'ask' gets included along with its many variants (ask/asked/asketh/asking etc.), which bumps up the number. Measured more scrupulously,

---

*See *Ulysses by Numbers*, by Eric Bulson (Columbia University Press, 2020).
†Milton's 22nd and 23rd lines being: 'What in me is dark / Illumine, what is low raise and support'.

Shakespeare's vocabulary turns out to be in the region of 17–20,000 words, which is at least 10,000 words fewer than Joyce's *Ulysses* lexicon of around 30,000. By which I mean that of the 260,430 words that make up the novel, 29,899 of them are unique Joycean coinages. An astonishing number.

Of course Shakespeare's impact on language and culture over the past 500 years has been far greater than that of Joyce's, and Joyce in the *Wake* acknowledges the playwright's global influence by renaming him 'Shapesphere', while elsewhere gently mocking him as 'Shopkeeper'.

Crystal estimates that most of us employ a vocabulary of at least 50,000 words, although that depends on what is meant by 'employ'. We all have active vocabularies (that is, the words we say and write) and passive, or receptive vocabularies (words we might not use often, or ever, in speech or writing, but which we recognise and understand when we see or hear them). The latter lexicon is likely to be larger than the former for most of us, who may recognise the Shakespearean coinage 'incarnadine' without ever using it ourselves.

Perhaps like me, when tackling for the umpteenth time a page of the *Wake*, you experience a sense of *déjà lu*, not simply because you've tried again and failed again (without failing better) to make sense of it all, but because—even if you've never before read that particular passage, or if you've read it and forgotten it, or if (like me) you can't be sure whether or not you've already read it—there's always a faint sense that whatever it is one is reading *has already been read*, if only by the author and the army of commentators who have since pored over every syllable.

Robert Anton Wilson, a huge fan of *Finnegans Wake*, passed on some excellent advice to would-be readers:

> The best way to approach *Finnegans Wake* is in a group. It has to be stalked like a wild animal, and you need a hunting party. I'd been reading *Finnegans Wake* alone for many years before I discovered this. The second thing is—it's best in groups. And the third law, which I discovered, is it's best in groups with several six packs of Guinness on the table. The more Guinness you drink the clearer *Finnegans Wake* gets.*

---

*From an interview here: http://maybelogic.blogspot.com/2009/04/robert-anton-wilson-on-finnegans-wake.html

45. 'A BOOK IN BROWN PAPER'

To mark the publication of the Faber booklet *Anna Livia Plurabelle* in 1930, Joyce came up with the following doggerel:

> Buy a book in brown paper
> From Faber and Faber
> To see Annie Liffey trip, tumble and caper.
> Sevensinns in her singthings,
> Plurabelle on her prose,
> Seashell ebb music wayriver she flows.

I expect nobody under fifty will understand Joyce's reference to brown paper. It used to be for discretely wrapping pornography from 'under the counter' in a dirty book shop. Perhaps it still is, if there are still dirty book shops.

Joyce was reportedly annoyed that the Faber publicity department made no effort to promote the booklet beyond issuing his poem as a mimeographed sheet. To make matters worse some smart-aleck at Faber added a chortling note to the poem:

> The Sales Department, puzzled as such departments are wont to be, have sought some light on the two James Joyce contributions to Criterion Miscellany. Below the explanations offered are passed on that you may be able to derive similar enlightenment.

There followed some witless etymological glosses that lacked entirely the bounce and fizz of Joyce's poem.

46. FINNEGANS 苏醒

Ulysses has appeared in French as *Ulysse* (1929), in Spanish (*Ulises*, 1949), Finnish (*Odysseus*, 1964), Slovenian (*Ulikses*, 1967), Greek (*Odysseas*, 1969–1976), Arabic (*Ulis*, 1982), Hebrew (*Uliss*, 1985), Russian (*Uliss*, 1993), Dutch (*Ulysses*, 1994) and Chinese (1995). The latter was translated by the husband and wife team of Xiao Qian and Wen Jieruo and published in three volumes, following a lengthy battle with the authorities. Priced at the equivalent of a school teacher's weekly wage, it sold 85,000 copies. 'In old age one should do something monumental,' said Xiao, who was eighty-five at the time.

Dai Congrong (b. 1971) spent eight years translating the first part of *Finnegans Wake* into Chinese and, at 775 pages, the heavily annotated result was already longer than the original. It was energetically promoted, with large yellow banners hung along Shanghai's elevated roadways, enormous billboards in most large cities and widespread media coverage. The yellow cover featured a photographic image of an owl made out of coffee beans, which has nothing at all to do with the novel but, in a nation of dedicated tea-drinkers, implied foreign sophistication. The initial print run of 8,000 copies sold out within a month but a second sold more slowly and the readership for the *Wake* in Chinese seems to have peaked at 13,000 in a country with a population, in 2019, of 1,398,000,000.

Dai Congrong reflected on the eight-year project, which left its mark:

> My body suffered from the work . . . I looked older than I should be. My eyes became dark, and my skin wasn't that good either.

Other translations were even more fraught. According to Sheng Yun, writing in the *London Review of Books* (7th April 2014), one of the translators involved in the Japanese version went missing, another went mad and a third person had to be roped in to finish the job.

An excellent account of the challenge facing translators is *Polyglot Joyce* (2005) by Patrick O'Neil, which features an intriguing section about the particular challenges involved in rendering *Ulysses* into Irish Gaelic, a translation by Breasal Uilsean and Séamas î hInnéirghe that appeared as *Uiliséas* and was published as twelve pamphlets between between 1987 and 1992.

Polyglot Joyce argues that translation enriches rather than dilutes or distorts the original text, and offers new portals of enquiry. O'Neill believes that all of the many translations of Joyce's work, or the work of any writer, can be taken together as a coherent object of study—a single 'polyglot macrotext' that calls for 'a transtextual reading', one which involves the original English language text and as many translations as possible. I've picked my way slowly through *Ulysses* in French on the strength of an 'O' level scraped by in the last century, but fluent command of at least six languages seems to be the minimum requirement for polyglotism, so the former Arsenal FC manager Arsène Wenger would be far better at reading Joyce transtextually than most of us because he speaks French, German, English, Spanish, and Italian, and has some knowledge of Japanese.*

Joyce was himself a notable polyglot, fluent in English, Italian (both Standard Italian and the Trieste Dialect), French, German, Norwegian and Latin, and able to hold his end up in conversation in Irish and Greek.

The very last thing Joyce published was his own Italian translation of 'Anna Livia Plurabelle', the final section of the *Wake*. He was helped in the task by the Italian-born French film critic Nino Frank (1904–1988) whose other claim to fame is that he coined the term '*film noir*'. Here's his memory of the process:

> We worked in Joyce's room, a characterless place that I have no recollection of, usually with him stretched out on the divan in his dressinggown ... I read and interpreted the text on my own, after which Joyce explained it to me word by word, revealing to me its various meanings, dragging me into the complex mythology of his Dublin. Then began the slow tennis of approximation; we tossed short phrases to each other like slow-motion balls through a rarefied atmosphere. In the end our procedure resembled incantation.†

---

*Ioannis Ikonomou (b. 1964) works as a translator at the European Commission and, astonishingly, speaks thirty-two modern languages, including twenty-one of the twenty-four official languages of the European Union (the three exceptions being Estonian, Maltese, and Irish). Among the other languages he speaks are Russian, Bengali, Persian, Turkish, Arabic, Hebrew, Amharic, and Mandarin. He has also studied a number of ancient languages, such as Old Church Slavonic, Classical Armenian, Sanskrit, Sogdian, and Assyro-Babylonian.

†From 'The Living Joyce' in *Portraits of the Artist in Exile: Recollections of James Joyce by Europeans* edited by Willard Potts (Harcourt Publishers Ltd, 1986)

'The slow tennis of approximation' is a keeper. The translation appeared in February 1940 in the Italian literary magazine, *Prospettive*. Joyce was delighted to receive a copy the following month, in the commune of Saint-Gérand-le-Puy, in the Allier department in Auvergne-Rhône-Alpes in central France, where he and Nora were staying at the Hotel de la Paix, visiting their grandson Stephen who was enrolled at a bilingual school nearby. The tedium of life in the commune was relieved by a brief visit from Samuel Beckett, but much of the time Joyce was alone. According to Richard Ellmann's biography:

> His long dark overcoat and large dark glasses made him a conspicuous figure, and the villagers referred to him as 'that poor old man' and could hardly be brought to believe in his international fame. Life in Saint-Gerand was less peaceful for Joyce than for others because of the abundance of dogs, which kept him at private war, his cane poised in defense and his pockets filled with stones—'My ammunition,' as he said. When asked why he disliked them, he replied, 'Because they have no souls.'

After Easter the Joyces moved to nearby Vichy, before the German Occupation prompted a final move to Switzerland in December, where Joyce would die a year later.

The Joyces' stay in Saint-Gerand is commemorated in a modest museum in the town library at 1 rue Maurice Dupont. Their website is charming.*.

---

*www.jamesjoyce-a-saintgerandlepuy.com

47. The Wake in the Willows

From Kenneth Grahame's *The Wind in the Willows* (1908) here's the moment when Ratty arrives staggering under the weight of 'a fat, wicker luncheon-basket':

> 'Shove that under your feet,' he observed to the Mole, as he passed it down into the boat. Then he untied the painter and took the sculls again.
>
> 'What's inside it?' asked the Mole, wriggling with curiosity.
>
> 'There's cold chicken inside it,' replied the Rat briefly; 'coldtongue-coldhamcoldbeefpickledgherkinssaladfrenchrollscresssandwich-espottedmeatgingerbeerlemonadesodawater—'
>
> 'O stop, stop,' cried Mole in ecstasies: 'This is too much!'

Since first reading the passage as a child I've casually collected this type of unspaced writing, the technical term for which is *scriptio continua*.* A favourite example is 'Iveneverbeensoinsultedinmyentirelife,' a blustering outburst by Edgar Naylor, the unlikable English hero of Cyril Connolly's only novel *The Rock Pool* (1936).

This brings us again to the ten one-hundred letter words in *Finnegans Wake*, each suggesting the rumble of thunder which is, in the cosmology adapted by Joyce from the 15th century Florentine savant Giambattista Vico, a signal that the whole cycle of history is about to begin again.

Here's the first thunderclap (which we first encountered as a prompt to memorisation in essay 34 and which we'll encounter again in essay 91 'Adventures in the skin game'):

> bababadalgharaghtakamminaronnonnbronntonnerronnuonn-thunntrobarrhounawnskawn toohoohoordenenthurknuk

This is made up from the words for thunder in Japanese (*kaminari*) Hindi (*karak*), Greek (*brontaô*), French (*tonnerre*), Italian (*tuono*), Swedish (*åska*), Portuguese (*trovão*) and Danish (*todenen*), and there may be others rumbling away in the background.

---

* Alternatively 'scriptura continua'. But shouldn't that really be scripturacontinua?

The sixth thunderclap, heard at the close of 'The Mime of Mick, Nick, and the Maggies', goes like this:

Lukkedoerendunandurraskewdylooshoofermoyportertooryzo-oysphalnabortan sporthaokansakroidverjkapakkapuk.

This relies on a polyglot range of phrases meaning 'shut the door' found in Danish (*luk døren*), Italian (*chiudi l'uscio*), French (*fermez la porte*), German (*Türe zu*), Modern Greek (*sphalna portan*), Russian (*zakroi dver'*) and Turkish (*kapiyi kapat*). Throw in the Finnish word for tavern (*kapakka*) and an echo of the German *kaputt*.

Marshall McLuhan used *Finnegans Wake* as the template for *War and Peace in the Global Village**, a study of warfare throughout history. He observed that each thunderclap in the *Wake* 'is a cryptogram or codified explanation of the thundering and reverberating consequences of the major technological changes in all human history'. His take, disputed by Joyceans but quite persuasive, runs thus:

Thunder 1: Paleolithic to Neolithic. Speech. Split of East/West. From herding to harnessing animals.

Thunder 2: Clothing as weaponry. Enclosure of private parts. First social aggression.

Thunder 3: Specialism. Centralism via wheel, transport, cities: civil life.

Thunder 4: Markets and truck gardens. Patterns of nature submitted to greed and power.

Thunder 5: Printing. Distortion and translation of human patterns and postures and pastors.

Thunder 6: Industrial Revolution. Extreme development of print process and individualism.

Thunder 7: Tribal man again. All choractors [*sic*] end up separate, private man. Return of choric.

Thunder 8: Movies. Pop art, pop Kulch via tribal radio. Wedding of sight and sound.

Thunder 9: Car and Plane. Both centralizing and decentralizing at once create cities in crisis. Speed and death.

---

* *War and Peace in the Global Village* by Marshall McLuhan and Quentin Fiore (Bantam, NY 1968; reissued byGingko Press, 2001)

Thunder 10: Television. Back to tribal involvement in tribal mood-mud. The last thunder is a turbulent, muddy wake, and murk of non-visual, tactile man.

Joyce was very frightened of thunder. When asked by Arthur Power why he was afraid yet his children were not, Joyce replied with contempt: 'Ah, they have no religion.'

That tenth and final thunderclap consists of 101 letters, so the sum total of letters in the ten rumbles comes to a palindromic 1,001, a Viconian recursion which I'll exploit as a way back to *The Wind in the Willows* and its celebrated illustrator Ernest Shepherd (who was also the artist responsible for *Winnie-the-Pooh*). His son Graham Shepherd, born in 1907, was also an illustrator and cartoonist and—here's the connection back to our man—it was he who introduced Louis MacNeice to the works of James Joyce when they were both Oxford undergraduates.[*]

The last chapter of *The Wind in the Willows* is, as it happens, entitled 'The Return of Ulysses'. Toad returns to Toad Hall, his ancestral home and evicts the stoats and the weasels who have temporarily taken the place over, just as Odysseus (or Ulysses) returns home to discover the palace is packed with interlopers and does much the same thing. While we're on the subject—if you recall the well-known group photograph, taken in Paris in 1923, of Ford Madox Ford, Joyce, Ezra Pound and the Irish-American lawyer and patron John Quinn, perhaps you'll agree that they appear to be auditioning for a stage version of *The Wind in the Willows* as, respectively, Badger, Mole, Ratty and the leader of the weasels.

[*]Graham Shepherd drowned on September 20th 1943 when his ship *HMS Polyanthus* was sunk by a German U-Boat. All but one of those aboard were lost—at least 7 officers and 77 crew. The sole known survivor died three days later when the ship that rescued him, *HMS Itchen*, was torpedoed with the loss of 230 lives.

48. ON STANLEY UNWIN

> Are you all sitty comftybold two-square on your botty? Then I'll
> begin.

The great Stanley Unwin, of course. Who else?

He was an intermittent feature of my childhood, on the radio and
on television, and appeared briefly as Gert Frobe's Chancellor in the
overblown film version of *Chitty Chitty Bang Bang* (1968). 'Professor' Stanley Unwin (his stage name—he was entirely unencumbered
with academic titles) devised a fluent Joycean spoken gobbledygook
he called 'Unwinese', deploying a modest range of tropes to render
plain speech engagingly semi-comprehensible. Syntax wasn't much
disrupted and there was no daunting theoretical substructure; he
simply wanted to amuse and delight his audiences, and this he re-
liably did. The addition of suffixes such as '-lode' and '-bold' made
ordinary words sound wonderfully mysteriolode and beautibold.

Unwinese was instantly recognisable, wonderfully imitable but
very hard to do well, and to be able to do so largely off-the-cuff (as
he did) was a rare gift, like speaking in tongues. He was an heir to
Edward Lear and the verbal equivalent of the cartoonist and kinetic
sculptor Rowland Emmett. You can listen online to a recording of
Unwin delivering his version of Goldilocks and the three bears, and
here's a transcript of the opening:

> Goldyloppers trittly-how in the early mordy, and she falolloped
> down the steps. Oh unfortunade for crackening of the eggers
> and the sheebs and the buttery full-falollop and graze the knee-
> clappers. So she had a vaselubrious, rub it on and a quick healy
> huff and that was that.

I always found it hard to believe that Unwin was unaware—or un-
winaware, or unawarybold—of *Finnegans Wake*, published in May
1939 but circulating in little magazines for many years before that
and, looking at his online obituaries, my hunch proved right. Unwin once told his close friend, the writer and broadcaster Michael
Pointon, that a particular phrase in *Finnegans Wake*—a 'troutling
stream'—had opened the door for him to a new way of language. The
phrase comes from the following passage in the *Wake*:

Stanley Unwin (1911–2002)

Yes may we not see still the brontoicthyian form outlined, even in our own nighttime by the sedge of the troutling stream that Bronto loves and Brunto has a lean on.

Further research confirmed that Unwin was introduced to Joyce's work while working in the Features Unit at the BBC during the war. He had previously been a wireless operator in the Royal Navy, was discharged due to chronic sea-sickness and, on joining the BBC as a sound engineer, was assigned to war broadcasts in various parts of the globe. To keep spirits up in perilous 'bangy-bangy, boomy-boomy' situations, he entertained members of the Unit with off-the-cuff 'performages' featuring such favourite phrases as 'Oh, folly, folly!' and 'deep joy'. Many of the phrases had their origin in the way his mother told him bedtime stories.

Compare Godlyloppers with this section of *The Mookse and the Gripes*, Joyce's re-telling in the *Wake* of Aesop's fable *The Fox and the Grapes*:

> Gentes and laitymen, fullstoppers and semicolonials, hybreds and lubberds! Eins within a space and awearywide space it wast ere wohned a Mookse.

Joyce's dense multi-lingual punning, his manic erudition and his belief that readers would contentedly spend a lifetime deciphering his work all contrast with Stanley Unwin's gentle, unpretentious and humane whimsy. Both men rely, in the examples given above, on an underlying fairy tale narrative familiar (one assumes) to their respective audiences. Joyce's 'Gentes and laitymen' reminds me of the children's' poem beginning 'Ladles and jellyspoons', although the latter requires no exegesis by tenured academics. Nor, come to that, does Unwinese.

There are other echoes of *Finnegans Wake* in Unwinese, such as his frequent use of 'childers' as a plural of children, a clear echo of Joyce's Chapelizod pub landlord H.C. Earwicker's initials standing for (among other things) 'Haveth Childers Everywhere'. Whenever I dip a toe into the *Wake* I like to imagine Unwin's light, affable mellifluous voice, and the gentle clack of his ill-fitting dentures. It helps.

Unwin was always in demand with producers and advertising agencies and parlayed an eccentric party piece into a long career. Could he make a living today? I doubt it. Pushier, rowdier talents prevail and the market for gently whimsical verbal dexterity seems to have evaporated.

He has a further claim to cultural significance as the narrator on what is now regarded as the first-ever 'concept album'. Released in May 1968, *Ogden's Nut Gone Flake* by Small Faces is a pop-culture artefact that pre-dates (by two days) and bears comparison with The Beatles' more celebrated *Sergeant Pepper's Lonely Hearts Club Band*. On side two Unwin tells the story of a man named Happiness Stan, who sets off in search of a half moon. I used the opening lines at the start of this essay.

Unwin lived for more than sixty years in the Northamptonshire village of Long Buckby. After he died there was a thanksgiving service at the village church of St Lawrence's with a valediction prepared by Unwin's family:

> Goodly Byelode loyal peeploders! Now all gatherymost to amuse it and have a tilty elbow or a nice cuffle-oteedee—Oh Yes!

He is buried in the churchyard there alongside his wife Frances, who pre-deceased him. Their gravestone bears the epitaph:

> Reunitey in the heavenly-bode—Deep Joy.

49. FINNEGANIGHT, ANYONE?

Bloomsday is a big deal on 16th June every year, whether it's devoted to high-minded cultural commemoration, rowdy booze-ups or something in between. It's a money-spinner too, not just in Dublin but around the world. So why is there no equivalent celebration dedicated to *Finnegans Wake*?

An obvious reason is that *Ulysses* is set on a particular day of the year while *Finnegans Wake* has no precise calendrical setting, although there are several contenders.

Joyce himself favoured 4th July, which happened to be his father John's birthday and the day on which he married Nora, in 1931. John Joyce (1849–1931) was the inspiration for the *Wake*'s main character HCE, and the reason so much of the book takes place in The Mullingar House in Chapelizod is because that's the pub where John had spent many hours as a young man.* His son wanted *Finnegans Wake* to be published on this day (as *Ulysses* had been published on his own birthday in 1922), but his publisher objected on the grounds that summer releases would get less attention from the reviewers.

In *Twelve and a Tilly: Essays on the occasion of the 25th anniversary of Finnegans Wake* (Faber and Faber, 1966), the Joycean scholar Nathan Halper argues that the night on which *Finnegans Wake* is set, or rather the night during which the dream of Humphrey Chimpden Earwicker (if that's what it is) takes place, must be that of Saturday 18th March, 1922. His argument is presented as a series of numbered statements based on almanacs, tide tables, phases of the moon, holy days, the Spring equinox and so on. This mathematical approach certainly has all the appearance of chilly intellectual rigour, like the *Tractatus Logico-Philosophicus*, but is also bonkers.

Other dates are available. Peter Reichenberg argued in the *James Joyce Quarterly* that at least part of the book is set on Saturday 7th April, 1928, which he calls 'Earwickersnight'. He bases this on the

---

*The Mullingar House is a pub in the Dublin suburb of Chapelizod (which contains the initials HCE (Humphrey Chimpden Earwicker) and ALP (Anna Livia Plurabelle) plus Izod (as in 'Iseult'). There's a plaque outside that says 'Home of all characters and elements in James Joyce's novel Finnegans Wake.' It was run for over 80 years by the Keenan family until sold by auction to a consortium of landlords in 1999. There is a Joyce death mask behind the bar but little else to connect the place with the *Wake*.

inclusion of some football results heard in the background on the radio in the Chapelizod pub:

> He's alight there still, by Mike! Loose afore! Bung! Bring forth your deed! Bang! Till is the right time. Bang! Partick Thistle agen S. Megan's versus Brystal Palace agus the Walsall! Putsch!

It's an elegant and ingenious deduction, although he makes no reference at all to Halper's earlier, more detailed, speculations. In any case Reichenberg's Earwickersnight would have to take place on a literary date which had already been snapped up—it's the day on which William Faulkner's *The Sound and the Fury* (1929) is set.

An illuminating blog by Peter Chrisp (*qv*) assembles and evaluates the various 'dream' theories surrounding the Wake, and is recommended.[*] As he points out, there's no record of Joyce himself ever suggesting that the whole novel is Earwicker's dream, but it was a view first advanced by the American critic Edmund Wilson.[†] Joseph Campbell and Anthony Burgess both perpetuated Wilson's view, which is attractive in its simplicity but doesn't bear close scrutiny.

Peter approvingly quotes a lecture by J.S. Atherton at the inaugural James Joyce Symposium, at the Gresham Hotel in Dublin on Bloomsday in 1967:

> I do not wish to deny any of the theories which have been put forward as to the identity of the dreamer: they are all true up to a point. For, as I see FW it is everyone's dream, the dream of all the living and the dead. Many puzzling features become clear if this is accepted. Obviously we will hear many foreign languages: Chinese will be prominent if we know Chinese; German if we know German, and so on . . . It is the universal mind which Joyce assumes as the identity of the dreamer; he, of course, is writing it all down but everyone else contributes.

So it's not just his dream, but ours.

Finnegans Wake was first published in book form on 4th May 1939 and, to mark the eightieth anniversary of the event in 2019, I organised a one-off literary cabaret called *Finnegnight*. The venue was a

---

[*] https://peterchrisp.blogspot.com/2020/12/the-dream-of-hcearwicker.html
[†] 'The Dream of H.C. Earwicker' in *The New Republic* (28th June 1939) later reprinted in *The Wound and the Bow*.

derelict former Conservative Club in Paddington, a place of rubble, old sofas, dampstained walls, wobbly chairs and multiple buckets collecting the rainwater that dripped, even on dry cloudless days, from the many holes in the roof. There was plenty of Jameson's and bottled Guinness and proper sandwiches (ham, cheese, fishpaste), black and white pudding, and fruitcake, and French Fancies.

Melanie Pappenheim sang the ballad 'Finnegan's Wake' accompanied on the violin by Alice Zawadzki, the author Tony White barrelled through the Willingdone Museyroom episode, the artist and publisher David Henningham sang 'The Ballad of Persse O'Reilly' while lobbing parsnips into the audience like grenades. The poet Dan O'Brien and actress Jessica St Clair performed a dialogue as Mutt and Jute, the composer and author Alba Arikha read a passage of *Finnegans Wake* in French translated by her godfather, Samuel Beckett; the author Alex Pheby read movingly from his novel *Lucia* and, to end of the evening, the writer, critic and broadcaster Jennifer Hodgson chaired what we called 'the settee salon' with a panel featuring *gorse* editor Susan Tomaselli and the authors June Caldwell and Eley Williams. Jenn's opening question was: 'When did you first not read *Finnegans Wake*?' to which Eley replied 'I've not been reading it since I was an undergraduate, and now I tend not to read it at least once or twice a year.' What followed was an exhilarating and hilarious alternative to the usual Joycean discourse, and a subversive take on the entire modernist canon. That's the way to do it.

50. Confession

—Now, just wash and brush up your memoirias a little bit.
—*Finnegans Wake*

I've been doggedly trying and failing to read *Finnegans Wake* since 1979—the year Kanye West was born—but as time goes by and the shadows gather I am close to abandoning for good any further attempt to complete this colossal, impossible text, this 'alphybetty-formed verbage'. My three copies are all by now dilapidated; one quite heavily annotated in places, the second weirdly bloated after being accidentally dropped in the shower and the third always by my bedside, within reach on insomniac nights, well-thumbed but largely unread. I also have a clutch of commentaries, among them Philip Kitcher's *Joyce's Kaleidoscope* (Oxford University Press, 2009) in which the author categorised *Wake* readers as 'those too intimidated to try to read it, those who have tried and failed, and . . . those who write about it.'

I've tried and failed *and* I'm going to write about it, and this essay will take the form of a confession to the world of something only a handful of people know about me. I want to tell you why I have never read in its entirety, and will almost certainly never read in its entirety, *Finnegans Wake*.

One problem with confessional writing is that while it all clearly matters a lot to the author, there's no reason it should it matter to the reader. Of course a sufficiently gifted writer will engage their readers' sympathies to the extent that whatever they (the writer) has experienced and cares to share will be of general interest—instructive, compelling, consoling, admonitory or heart-warming. I am not that kind of writer.

When I was eight years old my parents became members of an evangelical fundamentalist Christian cult called the Watch Tower, Bible and Tract Society of Pennsylvania, better known to the world as the Jehovah's Witnesses. You'll have heard of them, I expect. The Society is the world's largest publisher with a billion dollar property portfolio, but elects to regard itself as a religion (which came in handy for tax purposes until the law changed). It has around 8 million adherents in 240 countries. My parents' conversion was sudden, absolute and for me catastrophic, because for the next eight years I found myself in a closed and claustrophobic religious community within which everything not compulsory was forbidden.

It's hard to communicate to anyone outside the cult how very strange the convictions shared by (or imposed on) its followers are. Witnesses refuse to celebrate Christmas, Easter, birthdays or other holidays or customs, all of which they regard as 'pagan' (a vague but sufficient term applied to all the things they are told not to like); they don't recognise any version of the Bible apart from their own, they don't believe in the Holy Trinity or the immortal soul and they don't accept the legitimacy of any other religion, or system of government. They don't believe in evolution and don't approve of higher education, blood transfusions, homosexuality, competitive sport or beards. For decades they were militantly against vaccination, although the global pandemic has made them re-think that position.*

What Witnesses *do* believe in, and fervently, is the entire Protestant canon of scripture. They consider the Bible—or their particular version of the Bible, which is quite unlike any other version of the Bible—to be the final authority that underlies and informs all of their beliefs, and that it is scientifically and historically accurate in every last detail, completely reliable and to be taken absolutely literally because it's the word of God, and inerrant. They are dogged literalists who insist that whatever is in the Bible is true because it's in the Bible, and that whatever is in the Bible is in the Bible because it's true.

Growing up in the cult was to live in a paralysing state of boredom and fear. Boredom because of the interminable and unvarying

---

*Here's a list of some of the other things that Witnesses believe are pagan and therefore prohibited: Carnivals generally, the Olympics, New Year's Eve, Valentine's Day, Mother's Day, Father's Day, The Day of the Dead, Hallowe'en, birthdays, throwing rice and/or the bouquet at weddings, wedding marches, astrology, the Rosary, symbols on graves such as fish, anchor, dove and peacock, the Star of David, democracy, Lantern Festivals, mazes and labyrinths, the Cross (they believe Christ was put to death on a stake), Hell, clerical celibacy, Mary (the Mother of God), philosophy (yes—*philosophy*), Harvest Festivals, saying 'Bless you' when somebody sneezes, May Day, toasting, offering incense to the dead, throwing soil or flowers into a grave and drawing Halos on religious figures. Things deemed pagan that are nevertheless acceptable include wedding rings, wedding cake, calendars, piñatas, the Twist ('and other modern dances') and flowers at a funeral. This is a quite fantastically dingy religion.

prayer meetings every other day, and the constant doorstep evangelising, going from house to house in every street in our fading seaside
town; fear because the end of the world was nigh, and quite literally so. We all of us knew when this would happen because we had
been told when it would happen. It would happen in 1975. And we
all of us knew what it would be like. Fire would fall from a black sky
and there would be earthquakes and erupting volcanoes and tidal
waves; skyscrapers would topple and churches would burn and people would run around screaming and everybody apart from the Witnesses would be destroyed. These horrors were portrayed graphically
in Society publications that were the stuff of nightmare for me as a
child, and remain so to this day. I would be 16 years old in the year
the world was due to end and preparing for my GCSE 'A' Level examinations, after which I would be judged by Jehovah and then either
live forever with my parents and the rest of our congregation in an
earthly paradise, or be condemned to a permanent non-existence.

The Witnesses's Governing Body, a succession of anonymous be-
suited ill-educated men based in New York had, over the previous
century, regularly announced precise dates for the Apocalypse based
on measurements derived from the Great Pyramid. These deadlines
passed uneventfully and were then hastily reconfigured as a test of
faith. Some disappointed Witnesses dropped out, to be shunned by
the remaining faithful as apostates, while the zealots remained. A
few years later a new date would be announced and the whole sinister count-down would start all over again.*

---

*Armageddon was first predicted to take place in 1878 (when it was called 'The End
of the Harvest'), then again in 1881 ('A Revised End of the Harvest'), and again in
1914 (which would mark the end of human rule of the earth and happened to coin-
cide with certain events in Europe that would shape the century), then once more
in 1918 ('The New Terminus') and 1925 ('The Resurrection of the Patriarchs') and
finally in 1975. The prediction that haunted my childhood and adolescence began
in 1968, the year my parents were converted. Here's how the date was announced
in *The Watchtower* magazine (15th April 1968), which reads like a commentary on
the *Wake*'s key date of 1132:

> To calculate where man is in the stream of time, relative to God's sev-
> enth day of 7,000 years, we need to determine how long a time has
> elapsed from the year of Adam and Eve's creation in the year 4026
> B.C.E. From the autumn of that year to the autumn of 1 B.C.E. there
> would be 4,025 years. From the autumn of 1 B.C.E. to the autumn

There was, as you can probably imagine, a huge psychic strain involved in managing the daily secular demands of 'Caesar' (i.e. the world, which for me back then meant school, and homework, and mock examinations and all that) and everything else. Life in the real world, that is life outside of the cult, was something to be endured stoically and never enjoyed; there could be no *carpe diem* because there was no *diem* to *carpe*. I could never be sure that even my most modest plans would come to fruition, not even on the day they were made, because who knew what the rest of that day would bring? The most humdrum of activities—getting a haircut, going for a swim—still had to be undertaken, because life had to be lived as if it wasn't suddenly about to end in fire and brimstone. As a consequence, along with all the other Brothers and Sisters in our congregation of around sixty, and my parents, I was living in a state of constant jittery anticipation. But because I lacked my parents' wholehearted conviction, I knew that for me the most likely outcome of God's judgement would be personal oblivion. The result of this was that I lost any sense of myself in time. This was part of a more general sense of depersonalisation that took place during the years I was exposed to the dizzying banalities and boilerplate certainties of the Society's creed.

'Hier ist kein warum' ('Here there is no why') said an Auschwitz guard to Primo Levi; the Witness equivalent is 'Here there is no when.' I have no clear chronological memory of most of the time I spent in a trance of indoctrination because those years have merged into a single unhappy 'then', unpunctuated by any of the rites of passage that provide the structure for most lives, for most families. It was always 'now' for me, then. I wish I'd known Wittgenstein's view in the *Tractatus Logico-Philosophicus* that 'if we take eternity to mean not infinite temporal duration but timelessness, then eternal life belongs to those who live in the present' because I now see that the

---

of 1 C.E. is one year (there was no zero year). From the autumn of 1 C.E. to the autumn of 1967 is a total of 1,966 years. Adding 4,025 and 1 and 1,966 we get 5,992 years from the autumn of 4026 B.C.E. to the autumn of 1967. Thus eight years remain to account for a full 6,000 years of the seventh day. Eight years from the autumn of 1967 would bring us to the autumn of 1975, fully 6,000 years into God's seventh day, his rest day.

lack of temporal markers—birthdays, festivals, personal watersheds such as passing exams and any variation in the rigid, unvarying year-round pattern of prayer meetings and doorstep evangelising—was both part of the cult's process of indoctrination and a crude way of simulating the experience of eternal life through the suspension of time.

Jehovah's Witnesses today, as they did back in 1975, look at events in the world around them and everything they see supports their conviction that they are living in the End Days.

A conviction, you have to understand, is not the same thing as a belief. While a belief is something hard-won, and open to doubt, something that can be questioned and debated, a conviction is *not* open to doubt, is *never* questioned and *cannot* be debated. A conviction is not the same thing as the truth although my parents, like all Jehovah's Witnesses, always referred to their set of convictions as 'The Truth'. You couldn't argue with the truth, and you certainly couldn't argue with 'The Truth'. It would get you nowhere because reason cannot prevail when reason is not part of the conversation. Of course anything that's asserted without evidence can be rejected without evidence. I know that now, but I didn't back then.

My years as a Jehovah's Witness made me a stranger to myself, and to others. I shared few daily experiences with non-Witnesses, and had little in common with them. I knew only what I had been told to believe and the few scraps I picked up at school about the real world. I had no access to my private thoughts and feelings, and wasn't sure that I was even capable of having private thoughts, or feelings that were really my own and not those concocted and imposed by the ill-educated men in suits in Brooklyn. Or, if I had feelings, I didn't know how to think about them. I had to find a way to know what to feel. I had to learn how to think for myself, and how to have feelings about those thoughts. I had to find out who I was, starting from scratch. I needed, like Beckett's Hamm in *Endgame*, to find the 'heart in my head.'

So where did I go to find out?

Libraries, mainly, because there was no internet then.

We had few books at home any more apart from those published by the Watch Tower, Bible and Tract Society of Pennsylvania. We had a lot of those. My own school textbooks were carefully vetted and sometimes prohibited and I became a furtive reader, squirrelling books away as you might conceal cigarettes or drugs or a secret diary.

Joyce was waiting for me.

It was reading *A Portrait of the Artist as a Young Man* at the age of fifteen that really knocked me for six. I certainly wasn't the first unhappy adolescent to identify with the struggles of young Stephen Dedalus, and not the last, but I had a particularly intense personal investment in his rejection of God and faith and family. The coercive rhetoric of Father Arnall's sermon to the young boys of Clongowes Wood College during the Belvedere school retreat was wonderfully, hilariously ridiculous, and immediately familiar, the verbal incarnation of all that oppressed me in the Witness cult, and all that I had to reject:

> Now let us try for a moment to realise, as far as we can, the nature of that abode of the damned which the justice of an offended God has called into existence for the eternal punishment of sinners. Hell is a strait and dark and foul-smelling prison, an abode of demons and lost souls, filled with fire and smoke. The straitness of this prison house is expressly designed by God to punish those who refused to be bound by His laws. In earthly prisons the poor captive has at least some liberty of movement, were it only within the four walls of his cell or in the gloomy yard of his prison. Not so in hell. There, by reason of the great number of the damned, the prisoners are heaped together in their awful prison, the walls of which are said to be four thousand miles thick: and the damned are so utterly bound and helpless that, as a blessed saint, saint Anselm, writes in his book on similitudes, they are not even able to remove from the eye a worm that gnaws it.

Witnesses are told, and therefore believe, that there's no such thing as Hell, although Satan and his demonic hoards are very real, and a constant threat. That aside, Father Arnall's rhetoric was entirely familiar to me. That the walls of a place that doesn't exist were 'four thousand miles thick' (or at least 'said to be') was the same kind of eschatological piffle deployed by the Brooklyn Brotherhood. You doubt that? Here's part of a talk from just a few years ago by a senior Jehovah's Witness named Anthony Morris III, which you can find online:

Take a steel ball that is the size of the sun. Now thousands upon thousands of Planet Earths could go inside the circumference of a steel ball the size of the Sun. So this steel ball that's the size of the Sun, we're gonna put a fly on the top of it. That fly is gonna walk around that steel ball that's the size of the sun and walk around it until he wears it down to nothing. And that's just the beginning of eternity. It's just started see? And once you've captured that, the devil's finished! Eternity? With Jehovah himself in some cases, with others living on a beautiful paradise earth? What fool turns their back on that?*

As a schoolboy I read *A Portrait* (which was then on the 'A' Level English syllabus) with mounting excitement and euphoria. Stephen's eloquent rejection of God and church and state and family, expressed with chilly conviction and fearless intellectual arrogance, spoke to me, and thrilled me, and thrills me still. He—or rather Joyce—gave me a coherent way of seeing things, and, what is more, suggested a means of escape. A cold lucid indifference reigned in my soul. It remains to this day.

What did it avail to pray when he knew that his soul lusted after its own destruction? A certain pride, a certain awe, withheld him from offering to God even one prayer at night, though he knew it was in God's power to take away his life while he slept and hurl his soul hellward ere he could beg for mercy. His pride in his own sin, his loveless awe of God, told him that his offence was too grievous to be atoned for in whole or in part by a false homage to the All-seeing and All-knowing.

The big difference between Joyce and Lucifer is that Lucifer never denied the existence of the Almighty and, in challenging His heavenly primacy, actually affirmed it. Joyce, on the other hand, said there was no God, a very different kettle of theological fish. Brian Nolan (aka Flann O'Brien) described the author as 'a truly fear-shaken Irish Catholic' and that was me, then, apart from the nationality and religion. But I had in my possession something that Joyce hadn't had at my age. I had *A Portrait of the Artist as a Young Man*.

*I'm not making this up. It's here: https://youtu.be/_efY5rbkKg4. This can stand for all the quasi-theological claptrap I had to listen to in my formative years. This mediocre man can be found elsewhere on the internet. He has a particular obsession with homosexuals who wear 'tight pants'. A queer old josser indeed.

On my sixteenth birthday in March 1975 (which went otherwise unmarked), keenly aware of the imminent apocalypse and with a light-headed sense of transgression, I bought for £1.60 the Penguin edition of *Ulysses*, which I hid in my room. I struggled with it at first, as we all struggle, but managed to read it all before my next birthday, by which time I had been disfellowshipped from the cult and was therefore an apostate, quite literally an 'anti-Christ'. I left home for university, and my life in the world began.*

I found the Stephen of *Ulysses* far less compelling and sympathetic than his earlier incarnation in *A Portrait*. While I wouldn't go as far as Wyndham Lewis who, in *Time and Western Man* (1927), described the later Stephen as a 'small, pointless, oppressive character,' he seemed to me meaner, less heroic, less romantic. Perhaps we had both grown up.

In common with all atheists, including Joyce, I think about God all the time, and still tend to see the world in religious terms. Having rejected my parent's convictions (a rejection which broke their hearts and for which they have never forgiven me) I found myself with a god-shaped hole to fill and a leftover life to live. This would prove to be a life full of surprises, discoveries, setbacks and satisfactions, but one lived without any sense of imminence or momentousness, without the oppressive but powerfully motivating conviction that, whatever I did or didn't do, Jehovah would know about it and rejoice, or not rejoice. My everyday behaviour was no longer freighted with any particular significance, either for me or for my ex-god. I was like Ray Liotta at the end of *Goodfellas*, relocated to the suburbs of myself, 'an average nobody. I get to live the rest of my like like a schnook.'

---

*In July 1976 the Governing Body published the following small-print explanation of their 1975 balls-up in *The Watchtower* magazine:

> If anyone has been disappointed through not following this line of thought, he should now concentrate on adjusting his viewpoint, seeing that it was not the word of God that failed or deceived him and brought disappointment, but that his own understanding was based on wrong premises.

Not a word, of course on the source of these 'wrong premises'. The unaccountable mediocrities who ran the whole show back then are now all dead, and good riddance, but their successors continue to hold the lives of millions in thrall.

So I searched for other consolations, other palliatives, but when it came to the arts in general and to literature in particular, I could commit to reading only what I knew to be the *very best* novels and poetry. I was a zealot still, you see, but what I sought were secular incarnations of the divine. These I found, and continue to find, in *Ulysses*, a novel that tackles both a fundamental crisis of our time and my own condition, namely (in Max Weber's phrase) 'the disenchantment of the world,' the loss of any sense of completeness or security that accompanies the displacement of religion by the secular. Addressing this disenchantment and sense of insecurity through reading novels is still a high-stakes game—as the philosopher Julia Kristeva once noted, 'all literature is probably a version of the apocalypse.' Which brings me back to *Finnegans Wake*, and why I really can't be doing with it.

I understand what Joyce set out to do in his last novel and, while I recognise and admire his extraordinary achievement and while I think it's a work of quite astonishing beauty and integrity and nobility, a work of uncompromising genius, and fabulously original, and rewarding, and of enormous significance, I find it impossible to read because it fails for me to fill that god-shaped hole and this is because whenever I read the *Wake* I find myself cast back to my years in the cult and to the thousands of hours spent unhappily exposed to the Watchtower Bible & Tract Society's horrible, inane and baffling publications.

The *Wake* expects from its readers what an evangelical cult demands from its followers, namely that they devote themselves entirely to it. I cannot bring myself to do this because—and I'm keenly aware this is an unusual perspective—it's a form of submission that I find repulsive and distressing. It reminds me of how I used to have to think and behave when confronted with the publications of the Watch Tower, Bible and Tract Society of Pennsylvania. I wish that wasn't the case, but it is. *Non serviam.* *

*Interviewed in *The Joycean Society* (2013), Dora García's enchanting documentary film about a Zürich reading group dedicated to *Finnegans Wake*, the Joycean scholar Geert Lernout says of the book that 'Joyce programmed it in such a way that he invites you to that kind of religious fervour, where you turn it into a holy book . . . I'm not describing it as dangerous . . . Of all possible pathologies, it is one of the most benign ones.'

Successful readers of the *Wake* are to a unique degree creative collaborators with the author, activating the text through their engagement with it, and through sharing their discoveries with other successful readers. I, on the other hand, feel that I have let Joyce down.

His novel has judged me and found me wanting and now squats reproachfully by my bedside. The one book I'm sure I'll never read from cover to cover, it has come to stand for all the other books I haven't read, and will never read, efficiently undermining any claim I may have to being even above-averagely 'bookish'. It subverts any sense I have of myself as a Joycean.

The many years I have spent not reading *Finnegans Wake* make me think of all other things I have spent many years not doing, such as keeping in shape or learning to drive a car or speaking German or managing spreadsheets. It makes me think also of the many other ways in which I have failed over the years, in private and in public, as a son and as a partner and as a parent, as a colleague and an employee, as a friend, as a citizen. It reminds me of all my mean-spirited and thoughtless acts, or my failures to act, and of all the people I've disappointed or hurt or annoyed or disgusted, whether I meant to or not, and of all the people I've treated unfairly or unkindly or thoughtlessly or cruelly. Not reading *Finnegans Wake* makes me intensely aware of all my shortcomings, all my delinquencies, all my defining flaws—and that's a lot to have to deal with when faced with a Faber paperback.

And yet. And yet. From time to time I come across something from the *Wake* that fails to trouble me with thoughts of religious abjection and failure, and which sticks in my memory, not because it's easy to remember but because it's impossible to forget, such as the word 'meanderthalltale', or this lexical ear-worm:

— My name is Misha Misha but call me Toffey Tough.

I mean Mettenchough.

It persuades me that there may yet come a time when I give the *Wake* another go, then perhaps another, and in that sense I'm still a member of the congregation even though I don't attend any of the meetings. And I feel I feel I owe it to myself and to others to read the *Wake* because the meatheads of Brooklyn are still spreading fear and despondency. In March 2020 one Stephen Lett, a member of the Jehovah's Witnesses Governing Body, spoke about the Covid-19 pandemic in an online video. This is what he said:

> The events unfolding around us are making clear that we're living in the final part of the Last Days, undoubtedly, the final part of the final part of the Last Days, shortly before the Last Day of the Last Days.

I watch this gurning satchel-mouthed ignoramus on YouTube and I feel nauseous. My thoughts go back to my younger self in 1975, and to all powerless young people today who are exposed to this frightening, life-denying apocalyptic bullshit. I hope that for some of them, the bookish ones, the ones like me, Joyce's writing may offer a portal into the real world, with all its horrors. A liberation.

51. NOW GET THE LOOK

As a hard-up young man-about-Dublin, Joyce could not afford to dress elegantly but developed a stylish thrift-shop look featuring grey flannel bags, tennis shoes and a yachting cap ('Where's she moored, Commander?' quipped Oliver St. John Gogarty). A blackthorn stick completed the ensemble, accompanied by a superior and condescending manner. As Ulick O'Connor recalled in his biography of Gogarty:

James Joyce, Trieste, 1912

> [Joyce] was aloof in bearing and demeanour; but had a caustic tongue and a sense of showmanship that enabled him to keep apart from the herd and at the same time to impress his personality upon the public mind. *

In a letter to his brother Stanislaus dated 28th February 1905, Joyce, then established as a teacher of English in Pula, gave some excellent advice:

> The following from experience: grow a moustache, pretend to know everything, and dress magnificently.

Stan managed the first but floundered when it came to omniscience and dandyism. His elder brother, on the other hand, had already developed the manner and the look that would see him out.

In many of the photographs taken in the 1920s and 30s, Joyce wears Zylo spectacles—what today's fizzy fashionistas would describe as 'trademark eyewear'—a brand first introduced around the time the Great War broke out. They became unpopular when competitors

---

* *The Times I've Seen: Oliver St. John Gogarty: A Biography* by Ulick O'Connor (Jonathan Cape, 1963)

introduced the more comfortable nose-pad feature and production was discontinued entirely in 1929, no doubt to Joyce's annoyance.

Joyce's spectacles

While the design seems quaint to us today, Joyce's spectacles were bang up-to-date at the time, and he particularly favoured the Zylo 'Windsor' model, the frames of which were made of an early type of plastic called—no surprise here—'zylo', available in black, brown, blond and *faux* tortoise shell. You can still snap up 1920s originals for a pittance, but to acquire a pair of Joyce's own glasses you'll need deep pockets. A pair of his *pince nez* from the collection of his friend and fellow Dubliner Thomas Pugh were were sold at auction in December 2018. They came in a velvet-lined morocco case, stamped 'Yeates & Co, Opticians / Dublin' and were listed in the catalogue at €10–15,000.

A Borsalino hat

Joyce was also a great man for hats, both in life and on the page. The phrase 'high grade ha' is repeated several times by Mr Bloom in *Ulysses*— a reference to the worn inscription in the stained inner rim of his bowler. It's a high grade gag that a hat claiming such quality should be so visibly distressed, like the battered billy-cock with a tale to tell acquired by Sherlock Holmes in Conan Doyle's *The Blue Carbuncle*. I suppose *Ulysses* itself is a high grade ha, in the sense of 'funny ha-ha', but that may be straining a point.

Joyce favoured straw boaters* in the summer and Italian Borsalino hats all year round. The latter are still manufactured today by the firm that bears its founder's name.[†]

Giuseppe Borsalino was born in Alessandria in Italy in 1834, became a qualified Master Hatter in Paris and returned to Italy to set up a workshop, importing the latest hat-making technology from Stockport in England. In 1897, on a visit to the Battersby hat-making factory in London, he reportedly dipped his handkerchief into a vat of black liquid, thus acquiring the secret for making perfect bowler hats. When Giuseppe died in 1900 his son took over the company and rapid expansion followed. By 1909 Borsalino was manufacturing 5,500 hats annually, rising to two million a year in the 1920s. There has been long decline since but, according to the company website, today's Borsalino wearers include Johnny Depp (making the first of two appearances in *Multiple Joyce*), Leonardo Di Caprio, Denzel Washington, Justin Timberlake, Kate Moss, Nicole Kidman, Naomi Campbell and John Malkovich, all of them 'immortalized wearing the unique style of the living legend of the most prestigious brand of hats in the world.'

A final and essential element in the Joyce look is the conscientiously mismatched jackets and trousers. Questioned angrily about this affectation in Tom Stoppard's *Travesties*, Joyce explains: 'If I could do it once, I could do it every time. My wardrobe got out of step in Trieste, and its reciprocal members pass each other endlessly in the night.'

---

[*] The milliner John Shevlin is the only maker of real Panama hats in Ireland using (as he says on his Facebook page) 'quality straw from Ecuador' and trading as Shevlin Millinery in Dublin's Temple Bar district. Shevlin formerly had a workshop opposite the James Joyce Centre in North Great George's Street and was approached one day by somebody working there who pointed out that he looked a lot like Joyce (and he certainly does). Would he be interested in a lookalike gig? He was. Here's his website: www.shevlin.ie.

[†] www.borsalino.com.

52. THE METHOD, DEFINED

'Some of the means I use are trivial—and some are quadrivial.'

—Joyce, quoted in Frank Budgen's *James Joyce and the Making of Ulysses* (1934)

The ancient Romans used the word *triviae* to describe the place where one road forked into two, from *tri* (three) and *viae* (roads), literally meaning 'three roads' but also, in a broader sense, 'a public place'.

In describing his method to Budgen thus, the Jesuit-trained Joyce wasn't being glib or self-deprecating but was actually referring to the sense in which 'trivium' and 'quadrivium' together describe the seven liberal arts of the medieval period derived from the Greeks, namely grammar, logic and rhetoric (the trivium), and music, arithmetic, geometry, and astronomy (the quadrivium).

The meaning of 'trivial' has become pejorative, referring to something inconsequential, unworthy of serious consideration, commonplace and lacking in substance. But there's nothing remotely commonplace about the means Joyce uses, and his mention of 'quadrivial' has a confident swagger to it, a well-judged arrogance. What Coleridge said of Wordsworth comes to mind, that great artists create the tastes by which they are judged.

This prompts me to observe, no doubt trivially, that if there's a place in the universe for Finnegan Wake™ (and there clearly is), there should also be a place for Quadrivial Pursuit™, a board game that's far more elaborate and challenging than the original. A *Finnegans Wake* version would work in three dimensions, like the three-tiered chess board in *Star Trek*, using the text as a platform and navigating downwards (lexically) and upwards (narratively). It could take the world by storm.

53. WHAT A HAUHAUHAUHAUDIBBLE THING, TO BE CAUSE!

In August 1929, when Joyce was in London to consult an ophthalmologist, he met the philosopher and linguist C.K. Ogden (1889–1957), author of *The Meaning of Meaning* and inventor of Basic English, 'the international language of 850 words in which everything may be said'. Ogden was an admirer of Joyce and, in issue 46 of the quarterly journal *Psyche* (October 1931), he would render the last four pages of 'Anna Livia Plurabelle' at the end of *Finnegans Wake* into Basic English, while admitting that 'in places the sense of the story has been changed a little.'

At their first meeting Joyce suggested that Ogden should write an introduction to a forthcoming selection of passages from what was then entitled *Work in Progress*, material that would later appear in the *Wake*. Ogden in turn invited Joyce to come to a studio in the Orthological Institute in Cambridge to record the 'Anna Livia Plurabelle' section. The invitation was accepted.

The studio was so dimly-lit that Joyce could not make out the half-inch-high letters in the text and had to rely on whispered prompts throughout the recording. His performance impressed Ogden nevertheless. Joyce had a high, clear mellifluous voice and the recording, available online, deserves and repays repeated listenings.

The original recording was available as a 12-inch double-sided shellac disc with a label printed in green which reads 'THE ORTHO-LOGICAL INSTITUTE 10 KING'S PARADE, CAMBRIDGE'.

It was sold for 2 guineas and later pressings of the same recording were released by His Master's Voice, the Argus Book Shop and the Gotham Book Mart. This marked the beginning of a minor industry dedicated to the recording and transmission of Joyce's writings, what might be called the aural aura surrounding his works. Here are some of the many subsequent incarnations of Joyce as he is spoken.

On Bloomsday 1982, to mark the centenary of Joyce's birth, Ireland's national broadcaster RTÉ aired a superb radio production of *Ulysses*, dramatised and unabridged, which ran without interruption for 29 hours and 45 minutes. It was later released as a boxed set of

32 CDs and has been broadcast several times since. It seems to me definitive.*

Ten years later, in 1992, the intrepid Dublin-born writer and scholar Patrick Healy spent four days at Dublin's Bow Lane Recording Studios recording the complete text of *Finnegans Wake*. It's an engagingly ramshackle achievement, with plenty of fluffs and slips and hesitations (hardly surprising). It lasts for 35 hours and you can listen to the whole thing on www.openculture.com. You have to admire Healy for his tenacity in doing single-handedly (and single-mindedly) what is usually done by a string of readers taking turns—it's a bravura performance.

The following year BBC Radio broadcast an abridged dramatisation of *Ulysses* with a cast including Sinéad Cusack, James Greene, Stephen Rea and Norman Rodway, and a brisk running time of just under six hours.

A complete reading of the unabridged text of *Ulysses* was released as a set of 22 CDs by Naxos Records in 2004, performed by Jim Norton (father of the telly presenter Graham and fondly recalled as the choleric Bishop Brennan in *Father Ted*) and Marcella Riordan as Molly Bloom. Norton senior also recorded an abridged *Finnegans Wake* for the same label in 2009, again with Marcella Riordan. Reviewing it in *The Observer*, Robert McCrum said it was 'the perfect short cut for slackers, poseurs and insomniacs.'

On Bloomsday 2010 Frank Delaney (see essay 89, 'De minimus non shabby curate lex') launched his superb podcast series *Re:Joyce*, offering his followers a detailed page-by-page analysis of *Ulysses* and, two years later, on Bloomsday 2012, BBC Radio 4 transmitted a new nine-part adaptation of the novel dramatised by Robin Brooks and produced and directed by Jeremy Mortimer, narrated by Stephen Rea (who had already appeared in the 1993 radio adaptation and on screen as Leopold Bloom), with Henry Goodman as Bloom, Niamh Cusack as Molly and Andrew Scott (who would later be memorably cast as the hot priest in Phoebe Waller-Bridge's television comedy *Fleabag*) as Stephen Dedalus.

---

* A recent trend at arts festivals all over the world has been for non-stop live readings of *Ulysses* and *Finnegans Wake*. Is this even an idea, let alone a good idea? To re-purpose literary texts as a form of endurance theatre seems to me a lamentable development.

The most recent Joyce recording—and one with claims to being the best—was issued by Naxos on Bloomsday 2021. It's another unabridged *Finnegans Wake* clocking in at a brisk 29 hours 18 minutes, read by the Irish actor Barry McGovern (who was born in Eccles Street and now lives in Chapelizod), with the aforementioned Marcella Riordan. It's directed and produced by the composer Roger Marsh, who has overseen all the Naxos recordings of Joyce's novels and who also selected this recording's musical soundtrack, which includes Mozart, Bach, Wagner, Verdi and Bellini.

Of the others, the many others, let the British actor Patrick Horgan (1929–2021) stand for them all. He was the narrator in Woody Allen's *Zelig* (1983), played a Nazi officer in an episode of *Star Trek* (season 2 episode 21: 'Patterns of Force') and, as a committed Joycean, recorded an audiobook version of *Finnegans Wake* for the Library of Congress in 1985. This was a commission from the National Foundation for the Blind and not intended for public circulation, but some of it is available online. It may be damage to the original tape that means the opening lines drop the phrase 'from swerve of shore to bend of bay.'

54. SEXCALIBER HROSSPOWER

In the late 1920s and early 30s the future president of Ireland, Erskine Hamilton Childers (1905–1974), son of Robert Erskine Childers (author of *Riddle of the Sands*), worked at Drake's Travel in Paris. Drake's, based at at 11, rue de Castiglione in the 1st arrondissement, operated a fleet of Hispano-Suiza limousines.

Hispano-Suiza, founded in 1904, was, and still is, a Spanish automotive-engineering company. In 1923 its French luxury car arm became a semi-autonomous partnership—the Société Française Hispano-Suiza—and, while the Spanish factories moved increasingly to the production of trucks, buses and aircraft engines, the Bois-Colombes plant near Paris became the company's main luxury car plant. The magnificent limousines produced there were among the most expensive automobiles ever built, and proved especially popular with White Russian aristocrats who had fled their homeland after the Bolshevik Revolution. What has all this to do with Joyce?

In common with almost all the modernist writers of the 1920s, our man never learned to drive. There is, however, a photograph of him sitting at the wheel of an enormous open-top limousine—and it's an Hispano-Suiza—on page 77 of *James Joyce's Ireland* (Yale University Press, 1992) by David Pierce.

The picture was taken in 1932 near the medieval city of Feldkirch, on the border with Switzerland and Lichtenstein. Nora and Lucia sit in the back of the car and Joyce (in dark glasses and a straw boater) is in the driver's seat, his left arm propped casually over the door. To his right sits Lucia's nurse. In the bottom right hand corner of the image is the photographer's shadow, presumably the chauffeur's. We can assume Joyce hired the car from Drake's and quite possibly at a discount from Childers, a fellow expat Irishman.

What appears to be a jolly holiday snapshot is in fact a record of a particularly difficult time for the Joyce family. Lucia, then aged 25, had first exhibited signs of mental illness two years earlier, following her rejection by Samuel Beckett, with whom she was in love. At Joyce's 50th birthday party in February 1932 she threw a chair at her mother and her brother Giorgio had escorted her to an asylum.

From left: Lucia's nurse, Joyce, Nora, Lucia, shadowy chauffeur (Image courtesy Beinecke Rare Book and Manuscript Library, Yale University)

At the end of May that year she was diagnosed with hebephrenic psychosis by a Dr Gaston Maillard, who advised her parents that she should remain in his clinic at L'Haye-les-Roses.

In early July Joyce arranged for Lucia and her nurse to be smuggled out of the clinic, which is presumably when the photograph was taken. They travelled with Joyce and Nora to Feldkirch, where their friends Maria and Eugène Jolas were spending the summer. Eugène was a writer, critic, translator and co-founder of *transition*, the avant-garde literary magazine in which sections of *Work in Progress* (later *Finnegans Wake*) were first published. In his memoir, *My Friend James Joyce* (1941), Jolas recalls Joyce telling him at the time that 'Over there, on those tracks, the fate of *Ulysses* was decided in 1915,' a quote now reproduced in German on the walls of Feldkirch railway station concourse.*

In 1915 Joyce had been classified an 'enemy alien' in Trieste, which was then part of the Austro-Hungarian Empire. He obtained permission to leave and, accompanied by Nora and their two young children, boarded a train for Zürich. Officials boarded the train at Feldkirch to carry out border control checks, and Joyce narrowly es-

---

*The original German inscription read: 'Dort drüben auf den Schienen wurde 1915 das Schicksal des Ulysses entschieden'—James Joyce 1932 am Bahnhof Feldkirch.

'James Joyce Passage' in Feldkirch

caped arrest and detention—his brother Stanislaus had been arrested in Trieste and remained until the end of the Great War.

Feldkirch further commemorates its Joyce connection with a plaque at the Hotel Löwen, where the author stayed for three weeks. A tunnel passing beneath a road and some houses in the city centre, which Joyce must often have passed through on his way to the station, was officially renamed 'James Joyce Passage' in his honour on Bloomsday in 2004.

Lucia's condition worsened over the years. At the age of 43 she moved to Britain and was admitted to St Andrew's Hospital (formerly the Northampton General Lunatic Asylum for the Middle and Upper Classes), where she would spend the rest of her life, with rare visits from Samuel Beckett (just once, in the early 1950s), Maria Jolas and Harriet Shaw Weaver. The once vibrant and talented young woman, who danced as a toy soldier in Jean Renoir's film *La Petite marchande d'allumettes* (1927), who had an artist's temperament and an intensely intimate relationship with her father, became an isolated and unhappy recluse. Helen MacTaggart, a Joyce enthusiast, met her one afternoon in 1977:

> It was not a nice place to be. Lucia talked a lot and I got the impression she did not see enough people. She smoked non-stop and had quite a guttural, European accent, not an Irish lilt.*

A fellow inmate was The Honourable Violet Albina Gibson (1876–1956), the Dublin-born daughter of Lord Ashbourne, who had shot Benito Mussolini in Rome in 1926. She was arrested and later (at Mussolini's request) deported to Britain without charge and admitted to St Andrews. Her grave is close to Lucia's. The novel *Saving Lucia* by Anna Vaught, published in 2020 by the independent press Bluemoose Books, explores the lives of Lucia Joyce and Violet Gibson, and is recommended.

---

*Quoted in 'Alone at the end' by Vanessa Thorpe, published in *The Guardian* on 21st February 2010.

55. BESIDE THE SEASIDE

Day-trippers to the Kent resort of Margate can sit in the same seaside shelter where T.S. Eliot spent time connecting nothing with nothing and composing the third part of the twentieth century's greatest poem, the one that was published in the same year that *Ulysses* appeared. The shelter overlooks Margate Sands (and there's a phonetic connection between Margate and the London district of Moorgate, featured elsewhere in *The Waste Land*).

The Victorian structure is Grade II listed but was, on my last visit, in a rather weatherbeaten condition. There's no plaque, thank the stars, although I expect it's only a matter of time before a well-intentioned conceptual artist makes a 'playful intervention'. For the time being we can settle for an adjacent blockhouse urinal with the simple anagram *TOILETS* painted in black letters on the side.

James and Nora Joyce never made it to Margate, but in the summer of 1929 they did spend two months in the equally prosaic west country resort of Torquay, staying at the Imperial Hotel, an expensive establishment offering a lavish range of services (pools, a gym, a spa, sun beds, a sauna and squash and tennis courts, and massage), none of which the the two holiday-makers used. Joyce didn't much like the place, writing to a friend that it would have been better to book into a small guest house and to visit the Imperial for lunch.

He would spend his afternoons on the beach, languidly fingering pebbles. But there were odd bursts of energy, during one of which he vaulted over a wall and hurt his arm. In the evenings he would visit local pubs with his friend, the scholar and translator Stuart Gilbert, drinking cider (which he didn't much like) and listening to the simultaneous conversations going on around them which, to Gilbert's amazement, he seemed able to follow without difficulty.

Which locals would they have visited?

The nearest pub to the Imperial is The Hole in the Wall in Park Lane. It's a cosy-looking joint with an intriguing plaque on one wall, which appears to be a modern version of an earlier one that Joyce may have seen.

In 1815 the French Emperor Napoleon Bonaparte had surrendered to Captain Frederick Maitland of the *Bellerophon*, which brought him to England. ('Billy Ruffian' is a Joyce-grade coinage, surprisingly

Plaque in *The Hole in the Wall*, Torquay

not to be found in the Wake's Willingdone museyroom.) The Emperor was detained on board in Plymouth Sound during July while his fate was decided. Boatloads of sightseers would float expectantly around the *Bellerophon* and Boney would obligingly put in an appearance at around 5pm each day. Lightning artists—the paparazzi of the day—would knock out rapid sketches as he strolled Napoleonically around the deck.

A short distance from The Hole in the Wall is The Devon Arms, another traditional boozer. I can't find any more pubs within easy walking distance of the Imperial, but there may have been other places, now closed.

I can picture Joyce wincing at the sharp and musty taste of Devon scrumpy. Torquay, despite its prime location on 'the English Riviera' lacked much continental sophistication and a glass of white wine was not the sort of thing one could expect to find in any pub there, or anywhere else in Britain. Sherry at best, or perhaps port.

56. HIS ART BELONGS TO DADA

'What did you do in the War, Mister Joyce?'
'I wrote *Ulysses*. What did you do?'

Joyce's crushing response (as imagined by Tom Stoppard in *Travesties*) throws up some unoriginal yet still unsettling questions about the artist's relation to society. His apparent indifference to the Great War (which he spent, as it were, in an ivory bunker in Zürich) may be down to heartlessness, or self-absorption, or high-minded dedication to a greater cause.

What of the many other artists who fetched up in neutral Switzerland, and more particularly in Zürich, but who didn't come up with masterpieces? The multilingual city was home to a loosely-knit expat community of writers and painters, many of whom gathered at the Cabaret Voltaire, the night club founded in 1916 by the young German poet Hugo Ball and his partner Emmy Hennings. In a damp back room of a Spiegelstrasse bar originated the Dada movement which, with its combination of dance, music and recitations, was the *fons et origo* of modern performance art. As far as we know Joyce never spent an evening there, but if he ever did the onstage figure of Hugo Ball would have made an impression:

> *I wore a specially designed costume. My legs were encased in cothurns made of luminous blue card-board reaching up to my hips, so that I looked like an obelisk. Above this I wore a huge cardboard collar, scarlet inside and gold outside. This was fastened at the throat in such a manner that I was able to move it like wings by raising and dropping my elbows. In addition, I wore a tall blue and white striped hat.*

Tricked out as a cubist bishop, Ball delivered intense readings of his 'sound poems', a handful of which have proved to be both durable and influential. His poem 'gadji beri bimba' was performed by Talking Heads, and the influential Sheffield band Cabaret Voltaire took their name from the nightclub. Look online for a jaw-dropping clip of Marie Osmond, no less, reciting (apparently from memory and with tremendous conviction) one of Ball's sound poems, the one which begins like this:

> jolifanto bambla o falli bambla
> großiga m'pfa habla horem
> egiga goramen
> higo bloiko russula huju
> hollaka hollala
> anlogo bung
> blago bung blago bung
> bosso fataka
> ü üü ü

And so on.

While the Dada movement had a major cultural impact in Berlin, Paris, Cologne, New York, the Netherlands and Yugoslavia, the British art establishment tended to be sceptical about such continental goings-on. Critics such as Herbert Read and others were swift to observe that Lewis Carroll got there half a century earlier with 'Jabberwocky'.

But Ball's verses are far more radical and provocative than Carroll's engaging nonsense and should be read (or preferably heard) in a counter-cultural context, ideally in a dank nightclub with a rowdy young audience, and during wartime.

Disgust at the martial rhetoric and colossal bloodshed of the conflict beyond the Swiss border was intense. On 28th July 1916, as the Battle of the Somme raged, Ball read out the first Dada Manifesto:

> How can one get rid of everything that smacks of journalism, worms, everything nice and right, blinkered, moralistic, europeanised, enervated? By saying dada.
>
> Dada is the world soul, dada is the pawnshop. Dada is the world's best lily-milk soap.

Ball's sound poems were a heartfelt reaction to the Great War, an anguished and eloquent act of cultural cleansing: 'A line of poetry is a chance to get rid of all the filth that clings to this accursed language, as if put there by stockbrokers' hands, hands worn smooth by coins.' He was anti-modernist in his desire to do away with the rational discourse of modernism, to ditch the dictionary and to create a new language free of convention or association. In a calculatedly unreasoning response to the prevailing unreason, he set out to do

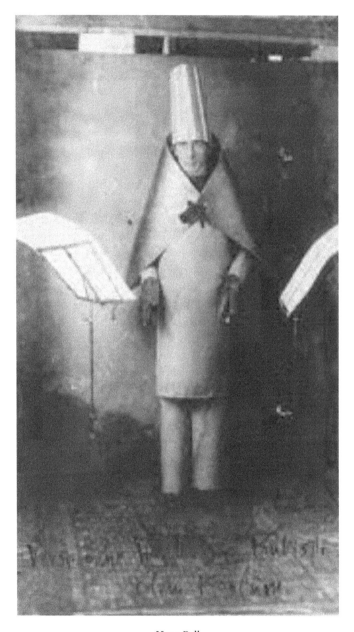

Hugo Ball

to language what the Allies and Central Powers were doing to the landscape of Flanders:

> All the words are other people's inventions. I want my own stuff, my own rhythm, and vowels and consonants too, matching the rhythm and all my own.

Humpty Dumpty comes to mind ('When I use a word [...] it means just what I choose it to mean—neither more nor less'), and Ball's ferocious linguistic innovations offer us a link between *Through the Looking-glass* and *Finnegans Wake*.

Ball gave Dada its theoretical heft and intellectual legitimacy, Tristan Tzara the momentum and commercial savvy. When the two men fell out over Tzara's entrepreneurial plans to systematise the movement and launch it internationally, Ball left Zürich and, after a stint in journalism, retired to the countryside to became something of a Catholic mystic before dying, aged 41, from stomach cancer. Of his first book *Flametti* he wrote: 'This little novel contains my whole philosophy on 200 pages. Love for those who are on their knees. For the outcasts, the crushed, the tormented.'

Originally published in Berlin in 1918, *Flametti* was written in three months in 1916 when Ball and Hennings, pre-Dada, were living in a state of grinding poverty as part of an itinerant Swiss theatrical troupe. The novel is largely set in the imaginary 'Fuchsweide' district of Zürich where an 'offbeat, fun-loving crowd' hang out in an atmosphere of 'unadulterated authenticity in the midst of a world of appearances, a miracle spawned by outrageous perversities.'

Flametti vividly depicts an impoverished ensemble of yodellers, a female impersonator, escapologist and giggling soubrettes who perform such vacuous crowd-pleasers as *The Harem*, *The Graveyard Thief*, *The Man with the Giant Mustache* and *The Water Sprites*. Max Flametti is the eponymous actor manager, and it's tempting to see him as a satirical portrait of Tristan Tzara—a bombastic ham, opportunistic fraud and energetic adulterer, evading creditors and the authorities while hustling nightclub owners for the next gig. Landing a season at the prestigious Krokodil bar he commissions a new piece about Native Americans called *The Indians* from a writer named Stanislaus Rotter (we'll come back to him), a verse melodrama that reflects the Dada movement's interest in primitivism.

The opening night of *The Indians* is a *tour-de-force* of grotesque comic description, and often hysterically funny. Here's an audience member at the Krokodil called Skullface:

> White makeup, eyes rimmed in red, her face ensconced on a goitery neck, her hindquarters restlessly wriggling back and forth on her chair, she looked around at the arriving gussets and tightened her garter, while shoving the sixth piece of cake between her golden teeth.

Then there's Fräulein Annie with her 'obstreperous boil' and dirt-clogged fingernails that she manicures with a toothpick, the onstage dancers 'in tango-coloured baby-doll tunics' and the throbbing beat of the orchestra: 'Mtata, mtata, umba, umba, umba, umba!' and 'Ptuuh dada dada da, umba, umba!' It's a chaotic gathering and, one assumes, not unlike a night at the actual Cabaret Voltaire: an energetic, shambolic, hit-and-miss programme of dance, music (especially jazz and African tribal drumming) and the spoken word: strident, radically experimental, offensive, brutal and silly.

The hard-up musical director Herr Meyer is clearly a self-portrait of the author, bankrupt by the end of the novel. Other characters come and go and some are tantalising: the aforementioned Stanislaus Rotter has 'rimless bloodshot eyes', sports *pince nez*, reads the *Daily Mail* and is haughtily condescending. Could this be a sly portrait of Joyce, using his younger brother's surname? If so this would be the first appearance of our man in somebody else's novel, and quite a find.

Catherine Schelbert's translation of *Flametti* is wonderfully idiosyncratic, perfectly capturing the period. It must have been a daunting task, but she tackles the Germanized Swiss idioms and Austrian dialect of the original with wit and gusto and I can think of no other novel with so many exclamation marks! Every utterance is a manifesto! *Flametti* is required reading for anyone with an interest in the origins of European modernism, who wants to know more about the city where much of *Ulysses* was written or who seeks an answer to the question: '*Was hast du im Krieg zu tun, Herr Ball?*'

57. An Italian modernist in Charlton

Joyce was twenty-five when he arrived in Trieste in 1906, accompanied by Nora Barnacle. They were unmarried and he had landed a poorly-paid teaching job at the Berlitz language school.

The following year he befriended one of his students, a Triestine businessman in his mid-forties named Aron Ettore Schmitz who, after the death of both of his parents, had married his cousin and become a partner in her father's business. This was a successful manufacturing company specialising in production of a marine paint which, applied to the hulls of ships, prevented the accumulation of barnacles. (Whether this was the basis for some chortling banter at Nora's expense is open to conjecture.)

Prior to meeting Joyce, Schmitz had spent ten years in England managing the company's London branch and living at 67 Charlton Church Lane, London SE7 7AB (the house now carries a blue plaque). His English must therefore have been pretty fluent, and I can't help but wonder whether he signed up for Berlitz English lessons simply as a way of passing the time.

Schmitz's name may fail to resonate but, under the literary pseudonym of Italo Svevo, he wrote *La coscienza di Zeno* (usually translated as *Confessions of Zeno*), first published at the author's expense in 1923 and now regarded as one of the greatest Italian novels of the 20th century. Joyce, an early champion, arranged for the book to be translated into French and it appeared thus in 1927, published by Gallimard. The French critics were extravagant in their praise, Italian critics followed suit and Svevo's literary reputation was secured.

Confessions of Zeno is among the first works of fiction to engage with the subject of psychoanalysis, a practice that Svevo regarded with scepticism because, like Karl Kraus, he regarded it as the condition for which it claimed to be the cure. The novel takes the form of Zeno Cossini's diary, published and prefaced by his doctor in a fit of pique after his patient suddenly cancels his course of treatment. Zeno, we are told, was apparently addicted to smoking until analysis led to the conclusion that what he was *really* addicted to was the masochistic pleasure of giving the habit up. It's a richly comic, deeply serious study of marriage and mortality and the fear of death, and of dying.

It's well known that Svevo, a Jew and an atheist, was the likely model for Leopold Bloom.* Less well known is the fact that Joyce took Svevo's wife Livia's name for the *Wake*'s Anna Livia Plurabelle. (Joyce wrote to Svevo in February 1924 to tell him just that.) A quarter of a century later a wonderful photograph taken by John McAfee and captioned 'Celebrating Bloomsday 1949' shows 'Mrs Livia Italo Svevo' (now a widow) with Joyce's brother Stanislaus and W.J. Sullivan sitting together in a restaurant. This was perhaps the true first Bloomsday, before the boozy goings-on at Sandycove in 1954.

---

*Joyce also had an acquaintance in Trieste named Leopoldo Popper, a Jew of Bohemian descent who had employed Joyce as an English tutor for his daughter Amalia. Popper managed the company of Popper and Blum, and it's possible that 'Leopold Bloom' combines Popper's first name and an anglicised version of Blum.

58. Tell me all. Tell me now. You'll die when you hear.

The operation was a success, but the patient died.

Joyce's life came to an end in a Zürich hospital in the early hours of Monday, 13th January 1941. He was a prematurely aged man of 58, and exhausted. He had been taken by ambulance to the Schwesternhaus zum Roten Kreuz the previous Friday suffering from stomach cramps and X-rays confirmed a perforated duodenal ulcer. An immediate operation was required.

What appears to have been a long-standing condition had remained undiagnosed for at least seven years. Joyce, afraid that he might have cancer, was worried about the cost of his treatment—'How are you going to pay for this?' he asked his son Giorgio, who reassured him. The operation was performed at 10 o'clock on Saturday morning and Joyce recovered consciousness in the afternoon. He seemed for a while to rally but on Sunday grew weaker. A blood transfusion became necessary and two Swiss soldiers from Neuchâtel donated their blood. This pleased Joyce who said: 'A good omen. I like Neuchâtel wine.'

Later that afternoon he passed into a coma, recovering briefly to ask that a bed be set up for Nora next to his. The doctors insisted that his wife and son go home, which they did. Joyce regained consciousness for the last time at around 1am, asking the nurse to call his family. He died alone at 2:15 am on Monday morning, Nora and Georgio arriving fifteen minutes later.

His body was interred in the Fluntern Cemetery, close to the Zürich zoo. In 1966 the remains were moved from an ordinary grave to a more prominent site, and the fine bronze sculpture by Milton Hebald erected. This portrays Joyce as an impish, attentive figure, legs crossed, an open book in his right hand, his slender cane propped against his hip, holding a cigar aloft.

Not long before his death he was asked whether he would ever go back to Dublin and his reply was reportedly 'Have I ever left it?' His actual last words are said to have been 'Does nobody understand?' but there appears to be no firm evidence to support this.

His final *written* communication was a postcard to his brother Stanislaus, postmarked 4 January 1941 and sent from the Pension Delphin, Muhlebachstrasses 69, Zürich. Stan was in trouble with the Fascist authorities in Italy and Jim sent the names and addresses of people who might be able to help him, including Ezra Pound and Curzio Malaparte. He signs off, in Italian, 'Saluti da tutti' ('Greetings from all of us').

Saluti da tutti.

59. CÉSAR ALBIN AND *MARITANA*

César Albin caricature of Joyce (1939)

This caricature of Joyce by César Albin dates from 1939 and was prompted by Paul Léon's remark that, when Joyce bent over, he resembled a question mark. It appeared in issue 21 of *transition* (21st March 1932) and was produced in consultation with the subject. It shows a shabby figure slouched interrogatively in dark glasses, a patched and threadbare suit and cobwebby hat, hands thrust into pockets, surrounded by rainclouds. At his feet a globe, dominated entirely by Ireland in general and the black stain of Dublin in particular. Rolled up in his back trouser pocket is the sheet music for 'Yes! Let Me Like a Soldier Fall' from the now all-but-forgotten three-act opera *Maritana* by the Waterford-born composer William Vincent Wallace, with lyrics by Edward Fitzball. Joyce refers to the song in the two *Dubliners* stories 'A Mother' and 'The Dead', and again in *Ulysses*.

First produced in London in 1845, *Maritana* was a great success in Dublin, Philadelphia, Vienna and New York, and was performed regularly throughout the following century. It remained popular until the 1950s by which time the public taste for such tuneful, sentimental music had waned. 'Yes! Let Me Like a Soldier Fall' is performed in Act 2 by the character Don Cæsar de Bazan, a jovial nobleman admired from afar by the gypsy street singer Maritana. He has been sentenced to death for duelling during Holy Week, but on the day of his execution a Royal pardon is intercepted by the King's villainous minister Don José, who offers Cæsar a soldier's death if he agrees to marry a certain lady of his acquaintance. Cæsar agrees and José brings the heavily-veiled Maritana to the prison, the plan being to make her a nobleman's widow, which—well, you get the idea. Cue the song:

> Yes! let me like a Soldier fall,
>   Upon some open plain,
> This breast expanding for the ball
>   To blot out ev'ry stain.
> Brave manly hearts confer my doom
>   That gentler ones may tell
> Howe'er forgot, unknown my tomb,
>   *I like a Soldier fell,*
> Howe'er forgot, unknown my tomb,
>   *I like a Soldier fell.*
>   *I like a Soldier fell.*
>
> I only ask of that proud race
>   Which ends its blaze in me,
> To die the last, and not disgrace
>   Its ancient chivalry!
> Tho' o'er my clay no banner wave
>   Nor trumpet requiem swell,
> Enough they murmur o'er my grave
>   *He like a Soldier fell,*
> Enough they murmur o'er my grave
>   *He like a Soldier fell,*
>   *He like a Soldier fell.*

A spirited 1957 production by the Kilrush Opera Society is available online and the song kicks in at 51:50. The opera was revived briefly by The Royal Dublin Society in 2006, with an orchestra conducted by Proinnsías Ó Duinn and singers led by Mairead Buicke and Robin Tritschler. It has since faded from view.

60. WHO WAS THAT MASKED MAN?

Joyce, James. James Joyce's death mask, the plaster-of-paris mask c.6 inches deep, 11 inches high, [January 1941]

—Sotheby's catalogue for the sale of English Literature, History, Children's and Illustrated Books and Drawings. (July 2001)

Like Napoleon's black felt tricorne hat, of which at least 19 are known to exist, there seem to be an awful lot of Joyce death masks currently in circulation. Two were made the day after he died, but they have proliferated since then.*

The National Library of Ireland successfully bid £55,000 for the mask listed above. It appeared to have an impeccable provenance, but the National Library's director Brendan O'Donaghue withdrew from the sale when it became clear that this was not one of the two originals, and not even a copy of one of the two originals, but a copy of *another* copy of one of the two originals—or possibly of one of three originals, as we shall see in a moment.

The Sotheby's catalogue entry claimed that the mask was one of two plaster casts made by the Swiss sculptor Paul Speck at the request of Carole Giedion-Welcker (1893–1979), an art-critic friend of the Joyces who had been at his bedside shortly after—or possibly shortly before—he died.

But (and the plot thickens) it appears that a *third* mask was made at the time, quite possibly without the knowledge of Giedion-Welcker or the Joyce family. According to the Sotheby's catalogue it remains unknown whether Speck made three original so-called 'negatives' at the same time, or used one of the two originals to make a third at a later date, which would technically be a copy. This third mask was acquired by one Edmund Brauchbar, a former pupil of Joyce's in Zürich, who arranged for his son Rudolph to forward the item to the United States in January 1942. Brauchbar subsequently donated it to the United States Library of Congress, where it remains to this day.

---

*Sotheby's in Paris announced that it would commemorate the bicentenary of Napoleon's death with a sale dedicated to what should be called Napoleoniana. With an estimated sale price of more than half a million pounds, the hat in question is thought to have been worn by the Emperor when he signed the peace treaties of Tilsit, thus carving up Europe into regions of French and Russian influence. Included in the sale was a death mask based on the original cast taken by doctors on the island of St Helena. Est., €400–600k.

Of the two wholly original plaster-of-paris masks, Giedeon-Welckerlater bequeathed one to the Zürich James Joyce Foundation (where it can be seen today) and the other to the Dublin architect Michael Scott, who arranged for it to be displayed at the Joyce Museum in the Martello tower at Sandycove, next door to his modernist house (see essay 76 'The Ondt and the Gripes'). At some point in the late 1950s or early '60s Scott used his original plaster mask to cast six bronze replicas, one of which can be seen (along with the original) in the Sandycove museum, another of which he gave to the film director John Huston in recognition of his role in establishing the museum. Huston in turn passed this mask for safekeeping to his son Tony, who wrote the script for his father's last film *The Dead* (1987), based on the final story in *Dubliners*. The Huston mask languished in a London bank vault until 1991, when Tony Huston presented it to the Rosenbach Museum and Library in Philadelphia, the former home of book dealer A.S.W. Rosenbach.

The Rosenbach Museum and Library also owns the autograph manuscript of *Ulysses* for which Rosenbach had paid $1,975 (much less than the author considered it was worth). Rosenbach later sent Joyce a telegram asking him if he had any other materials for sale, but misspelled *Ulysses*, prompting Joyce to dash off some irritable doggerel in a letter to Harriet Shaw Weaver (24th May 1924):

> Rosy Brook he bought a book
> Though he didn't know how to spell it.
> Such is the lure of literature
> To the lad who can buy and sell it.

To confuse matters the Sotheby's catalogue stated:

> Provenance of present example: Carola Gideon-Welckler; Michael Scott (the Irish architect and founder of the James Joyce Tower, Sandycove, Dublin); the film director John Huston (as a token of appreciation for his efforts in helping the museum); his son Anthony Huston; present owner. The mask was on display at the Rosenbach Foundation from 1992 to 2000.

But this wasn't the same mask that Huston had given to the Rosenbach, which remains to this day in the Rosenbach. The mask up for auction, rather quaintly described by the Sotheby's cataloguer as 'the final visage of one of the greatest authors of the twentieth century,' appears to be one of no fewer than *six* additional plaster masks which (according to Sotheby's) 'were apparently made by Swiss sculptor Victor Dallo under the direction of Paul Speck.' These probably date from the early to mid-1950s and three of the six are known to be in the Zentralbibliothek, the University of Lausanne and the University of Basle. That leaves three unaccounted for (or two, not including the Sotheby's mask). What a mnice old mness it all mnakes!

To recap: the two *original* masks—the ones taken from Joyce's dead head—are in the James Joyce Foundation in Zürich and the Joyce Museum in Sandycove. The third, by the same maker but almost certainly created at a later date, is in the Library of Congress in Washington DC.

In yet a further thickening of the plot another version of the mask, this time made in Irish silver, went on display at the Hunt Museum in Limerick in 2012. At the time this was also, and wrongly, claimed to be one of the two originals (which were not, of course, made from silver). Obviously made at a much later date, it had been in store in Limerick on long-term loan from the Irish billionaire Tony Ryan (1936–2007), the co-founder of Ryanair.

In 2017 the Birmingham foundry Lunt's Castings produced a limited edition of 12 further bronze masks, one of which went up for auction in October 2020 at an estimate of €1,500–€2,000. I think that brings the total to at least 28 death masks, of which at least seven are currently on public display in different parts of the world. The others—however many of them there may be—are presumably in private hands. There's one behind the bar at The Mullingar House in Chapelizod and perhaps Bono has a few, or Michael Flatley.

The July 2001 auction cited at the start of this essay included another unique and far more significant item. Here's part of the catalogue entry:

> A heavily revised and substantially complete early working draft of the "Eumaeus" chapter, a largely continuous and fluent text written in Joyce's cursive and 'personal' hand in black ink (the earliest hand), with extensive revisions, insertions and additional passages, some interlinear, but the majority drafted in the margin or on facing (previously blank) pages, sometimes lengthwise, in (chiefly later hands of) red, black and green ink and pencil, every page heavily "deleted" by the author in characteristic fashion with

large crosses in red or blue crayon or pencil; written in a small lined exercise book, a pencil inscription (possibly in Joyce's hand) on the first page: "Miss Collins, 18 r. Michodiere, 18 de la Sourdiere (rue S Honore,—" [possibly the name and address of the typist used to type up the subsequent 'fair copy'] 48 pages, text written on 44 pages, 4 pages blank, 24 leaves, 8vo (c.210 × 153mm.), with narrow white silk bookmark, purple paper wrappers with label lettered "EUMEO" modern white vellum folder lettered in gilt, in slipcase, [some portions possibly Trieste, between 1916 and 3 July 1920; other portions and many revisions and markings, Paris, summer and autumn of 1920]

This previously unknown autograph manuscript, one of the earliest complete working drafts of any *Ulysses* episode, was the property of a private collector who had acquired it from the former French Ambassador to Bern. The item had 'minor soiling or fingermarks (probably from authorial use)' which makes one wonder whether there's any DNA to be sourced from the paper.

The previous year Christie's had sold a 'Circe' manuscript to the National Library of Ireland for £1.4 million. The 'Eumaeus' episode went to a private buyer for £861,250 ($1,213,540), which was slightly below the Sotheby's estimate. The bronze death mask went for £41,650.

61. A Portrait of the Artist as a Disappointed Man

Bruce Frederick Cummings (1889–1919) wrote under the magnificent nom-de-plume of Wilhelm Nero Pilate Barbellion and is best remembered, though not adequately admired and respected, as the author of *The Journal of a Disappointed Man* (1919).

The *Journal* is a record of his daily life from the age of 15 and the first entry reads: 'Am writing an essay on the life-history of insects and have abandoned for the time being the idea of writing on "How Cats Spend their Time". Cummings was a born naturalist and this childhood interest led to his becoming a professional entomologist, employed in the classification of insects at the Natural History Museum in South Kensington. But without a university degree and from an impoverished provincial background, with few connections or advantages and no sense of entitlement, he found himself struggling on the margins. This struggle informed the sense of disappointment that would be the making of him as a writer.

He was 26 years old and the Great War was at its height when in 1916 he was summoned to attend an army medical. His own physician had given him a sealed envelope to pass to the army doctor which remained unread during the examination, but on his way home he opened it and discovered that he had been diagnosed with multiple sclerosis, although the army doctor had not needed this confirmation before declaring him unfit for military service.

He lived long enough to complete and oversee publication of *The Journal of a Disappointed Man* in March 1919. This featured an introduction by H.G. Wells, a fervent admirer who was believed by some readers at the time to be the actual author. Wells noted that Barbellion's scientific writing had 'the grace, the power of handling, the breadth of reference of literature' and, by implication, that his literary writings had a corresponding scientific precision and weight. Writing as Barbellion, Cummings engages head-on with (as Wells put it) 'the tragedy of his hopes and of the dark, unforeseen, unforeseeable, and inexplicable fate that has overtaken him.'

For the seven months left to him following publication Cummings was able to enjoy, briefly, a degree of literary celebrity and to finish two more books. Thanks to the efforts of Ray Davis, a Barbellion admirer in California, the author's complete works are available to read online.* I wrote to Ray to ask him why he'd committed to this project and this prompted the following observations about the writer and his connections to Joyce, which he has kindly allowed me to to share with you here:

> Barbellion claimed instant fellowship with (what he lived long enough to read of) James Joyce. They shared pride and poverty, compulsive truth-telling, retreats into silence, and a sense of exile.
>
> More particularly they were both intellectually ambitious provincials stuck on the periphery of *longue durée* cultural shifts.
>
> Bruce Cummings was born to be a naturalist in the grand old tradition, devoting his passions and skills to the present-to-hand reality of plants, beasts, and earth on the ground. He should've sailed on the Beagle or explicated the ecology of the English countryside, but such escapades had already become a gentleman-scholar's game and would soon become the niche of pop-science writers like Barbellion's champion H.G. Wells. 'Real' working-class science instead took place in urban offices and urban labs for the greater profit of industry or government.
>
> Although I sense a leap in energy and happiness whenever Cummings returned to the countryside, he never himself described that dichotomy in so many words. Instead, like other brilliant articulate failures, he redirected himself from his first vocation to literature. He would still observe, analyze, and describe, but specimens would be human and he would be first on the dissection table.
>
> James Joyce faced similar blockages but his vocations were spiritual and literary from the start, and due to whatever combination of history, capability, and opportunity Joyce became more explicitly aware of his dilemma, formed vaster ambitions, and lived to fulfil them.
>
> We have no way to know where Cummings would've gone next, or if he would have been able to publish even one book without the sales hook of his early death. On the other hand, would Joyce be remembered if he'd died at Cummings's age, with only *Chamber Music* to his name? At the very least, Cummings's publications provide a unique testament of Dedalus-in-progress, drowned before flight, as I reckon most members of the extended Dedalus clan have been.

---

* www.pseudopodium.org/barbellionblog.

More particularly still, they share a certain attitude.

Embodied/embedded/naturalist philosophers and scientists, much as I love 'em, often speak of human experience in ways which would (thoughtlessly for the most part, sincerely for the horrifying part) dismiss the blind, the deaf, the pained, the frail, the immobilized, the illiterate, or the starving as not-really-human. (Other philosophers seem willing to dismiss any non-philosopher, no matter what shape they're in, as subhuman, so it may just come with the territory.) Those philosophers, theologians, and mystics who do admit the existence of suffering also tend to deny the existence of anything else, with sweet nothing our only transcendence.

In literature there's a minor muscular-secular-hedonist tradition, viz. that hearty medico buck Oliver Gogarty, but from Rochester through Zola what's labeled Naturalism leans grim and nihilist. Early critics received Joyce's first books (and Barbellion's *Journal*) accordingly, sometimes awarding them extra-naturalistic points for having come straight from the whoreson's mouth of a native informant. (Richard Wright's helpfully titled *Native Son* would be a later example of such critical reception.) And it's true that Joyce and Cummings, like Flaubert and Ibsen, were to varying extents out for revenge.

They were not, however, out for nothingness, and desperate though their circumstances might be, their works were above all else lively: liveliness was their chief defence. Flaubert and Ibsen had violently and despairingly alternated between Romantic/Naturalist inflationary/deflationary antitheses; learning from their examples, Joyce achieved a bizarrely cheering synthesis, and reconstructed the incarnate spirituality of the Church as inspirited carnality.

As for Barbellion, naming his posthumous-to-be collection *Enjoying Life* (1919) exhibited a sense of humour but not sarcasm. He did 'enjoy life' and, dutifully recording his own disgust, pain and hopelessness was another method of enjoyment.

Most particularly they were drawn to a certain technique whereby enforced isolation, quotidian (if not downright nauseating) realism, and defiant vibrancy might merge.

Barbellion on Joyce's *Portrait*: 'He gives the flow of the boy's consciousness—rather the trickle of one thing after another . . . It is difficult to do. I've tried it in this Journal and failed.'

Deliberate production of personality-tinted-or-tainted discourse is at least as old as classical rhetoric. 'Stream of consciousness' is only its most recent technique, and in a way the most limited.

As Barbellion noticed, it's also misnamed. What it transcribes isn't a stream, or consciousness, and definitely not silently meditative abstraction staring into an abyss on unframed dust-free mirrors, but an inner monologue. Whereas William James wanted to emphasize continuity, linear speech is forced to present one damned blessed word after another. Memories can't be conveyed without hints of obsession; nonverbal perceptions can't be conveyed without a hint of focus.

Most crucially, an inner monologue takes place in solitude, when the only thing hopping is our antsy brain. Like poetry, it makes nothing happen. Engaging in dialogue with company or trying to learn a novel practice or becoming absorbed in almost anything other than our unlovely self forces (and allows) us to drop the burden of our inner chatter. Which doesn't mean our book has to stop: although the only time you talk to yourself is when you're not talking to anyone else, the only time you reveal yourself is always. If the 'stream' is interrupted, we can simply flip to free indirect discourse (personality-tinctured third-person-limited) or drama (a report of direct speech) or narrative with a heavy tincture of narrator (that tried-and-true device common to Swift's satires, nineteenth-century dialect comedy, and the 'Nausicaa' and 'Eumaeus' episodes of *Ulysses*).

Given those limitations, a journal or diary is a natural home for inner monologue. Similarly, Joyce's 'stream of consciousness' is tailored to the occasion of *Ulysses*, a day of excruciatingly extended emotional isolation for both male leads, and suits Molly only once she's trapped by insomnia in the dead of night.

But within those limitations, the inner monologue has a peculiar strength: it makes nothing happen. In the midst of sweet-fuck-all it spills a past, a present, alertness, misunderstandings, hopes, vexations, half-quotes, dumb jokes, old clothes, an embedded life dragging world and culture along in its rat's-nest-tangle. In either fiction or journal, no matter how dismal the life might objectively appear (as if there were anything objective about it), it exhibits a liveliness worth living.

Joyce was, like Barbellion, a disabled writer, although seldom regarded as such, despite being virtually blind in his later years following an interminable succession of extremely painful eye operations.

In 2020 my friend Jake Goldsmith set up the Barbellion Prize, 'dedicated to the furtherance of ill and disabled voices in writing'. It's awarded annually to an author whose work, in the opinion of the judges, best represents the experience of chronic illness and/or disability. Jake, who has cystic fibrosis and a complex range of other conditions, named the prize in homage to an author who exemplified the sort of work that can be produced under such terrible circumstances, and as a testament to the power of writing to contend with the realities of illness.

The Barbellion (never, I'm sure, to be known as 'the Barbie') is awarded to a work in any genre—fiction, memoir, biography, poetry, or critical non-fiction—from around the world, in English, in translation, traditionally published, or self-published. The inaugural prize was won by the American painter and author Riva Lehrer for her powerful memoir *Golem Girl*.

Many writers and artists, like the rest of us, experience some form of physical or mental disability in their lives. Or, to put it another way, it's hard to think of any writer or artist who enjoyed unremitting mental and physical good health. Barbellion can stand for them all, and the last word goes to him:

> To me the honour is sufficient of belonging to the universe—such a great universe, and so grand a scheme of things. Not even Death can rob me of that honour. For nothing can alter the fact that I *have* lived; *I have been I*, if for ever so short a time. And when I am dead, the matter which composes my body is indestructible—and eternal, so that come what may to my 'Soul', my dust will always be going on, each separate atom of me playing its separate part—I shall still have some sort of a finger in the pie. When I am dead, you can boil me, burn me, drown me, scatter me—but you cannot destroy me: my little atoms would merely deride such heavy vengeance. Death can do no more than kill you.

62. WHY HE'D NEVER WORK FOR GOOGLE

There's a popular view, regularly recycled by lazy hacks, that runs something like this: if [insert name of great artist from the past] were alive today he or she would be working as [insert some contemporary occupation]. The most frequently recycled version of the trope being that if Shakespeare were alive today he'd be writing scripts for telly soap operas, a very moot assertion that implies the soap writers of today could punch their weight against any Elizabethan playwright. As if.

A variant on this was the headline to a *Guardian* essay by the novelist Tom McCarthy in March 2015:

> If James Joyce were alive today he'd be working for Google.

McCarthy doesn't actually say or imply anything as crass as that in his piece so we can assume this is click-bait added by a *Guardian* sub-editor. What McCarthy actually says is more interesting:

> If there is an individual alive in 2015 with the genius and vision of James Joyce, they're probably working for Google, and if there isn't, it doesn't matter since the operations of that genius and vision are being developed and performed collectively by operators on the payroll of that company, or of one like it.

Despite his lengthy stint as an English language teacher in Trieste (a shadowy and poorly-regulated profession that's a bolt-hole for the unreliable, the unprofessional and the disengaged), Joyce was virtually unemployable. He briefly and unsuccessfully managed a Dublin cinema and dabbled in various madcap commercial schemes that never got off the ground—exporting tweeds, editing *The Irish Beekeeper** and so on. No, if Joyce were alive today he'd be an impover-

---

*In December 1903 Joyce offered to translate Maurice Maeterlinck's *La Vie Des Abeille* (*The Life of the Bee*, 1901) for the *Irish Bee-Keeper*, and was employed very briefly as a sub-editor. The pages of the journal would later turn up on a book-cart in *Ulysses*. The Belgian polymath Maeterlinck was the first to observe that bees have a complex language, sharing details of remote food sources through their movements and hum frequencies. I warmly recommend a marvellous essay, easy to find online, called 'Beelines: Joyce's Apian Aesthetics' by Rachel Murray. ('The low-level hum of bees circulates through a number of texts in the author's *oeuvre* [. . .] culminating in the swarm of hymenopteran references in *Finnegans Wake*.')

ished writer, and a great one, published by some tiny independent press in Dublin or Berlin or Paris. Admired by a handful of discerning readers and editors and critics, he would be an influential part of the current rebooting of modernism by writers under forty. He isn't working for Google because he's already got a job.

63. ON MARY ELLEN BUTE

In his influential *Novels into Film* (1957), Professor George Blustone argued that 'Proust and Joyce would seem as absurd on film as Chaplin would in print', his view being that whatever was particularly filmic about a film or novelistic about a novel 'cannot be converted without destroying an integral part of each.' He's right, up to a point, although I wonder if he ever got around to watching Howard Hawks' 1946 production of Raymond Chandler's *The Big Sleep*, an admittedly rare example of a great novel being turned into a great film. Blustone's view was that 'the great innovators of the twentieth century, in film and novel both, have had so little to do with each other, have gone their ways alone, always keeping a firm but respectful distance.'* Had he looked beyond Anglophone cinema, at Renoir in France and Eisenstein in Russia for example, or had he written the book twenty years later, he might have arrived at a different conclusion. I somehow doubt he ever saw *Passages from James Joyce's Finnegans Wake*, directed by Mary Ellen Bute (1906–1983).

She was a pioneer in American abstract and animated filmmaking and, along with Maya Deren, one of the first female experimental film directors. Over a thirty-year career she made fifteen shorts, most of them less than five minutes in duration and a few of these can be found on online, notably *Tarantella* (1940), a series of dazzling, syncopating kinetic abstractions. Unlike many male film pioneers and experimental directors of her generation she is in danger of being completely forgotten.

Passages from James Joyce's Finnegans Wake (1965–67) is her *magnum opus*, a 92-minute live-action feature which took three years to complete. It has a gorgeous score by Elliot Kaplan, luminous cinematography by Bute's husband Ted Nemeth and a screenplay by Mary Manning Howe (1905–1999) who had previously written *The Voice of Shem* (1957), 'passages from *Finnegans Wake* freely adapted for the theatre.'†

---

*Blustone's study is confined to six films: *The Informer* (1935), *Wuthering Heights* (1939), *The Grapes of Wrath* (1940), *Pride and Prejudice* (1940), *The Ox-Bow Incident* (1942), and *Madame Bovary* (1949), all mainstream Hollywood productions.
†Mary was a childhood friend (and later lover) of Samuel Beckett, who appears as a character named Ego Smith in her 1931 play *Youth's the Season*. She and her mother

Mary Ellen Bute

Manning was an actress and playwright who worked with Yeats at Dublin's Abbey Theatre and in the 1930s was an active member of the first film societies in Dublin. On moving to Boston she founded the Poets' Theatre in Cambridge, which attracted, among illustrious others, Frank O'Hara, John Ashbery, Edward Gorey, W.S. Merwin, V.R. Lang, Gregory Corso and Samuel Beckett.

Shot in a small New York film studio owned by her husband and on location in Dublin, Bute's film is daring in its use of experimental techniques and features animated sequences, double exposure and archive footage run backwards,forwards, and even upside-down. It's an odd, uneven, often baffling version of an equally baffling novel. The sound recording is occasionally muddy (and activating closed caption subtitles on a laptop throws up a spectral version of the *Wake* that could be published in its own right) but it's certainly worth watching, and watching again. It's as wayward and original a piece of cinema as *Citizen Kane* or rather, given its minuscule budget and improvised air, its lack of access to studio resources or major actors,

Susan Manning feature in Beckett's novel *Dream of Fair to Middling Women* as 'the Fricas', or harpies.

it resembles some of Welles's later, more personal and idiosyncratic projects.

The pre-credit titles, sourced in Joseph Campbell's *A Skeleton Key to Finnegans Wake* (1944), are as good a summary of the novel as any I've ever read:

> *Finnegans Wake* deals with the night world, with the subconscious, and with dreams. Joyce felt that during the night man must redeem himself by means of a quest; must refresh his powers through sleep, which takes him beyond himself into a world without definition. Man's goal is lucidity, a fresh awakening. The quest carries him through all history, which seems to be a constant process of waking. It is some of this universal element we have tried to capture in this first film based on any of Joyce's major works. Finnegan—otherwise known as H.C. Earwicker or Here Comes Everybody—has two sons, Shem and Shaun, who are also conflicting parts of himself which invade him; and his daughter Iseult, who is a younger manifestation of his wife, Anna Livia Plurabelle (ALP), who is also his soul and the River Liffey. Finnegan must come to terms with these parts of himself, realize the dangers inherent in their extreme forms, and experience his "reunited selfdom," in order to "Wake" up.

The film is dedicated to Frances Steloff (1887–1989), founder of New York's Gotham Book Mart, a hub for avant-garde literature and literati from 1920 until its closure in 2007. Joyce himself used to order books direct from the store and, although they never met, Steloff was one of the founders of the James Joyce Society, which used to gather at the Gotham.

Most of the cast, recruited from an off-Broadway production of Brendan Behan's *The Hostage*, have left no mark on film history beyond this one picture. Martin J. Kelly is handsome and engaging as Tim Finnegan/HCE, Jane Reilly plays Anna Livia Plurabelle and John V. Kelleher is a white-haired American television announcer with a silky, sonorous voice. One name that stands out in the end credits is that of the film editor Thelma Schoonmaker. This was her first professional job; the following year she would edit Martin Scorsese's debut feature *Who's That Knocking at My Door* (1967) marking the start of a collaboration with the director that would continue for the next six decades.

Passages from James Joyce's Finnegans Wake

Graham Greene saw the film in Antibes when it was first released and described it to a friend as 'a deadly bore in spite of the shocks that made people yell out "dégoûtant." One came out depressed with a headache.' This is harsh. The film has by now acquired a cultural lustre that makes it among the most fascinating and rewarding of all Joycean adaptations.

Mary Ellen Bute's final years were spent in stylish poverty. In her seventies, amicably separated from Ted Nemeth and having depleted her inheritance, Mary Ellen Bute lived at a Salvation Army residence for women located in New York's fashionable Gramercy Park. During that period Bute lectured and presented her films at numerous East Coast, midwestern and Canadian venues, trying to raise enough money to finish a film about Walt Whitman. Easily recognised by her yee-haw Texan accent, resounding laugh, red hair and high heels (she was just over five feet tall), she still enjoyed dressing up, sometimes in a sequinned split skirt or leopard print leather pants.*

Before *Passages from James Joyce's Finnegans Wake* there had been two attempts to film *Ulysses* that never got off the ground. When

---

*From *Notable American Women: A Biographical Dictionary* (Belknap Press, 2005) edited by Susan Ware and Stacy Braukman, Volume 5, page 9.

the Russian director Sergei Eisenstein visited Joyce's apartment in Paris in November 1929 they exchanged thoughts on a film adaptation which the director was keen to develop, but nothing came of it. In Hollywood Warner Brothers bid unsuccessfully for the film rights in 1931, with Charles Laughton considered for the role of Bloom.*

The most noteworthy *Ulysses* adaptation to date is *James Joyce's Ulysses* (1967), a British-American co-production nominated for an Academy Award for Best Adapted Screenplay.† Adapted by Fred Haines and Joseph Strick, who also directed, it's a rough and ready, low-budget production with a terrific cast including Milo O'Shea (Leopold Bloom), Barbara Jefford (Molly), Maurice Roëves (Stephen) and T.P. McKenna (Buck Mulligan).‡ It was an inspired decision to shoot the film on the streets of 1960s Dublin and not as a period drama (which of course, in a sense, it now is). It was also wisely decided to cut the proposed 18 hours' running time to a more conventional feature length.

The American cinema critic Roger Ebert rated it the second-best film of 1967 after *Bonnie and Clyde*, and *Life* magazine, in a four-page feature, described it as 'a superb film from Joyce's cryptic classic.' Other critics were unconvinced, dismissing it as 'an act of homage in the form of readings [. . .] plus slides' (Pauline Kael) and 'a facile and ludicrous reduction' (Stanley Kauffmann). I side with Ebert. The film was promptly and predictably banned in Ireland for being 'subversive to public morality,' a ban that would remain in place until the first public screening in February 2001, with the director in in attendance. In New Zealand, the film was restricted to adults over 18 in, can you believe, *gender-segregated audiences*. Although the British Board of Film Censors insisted on very significant amendments, it

---

*I sometimes wonder what might have been the cinematic outcome if Orson Welles and Herman J. Mankowitz had settled on Leopold Bloom rather than Charles Foster Kane as the subject of Welles's debut film for RKO Studios, although the only character in the novel Welles could have played was Blazes Boylan.

†Stirling Silliphant's screenplay for *In the Heat of the Night* (directed by Norman Jewison) won. In all, five Academy Awards went to this movie, including Best Picture and Best Actor (Rod Steiger).

‡Barbara Jefford would later provide voiceovers for three different Bond girls—Daniela Bianchi (as Tatiana Romanova in *From Russia with Love*), Molly Peters (Patricia Fearing in *Thunderball*) and Caroline Munro (Naomi in *The Spy Who Loved Me*).

played at London's Academy Cinema in Oxford Street for sixteen months.

Strick went on to direct *A Portrait of the Artist as a Young Man* (1977) which, while faithful to the original novel, seems at times to be rather overawed by it.

Nobody has a bad word to say about John Huston's last film *The Dead* (1987), based on the final story in *Dubliners*, a lustrous, stately and faithful take on the original with a superb cast. A later film, *Bloom* (2003), based on *Ulysses*, was written and directed by Sean Walsh and featured Stephen Rea (very good as Bloom), Angeline Ball (Molly), Hugh O'Conor (Stephen) and Alvaro Lucchesi (Buck Mulligan).

Finally one to avoid, unless you relish the prospect of Ewan McGregor playing Joyce ('the World's Sexiest Writer Had One Inspiration . . .'). *Nora* (2000) directed by Pat Murphy, was adapted from the fine biography of Nora Barnacle by Brenda Maddox, and Susan Lynch is excellent as Nora but—ah what the hell. You'll like this kind of thing if it's the kind of thing you like. Joe Leyden of *Variety* judged it 'a handsomely produced but prosaic period piece aimed at upscale, literary-savvy auds.' It took me a moment to realise that 'auds' is, or are, audiences. Obvs.

64. GRACE

The Hollywood star Grace Kelly (1929–1982) was proud of her Irish roots and in 1961 visited a tiny cottage overlooking the Leg of Mutton lake at Drimurla, County Mayo. This was the former home of her grandfather John Kelly, who had left Ireland during the Great Famine and emigrated to the United States where he founded what later became one of Philadelphia's leading construction companies. Grace had married Prince Rainier III in 1956 so this sentimental trip to Drimurla was every bit as intimate as the picnic in *Citizen Kane*— not a private pilgrimage, but a State Visit of Their Serene Highnesses The Prince and Princess of Monaco, plus entourage.

Following this trip she developed a keen interest in all things Irish and began to assemble a library of works by and about Yeats, Joyce, Wilde and Swift, and volumes of Irish history, politics, geography and folk tales.

After her death in a car accident in 1982, Prince Rainier invited George Sandulescu (b. 1933), an English lecturer at the University of Turin, to inspect the contents of the two large bookcases containing his late wife's collection. Two years later, with the support of Virginia Gallico (widow of the writer Paul Gallico) and Anthony Burgess, who had settled in Monaco as a tax exile in 1976, the Princess Grace Irish Library was opened, occupying a three-storey villa a short walk from her former Palace home on the Rock of Monaco.[*]

Sandulescu ('Greek by origin, Romanian by birth, Swedish by nationality, British by education, Italian by profession [and] Monégasque by residence') was appointed Director of the Library from its foundation until 1996. He later recalled Princess Grace's attendance at a Joyce event he had organised in Monaco shortly before her death:

> She came at 3 o'clock and we expected her to stay at most a couple of hours. She finally left at midnight and she'd taken part in all the

---

[*] Here's the address, if you happen to be passing:

> 9 rue Princesse Marie-de-Lorraine
> Monaco-Ville
> MC 98000
> Principality of Monaco
> Phone :+377 93 50 12 2

literary discussions, but we didn't know that she'd been collecting Irish books.*

Thanks to generous donations by the Irish government and Irish exiles abroad (including Samuel Beckett), the Library now has a fine collection of books by and about Irish authors, and organises monthly invitation-only lectures throughout the year, where whiskey and stout are served. On 15th July 2015, for example, the magnificently-named Professor Tina Waldeier Bizzarro (Department of History of Art, Rosemont College, Pennsylvania) and Susan Kelly Vonmedicus (Artist, Pennsylvania) presented 'The History of Irish Book Illumination of the Golden Age (600–800 CE)'.

The Library's 2016 writer-in-residence was Liz Nugent (b. 1967), 'the award-winning author of the No 1 bestseller, *Unravelling Oliver*'. Her latest novel *Lying in Wait* is 'another absorbing, twisty, brilliantly observed story of murder in high places'. This, from the author's website:

> The last people who expect to be meeting with a drug-addicted prostitute are a respected judge and his reclusive wife. And they certainly don't plan to kill her and bury her in their exquisite suburban garden.

Now you might expect me to question the cultural priorities of the Princess Grace Irish Library in selecting Liz Nugent above other more respectably 'literary' names for the post of writer-in-residence. But I shan't, because I've read her first novel and think it's terrific.

---

*In 'Monaco, the Irish Library of Princess Grace' by Sally Ogle Davis (*Washington Post*, 15th January, 1989).

65. IN CAMERA

1922 saw the publication of *Ulysses* in February and *The Waste Land* in October (in the first issue of *The Criterion*, edited by Eliot himself, of which only 600 copies were printed—it would not be published in New York until December). These two texts are among the greatest achievements in prose and poetry of the modernist movement, and some crabbier critics might argue that it's been largely downhill since then.

It was also a remarkable year for the well-established medium of cinema. June saw the US première of Robert Flaherty's seminal *Nanook of the North*, the first commercially successful feature-length documentary and, in November, the first two-tone Technicolor movie *The Toll of the Sea* was released. The highest-grossing film of the year was *The Adventures of Robin Hood* starring Douglas Fairbanks, and among other 1922 releases which remain in circulation today were *Blood and Sand* (starring Rudolph Valentino), Fritz Lang's *Dr. Mabuse, der Spieler* (*Dr. Mabuse the Gambler*), *Flesh and Blood* starring the protean Lon Chaney, *Foolish Wives* directed by and starring Erich von Stroheim, Murnau's atmospheric chiller *Nosferatu, eine Symphonie des Grauens*, and King Vidor's *Peg o' My Heart*.

Along with the usual potboilers, westerns and one-reel comedies there were screen adaptations of F. Scott Fitzgerald's *The Beautiful and the Damned*, Defoe's *Robinson Crusoe*, Arnold Bennett's *The Card*, Ellen Wood's *East Lynne*, *Macbeth*, *The Count of Monte Cristo*, *Oliver Twist*, *The Prisoner of Zenda*, *The Scarlet Letter* and *Vanity Fair*.

These and other adaptations reflected a tendency for film producers to seek a degree of social and cultural respectability through prestigious association, and to attract profitable 'high hat' audiences—metropolitan, sophisticated and with more 'advanced' tastes. Further down the bill were crowd-pleasing shorts by Chaplin and Keaton, and a spoof of that year's Valentino hit entitled *Mud and Sand* starring Stan Laurel (still a solo act) as 'Rhubarbo Vaselino'.

Joyce's professional connection with cinema is well known. Prompted by his sister Eva's observation that there were 21 cinemas in Trieste but none at all in Dublin, Joyce secured the backing of a group of Triestine businessmen who had already opened cinemas in Hungary and Italy and now had plans for new picture houses in Dublin, Belfast and Cork. He travelled back to Dublin in 1909 to set up the Cinematograph Volta, a 420-seat venue at 45, Mary Street. Ireland's first dedicated cinema, it's long-since demolished but there's a plaque attached to Penney's, the modern department store that now occupies the site.

The Volta opened for business on the afternoon of Monday 20th December 1909, and the event was reported the following day in *The Freeman's Journal*:

> Yesterday at 45 Mary street a most interesting cinematograph exhibition was opened before a large number of invited visitors. The hall in which the display takes place is most admirably equipped for the purpose, and has been admirably laid out. Indeed, no expense would appear to have been spared in making the entertainment one deserving of the patronage of the public. Perhaps its special feature is that it is of Italian origin, and in that respect somewhat out of the ordinary [. . .] For an initial experiment it was remarkably good, remembering how difficult it is to produce with absolute completeness a series of pictures at the first stage of their location in new surroundings the occasion may be described as having been particularly successful. The chief pictures shown were "The First Paris Orphanage," "La Pourponniere," and "The Tragic Story of Beatrice Cenci." The latter, although very excellent was hardly as exhilarating a subject as one would desire on the eve of the festive season. But it was very much appreciated and applauded. An excellent little string orchestra played charmingly during the afternoon. Mr. James Joyce, who is in charge of the exhibition, has worked apparently indefatigably in its production, and deserves to be congratulated on the success of the inaugural exhibition.

Not mentioned in the newspaper report are two other films screened that day. The first was *Bewitched Castle* (likely to be a short by George Méliès better known as *Haunted Castle (Le Château hanté)*, dating back to 1897). The second, *Deviled Crab*, was an Italian comedy short made in 1909 and originally entitled *Cretinetti ha ingoiato un gambero* (literally 'Cretinetti has swallowed a prawn'), released under the English title *Foolshead Swallows a Crab* before it appeared at the Volta under its new title. It's unclear at what point

the film was renamed—could Joyce himself have had a hand in it?*
The original English title offers a coincidental link to the moment in
the 'Lestrygonians' episode of *Ulysses* when Bloom mulls over what
to have for lunch in Davy Byrne's pub:

> Like a few olives too if they had them. Italian I prefer. Good glass
> of burgundy take away that. Lubricate. A nice salad, cool as a cu-
> cumber, Tom Kernan can dress. Puts gusto into it. Pure olive oil.
> Milly served me that cutlet with a sprig of parsley. Take one Span-
> ish onion. God made food, the devil the cooks. Devilled crab.

Crabs, having neither fins nor scales, aren't kosher, although Mr
Bloom, an unobservant Jew who has breakfasted on pork kidneys,
would not be put off by that. Is this conceivably a cryptic reference
by Joyce to the programme at the Volta? Get weaving, Joyceans.

A digression. While researching the Volta opening programme
I came across a silent comedy called *Deviled Crabs* dating from
1917, one of 78 'electrically convulsing fun shorts' produced and dis-
tributed between 1916 and 1918 by the Jaxon Film Corporation of
Jacksonville, Florida. While *Deviled Crabs* is obviously not among
the films screened at the opening night of the Volta in 1909, I include the following synopsis from *Moving Picture World* (6th October, 1917), for reasons that will be immediately apparent to readers
of *Finnegans Wake*:

> Pokes, a hod-carrier, has been discharged by Jabs, the contractor,
> and on his way home he stops at the saloon to drown his sorrows
> and partakes freely of devilled crabs and beer. When he arrives
> home his wife seats him before the fire to rest while she prepares
> supper. Strange sights appear to Pokes. The devil, with Jabs' face,
> comes out of the fireplace and Pokes signs a bond selling himself
> to Satan for a rousing good time. His clothes immediately change
> and money rains on him. Pokes has a great time, but the devil is

---

* 'Cretinneti' was one of several characters devised by the French performer André
Deed (1879–1940). As one of the earliest stars of Italian cinema he appeared in
248 comedy shorts between 1905 and 1938, although his star waned after the Great
War and the man who had once acted for Georges Méliès ended up employed as a
warehouseman at the Pathé film studios at Joinville-le-Point. From what I've seen
of his work he's not a patch on the dapper Max Linder, or Chaplin, or the great
Buster Keaton. There's nothing subtle about his crude pratfalls, constant physical
violence and histrionic gurning rages; there's no charm, no depth.

always at his elbow. Finally, he decides to rid himself of Satan or Jabs, whichever it is, and hides under the haystack, but it immediately catches fire and Pokes wakes with a wild cry to find that he has poked his feet into the blazing fire. His wife puts out the flames and says, "Come to supper, we have nice deviled crabs." Pokes' reply is left to the imagination, but there are a lot of broken dishes in the yard the next morning.

Is it remotely conceivable that the drunken hod carrier Pokes is a distant cousin to 'this man of hod, cement and edifices' Tim Finnegan? Is it also possible that Joyce had Pokes and Jabs in mind when he came to create the duos of Mutt and Jute or Glugg and Chuff in *Finnegans Wake*?

The Volta was not a commercial success—many of the films screened were Italian or French productions which came complete with Italian intertitles, so a synopsis in English had to be printed and handed out to audiences. This, mark you, in a city where the tram routes had symbols for the benefit of the illiterate. It must have been a dispiriting experience, straining in the gloom to decipher the crib sheet. The programme ran on an hourly cycle between 5pm and 10pm. Dubliners stayed away in droves and Joyce returned to Trieste to face his backers. The Volta was subsequently sold to the British Provincial Cinema Company and struggled on, finally closing in 1919. It re-opened after the war as the Lyceum Picture Theatre, but was never particularly successful and the curtain came down for the last time in 1948.

66. A NIGHT IN VIENNA

A favourite scene in my favourite film. In Carol Reed's *The Third Man* (1949) Holly Martins (Joseph Cotton), a writer of lowbrow cowboy fiction, faces a grilling from the Viennese audience at a British Council lecture chaired by the increasingly flustered chairman, Crabbin (Wilfrid Hyde-White). It soon becomes clear that the floundering Martins is, as described earlier by the English army officer Calloway, 'just a cheap scribbler with too much drink in him.'

> MARTINS: Well, yes. I suppose that is what I meant to say.
> CRABBIN: Of course, of course, of course.
> MAN: Do you believe, Mr. Martins, in the stream of consciousness?
> MARTINS: Stream of consciousness . . . well . . . well . . .
> MAN: What author has chiefly influenced you most?
> MARTINS: Grey.
> WOMAN: *Grey?* What Grey?
> MARTINS: Zane Grey.
> CRABBIN: Oh, that is Mr. Martins' little joke, of course. We all know perfectly well that Zane Grey wrote what we call Westerns— cowboys and bandits.
> MAN: Mr. James Joyce, now, where would you put him?
> MARTINS: Oh, would you mind repeating that question?
> MAN: I said, where would you put Mr. James Joyce? In what *category?*

The man—an intense and intimidating Viennese intellectual with the look of Karl Kraus—pronounces 'category' with stress on the second syllable—*cat-AY-goree* (just as it's pronounced in Joyce's limerick in essay 10)—which always makes me smile. Martins' humiliation as his audience rapidly evaporates is excruciatingly funny, as is Crabbin's cold-sweat embarrassment. It's clear from the scene that by 1949 Joyce was firmly established as shorthand for all that is intellectually challenging, and (we can assume) recognised as such by a large popular audience who may never have even heard of *Ulysses*.

Greene admired Joyce and 'especially for his short stories', as he said to his friend the Irish short story writer Sean O'Faolain, on a pilgrimage to the Martello Tower in Sandycove.[*]

---

[*]Reported in *Conversations with Graham Greene* by Henry J. Donaghy (University Press of Mississippi, 1983).

67. BONJOUR, JACQUES

Cinephiles of a certain vintage who remember London's many repertory cinemas before the arrival of videotape and DVDs and multiplexes, who can recall a time when when it was not so much permitted as obligatory to smoke during a screening and who used to hang out between films in the scruffy bar at the National Film Theatre with its display of framed Hollywood mugshots (alphabetically arranged from A to Z), such ageing movie buffs may also call *Ghost Dance*, a low-budget British film directed by Ken McMullen and released in 1983. Described as 'a journey into beliefs and myths surrounding the existence of ghosts and the nature of cinema' it was noted by the *New York Times* for its 'near-perfect opacity'. I saw it one Sunday afternoon at the Everyman cinema in Hampstead and was agreeably bewildered. I knew very little about Jacques Derrida at the time, who featured prominently in the film, despite his status as the leading French thinker of the period.

Derrida famously questioned the assumptions of the Western philosophical tradition, and of Western culture in general, in a process known as 'deconstruction' which—despite what right-wing critics said then—was not a destructive or iconoclastic process, but rather one of questioning and problematising the assumptions that lay beneath our culture, our institutions, our values. It was a necessary and beneficial assault on complacency and, as such, continues to infuriate the same right-wing critics.

What I recall most clearly in *Ghost Dance* is a brief exchange in a Paris café between the Scottish actor Robbie Coltrane and Derrida himself. It went like this:

> COLTRANE: Bonjour Jacques.
>
> DERRIDA: Bonjour Robbie.

Actually I've just watched the film online for the first time in forty years and I'm completely wrong—this exchange *does* occur, but it's not between Derrida and Robbie Coltrane. It's between Derrida and an unnamed American Professor played by John Annette, and it takes place in Le Select in Montparnasse. Derrida, drinking coffee alone, is joined by the Professor and his student Pascale (played by Pascale Ogier) and the dialogue goes like this:

PROFESSOR *(to Derrida)*: Perhaps you could talk to her about some of her ideas?

DERRIDA: Of course, of course. But we don't have much time. Briefly Pascale, what's the idea behind your idea?

PASCALE: The idea behind my idea . . . is that I have no idea.

DERRIDA: Ah. I see. We'll talk about it tomorrow.

There's the 1980s for you, in a nutshell. Derrida (and this my real point) has a central role in contemporary Joyce studies—or had, because his stock in this respect, it's fair to say, has fallen since his heyday.

The year after *Ghost Dance* was released Derrida was invited to deliver the opening address to the Ninth International James Joyce Symposium in Frankfurt. His lecture was the entitled *Ulysse gramophone: Le oui-dire de Joyce*, translated into English as 'Ulysses Gramophone: Hear Say Yes in Joyce', a clunky attempt to capture the simultaneous meanings of '*oui dire*' ('saying yes') and '*ouï-dire*' ('hearsay').

Derrida had made a close reading of *Ulysses* and had plenty to say. He cited Joyce's writing as the first example of deconstruction, an immodest enough claim from the originator of deconstruction. In an earlier piece (*Deux mots pour Joyce*) Derrida had claimed that Joyce and the philosopher Edmund Husserl embodied two kinds of writing: Husserl offered a language of maximum 'univocity', one that embodied history and memory with great clarity, whereas Joyce, on the other hand, aimed for maximum 'equivocity', in which every element of language was both concentrated and made to yield the maximum amount of signification. Derrida described *Finnegans Wake* as an '*acte de guerre babelien*', and that Joyce's 'babelization' was more representative of the cultural conditions of language than Husserl.

That Joyce was an exemplar for Derrida and at the heart of his own textual practice is good to hear, but I'm reminded of Molly Bloom's response to her husband's attempt to explain 'metempsychosis':

—O, rocks! she said. Tell us in plain words.

68. BONO WILL NOW SAY A FEW WORDS

From the *Irish Times* (16th July 2013):

> A mixed assembly of diplomats, city councillors, writers and a rock star gathered on the Promenade des Anglais in Nice yesterday to commemorate James Joyce's brief stay at the Hôtel Suisse in 1922.
>
> Mr Kavanagh and Mr Estrosi pulled a cord and the curtain fell from the commemorative plaque. "We raised a glass of Jameson to Jimmy Joyce," said Pierre Joannon, the honorary Irish Consul General on the Côte d'Azur.

Jimmy Joyce? What nauseating chumminess. Nobody ever called James Joyce 'Jimmy'—*nobody*. His father called him Jim and Nora called him Jim, as did members of his immediate family and, come to that, Ezra Pound, but to the rest of the world he was either James or Mr Joyce or Monsieur Joyce or Signor Joyce or Herr Joyce. Never Jimmy.[*]

Present with Pierre Joannon were the Mayor of Nice Christian Estrosi, the Irish Ambassador Paul Kavanagh and the rock singer Bono, who wore a straw hat and sunglasses and an orange shirt. Bono was accompanied by his friend, the Irish artist Guggi (aka Derek Rowen), a former member of the post-punk band The Virgin Prunes.

The connection between Joyce and the Hotel Suisse is slight; the author stayed there from 17th October to 12th November 1922. The Joyce scholar Danis Rose (*qv*) was the first to establish a connection between *Finnegans Wake* and Nice, and another scholar, Vincent Deane, discovered further evidence when he helped to edit Joyce's

---

[*] Pierre Joannon (b.1943) is a writer, historian and Franco-Irish diplomat, a former member of the Board of Trustees at the Princess Grace Irish Library in Monaco (see essay 64 'Grace') and he has, since 1973, acted as Irish consul général for the Provence-Alpes-Côte d'Azur region. He has written books on Yeats and Michael Collins, and holds honorary Irish citizenship. He has the Légion d'honneur and a clutch of other honours. In 1967 he contributed to the far-right publication *Défense de l'Occident* (*Defense of the West*) a French journal promoting neo-Fascist ideas and Holocaust denial, founded by Maurice Bardèche (1907–1998) and published from 1952 to 1982. According to the website wikispook.com he was more recently associated with a secretive right wing political group known as Le Cercle, the kind of covert organisation beloved of conspiracy theorists but not, for that reason, one to overlook. Joannon attended Le Cercle events in Bonn and Capetown in 1983 and 1984.

notebooks. Deane mentioned the link to a local businessman called Michael Lillis and this led to a lunch at which plans for a plaque were agreed. Present at that lunch were four couples: Michael Lillis and his wife Caroline, Pierre and Annick Joannon, the poet John Montague and his wife Elizabeth Wassell, and the U2 manager Paul McGuinness and his wife Kathy Gilfillan.

At the subsequent unveiling of the plaque Bono of the U2 band had something to say, and this is what he said, as recorded (presumably on a camera phone) by one Michael Kiefer:

> Um er um I'm here to serve someone who is impossible to serve by way of ceremony or . . . er . . . rhythm certainly of rhythm because James Joyce cut all the rhythms he could . . . um . . . er . . . to such a wonderful occasion as this . . . um . . . it's it's it's hard to know how to, how to, speak about him. All I would say is this: what U2 tries to do in . . . in . . . in . . . in music and words he . . . he could do with just words and and the thing that I envy most of course is the humour. Um. It's . . . it's just hard to be that funny when you're . . . er . . . singing out front with a very serious rock band like U2 . . . um . . . so I envy the humour of Joyce, which he used as a, as a, as a weapon and I think also to say that we still have that reverence for the word here with us. Um John Montagu (*applause*) who (*inaudible*) and who can much much better express um . . . er . . . his love and conviction [*sic*] for James Joyce than I . . . um . . . who consider myself just a . . . an annoying fan of James Joyce, the one who follows him around and, were he still with us, I would be buying his drinks and then spilling them on him, offering to clean up the mess, pay the bill, writing a poem and being ignored, what he would think fit.

Bono, to be fair, makes a far better fist of unveiling a plaque to Joyce than I would belting out rock anthems to a stadium full of adoring fans, but I'm still irritated by Pierre Joannan's reference to 'Jimmy Joyce', and what's wrong with kicking a man when he's up?[*]

It's been claimed that the view from the Joyces' hotel bedroom window at the Hotel Suisse may have inspired the opening passage

---

[*]While we're in the world of rock music, Stewart Copeland (b. 1952), former drummer with The Police, claims to be obsessed with Joyce and wants 'to write the opera of *Finnegans Wake*', according to an interview in the Irish *Herald* (20th August 2014). 'In fact, I've half written the libretto.'

of *Finnegans Wake* ('from swerve of shore to bend of bay') but I doubt it. Plaques commemorating addresses at which Joyce worked on *Finnegans Wake* might just as well be screwed to walls in Amsterdam, Antwerp, Bognor Regis, Brussels, Copenhagen, The Hague, Le Havre, Llandudno, London, Nice, Ostend, Paris, Rouen, Saint-Malo, Torquay, Tours and Zürich. A plaque on all his houses.

69. MONUMENTAL COCK-UP

'A man of genius makes no mistakes; his errors are volitional and are the portals of discovery' wrote our man, with characteristic immodesty. He might have added that if you're looking for an epic balls-up, bankers are a corresponding portal.

The unattractive object pictured overleaf is one of 10,000 commemorative coins minted in Germany in 2013 for the Central Bank of Ireland. It depicts a trepanned, jug-eared, pointy-chinned Cyclopean Joyce and, in the kind of lettering usually seen on the covers of chick-lit paperbacks, the first two sentences from the 'Proteus' episode of *Ulysses*:

> Ineluctable modality of the visible: at least that if no more, thought through my eyes. Signatures of all things that I am here to read. Seaspawn and seawrack.

The launch, a private event held in Joyce's *alma mater* University College Dublin, was hastily followed by a red-faced press release, part of which read:

> The Central Bank acknowledges that the text on the Joyce coin does not correspond to the precise text as it appears in *Ulysses* (an additional word "that" has been added to the second sentence). While the error is regretted, it should be noted that the coin is an artistic representation of the author and text and not intended as a literal representation.

You'll note the evasive passive wriggles of 'the error is regretted' and 'it should be noted'. I'm keen to learn, perhaps from the chump who wrote this piffle, how a misquotation can be flourished as an 'artistic interpretation' as opposed to 'a literal representation', by which I suppose is meant 'an accurate transcription of the original text'. They want it both ways, these damned bankers—to enjoy the prestige-by-association of Joyce, a notoriously 'difficult' writer that otherwise literate people are unashamed to admit never reading, as though this were evidence of their own robust common sense and, at the same time, arrogantly to assert that he is nothing more than

Ineluctable modality of the risible

grist to their aesthetic mill, subordinate to the condescending 'interpretation' of a boorish commercial concern.[*]

---

[*]Prior to the advent of the euro the Central Bank of Ireland issued three series of
banknotes: Series A (1928–1977), Series B (1976–1993) and Series C (1992–2000).
The latter (*Nótaí bainc sraith C*) featured famous Irish historical figures and the
£10 note, designed by Robert Ballagh and in circulation from 1993 to 2002, included on the back a River Liffey mask by the sculptor Edward Smyth (1749–1812)
taken from the frontage of the Custom House in Dublin. A nineteenth century
map of the city and the opening words of *Finnegans Wake* also feature. On the
front there's a portrait of a middle-aged Joyce with a background featuring Dublin
and Wicklow, and particularly Dublin Bay. Has there ever been a more lavishly
literary banknote? Ballagh (born 1943) represented Ireland at the 1969 Biennale
de Paris. A fine artist, he has also designed sets for Riverdance, Beckett's *Endgame*
(1991) and Oscar Wilde's *Salomé* (1998). He has also designed over 70 Irish postage
stamps.

The text on the coin misquotes the thoughts of Stephen Dedalus as he walks alone along Sandymount Strand, his mind calmly racing:

> Ineluctable modality of the visible: at least that if no more, thought through my eyes. Signatures of all things I am here to read, sea-spawn and seawrack, the nearing tide, that rusty boot. Snotgreen, bluesilver, rust: coloured signs.

Let's agree that it's an odd choice of text by any measure, and what in Erin's name it has to do with coinage is anyone's guess. Joyce's writings offer plenty of quotable zingers, so one wonders who settled on this one, and how. No blame can be attached to the artist, Mary Gregoriy (*sic*), who clearly had no say in the choice of the original quotation because, as she admitted on her blog:

> I have not really read a book for such a long time—too busy at the mo.

So perhaps a cohort of sleek Irish bankers with literary leanings met for a long lunch, or several long lunches, to wrangle learnedly over a shortlist submitted by a panel of respected Joyce scholars and well-read numismatists. Or perhaps their spouses, over tea and cake at some convivial book club? Or maybe their children? Or a bunch of lads in the pub with blindfold and pin?

Having settled on the text for Gregoriy to render in her squiggly 'hair writing', did nobody think to check, and then sign off, the final version? Wasn't there a preliminary drawing? Did no memos circulate? Were there no emails between artist and client and mint? If some official responsible for signing it off *did* sign it off, shouldn't they get a bollocking? I'm a firm believer in blame culture, and especially in the financial sector.

Nobody, however, is likely to care enough to apportion or accept blame, and I expect everybody at the bank is privately congratulating themselves over the enormous amount of coverage the error received and, in a misguided access of optimism, the boom in sales of the coin itself. But who in their right mind and with the slightest interest in Joyce would want to own this vulgar and preposterous ten euro coin costing, quite incredibly, *forty-six* euros? The total issue has been valued by the Irish Central Bank at €4,600,000, although the literal face value (or purchasing power) is fixed at €50,000. There's an artistic interpretation for you. Stephen Joyce, never one to exaggerate, described the coin and the circumstances surrounding its issue as 'one of the greatest insults to the Joyce family that has ever been perpetrated in Ireland'.

If the literary arbiters at Central Bank need an alternative *Ulysses* quotation for any future numismatic insult to the Joyce family they could do worse than choose what is quite possibly the most beautiful sentence ever written. It describes the sky over Dublin on the night of 16th June 1904 as seen by Leopold Bloom, in the back garden of his house at 7, Eccles Street:

> The heaventree of stars hung with humid night blue fruit.

Even a banker couldn't make a hash of that.

70. Sail again. Sail better.

But what about the fighting navy, says Ned, that keeps our foes at bay?

—*Ulysses*

The Irish Navy has a fleet of four Offshore Patrol Vessels (OPVs), all of which are members of the Samuel Beckett-class (and that odd hyphen conforms to naval practice, apparently). The Samuel Beckett-class. Let that sink in.

The fleet consists of four vessels:

P61 LÉ SAMUEL BECKETT
P62 LÉ JAMES JOYCE
P63 LÉ WILLIAM B YEATS
P64 LÉ GEORGE B SHAW

It's odd to see Joyce playing second fiddle to Beckett. The two men are eternally paired, but never as equals. Beckett is always subordinate to Joyce—he's like like Sancho Panza to Don Quixote, Watson to Holmes, Estragon to Vladimir.

'The naming of a naval vessel is a hugely significant event as it lays the foundation of the ship's character and spirit.' That's what it says on www.military.ie, where we are also reminded that Irish Naval vessels have traditionally been named after female figures in Irish mythology—the five other boats making up the rest of the fleet are named *Eithne*, *Orla*, *Ciara*, *Róisín* and *Niamh*.

Designed by Vard Marine and constructed by Babcock Marine of Appledore in North Devon, the first ship of the class was completed in November 2014 and delivered to the Naval Service in mid-2015. The official naming and commissioning ceremony was held at Dún Laoghaire on 1st September 2015. The crew of 44 included six officers, all under the command of Lieutenant Commander Mike Brunicardi.

During the Covid pandemic the LÉ JAMES JOYCE was moored on Sir John Rogerson's Quay in Dublin, operating as a COVID-19 Community Testing Centre on behalf of Ireland's Health Service Executive and National Ambulance Service. The vessel was deployed for a special turn of duty on Bloomsday 2021 when, early in the morning, it sailed past the Martello tower in Sandycove bearing aloft the

Munster flag of three crowns on a blue field, a reference to the 'Cyclops' episode of *Ulysses* in which the Citizen (a xenophobic and anti-Semitic nationalist, mark you), asserts that Ireland's lot will only be improved 'when the first Irish battleship is seen breasting the waves with our own flag to the fore'. A rather unsettling gesture, don't you think?

By way of contrast the 'luxury cruise ferry' *Ulysses*, pride of the Irish Ferries fleet on the Dublin to Holyhead/Rosslare/Cherbourg route, boasts (such vessels always 'boast') the following features, according to the company's website:

- Sandycove promenade deck
- Cyclops Family Entertainment Centre (which sounds frankly terrifying)
- James Joyce balcony lounge
- Leopold Blooms [*sic*] Bar
- Boylan's Brasserie (where the menu includes 'Boylan's signature avocado spread')
- Ulysses walking tour [on a *ship*?]

Is there, while we're navigating the subject, any more haunting vessel in literature than the one which closes the 'Proteus' episode of *Ulysses*? Stephen Dedalus has left the school where he teaches and, walking along the shore, is suddenly struck by a need to wipe his nose. But he remembers that he has earlier that morning lent his snotrag to Buck Mulligan to clean his razor:

My handkerchief. He threw it. I remember. Did I not take it up?

His hand groped vainly in his pockets. No, I didn't. Better buy one.

He laid the dry snot picked from his nostril on a ledge of rock, carefully. For the rest let look who will.

Behind. Perhaps there is someone.

He turned his face over a shoulder, rere regardant. Moving through the air high spars of a threemaster, her sails brailed up on the crosstrees, homing, upstream, silently moving, a silent ship.

71. BRONZING A GENT

Death masks, traditionally made of papier-mâché, are fragile objects and there are more durable commemorations, the earliest of which in Joyce's case, and perhaps the best, is the bronze statue placed over the author's final resting place in Zürich's Fluntern cemetery. Installed in 1966, it's the work of sculptor Milton Hebald (1917–2015) who was, Anthony Burgess wrote in 1971, 'without doubt the most important living figure sculptor.'

Burgess had skin in the game. In 1970 he and his second wife Liana bought a house from Hebald in Bracciano, near Rome, the city in which the sculptor had lived for fifty years. Burgess himself sat for Hebald that year and his rather lumpy bust can be seen on the front cover of both volumes of Burgess's autobiography, *Little Wilson and Big God* (1987) and *You've Had Your Time* (1990). Of the Fluntern cemetery sculpture, he wrote: 'if literary men, generally speaking, are devoted to Hebald more than any other living sculptor, it is because he has mediated wonderfully between the world of stone and metal and that of words.' Before casting the original full-size statue in 1966 Hebald produced a series of twelve maquettes, one of which went to Giorgio Joyce (who had the same build as his father and served as a model for Hebald). This is now at the Joyce Foundation in Zürich; there's another in Buffalo and the rest appear to be in private hands. A further twelve models were produced in 1981. Rarer than Joycean death masks or signed first editions of *Ulysses*, one of them came up for auction in London some years ago. I can think of no classier paperweight. Hebald also reportedly did some *Ulysses*-inspired statues, including a couple of Molly Blooms, but details are scarce.

Hebald was never a particularly high-profile artist in his lifetime, although he has a very visible presence in his native New York, where more than twenty original works grace public spaces. In 1961 'Zodiac Screen', his enormous bas-relief (220 feet long and 24 feet high and regarded as the world's largest sculpture) was installed at the entrance to the Pan Am terminal at what later became John F. Kennedy International Airport. It remained in place for thirty years until the airline went bust and it now belongs to the New York Transit Authority, dismantled and in store, its condition uncertain. By a happy coincidence—although this has nothing at all to do with Joyce—Hebald's daughter Margo, an architect, designed Terminal One at Los Angeles International Airport.

What of the other public monuments, all of which occupy a place on the broad spectrum of commemoration between shoddy Bank of Ireland coins and Irish Navy vessels?

Placed opposite the General Post Office in the centre of Dublin, a life-sized bronze figure of Joyce by the American painter, sculptor and actor Marjorie Fitzgibbon (1930–2018) leans nonchalantly on a slender cane, one hand pocketed. Irritatingly described in an online guide to Dublin as 'one of the city's iconic monuments' it was promptly dubbed 'The Prick with a Stick' by locals alert to any whiff of pretension. It is one of a number of sculptural commemorations in the city, including a plinthed bust (also by Marjorie Fitzgibbon) on St. Stephen's Green, facing Newman House, part of Joyce's alma mater University College.

A reclining figure representing Anna Livia Plurabelle designed by Éamonn O'Doherty can be found in Croppies Memorial Park near Houston Station. Known variously as 'The Floozie in the Jacuzzi' or 'The Whore (pron. Whoo-er) in the Sewer', it was originally located in O'Connell Street but was moved in 2001 to make room for the huge Spire of Dublin ('The Stiffy on the Liffey'), a 400 foot tall stainless steel spike built on the former site of Nelson's Pillar (which features in *Ulysses*: 'SOME COLUMN!—THAT'S WHAT WADDLER ONE SAID'). Another Dublin erection honouring our man is the fine statue by Rowan Gillespie in the garden of the Merrion Hotel, which ingeniously doubles as a sundial with Joyce as the gnomon, casting his shadow on panels containing lines from *Ulysses* that record Mr Bloom's movements on 16th June.

Further afield there's another bronze figure of Joyce by the Canal Grande in Trieste. It's a walking figure and, although life-size hardly life-*like;* it resembles Labour leader Keir Starmer with a Groucho moustache. Another sculpture (seated) by Mate Čvrljak can be found at the Caffè Uliks in Pula, Croatia, where Joyce lived for a while in 1905. In Szombathely, Hungary, home of Bloom's father Rudolf Virág, there's a figure ambiguously emerging from, or blending into, the wall of a building on the main square.

There's a more recent cast bronze sculpture called *Ulysses Sleeps* by the artist John Coll, in an edition of nine priced at €16,000 each. It takes the form of a flat vertical slab from which a version of Joyce's death mask emerges, engraved with a street map of Dublin. It looks like Han Solo after he's been frozen in carbonite.

72. ARTISTS OF THE PORTRAIT

Joyce is the least visual of great novelists. His descriptive passages of landscape or the sky, or the physical appearance of his characters, are vague and often cursory. Only one work of art is mentioned in *Ulysses*, namely *The Bath of the Nymph*, 'Given away with the Easter number of Photo Bits: Splendid masterpiece in art colours.' Framed, it hangs above the Blooms' marital bed and acquires the power of speech in the 'Circe' episode.

This isn't a piece of kitsch dreamt up by Joyce but a real painting, *Il bagno delle ninfe* by the Milanese artist Francesco Hayez (1791–1882). You can look it up online and, if so inclined, order a copy to hang above your own bed. *Photo Bits* was a mildly pornographic magazine published weekly between 1898 and 1914, which specialised in fetishist writing. The serial story 'Peggy Paget's Patent Paralyzing Pedal Props' first appeared in 1910 (the title is a giveaway) and the magazine also featured advertisements for 18-inch high-heel shoes.

Joyce's taste in visual art was very conservative. According to his friend Arthur Power the only picture on display in Joyce's apartment, apart from family portraits, was a reproduction of Johannes Vermeer's 'View of Delft' (1660), which hung over the fireplace and which Joyce admired very much.[*] He had no interest at all in contemporary artists such as Braque and Picasso. Artists, on the other hand, have long been interested in Joyce.

Among the many painters inspired by Joyce's writings is Henri Matisse (1869–1954), who reportedly disliked *Ulysses* but was willing, for a fat fee of $5,000, to produce a series of six images for inclusion in a deluxe version of the novel published in 1935 in an edition of 1500. Of these, 250 were signed by both the author and the artist. To Joyce's disgust the Matisse images were based on episodes in the Homeric original, which may have been down to the fact that Matisse had not read the novel. The artist sought to assuage publisher George Macy's concerns that his etchings bore no relation to the text: 'These 6 plates are really the product of reactions of my mind before Joyce's work, in which I chose the scenes having a correspondence in Homer's work.' A copy that come up for auction in 2019 went for £13,750.

---

[*] Arthur Power, *Conversations with James Joyce (Barnes & Noble Books*, 1974).

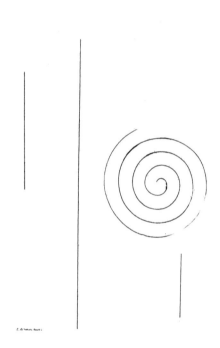

Brâncuși's portrait of Joyce

In 1929 the Romanian artist Constantin Brâncuși (1876–1957) made a minimalist portrait of the author consisting of a clockwise spiral and three vertical lines, which was used as the frontispiece for the 'Work in Progress' pamphlet *Tales Told of Shem and Shaun*, published that year. Joyce described it in a letter to Valery Larbaud (30th July 1929) as 'Brâncuși's whirligig'.

Another, more conventional, Brancusi portrait featured on the 1982 centenary stamp issued by the Irish Post Office. (Joyce has featured multiple times on Irish stamps, and on others issued in Belgium, Nicaragua and St Vincent & the Grenadines and elsewhere.)

In the last year of his life the Hungarian artist László Moholy-Nagy (1895–1946) created the schema below, a visual representation of *Finnegans Wake*, for a book prepared by his colleague at the Institute of Design, Leslie L. Lewis.

László Moholy-Nagy's schema for *Finnegans Wake*

Made between 1957 and 1961 (probably), *Joseph Beuys Extends Ulysses by Six Further Chapters on behalf of James Joyce* is a series of six A5 notebooks, each of 750 pages and consisting of 355 pencil and watercolour drawings. All six notebooks are part of the collection of the Hessisches Landesmuseum Darmstadt, the first two bound for presentation purposes and the others still in their original condition. Beuys (1921–1986) had a profound admiration for Joyce and once said that he wanted to 'do' *Finnegans Wake* again. His own copy was heavily annotated.*

I've already mentioned Richard Hamilton's series of images inspired by *Ulysses* (see essay 11 'Carry on Drawing'). His fellow pop artist Peter Blake (b. 1932) made a series of etchings entitled *James Joyce in Paris* in the mid-1980s, although his most well-known work will always be the cover for the Beatles album *Sgt. Pepper's Lonely Hearts Club Band* (1967), co-created with the rarely-credited American artist Jann Howarth (b. 1942). Featured in the cohort of collaged celebrities is a very indistinct image of James Joyce. He's in the second row on the right, just beneath Bob Dylan and above Lawrence of Arabia.

In 1980 the Argentinian conceptual artist Marta Minujín created *James Joyce Tower*, a replica of the Sandycove Martello tower using 5,000 loaves of bread. More recently the artists Joseph Kosuth with his neon wall-installation *Ulysses: 18 Titles* (1998) and Lawrence Weiner in his mural *Opus # 843* (2004), both referenced Joyce's prose while avoiding anything as literal as representation. The US abstract expressionist Robert Motherwell (1915–1991) did something similar with his *Ulysses Suite*, a series of 62 etchings which can be yours for $25,000.

For a few dollars less you can get a fine copy of the 1988 edition of the novel, published by Arion Press in San Francisco. This folio volume, bound in half-white pigskin over white speckled blue cloth, contains forty of the 62 Motherwell etchings on twenty folded leaves. From a limited edition of 150 and 25 (1–XXV) *hors de commerce* copies, 'printed on Perpetua type on French mould-made Jonannot paper'.

The great American artist Cy Twombly (1928–2011) frequently quoted lines of text in his work and apparently had many editions of Joyce's *Chamber Music* and *Pomes Penyeach* in his extensive library.

Another American artist, Charlene Matthews, spent two years making *38 Poles*, an artwork consisting of all 18 episodes of *Ulysses*

---

*A very good piece on Beuys and Joyce by Dr.Christa-Maria Lerm Hayes was published in *Circa Art* magazine (1st June 2003) and is available online.

spelled out *in capital letters* on 38 seven-foot-tall poles, each one two inches in diameter. (Faced with which I tend to think, if not to say out loud, that I know a lot about art, and I know what I don't like.)

Images from the 'Nulysses' series by Philip Maltman (Indian ink on paper, all 23cm x 21cm). 'Lestrygonians', 'Sirens', and 'Circe' (*left, from top*); 'Ithaca' (*right*)

Philip Maltman (born 1959) is a Scottish artist who now lives in London. We've never met, but it was Philip who provided the cover image for my book *About a Girl* (CB editions, 2016), a painting prompted by his admiration for Eimear McBride's debut novel *A Girl Is a Half-formed Thing*. His artistic influences are, he says, Constable, Turner, Monet, Rauschenberg, Motherwell and Twombly; the writers he most admires apart from McBride are James Salter, Laura Beatty, John Clare, and above all Joyce, whose writing is a regular inspiration. Maltman's Joyce-related work features stand-alone pieces and several series, including 'Finnegans Cake' (1992, a collection of 63 paintings in oil as responses to readings of the *Wake*), 'Nulysses' (1993 onwards) and an untitled suite of 18 Joyce-inspired abstract paintings. I asked him what prompted his responses to Joyce's writing and he replied:

> I think with Joyce, and *Ulysses* in particular, there is an atmosphere first, and that has been created by repeated reading. I saw Joseph Strick's film at the Academy in Oxford Street in 1967 which sort of imprinted itself on my idea of this atmosphere. I think I also unashamedly wanted to be someone who appreciated Joyce and all that that intellectually entailed. He was, and still is, a controversial and 'difficult' figure and I respond to that for some reason. There are many exotic descriptive passages in *Ulysses* and if I like a passage then I will note it down. e.g. 'Wavewhite wedded words shimmering on the dim tide' (from the 'Telemachus' episode).

Maltman's technique involves writing the chosen passage out in crayon or paint on a surface and then, working rapidly and usually in one sitting, directly responding to the individual words, with the paint eventually obliterating the whole text. Occasionally recognisable images or symbols may appear in what are essentially abstract works incorporating those texts. The original words are then re-written on the periphery of the work.

Seamus Heaney was an admirer of the 'Nulysses' series, writing to the artist:

> You play good tunes upon the Joycean keyboard, and you (tr)eat with relish the inner and outer stuff of words. It works well as a dialogic event, with Jemser on the receiving/prompting end of things[.]

Finally there's the conceptual artist Simon Popper who, in 2006, was shortlisted for the sixth (and final) Beck's Future Award, 'the younger, edgier cousin of the Turner Prize'.* For the related show at the Institute of Contemporary Art in London, Popper created an installation entitled *Borromean / Sinthome* consisting of 1,000 specially-printed green-wrapped copies of *Ulysses* in the same format as the original Shakespeare and Company first edition, but with all the words therein rearranged in alphabetical order, followed by all

---

* The prize was, for the first time, judged by a panel made up entirely of artists: Jake and Dinos Chapman, Martin Creed, Cornelia Parker, Gillian Wearing and Yinka Shonibare. They chose as the winner the artist and film-maker Matt Stokes for *Long After Tonight*, a film about Northern Soul dancers.

the punctuation marks, grouped as commas, semi-colons and so on. The books were neatly arranged in stacks on the floor of the gallery. A model railway completed the piece, a circle of track around which a little locomotive tirelessly pulled three carriages adorned with the logo 'Blum and Popper' (see the footnote to essay 57 'An Italian modernist in London').

Popper's work took its title from the French psychoanalyst Jacques Lacan's seminars on Joyce's writing in which he—Lacan—developed the model of Borromean rings, three interlocking circles that offer a map of human subjectivity, each ring representing one of three Lacanian components of reality: the Symbolic, the Real and the Imaginary (abbreviated as SRI and if this leaves you floundering then do look them up online and we can flounder together).

Lacan extends this model of the Borromean knot to include a fourth 'ring' known as the *sinthome*, the term deriving from the Latin spelling of the Greek origin of the French word *symptôme* (i.e. 'symptom'). Since meaning is already present within Lacan's Borromean knot, at the intersection of the Symbolic and the Imaginary, the function of the *sinthome*—loosely knotting together the Real, the Imaginary and the Symbolic—is, according to Lacan, *beyond meaning*.

Just as Lacan's theory is impenetrable without the basic code that informs his philosophy, Popper renders the text of *Ulysses* entirely meaningless and nonsensical by reducing it to its root code, to the absolutely rigid alphabetical arrangement of its entire lexical content. I admire Lacan but confess to finding his approach to Joyce opaque and unproductive, partly because he often seems to me to be stating the self-evident but mostly because I entirely lack the kind of intelligence that can engage with such an approach.

I have one of Popper's alphabetised *Ulysses* and I like it very much. Not least because one occasionally comes across a single word which triggers a memory of its appearance in the original novel. According to the critic David Bussel, Popper's work is 'an invitation to delinquency', and I'm all for that.

73. AND THE WINNER IS . . .

What connects the performers Martin Freeman, Ralph Fiennes, Alan Rickman, Barry Humphries, Michael Sheen, Russell Brand, Rory Bremner, Will Ferrell, Eddie Izzard and Michael Palin? Apart from the fact that, Izzard aside, they all opt for he/him pronouns?

Give up?

The answer is that they have all attracted the approval of the judges who select worthy recipients of The James Joyce Award, given by the Literary and Historical Society of University College Dublin (UCD) 'for those who have achieved outstanding success in their given field.'

Surprisingly the awards aren't known as the 'Jimmys', thus removing any slight vestige of dignity from what seems on first sight, and on subsequent sights, to be an exercise in random celebrity bagging.

Which *writers* have received this, 'the highest award that an Irish University society can give'? I shan't keep you in any suspense for a moment longer. Here they are, alphabetically:

Bill Bryson, J.K. Rowling, DBC Pierre, Salman Rushdie, Sue Townsend, Yu Hua, Seamus Heaney and Roddy Doyle.

They could hardly have overlooked Heaney, but . . . what about the rest? How was this eclectic selection arrived at? I suspect—and this is a wild guess—that some other writers, and not only Irish writers, on being sounded out about the honour, must have politely turned it down, perhaps having second thoughts about joining a cohort of honourees that includes the skateboarder Tony Hawk, the World Snooker Champion Ken Doherty and *The Who* singer Roger Daltrey, all recipients of (I repeat, neutrally) 'the highest award that an Irish University society can give'.

For a more recent literary recipient of this prize see essay 64 'Grace'.

74. DO BOOKS FURNISH A ROOM?

On 1st January 2012 all of Joyce's works published during his life-time entered the public domain in the United Kingdom, Republic of Ireland and European Union (except in Spain, but we don't have to go into that). This prompted a publishers' feeding frenzy and, while the sudden availability of cheap and sometimes *very* cheap paper-back editions was welcomed by hard-up Joyceans, the appearance of weird and wonderful 'collectors' editions' was another matter. Oddly, given the vagaries of the Estate as run by Stephen Joyce, there were already some jaw-droppingly freakish editions in circulation.

Next to me on the desk as I write is a green leatherette flap-topped box containing ten uniform miniature volumes, also bound in green leatherette, of Joyce's 'complete published work' produced by the Bath-based printer Robert Frederick in 1995. This spectac-ularly unattractive object has become something of a cult among Joyceans, and an unlikely collector's item. In a bold editorial move by Frederick, *Dubliners* is re-titled *Great Collection of Short Stories* with each of the stories appearing in alphabetical order, while *Ulysses* is split into three volumes with the 'Circe' episode (the longest in the original novel) relocated in the text so that all three have a uniform appearance. I could go on, but this seems to me as good a point as any to take a look at copyright (although some of you without much interest in the subject, which is to say all of you, may wish to skip to the next essay, or the one after that).

In the United Kingdom an author's works published posthu-mously remain under copyright for 50 years following the year of first publication. Other E.U. countries have different terms. The Re-public of Ireland, for instance, makes no distinction between work published in the author's lifetime and posthumously-published material—in either case it's based on the author's life plus 70 years. Under this provision, *Ulysses*, *Stephen Hero*, and *Giacomo Joyce* all entered the Irish public domain on 1st January 2012.

In the United States things are very different and, rather astonish-ingly given that he's been dead for far longer than he was alive, some of Joyce's individual works have yet to enter the public domain. Few of us will be here to celebrate when the 1961 edition of *Ulysses* comes out of copyright in 2057; the *Selected Letters* (published in 1975) won't enter the public domain until 2071 and *The James Joyce Archive* in

2073, which may well post-date human existence on our planet.*

If—and I realise it's a staggeringly colossal 'if'—if you're keen on learning more about copyright variants for Joyce's work I heartily recommend the website of the James Joyce Foundation at the University of Tulsa.

If on the other hand you'd prefer to turn your back on the internet for a while and assemble a modest library of essential Joyce reference books (with a focus on *Finnegans Wake*), how should you set about it?

First place goes to Richard Ellmann's magnificent biography *James Joyce*, originally published in 1959, revised in 1982 and unlikely ever to be excelled. Anthony Burgess described it as 'the greatest literary biography of the century', an honour that might be shared with Ellmann's equally magnificent biography *Oscar Wilde* (1987). As for other books, I emailed a few scholars and enthusiasts and they were surprisingly unanimous in suggesting the following baker's dozen:

— *Our Exagmination Round His Factification for Incamination of Work in Progress* (Shakespeare and Company, Paris, 1929). A collection of critical essays (and two letters) by writers who knew Joyce personally. Samuel Beckett's contribution 'Dante . . . Bruno. Vico . . Joyce' was his first appearance in print. Republished in paperback by Faber and easy to find.
— *A Skeleton Key to Finnegans Wake* (first published in 1944) by Joseph Campbell and Henry Morton Robinson. A foundational study.
— *A Census of Finnegans Wake* by Adaline Glasheen (Faber & Faber, 1957). Another ground-breaking work. (I originally wrote 'trailblazing' but am told this is actually a bit off as it has colonial associations. In all important respects and in spite of my age, class, background, education and appearance I'm about as woke as you can get.) Glasheen's book is an absolute wonder.
— *Letters* Volumes I, II, and III edited by Stuart Gilbert (vol. I) and Richard Ellmann (Vol. II and III). Originally published in 1957 and subsequently reprinted. Not cheap, although a more affordable *Selected Joyce Letters* was published by Viking Press in 1975 and can be picked up easily.
— *The Books at the Wake* by J.S. Atherton (Faber, 1959) Out of print but also easy to obtain. I love this book, but see the note on the graphic

---

*In the case of *Stephen Hero*, the early draft of what became *A Portrait of the Artists as a Young Man*, there were later additions to the original 1944 publication that appeared in 1955 and 1963, copyright on which will continue until 2051 and 2059 respectively.

novel by the author's daughter, Mary Talbot, in essay 97 *Allez, sa-lopard!*
— *A Concordance to Finnegans Wake* by Clive Hart (Paul P. Appel Publications, 1963, re-issued by University of Minnesota Press, Minnesota, 2009). Rated by Joyce scholar Fritz Senn as one of the most important and useful tools ever compiled.
— *A Shorter Finnegans Wake*, edited by Anthony Burgess. (Faber, 1969). For many readers this is a very good way in. The text is a third of the length of the original and Burgess offers a punchy introduction, illuminating commentary and brisk synopses of the selected passages. He makes it all seem straightforward.
— *The Finnegans Wake Experience* (Irish Academic Press, 1981), also by Roland McHugh. Described to me by Peter Chrisp as 'the first eyewitness report from the inner sanctum of Wake studies' and it includes this observation:

> Grasshopper sexuality is primarily acoustic: a female will walk away from a silent male towards a loudspeaker emitting male song. So each male surrounds itself with a fluid territory which it keeps saturated with its own song. I eventually discovered that professors at James Joyce symposia behaved similarly . . .

— *Portraits of the Artist in Exile: Recollections of James Joyce by Europeans* (Harcourt Trade Publishers, 1986) edited by Willard Potts. Memories and observations by those whose paths crossed Joyce's during his peripatetic European years.
— *James Joyce's Finnegans Wake: A Casebook* by John Harty, III. A collection of essays published by Routledge Library Editions in 1991 which includes 'A Working Outline of Finnegans Wake' by Bernard Benstock, the textual equivalent of sat nav.
— *How Joyce Wrote Finnegans Wake* (University of Wisconsin Press, 2007) edited by Luca Crispi and Sam Slote, an absorbing collection of essays explaining the growth of each chapter.
— *A Guide through Finnegans Wake* (University Press of Florida, 2009) by Edmund Lloyd Epstein. A take on the *Wake* aimed at the non-specialist, educated lay reader. Sam Slote (*qv*) described it as 'a thorough, but reductive, summary of a narrative line that is presented as if it were the essence of the Wake distilled and unencumbered by linguistic tomfoolery.'* It's best read in tandem with . . .

---

*"A Guide Through Finnegans Wake", review by Sam Slote. *James Joyce Quarterly* (The University of Tulsa) Volume 47, Number 1, Fall 2009 pp. 149–151.

— *Lots of Fun at Finnegans Wake: Unravelling Universals* by Finn Fordham (Oxford University Press, 2013). Cited in essay 42 ('Jabberwakey') this descriptive approach to the novel is warmly recommended.

— And then there's no end of free online stuff, notably *Annotations to Finnegans Wake* by Roland McHugh (available gratis at fweet.org). See essay 37.

The enormous quantity of critical writing about Joyce is intimidating for the newcomer and the non-academic, and it's hard to know where to begin and what to avoid (and quite a lot of it *is* best avoided if you value your sanity). An online bibliography curated by Liam Lanigan, Assistant Professor of English at Governors State University, Chicago, is tremendously useful, and recommended. You can see extracts for free at www.oxfordbibliographies.com. In his brief introduction Lanigan recommends *James Joyce in Context* edited by John McCourt (Cambridge University Press, 2009) as the best overview of current critical approaches, and most likely to appeal to the general reader. He also singles out Fritz Senn's *Inductive Scrutinies* (Johns Hopkins University Press, 1995), noting that 'advanced readers may find [it] more rewarding, although his prose always remains jargon-free and accessible.' Shouldn't that 'although' be 'because'? Unless that's a poker-faced reference to the rebarbative opacity of much academic writing, and I'm keenly aware that 'rebarbative opacity' is in itself an example of the kind of language I'm supposed to be attacking, but I'm writing this quite late on a Friday night and am at least two drinks ahead of you, whoever you happen to be.

I'm also keenly aware, and more so every day, that 2022 will see a veritable avalanche of books to mark the *Ulysses* centenary. Leading the field are John McCourt's *Consuming Joyce: 100 Years of Ulysses in Ireland* (published by Bloomsbury) and *Annotations to James Joyce's Ulysses* by Sam Slote, Marc A. Mamigonian, and John Turner, published by Oxford University Press at an eye-watering £125. The latter is particularly alluring, with 12,000 annotations and '20 contemporaneous maps' spread over more than 1,200 pages. It's published on 1st February, the day before Joyce's birthday, and is likely to give *Multiple Joyce* a run for its money.

75. THE CATS OF COPENHAGEN AND FINN'S HOTEL

In the same month—January 2012—that most of Joyce's major works entered the public domain in the Republic of Ireland, the Dublin-based Ithys Press announced publication of *The Cats of Copenhagen*, the first appearance in print of what they called 'James Joyce's story for children', with original pen and ink illustrations by Casey Sorrow, letterpress typeset by Michael Caine and handmade paper marbling and binding by Christopher Rowlatt. Here's the spec:

> The Lettered de-luxe issue, printed on the last sheets of Crisbrook Waterleaf from the renowned and now historic Barcham Green handmade papermakers, is in loose imperial quartos, with paper-wrappers of Christopher Rowlatt's hand-marbled fantasia and presented in a vibrant cloth-covered slip-case.

> The Numbered issue, printed on Fedrigoni Freelife Vellum, is in double-elephant sextos and hand-bound in one-quarter cloth over marbled boards.

Phwoar! You had to act fast to be the proud owner of 'a rare, special edition of 200 copies, limited to 26 Lettered copies, 170 Numbered copies & 4 copies Hors Commerce'. The price? Between €300 and €1,200, depending on the degree of splendid gorgeousness.

However *The Cats of Copenhagen* was certainly not, as Ithys optimistically claimed, 'James Joyce's story for children' but simply a few lines lifted from a short letter from Joyce to his four-year-old grandson Stephen, dated 5th September 1936 and one of many items making up a bequest to the Zürcher James Joyce Stiftung (Zürich James Joyce Foundation) by Hans E. Jahnke, the son of Giorgio Joyce's second wife, Asta.

Somebody must have taken the trouble to copy out the 242 words—ten minutes well spent—and then passed the text to Ithys Press who, for doubtless unimpeachable reasons, chose not to notify the Foundation of their intention to publish. Fritz Senn, speaking with quiet fury on behalf of the Zürcher James Joyce Stiftung, regarded this as intellectual property theft:

> We have been completely overlooked and ignored. It's only common decency to ask the owner. We are outraged. We have had no

hand in this unfair thing and feel not just ignored but cheated [. . .] This is to state that the Zürich James Joyce Foundation was left completely in the dark, it never permitted, tolerated, condoned or connived at this publication, and it rigidly dissociates itself from it.

Responding to the Foundation's statement Ithys Press publicist Anastasia Herbert said, disingenuously, that she had not informed the Foundation of her plans to publish because this would have led to intervention by the Estate, which had already prevented the publication by Cork University Press of *Irish Writing in the Twentieth Century* which (she claimed) 'caused serious problems'. For her the issue was straightforward: Joyce was out of copyright so this short text was up for grabs.

Fritz Senn also had a straightforward take on the situation: 'Copyright has been lifted only, we believe, from the published material. All the huge amount of non-published material we believe is still under copyright, so this is, we believe, an infringement of that.' He was also understandably concerned that the Joyce Estate might sue the Foundation in defence of their shrinking copyright.*

Herbert was again unapologetic. She dismissed the Foundation's objections, insisting that her publication was entirely legal and valid, and that any attempt to interfere with her business was 'both unlawful and morally reprehensible.' *The Cats of Copenhagen* was (according to Ithys) 'exquisite, surprising, and with a keen, almost anarchic subtext.' And she made it absolutely clear that they really, *really* weren't in it for the money:

> The book was conceived not as a commercial venture but as a carefully crafted tribute to a rather different Joyce, the family man and grandfather who was a fine storyteller, much like his own father John Stanislaus.

As it happens this emphatically uncommercial, carefully-crafted tribute would appear later that year as a money-spinning mass mar-

---

*The Joyce Estate was managed at this point solely, and with a whim of iron, by the author's grandson Stephen Joyce (see the next essay). In 2000 the *Irish Times* reported the case of a 23-year-old Irish composer named David Fennessy, who asked for permission to use 18 words from *Finnegans Wake* in a three-minute choral piece. Stephen Joyce refused because, he said: 'My wife and I don't like your music'.

ket paperback in the United States and would subsequently be translated into French, Czech, Dutch, Spanish, German, Chinese, Danish, Greek and Italian. As the Estate of T.S. Eliot knows, there's money in cats.

Ithys Press went on to publish *Finn's Hotel* in 2013, 'a wonderful, serio-comic collection of 'little epics' that James Joyce wrote in 1923,' although Joyce scholars know that these were drafts never intended for publication and are certainly not, as Ithys claimed, 'a lost link in the Joyce canon.' The Ithys press website insisted, again optimistically, that the texts 'form the true and hitherto unknown precursor to the multi-modulated voices of the Wake.' Describing these short sketches as 'vignettes', Danis Rose made a claim for this material to be accorded recognition as the basis for what later became *Finnegans Wake* and as a separate work in its own right. Very few Joyce scholars agreed with him.

The existence of the 'epiclets' making up *Finn's Hotel* had been known to Joyceans for decades and some of them had already been included in *A First-Draft Version of Finnegans Wake* edited by David Hayman in 1963. Hayman, writing in *The New York Times* (14th October 1992), emphatically rejected Rose's claim that *Finn's Hotel* was a standalone work and not simply Joyce's rough sketches for *Finnegans Wake*: 'He is seriously misrepresenting what he has [. . .] This is a hoax,' he said. Ithys sneered at 'the small and congenitally contentious world of Joycean textual criticism' and posted this on their website:

> Why is there a controversy about the publication of *Finn's Hotel*?
> Joyce scholars, like most academics, are notoriously contentious
> and argumentative and they don't particularly like radical new
> ideas, unless of course it is their own new, radical idea. But to crit-
> icise is a defining aspect of their profession after all, much like the
> opposition in a parliament in a less than terribly civilised state.

I'm reminded of the so-called 'Poetry Wars' of the 1970s, in which a bunch of Arts Council-funded radicals took on the Arts Council. It was described by one bemused observer as 'a knife fight in a phone booth'. If you want to read the sketches making up *Finn's Hotel* for free they're available online as part of the enormous James Joyce Digital Archive.

The Ithys publication involved roping in some big-hitters, with a preface by Rose himself (who just happened to be a director of Ithys and the driving-force behind the publication) and an introduction by the Irish poet, novelist and critic Seamus Deane. In what was emerging as standard practice the book appeared first in an alarmingly expensive deluxe edition (€2,500), then in pricey numbered editions and, later on, in mass market paperbacks in the United States, followed by translation into Spanish, Italian, Greek, Portuguese, German and Polish.*

Of greater interest to Joyce collectors is a box set of seven pamphlets featuring 'Work in Progress' texts that would eventually appear in *Finnegans Wake*. Conceived by Owen Griffith & Michel Sauer, only 500 sets were were produced by Ian Gunn's Split Pea Press in Edinburgh, the collection consisting of 'Anna Livia Plurabelle', 'The Mooske and the Gripes', 'The Muddest Thick That Was Ever Heard', 'The Ondt and the Gracehoper', 'Haveth Childers Everywhere', 'The Mime of Mick, Nick and the Maggies' and 'Storiella as She is Syung'.

Working with the designer Griffith, the artist Michel Sauer created a series of 76 tiny sculptural stamps using sheet zinc, each one formed from a number of interlocking planes and each of which could be inked up and used as a printing block. The prints made with these small blocks formed faintly-coloured images that appear throughout the series, illuminating the text without distracting the reader from it.

The seven booklets were set in Times Roman 10pt and printed on Vol19 Bookwove, bound with 216gsm Modo Papetua 'Smoke' (a soft blue-grey colour) covers. They were sold at £35 a set although the slip cases were costly to produce and the hand stitching was also expensive. The number of copies actually prepared for sale was around 200, which was what Gunn calculated he needed to sell to break even.

---

*Danis Rose (pseudonym of Denis O'Hanlon) is a noted scholar of *Finnegans Wake* (see essay 29 'Father Jack Hackett and a note on editions'). His 'reader's edition' of *Ulysses* makes some editorial decisions even bolder than Hans Walter Gabler's. For instance Joyce's description of Henry Price 'basket and fancy goods, chinaware and ironmongery, manufacturer, 21,22,23 Moore Street' becomes, in Rose's version, 'china merchant, 16 A South City Market.' Make sense of that who will.

Many were in fact given away to Joyce scholars and, according to Griffith, only around 150 were sold.

The edition appeared on the day Joyce came out of copyright in Europe. The very first set, copy 1 of the planned 500, was sent to Stephen Joyce, who apparently liked it very much.

According to Griffith 'the overall intention was to produce something which was as far as possible from a "luxury item." While still having something that did not fall to pieces when you looked at it from halfway across a small room. The Smoke has faded beautifully, even in the Scottish light.' A very collectible edition, and rare. They now fetch around £500 a set.

Split Pea Press is, according to its dormant website, 'undergoing a metamorphosis' but there are a few things available online including the very useful *Ulysses Tables*, a free PDF collating all the English language editions of *Ulysses* and the page number system adopted by the Hans Walter Gabler edition of 1984, a document developed from their earlier *Ulysses Pagefinder* (1987). Split Pea Press has produced other Joyce-related material, including a recreation of *The Dublin Evening Telegraph* for 16th June 1904.*

---

*These and other documents can be found on:
www.riverrun.org.uk/joycetools.html

76. THE ONDT AND THE GRIPES

> The Gripes had light ears left yet he could but ill see. He ceased.
>
> And he ceased, tung and trit, and it was neversoever so dusk of both of them.
>
> —*Finnegans Wake*

There are few more evocative literary locations than the Martello tower in Sandycove, accessible without charge and, in normal times, open to the public 365 days a year. It offers two attractions for visitors as the place where Joyce lived (very briefly) and as the setting for the opening pages of his masterpiece.

'Geragh' is the name of the modernist house next to to the tower, designed and built by Michael Scott (1905–1989), widely regarded today as the most important Irish architect of the 20th century.

He bought the site overlooking Dublin Bay in order to create a home for his father, but then decided to design a place of his own. 'I thought of the house as a series of descending circles—each one wider than the other,' he later explained, the choice of circles being 'my tribute to the Tower and to James Joyce.'

Descending circles sounds more like Dante's Inferno, but a search for images of 'Geragh' online reveals a light, bright and streamlined residence with marvellous sea views and spacious, uncluttered, utterly inhabitable interiors. I can think of few lovelier places to live.

Appointed President of the Architectural Association of Ireland in 1937, Scott made a name for himself by designing the Irish Pavilion for the 1938 New York World Fair, selected by an international jury as the best building in the show ahead of work by such luminaries as Alvar Aalto and Oscar Niemeyer. That same year he founded Michael Scott Architects and designed the Sandycove house, which was reportedly a day's work.

He purchased the adjacent Martello Tower in 1954. This had been Joyce's home between Friday 9th and Thursday 15th September 1904, shared with Oliver St John Gogarty and the visiting Englishman Samuel Chenevix Trench, cast in *Ulysses* as the interloper Haines.

With financial assistance from the film maker John Huston, the building was officially opened as a museum on Bloomsday 1962 by Sylvia Beach. The site expanded over the years and in 1978 a new exhibition hall was added. Samuel Beckett, unable to attend the opening ceremony, donated a necktie Joyce had given him in the 1930s. This joined other exhibits in the former gunpowder magazine including a Clogowes College pandybat, a photograph of the Gold Cup winner Throwaway, a pot of Plumtree's Potted Meat, a piece of Nelson's pillar and Joyce's cane (donated by Maria Jolas).

Scott is an important if low-key figure when it comes to the management of Joyce's legacy in Ireland. Another important figure, far more visible, had a more contentious role.

On New Year's Eve 2012 there appeared on UbuWeb, the online archive of all things avant garde, a brief message: 'Fuck you Stephen Joyce. EU copyright on James Joyce's works ends at midnight.' Accompanied by a link to an *Irish Times* article detailing the change in copyright status, the message reflected a widespread contempt for the sole descendant of James Joyce who had, until then, been in sole charge of his grandfather's literary Estate.

Stephen James Joyce, the son of James and Nora Joyce's son Giorgio and his wealthy American wife Helen Kastor Fleischman, was born in 1932. He spent a happy childhood in Paris and was very close to his grandparents, 'Nonno' and 'Nanna', who were very close to him. (This is unsurprising because, as some wit once observed, grandparents and grandchildren share a common enemy.) In the late 1930s Giorgio and Helen's marriage foundered and they became estranged. She suffered a complete nervous breakdown and he all but disappeared, so young Stephen was largely cared for by his paternal grandparents. His aunt Lucia, Georgio's sister, had been committed to a series of private institutions since the year Stephen was born.

Following the fall of France, James, Nora and Stephen moved to Saint-Gérand-le-Puy and later to Zürich. Giorgio was by now a chaotic drunkard so James and Nora became the main carers of his eight-year-old son. The three remained in Switzerland but money was short and it was a difficult time for them. Joyce died in 1941 and in 1946 the 14-year-old Stephen left for the United States, eventually fetching up at Harvard University where he studied international relations. On graduating he joined the Organisation for Economic Co-operation and Development (OECD), working in their Paris offices.

Giorgio Joyce remained in charge of his father's estate, although the day-to-day business of handling permissions and copyrights was managed by the Society of Authors. When Giorgio died aged 70 in

1976 Stephen took over control of the Estate from the Society of Authors, retiring from the OECD in 1991 to live with this wife Solange on the Île de Ré near La Rochelle and dedicating his life to managing his grandfather's literary legacy. Thus began a difficult period for Joyce scholars everywhere, who found Stephen Joyce erratic, capricious and unpredictable.

He always claimed that his sole aim was to protect the integrity of his grandfather's works. 'I am a Joyce, not a Joycean,' was his riposte to academics. Obstructive and combative, he would demand enormous sums from individuals and institutions seeking copyright permissions and, if such sums could not be wrung from hard-up researchers or impecunious faculties, permission was flatly refused, sometimes without explanation. When the late Michael Groden, an American scholar, applied for copyright permission to use Joyce's texts as part of a hypermedia project the Estate initially demanded payment of two million dollars.

In 2004 (the year which would mark the centenary of the day on which *Ulysses* was set) Stephen Joyce threatened the Irish government with a lawsuit if it staged any readings on 16th June. The readings were therefore promptly cancelled. He informed the National Library of Ireland that that an exhibition of his grandfather's manuscripts would amount to a copyright violation and the Irish Senate had to pass an emergency amendment in order to thwart him. His antagonism resulted in the Abbey Theatre cancelling a planned production of Joyce's play *Exiles*.

An atmosphere of trigger-happy litigation surrounded the estate for decades. Cork University Press, for example, on seeking permission to include some of Joyce's work in an anthology, became embroiled in a prolonged and expensive legal action that hampered their activity as a highly reputable academic press for years afterwards. Innumerable public readings of Joyce's works were prohibited. In 2006, for instance, the *New Yorker* reported that Stephen Joyce had informed Adam Harvey, a performer and self-declared 'Joyce geek' who had committed a chunk of *Finnegans Wake* to memory that he had almost certainly 'already infringed' copyright, although in the eyes of the law he most certainly had not.[*]

---

[*]Harvey (born 1974) has been performing works prompted by *Finnegans Wake* since 2001, when he delivered a memorized interpretation of 'Shem the Penman'

On his aunt Lucia's death in 1982 he destroyed all her correspondence, although it reportedly post-dated the death of her parents and never referred to them. He also destroyed postcards and a telegram from Samuel Becket, admittedly at Beckett's request. While Stephen Joyce was entirely within his rights to do so one cannot help but feel a sense of sadness and anger that Lucia's fragile purchase on the world was thus further diminished. It has taken the work of novelists and biographers to give her a cultural afterlife.

While many literary legacies are run with a combination of rigour and caprice—the Eliot estate under the diligent grip of the poet's widow Valerie, for instance—what was peculiar about the Joyce estate for decades was the poisonous atmosphere surrounding its management, which spread throughout the world of Joycean scholarship and hampered or thwarted a generation of scholars. If Stephen Joyce were alive today the book you are holding would never have been published. He had no children and with his death on 23rd January 2020 the Joyce line came to an end.

for the North American James Joyce Conference at UC Berkeley. He has since then expanded his repertoire to include 'Anna Livia Plurabelle', 'The Mime of Mick, Nick and the Maggies' and other passages.

77. First among sequels

When I first heard that a sequel to *Ulysses* was being written my heart sank. When I learned that the author taking on the challenge was the poet Chris McCabe, my spirits rallied because (I thought) if anyone can do it, he can. And my enthusiasm spiked at news that the book would be published by Henningham Family Press, an indie run by the artists Ping and David Henningham, creators of some of the most beautiful and affordable contemporary editions you'll ever see: hand-bound, superbly designed and type-set on gorgeous paper.* So my hopes were running high and, waiting impatiently for my copy to arrive, I amused myself by coming up with possible titles, finally settling on

TWOLYSSES

Dedalus (as it was in fact entitled) was published on Bloomsday 2018. The title, I assumed, was a nod to the 1924 French translation, by Ludmila Savitzky, of *A Portrait of the Artist as a Young Man*. Joyce approved of her suggestion to call it *Dedalus*, and so it remained until Folio published a revised edition in 1998 as *Portrait de l'artiste en jeune homme*.

I read McCabe's book and wrote about it for the *Literary Review*. Here's what I said:

> In dismantling and reassembling Joyce's original, McCabe has created a brilliantly complex and original work of fiction that is much more than a pastiche or mere homage.

> As a poet himself, McCabe has a sure feel for Joyce's prose style, or styles. Not simply in the use of Joycean compounds—the first page gives us seasand, airdew, dawnblue, catpurrs, sourbreath and eggwhites, nor in confidently adopting the stream of consciousness technique (which these days seems slightly quaint). The challenges were to own the antecedent material rather than to borrow it, and then to do something new with it, and not to fly too close to the sun.

> The 18 short episodes in *Dedalus* correspond to Joyce's original from 'Telemachus' to 'Penelope' but, rather than recycle the original's Homeric substructure, McCabe chooses instead to map his

---

*www.henninghamfamilypress.co.uk.

sequel against the five acts of *Hamlet*, with Stephen Dedalus as the Prince.

Part I adheres most closely to the circadian structure of *Ulysses*. Waking on the morning of Friday 17th June 1904, a hungover Stephen staggers down the Martello tower stairwell for some brittle exchanges with the English interloper Haines, while Buck Mulligan swims nearby at the 'Forty Foot'. Meanwhile in Eccles Street Leopold Bloom is once again preparing breakfast for Molly and teasing the pussens.

There are no unresolved plot points in *Ulysses* because there's barely any plot at all, but McCabe shrewdly picks up on some suggestive leads. Sundry consequences of Paddy Dignam's funeral and the Epsom Gold Cup winner the previous day are lighted on, we find out more about Stephen's feelings for his dead mother and about Bloom's excruciating awareness of his cuckold status.

The author comes into his own in Part II when he abandons straightforward pastiche and, prompted by the modern significance of 'platform' in the *Hamlet* stage direction 'A platform before the castle', begins to reconfigure his novel as a 1980s Text Adventure Game, the characters becoming (in the publisher's words) 'cultural types pasted into Digital Age storytelling'. This is a dazzling departure.

Between each of the three sections there is a series of cryptic Google-style maps reflecting the way modern-day Dubliners navigate their city. These maps resemble, and appear to function as, two-dimensional museum vitrines; a virtual Joyce museum with interactive displays, perhaps located in a castle, quite possibly in Denmark. These also appear to represent a layer of the subconscious beneath the Joycean stream, an equivalent to Eimear McBride's rendering of thought at the point before it becomes articulate speech. The effect is like a series of superimposed acetates featuring Homer and *Ulysses* and *Hamlet*, then computer gaming and, on top of all that, present-day metadata. This is genuinely, startlingly, wonderfully new.

McCabe's invention impresses, and never flags. His take on 'Wandering Rocks' features voices from modern-day Dublin (a Ryanair hostess, an I.T. help desk advisor, a boy scout and a Molly Bloom impersonator); 'Sirens' is a visual riot of phrases, words and letters while 'Cyclops' consists of a series of circular calligrams which diminish in size as the speaker's monocular chauvinism intensifies. (Concrete poetry has found a place in the experimental novel ever since *Tristram Shandy*.) In 'Circe' Stephen discusses his feelings about Joyce with a modern therapist and in 'Ithaca' McCabe interviews himself about his relationship with his late, alcoholic father. There are lipogrammatic fragments in which all vowels are excised to produce a kind of Oulipian text speak which at one point appear to dismiss the book itself as a 'frtlss nd ftl xrcs.' Far from being fruitless and futile—although readers unfamiliar with *Ulysses* will struggle—*Dedalus* offers huge rewards for the initiated.

Joyce sets his would-be followers a very high bar. The original 'Lestrygonians' episode, as we saw earlier, has Joyce's Bloom, hungry before lunch, looking at women's silk petticoats in a shop window:

> A warm human plumpness settled down on his brain. His brain yielded. Perfume of embraces all him assailed. With hungered flesh obscurely, he mutely craved to adore.*

Now here's McCabe's Bloom, also pre-prandial:

> Scent and salivation plumed through the thoughts of Bloom. Maybe buy some buns, walk down to the quay.

This is less richly textured, less suggestive—while 'plumed' adds some depth (and harks back to the original's 'plumped') I'm not convinced that 'salivation' (with its perhaps deliberately distracting echo of 'salvation') works here. This is not to criticise McCabe but to remind ourselves of what a genius Joyce was. It's the difference between perfume and scent, their respective complexity, their lingering *sillage*; McCabe's prose, perfectly serviceable and consistently very fine, does not always support the scrutiny that Joyce's does. But that's the case with practically every other writer in history.

And now that McCabe has proved it can be done, and done well, why not another sequel, set on the 18th June? Or perhaps a prequel?

---

*See essay 40 'Sillage'.

78. 'AND WORDS. THEY ARE NOT IN MY DICTIONARY'

Essential reading for any Joycean with a taste for lexicography is 'Comings and goings: Joyce's words in the Oxford English Dictionary' by John Simpson, former chief editor of the *OED*.* Joyce was himself an avid reader of dictionaries and would no doubt be delighted to learn that—as announced in June 2019—he ranks high on the Oxford English Dictionary's online list of most quoted sources.

He is, for example, the only source since the mid-17th century of the obscure word 'peccaminous' meaning 'full of sins, sinful', which he used in *Ulysses* ('A volume of peccaminous pornographical tendency entitled Sweets of Sin') and again in *Finnegans Wake* ('To put off the barcelonas from their peccaminous corpulums').

After starting work on the Third Supplement to the *OED* (OED3) in the year 2000, the lexicographers added more than 650 new examples of Joycean usage, part of a process that took ten years and which raised the total number of Joyce citations in the Dictionary to 2,311. The main volunteer reader was a retired schoolmaster from Faversham in Kent named R.A. Auty, who undertook to read the entire works of Joyce (apart from, he insisted, the *Wake*). He submitted thousands of handwritten slips on which were entered 'illustrative examples for any word or meaning that occurred in Joyce and was not already entered in the Dictionary.'

Things started to slow down after that, and just 161 new citations were added between 2010 and June 2019, when the total peaked at an impressive 2,472. As of December 2012 the James Joyce Online Notes site recorded 2,464 Joyce quotations and 423 Joyce 'First Uses'.

But over that same period Joyce's 'First Use' count has fallen fast—faster, in fact, than that of many other high-profile writers cited in the past. Why is that?

Firstly, according to Simpson, it was the increasing availability of online historical texts that gave researchers the ability and opportunity to search instantaneously through a colossal number of alternative sources.

The second reason was to do with Joyce's method of composition. Even before *Finnegans Wake* he was regarded as being lexically in-

---

*See http://www.jjon.org/joyce-s-words/oed.

novative to a quite extraordinary degree but, as Simpson points out, there is a greater understanding today 'that he actively sought out the ephemeral language of his time—and particularly of Dublin in his time—copying excerpts into his notebooks and assimilating these into his works.'

So now that the *OED*'s hard-working editors are able to uncover and rediscover for themselves some of the hidden layers of language that Joyce tapped into, the author himself is no longer the centre of attention. It's his sources that interest etymologists. Which may explain why the *OED* does not record that the earliest use of the word 'television' in literature is in *Finnegans Wake*, originally appearing in *transition* magazine in 1927:

> Television kills telephony in brothers' broil. Our eyes demand their turn. Let them be seen!*

Another frequently-cited high profile source in *OED* citations was W.H. Auden, and another digression is called for here.

In the fourth issue of *The W.H. Auden Society Newsletter* (October 1989) a young Toby Litt, long before he achieved fame as a novelist, contributed a dazzling essay entitled 'From "Acedia" to "Zeitgeist": Auden in the 2nd Edition of the *OED*'. Litt began his piece with a mischievous quotation from Auden, taken from an interview in 1971:

> One of my great ambitions is to get into the *OED* as the first person to have used in print a new word. I have two candidates at the moment, which I used in my review of J.R. Ackerley's autobiography. They are 'Plain-sewing' and 'Princeton-First-Year'. They refer to two types of homosexual behaviour.

Auden's ambition was realised posthumously with the appearance in 1989 of the twenty-volume 2nd edition of the *Oxford English Dictionary* (available online as 'OED3'), from which the following definition of 'Plain-sewing' is taken:

> Designating a form of male homosexual activity in which the penis is rubbed against the thighs or stomach of a partner. **1969** W.H. AUDEN in *N.Y. Rev. Bks.* 27 Mar.3/4

---

*My thanks again to Peter Chrisp, who blogged about this appearance here: http://peterchrisp.blogspot.com/2015/03/television-in-finnegans-wake.html

The source was Auden's *New York Review of Books* review of J.R. Ackerley's *My Father and Myself.** A second citation comes from the *TLS*, with a discreetly explicit Latin tag:

> **1980** *Times Lit. Suppl.* 21 Mar. 324/5 'Princeton-First-Year' is a more condescending version of the term 'Princeton Rub'; that is, *coitus contra ventrem.*

When it comes to 'plain sewing' as a euphemism for masturbation, the *OED* has it both ways:

> plain sewing. (a) Needlework which is functional or practical rather than decorative; (b) slang [popularized by W.H. Auden (compare quot. 1980)] , a sexual activity of homosexuals involving mutual masturbation.

One assumes the 'plain sewing' refers to the rhythmic back-and-forth motion of the hand when innocently stitching fabric or when, perhaps just as innocently, mutually masturbating.

Auden enriched the language of the tribe far beyond the subversive promotion of mid-century gay slang. He appears 766 times in the second, four-volume *OED* Supplement (published from 1972 to 1986), including quotations from works co-written with Christopher Isherwood, Louis MacNeice and Chester Kallman. Most of these citations are not (as you might think) for being the first person to have used a particular word in print, but are included to show either a change or extension of meaning. While this is an impressive total, Shakespeare—by far the most frequently quoted single author—is the source of 33,300 quotations, of which 1,600 come from *Hamlet* alone.

That Auden came to feature so prominently in the *OED* is largely down to the four years he spent as Professor of Poetry at Oxford between 1956 and 1961. During this time he became an acquaintance of R.W. Burchfield, a lecturer at Christ Church (Auden's old college) who was, from 1957, the editor of the second supplement to the *OED*. Burchfield had a low opinion of the poet's linguistic scholarship but decided nonetheless that Auden should be among the major writers whose work merited special attention from the compilers.

---

*'Papa Was a Wise Old Sly-Boots' *New York Review of Books*, 27th March 1969.

Of Auden's 766 citations, 110 are *Hapax legomena* or so-called 'nonce-words' or original coinages, of which around half are hyphenated compounds such as 'angel-vampire' and 'swan-delighting', poetic figures that have never entered mainstream English. A further twenty-two appear under sub-headings as additional definitions of words already in existence.

There are in all twenty-eight citations (including 'Princeton-First-Year') for which Auden is credited as the first writer to use the word in print, a lexical horde that in part reflects the poet's camp and ramshackle character.

Toby Litt writes:

> Among Auden's more notable citations are the first pejorative use of 'queer', the first printed use of 'ponce' to designate an effeminate homosexual, of 'toilet-humour', of 'agent' in the sense of a secret agent or spy, of 'dedicated' to mean a person 'single- minded in loyalty to his beliefs or in his artistic or personal integrity', of 'shagged' meaning 'weary, exhausted', and of 'stud' for a person 'displaying masculine sexual characteristics'. Further curiosities are the first printed appearance in English of the surrealist term '*objet trouvé*' and the first printed use of 'What's yours?' as an invitation given by the person buying the next round of drinks.*

'Bot' (as the colloquial abbreviation of 'bottom' and nothing to do with today's online trolling) is illustrated by quotations from Joyce, Auden, and the childhood language collectors Iona and Peter Opie: 'Spank your bare bot right well, miss, with the hair-brush' (*Ulysses*); 'The cute little botts [*sic*] of the sailors' (from Auden's 1951 collection *Nones*) and 'A kick up the bot for being a clot' (the Opies' *Lore & Language of Schoolchildren*, 1959).

Not included in the Litt list, but noted by Edward Mendelson in his introduction to the reprint of Auden's *The Prolific and the Devourer* (1939), is the poet's use of the term 'apolitical', its first appearance in print. Other Auden-sourced coinages include 'Mosleyite', 'Disneyesque' and (from 1941) 'butch', in the sense of aggressively masculine. What would we do, where would we be, without him?

---

*Toby Litt was right; the compilers of the *OED* were not. See 'The Record Book of Guinnesses'.

79. Out of the Audenry

Let's stick with Auden as one of the handful of 20th-century Anglo-phone writers who could give Joyce a run for his money. The poet makes a blink-and-you-miss-it appearance in *Finnegans Wake* as a pun on Odin, father of the Norse gods:

> I forget to bolt the thor. Auden. Wasn't it just divining that dog of a dag in Skokholme as I sat astrid uppum their Drewitt's altar, as cooledas as cul-cumbre.

Joyce (who was 25 and living in Trieste with Nora and their two young children when Auden was born in February 1907) was clearly aware of the young poet, who was his Faber stablemate, but I don't know if he ever read any of the books Auden published between 1930 and Joyce's death in 1941.[*] Auden certainly knew Joyce's work, and in the poem 'Letter to Lord Byron' (1937) said, tongue in cheek, that his writing was 'as innocent as grass' compared with the subversive depravity of Jane Austen, whose novels revealed 'the economic basis of society.' He also shared some thoughts on the author of the *Wake* in a magazine article published three months after Joyce's death.[†] This unusual piece opens with a lengthy quote from Nietzsche's *The Case of Wagner*.[‡] Joyce (says Auden) was, like Wagner, a 'master' and a virtuoso whose hand never falters. But then, damning with loud praise, he poses the bizarre question: 'Has that which Joyce does with such consummate skill anything to do with art?'

The answer is no, and Auden sets out to tell us why:

> All art before the nineteenth century was based on a pair of contrasts: the contrast between Chaos and Order, Fate and Free-Will; and the contrast between the Inferior and the Superior Man, the Churl and the Hero, i.e. between the man who is the passive slave of circumstance, incapable of creating order out of chaos, and the

---

[*] Joyce was a Faber author before Auden. His pamphlet *Anna Livia Plurabelle* was published in May 1930. Auden's *Poems* (1930) appeared four months later, on 18th September 1930.

[†] Published as *Der Fall Wagner* (1888). Auden uses the English translation by Thomas Common.

[‡] Writing in *Common Sense* (March 1941), an essay included in *The Complete Works of W.H. Auden: Prose Volume II 1939–1948* edited by Edward Mendelson (Faber and Faber 2002).

man who consciously asserts his will against the Accidental, and creates order for himself and for others.

During the nineteenth century Christian belief began to loosen its grip on artists and the public who became, in Auden's view, one of three things:

1. liberal optimists, who abandoned belief in Original Sin and saw the Good Life as possible for all;
2. pagans, who abandoned belief in Free Will and saw the Good Life as possible only for *some*: 'the intellectual, the proletariat, the aryan'; and
3. romantic pessimistic determinists, who abandoned belief in Grace and saw the Good Life as impossible to achieve 'and declared that we were lying in the swamp of the Accidental *all together*.'

In the first category Auden places Walt Whitman, in the second Wagner 'and perhaps D.H. Lawrence,' in the third Proust and Joyce. The latter he describes as 'a man conscious of possessing great energy, who believes that order neither exists nor is possible, and attempts to deduce what he thinks would be worth doing with his energy. If order cannot be created, then no action can be worthwhile; and the only proper occupation for a man [. . .] is in a passive recording of the flux.'

That sounds more like Beckett than Joyce, both in its phrasing and as a method. Even by Auden's cranky standards this is a strange take and, as is often the case in his prose writings, it reveals more about him than his ostensible subject. Did he really think there was no order in *Ulysses*, a novel with a structure derived from classical mythology and an organising schema of astonishing complexity and precision? It's hard to see how Auden can infer from it that Joyce thinks no action can be worthwhile, a view which would certainly come as a surprise to Joyce, who said of his own writing:

> The important thing is not what we write, but how we write, and in my opinion the modern writer must be an adventurer above all, willing to take every risk, and be prepared to founder in his effort if need be. In other words we must write dangerously: everything is inclined to flux and change nowadays and modern literature, to

be valid, must express that flux . . . A book, in my opinion, should not be planned out beforehand, but as one writes it will form itself, subject, as I say, to the constant emotional promptings of one's personality.[*]

I'm disheartened by Auden's take on Joyce's passivity because (as the poet Glyn Maxwell wrote) it 'seriously diminishes the appreciation of one of the language's greatest modern artists for another, and feels like an over-extension of Auden's habits.'[†] Maxwells's view is that Auden and Joyce had temperaments that were respectively Apollonian and Dionysian, and that when Auden rejects 'a passive recording of the flux' he is expressing less a literary judgement than 'a temperamental yearning for absolutes.'

Even without over-extension, Auden's habits were certainly unusual. What in his lifetime was regarded with affectionate forbearance as the eccentric behaviour of a genius strikes us today as evidence of somebody with an Autism Spectrum Disorder.

The 'temperamental yearning for absolutes' often found expression in a tendency—or compulsion—to impose rigid templates of order on experience. This is most evident in his prose, and the Auden scholar Tony Sharpe assembled some examples: 'A poet may write bad poetry in three ways' (*Forewords & Afterwords* p. 224); 'There are four things Lawrence does supremely well' (*Prose* II p. 318); 'To a situation of danger and difficulty there are five solutions' (*Prose* I p. 96); 'For a complete life a man requires six kinds of love' (*Prose* II p. 321), and so on.[‡] It's a characteristic Auden strategy to employ such 'non-negotiable' taxonomies to clarify his position while simultaneously complicating the reader's response. In adopting this anarchic pedagogue persona he startles his readers into attention, dazzling them with an erudite flourish which can then be explored on its own terms. A favourite example: the four kinds of critic he hoped a poet might

---

[*] *Conversations with James Joyce* by Arthur Power (Dalkey Archive Press, 2020).

[†] 'Putting the world to rights', Glyn Maxwell's review of *The Complete Works of WH Auden: Prose, Volume II 1939–1948* edited by Edward Mendelson (*The Guardian*, 14 Sep 2002)

[‡] Tony Sharpe 'Auden's Prose' in *The Cambridge Companion to Auden*, (Cambridge University Press, 2005) p.116.

never turn into, namely 'a prig, a critic's critic, a romantic novelist or a maniac.' Of these the fourth-named is 'the commonest of his kind [...], the man who believes that poetry is written in cyphers.'*

Auden's view is that the novelist who deals with human nature must at all costs avoid any suggestion of the exceptional or the heroic, which strikes me as an extraordinarily narrow view of literature and, come to that, of what constitutes the heroic. He argues that 'if the subject is the Mass Man thinking Mass thoughts as he performs Mass actions in the course of a disorganised day', then concessions must be made to human weakness, and so 'a purely arbitrary frame work, preferably one for which he is not responsible, must limit the weight of the book to that of a small ham.'

He's lost me there. What's *ham* got to do with it? Auden once compared love to 'the ham in a temperance hotel' and I like that line very much without really understanding it, but as a measure of literary worth, as part of a hypothetical critical charcuterie, I don't think it will do.

Auden insists that Joyce is a 'supreme master' only for those of us who accept the flux as 'the Thing-in-Itself' (from the German *Ding an sich*, a philosophical term introduced by Immanuel Kant to describe objects as they are, independent of observation). He shrugs off the achievement of the greatest prose writer of the century by saying that 'apart from the haunting beauty of accidental phrases with an accidental dream-like appeal, he ceases to interest as soon as he ceases to shock.' Those 'accidentals' are withering, but he's not done yet. Joyce's value, he concludes, is not aesthetic but political, 'to reveal to each of us those layers of his soul which are susceptible to the ambiguous and hypnotic Hitlerian cry.'

This strikes me as nuts.

Auden would, perhaps surprisingly, include many references to *Finnegans Wake* in *The Age of Anxiety* (1947), his 'baroque eclogue' in which four strangers—Malin, a Canadian airman; Quant, a clerk; Rosetta, a buyer for a department store and Emble, a young naval recruit—meet in a New York bar to share and explore their lives and hopes and thoughts on the human condition while getting smashed. Weaving back to Rosetta's apartment, they drink more and dance be-

---

* *Making Knowing and Judging—An Inaugural Lecture Delivered Before the University of Oxford on 11th June 1956* (Clarendon Press, 1956).

fore the two older men leave together and young Emble declares his love for Rosetta before passing out on her bed.

In 'The Seven Stages', the second of the six sections making up the poem, there are distinct echoes of the *Wake*, such as when Quant recalls 'Shilly and Shally the shepherd kings', a reference to the twin Earwicker brothers Shem the penman and Shaun the postman,* who can be seen as incarnations of Joyce (Shem) and his brother Stanislaus (Shaun). Like their protean father they go by many names in the *Wake*, such as Caddy and Primas, Mercius and Justius, Dolph and Kevin and Jerry and Kevin, and are further contrasted with the Biblical pairings of Jacob and Esau, Cain and Abel, and Saint Michael and the Devil, as well as the twin founders of Rome, Romulus and Remus. On top of all of which they *also* represent the binary oppositions of time and space, and tree and stone. How's that for an *active* recording of the flux?

*Try saying this sentence after a few pints of Guinness.

80. *NÅR VI DØDE VÅGNER*

When Susan Tomaselli launched the Dublin-based literary journal *gorse* in June 2014 she announced that it would run for just eighteen issues, each corresponding, though not closely, to an episode of *Ulysses*. At the time of writing it has reached issue 11 which, breaking with the established format, comes in the form of a box packed with extraordinary things. Every beautifully produced issue is a keeper, with gorgeous cover designs by Niall McCormack and an astonishing cohort of contributors.

gorse builds on the tradition of the so-called 'little magazines' of the 1920s and 30s which offered a home to many of the modern movement's key writers. Tomaselli's editorials are always a highlight of each *gorse* and here, with her generous permission, is the one that appeared in the very first issue:

Where the Dead Voices Gather by Susan Tomaselli

'*Mr Yeats has been speaking to me of your writing.*' In December 1913, Ezra Pound wrote to James Joyce asking permission to include a poem of his, 'I Hear an Army', in the anthology *Des Imagistes*. Joyce, living in self-imposed exile in Trieste and struggling to make ends meet—he had yet to make money from his writing—readily agreed. 'This is the first time I have written to any one outside of my own circle of acquaintance (save in the case of French authors) . . . I am *bonae voluntatis*—don't in the least know that I can be of any use to you—or you to me. From what W.B.Y. says, I imagine we have a hate or two in common—but thats [*sic*] a very problematical bond on introduction.'

Joyce sent Pound more work and Pound, drawn to Joyce's tribulations with censorious publishers—it took Joyce almost ten years for *Dubliners* to be published without expurgation—took up the cause. Acting as Joyce's unpaid agent, Pound used his connections as literary correspondent and editor to shepherd *A Portrait of the Artist as a Young Man*—as a serialisation in Harriet Shaw Weaver's *The Egoist* in 1914—and parts of *Ulysses*—first serial publication in *The Little Review* in 1918—into print.

'Enter a skinny, shabby Irishman and a natty, quietly sinister American,' as Kevin Jackson describes them, 'hellbent on exploding everything that realistic fiction and Georgian poetry held dear . . . Language has rebelled against the tyranny of subject matter and

Photomontage of Joyce, Ford Madox Ford, John Quinn and Ezra Pound (detail)
by G.R. Morris from Herbert Gorman's *James Joyce: a definitive biography*

character, and become the leading character in its own right. The
horror!'

As the 'unconscious mind, like the city, spends its time recycling
events,' so too did the moderns reuse the 'debris of previous literature.' Pound and co. picked up signals from ancient sources, re-
making it new.

'I want a place I and T.S. Eliot can appear once a month and where
Joyce can appear when he likes, and where Wyndham Lewis can
appear if he comes back from the war,' writes Pound to *Little Review* editor Margaret Anderson in 1917. Those places, the 'little
magazines'—*The Little Review, The Dial, Poetry, Broom, The Egoist*

and others—were crucial in getting the work of the 'men of 1914' (as Lewis dubbed himself, Eliot, Pound and Joyce) in print. Often publishing outside of the mainstream and challenging the very notions of what literature could be, they were the perfect venues for the exiles to explore new modes of writing. More significantly, the little magazines welcomed important work other editors had dismissed or ignored. They fast became hotbeds for innovation in new forms: first surrealism, then modernism.

Their relationship, though, cooled—Pound had no love for Joyce's new 'Work in Progress', Joyce was alarmed (and rightly so) at Pound's politics. The reversal of support from a former champion was disappointing, but Joyce was to find other encouragement in American expatriates Eugene and Maria Jolas. The Jolas' *transition* journal ran extracts from André Breton's *Nadja* and the surrealist manifesto 'Hands Off Love', introduced Kafka to an English readership with 'The Sentence' and 'Metamorphosis', ran Dadaist work by Hans Arp and Kurt Schwitters, published bits of Hart Crane's 'The Bridge', some of Gertrude Stein and early Samuel Beckett, and much of *Finnegans Wake* as 'Work in Progress'.

The frontline of the avant-garde in Paris, *transition* was the firecracker the middle class, middlebrow patrons of the arts needed: their 1929 manifesto was incendiary stuff.

A dismantled syntax, a new multilingual tongue, *transition* was a perfect fit for James Joyce's buckled style. 'The same people,' writes Peter Conrad, 'did not think in paragraphs or logical, completed sentences, like characters in nineteenth century novels. Their mental life proceeded in associative jerks and spasms . . . The modern mind was not a quiet, tidy cubicle for cognition. It thronged with as many random happenings as a city street; it contained scraps and fragments, dots and dashes, like the incoherent blizzard of marks on a modern canvas which could only be called an 'impression' because it represented nothing recognizable.'

Joyce, Gertrude Stein and the other *transition* contributors were employing English in radically new ways, bending and regenerating a language made dull by age and usage. 'Joyce,' says Peter Gay, 'pushed the dissection and reconstitution of prose to an extreme that nobody could surpass without landing in sheer incoherence.' *Finnegans Wake* could not serve as a model for later subversive writers, Gay continues, but 'it remains—and will remain—a solitary monument to a bold, learned, and unduplicible venture, serving as Joyce always did to affront dominant literary pieties.'

PROCLAMATION

TIRED OF THE SPECTACLE OF SHORT STORIES, NOVELS, POEMS AND PLAYS STILL UNDER THE HEGEMONY OF THE BANAL WORD, MONO-TONOUS SYNTAX, STATIC PSYCHOLOGY, DESCRIPTIVE NATURALISM, AND DESIROUS OF CRYSTALLIZING A VIEWPOINT...

WE HEREBY DECLARE THAT :

1. THE REVOLUTION IN THE ENGLISH LANGUAGE IS AN AC-COMPLISHED FACT.

2. THE IMAGINATION IN SEARCH OF A FABULOUS WORLD IS AUTONOMOUS AND UNCONFINED.
(*Prudence is a rich, ugly old maid courted by Incapacity... Blake*)

3. PURE POETRY IS A LYRICAL ABSOLUTE THAT SEEKS AN A PRIORI REALITY WITHIN OURSELVES ALONE.
(*Bring out number, weight and measure in a year of dearth... Blake*)

4. NARRATIVE IS NOT MERE ANECDOTE, BUT THE PROJEC-TION OF A METAMORPHOSIS OF REALITY.
(*Enough ! Or Too Much !... Blake*)

5. THE EXPRESSION OF THESE CONCEPTS CAN BE ACHIEVED ONLY THROUGH THE RHYTHMIC " HALLUCINATION OF THE WORD ". (Rimbaud).

6. THE LITERARY CREATOR HAS THE RIGHT TO DISINTE-GRATE THE PRIMAL MATTER OF WORDS IMPOSED ON HIM BY TEXT-BOOKS AND DICTIONARIES.
(*The road of excess leads to the palace of Wisdom... Blake*)

7. HE HAS THE RIGHT TO USE WORDS OF HIS OWN FASH-IONING AND TO DISREGARD EXISTING GRAMMATICAL AND SYNTACTICAL LAWS.
(*The tigers of wrath are wiser than the horses of instruction... Blake*)

8. THE " LITANY OF WORDS " IS ADMITTED AS AN INDEPEN-DENT UNIT.

9. WE ARE NOT CONCERNED WITH THE PROPAGATION OF SOCIOLOGICAL IDEAS, EXCEPT TO EMANCIPATE THE CREATIVE ELEMENTS FROM THE PRESENT IDEOLOGY.

10. TIME IS A TYRANNY TO BE ABOLISHED.

11. THE WRITER EXPRESSES. HE DOES NOT COMMUNICATE.

12. THE PLAIN READER BE DAMNED.
(*Damn braces ! Bless relaxes !... Blake*)

— *Signed :* KAY BOYLE, WHIT BURNETT, HART CRANE, CARESSE CROSBY, HARRY CROSBY, MARTHA FOLEY, STUART GILBERT, A. L. GILLESPIE, LEIGH HOFFMAN, EUGENE JOLAS, ELLIOT PAUL, DOUGLAS RIGBY, THEO RUTRA, ROBERT SAGE, HAROLD J. SALEMSON, LAURENCE VAIL.

transition: manifesto

'*In the buginning is the wood, in the muddle is the sound-dance and thereinoften you're in the unbewised again.*'

One of the finest Irish novels of 2013, Eimear Mcbride's *A Girl Is a Half-formed Thing*, was ignored for nine years, dismissed as be-ing too experimental. English indie publishers Galley Beggar Press took a punt with it and it went on to win the Goldsmith's Prize, a prize that embraces the enthusiasm of Laurence Sterne—another great Irish innovator—and rewards 'fiction that breaks the mould or opens up new possibilities for the novel form.' Novels that are novel.

Another, Donal Ryan's *The Spinning Heart*, a novel in voices, was re-jected forty-seven times before being rescued from the 'slush pile' by a beady-eyed intern and published to international acclaim by Irish independents Lilliput Press. They—McBride and Ryan, Galley Beggars and Lilliput—are stories of our time.

Donal Ryan has said we are in the eye of a publishing storm; we think he's on to something. The optimism of the 50s, and the spirit of Ireland's own little magazines—*The Bell*, *Threshold*, *Atlantis*, *The Dublin Magazine*—is alive and well in the *Dublin Review* and *The Stinging Fly*, and in newcomers *The Moth*, *The Penny Dreadful*, *South Circular*, *The Bohemyth*. Though the James Joyces, the Ezra Pounds, the Gertrude Steins, the Ernest Hemingways of today would still be deemed uncommercial (well, perhaps not Hemingway), praise be the independents and the little magazines, for giving voice to innovation, for ushering exciting and unusual authors into print.

For all our talk of the ghosts of Ezra Pound and James Joyce, *gorse* does not wish to raise the dead. We are not nostalgic for the past, but look for the potential in literature today—we believe in the art of words. But we are not only for the novel; we champion the unconventional and the under-recognised, writers exiled in their own countries.

'I hear an army charging upon the land . . .'

Susan Tomaselli's rousing editorial concludes with a line from one of Joyce's best poems, and here it is in full:

> I hear an army charging upon the land,
>   And the thunder of horses plunging, foam about their knees:
>
> Arrogant, in black armour, behind them stand,
>   Disdaining the reins, with fluttering whips, the charioteers.
>
> They cry unto the night their battle-name:
>   I moan in sleep when I hear afar their whirling laughter.
> They cleave the gloom of dreams, a blinding flame,
>   Clanging, clanging upon the heart as upon an anvil.
>
> They come shaking in triumph their long, green hair:
>   They come out of the sea and run shouting by the shore.
> My heart, have you no wisdom thus to despair?
>   My love, my love, my love, why have you left me alone?

81. Mystery of the Wax Museum

easily representative, what with masks, whet with faces, of all sections and cross sections.

—Finnegans Wake

With some it's clowns or spiders, with Joyce it was thunder and dogs, but with me it's automatonophobia—an irrational fear of anything that falsely represents a sentient being. This includes, but is by no means limited to, ventriloquists' dummies, clothes shop mannequins, scarecrows and—particularly—waxworks.

If you ever somehow managed to persuade me to visit Madame Tussaud's I would not have a good time, and you'd notice it. Everybody would notice it.

This is not an affectation, not an attempt to make me appear complex or interesting, but a deep-rooted and abiding disquiet when confronted with almost any simulacrum of the human form, whether it's the Cybermen in *Dr. Who* (far more terrifying than the Daleks) or street mimes masquerading as statues (although actual statues are not a problem for me). I recall being scared witless as a child by the final episode in Robert Hamer's supernatural portmanteau film *Dead of Night*, and if you've ever seen *that* you'll probably share my fear.

The waxwork exhibition mentioned in *Ulysses* ('prop. A. James at 30 Henry street') is the fictional precursor to Dublin's real-life National Wax Museum Plus, which opened in 2008 at the tail end of the Irish economic boom. I've never visited the place, of course, but have explored it online, with mixed feelings, navigating representations of the Irish pop duo Jedward, actor Colin Farrell, Tolkien's Gollum and, inexplicably, Spongebob Squarepants.

In the Great Irish Writers room ('a salute to the literary legacy of our nation's greatest writers [. . .] forever immortalised in wax and ready to greet you at the entrance of the museum') can be found the blokeish cohort of Joyce, Beckett ('one of our favourite wax figures, the detail and likeness is second to none'), Wilde, Yeats, Sean O'Casey and George Bernard Shaw. They stand together or sit apart, stoically enduring the momentary attention of shrieking teens on their cultural odyssey from Jedward to Spongebob.

The Beckett figure really is second to none and, automatonophobia notwithstanding, I'd happily commission a duplicate to have one around the house, a permanent, taciturn, low-maintenance trophy guest. The Joyce figure sits alone, cross-legged, a book balanced in the crook of his knee, wearing a bow tie and a dark buttoned-up two-piece suit. He has a stiff and lifeless appearance, although this is to be sure a defining—*almost* reassuring—feature of all waxworks. I tend to picture the real Joyce as lounging, draped over an armchair or chaise lounge, his body supple, boneless even; this ramrod figure seems simultaneously concussed and tense, braced for a sudden, shocking and involuntary movement which would have me screaming the house down.

The original museum in Parnell Square was quite an austere affair with no sign of Spongebob but plenty of political figures to marvel at, including the latest Taoiseach incumbent. When its owner sold the building in 2005 the contents went into store but the warehouse premises were subject to regular break-ins, vandalism and theft. In 2007 dozens of figures including Hannibal Lecter, Fred Flintstone, the Teletubbies and Gollum were abducted, along with guitars used by 'The Edge' of U2. Clothes were also taken and figures of Stalin, Hitler, Churchill, De Gaulle and Roosevelt were stripped. Replica uniforms from the Easter Rising and the Second World War were also stolen. The new owner Kay Murray lapsed into unconscious wit when she reportedly said:

> They're really worth nothing to the person who has them, they're of no material worth.

The cultural theorist Walter Benjamin, who saw modernity as 'the ephemeral incarnate', was fascinated by a particular wax effigy at the Musée Grévin in Paris, that of a female figure adjusting her garter. Benjamin must have directed his male gaze at her much as Bloom directed his at Gerty MacDowell on the beach at Sandymount Strand. Of the Grévin waxwork, Susan Buck-Morss says:

> Her ephemeral act is frozen in time. She is unchanged, defying organic decay.*

---

* *The Dialects of Seeing: Walter Benjamin and the Arcades Project* by Susan Buck-Morss (MIT Press, 1989)

Ulysses is the literary equivalent of that frozen wax figure—the accumulating inconsequentiality of Mr Bloom's ephemeral thoughts and acts and feelings are permanently preserved, suspended in the aspic of atemporality. The long-gone city on the Liffey is likewise captured in time, now and forever.

Joyce himself visited Madame Tussaud's in London in 1931, with Nora's sister Kathleen. She said to him, 'I want to see you here.' He replied, 'You never will.'

82. Record Book of Guinnesses

An Irish queer, quipped Brendan Behan, is someone who prefers women to beer. As a thirsty young heterosexual in Dublin, Joyce briefly favoured sack (sherry fortified with brandy) before committing to porter, and as he got older he learned a lot about other types of booze. In Trieste he drank absinthe, whiskey and the local prune liquor, sligovic; late in life while staying in Saint-Gérand-le-Puy he would drink *l'eau de vie de sorbet* 'a caustic and potent solution no longer consumed by anyone except peasants and animals.'* He knew a lot about alcohol and he knew what he liked, stating that white wine was like electricity while 'red wine looks and tastes like a liquified beefsteak.' His favourite tipple was, most observers agree, a Swiss white wine called Fendant de Sion, the taste of which he compared to the urine of a noblewoman.

In April 2004 the Sion-based Provins Valais—possibly unaware of the aristocratic piss association—launched its red and white *Cuvée James Joyce*, 'a fruity white wine grown from the Chasselas grapes'. The makers sought legal advice, were assured there was no breach of copyright in using the author's name and had already exported 18,000 bottles to Ireland when Stephen Joyce, on behalf of the Estate, secured an injunction to block further sales. Provins Valais promptly submitted a counter plea for damages. Stephen Joyce was, as we know, a litigious and unpredictable character and his action in this case was arbitrary and perverse. Perhaps he mistakenly thought that Fendant de Sion was the wrong wine, because his grandfather also drank Neuchâtel wine (another Swiss white) in his final years.

In the *Dubliners* story 'Grace' (1914) Joyce came up with 'peloothered' as a word for intoxication. He was throughout his life a heavy drinker, often peloothering to the point of collapse and being carried home by friends (one one occasion pushed in a wheelbarrow). Was he an alcoholic? His biographers tend either to gloss over the binge drinking, or treat his 'Bacchic indulgence'† with forbearance and even admiration, offering the mitigation of genius

---

*This and other details come from 'Joyce's Drinking' by Austin Briggs. *James Joyce Quarterly* Vol. 48, No. 4 (Summer 2011). Perhaps the last word on the subject, and quite troubling.

†The phrase used by John McCourt in *The Years of Bloom: James Joyce in Trieste, 1904–1920* (University of Wisconsin Press, 2000).

by way of explanation and even justification. Joyce himself told Jung he was a man 'inclined to extravagance and alcoholism,' and Nora was regularly dismayed by his frequent binges. The catastrophic impact of his drinking on their children, rarely touched on, is self-evident: Giorgio became an unhappy drunk in later life and Lucia's complex health problems were exacerbated by her early addiction to champagne and the barbiturate Veronal.

One apparently long-established link between Joyce and booze actually dates back only forty years to Bloomsday 1982 when, to mark the centenary of Joyce's birth, the *Irish Times* carried a full-page Guinness advertisement which included this claim:

> When it came to writing slogans James Joyce proved himself no slouch.
>
> He suggested replacing 'Guinness is Good for You' with 'Guinness –The Free, The Flow, the Frothy Freshener!'

Really? We'll come back to this in a moment. As one of the many thousands of visitors to Dublin that June I drank two or three pints of Guinness in the course of Bloomsday evening. Perhaps four, or five even. It was a Wednesday as I recall, and the following day, feeling rather shaky, I went to an exhibition at the Guinness brewery in St. James's Gate. I still have the programme somewhere. It was called, I remember, 'Wine of the country,' a phrase that appears in the 'Cyclops' episode of *Ulysses*, the one in which Bloom encounters the one-eyed bigot nationalist in Barney Kiernan's pub.

> — Give it a name, citizen, says Joe.
>
> — Wine of the country, says he.
>
> — What's yours? says Joe.
>
> — Ditto MacAnaspey, says I . . .
>
> — Three pints, Terry, says Joe.

Oddly enough the earliest use of the phrase 'what's yours?' as an invitation to have a drink was at one time attributed in the *Oxford English Dictionary* to none other than W.H. Auden, which proves that the original compilers hadn't read *Ulysses*. (See essay 78 'And words. They are not in my dictionary'.)

That Guinness advertisement snagged the attention of Joyce scholar Catherine Gubernatis Dannen, who researched the company archives and found that there was no evidence whatsoever to prove that Joyce came up with his own slogan for Guinness stout, and that the story dated back to no earlier than 1982, when the company jumped on the centenary bandwagon. The advertising campaign was designed to improve the company's relations with the Irish public at a time of stagnant sales. Dannen adds:

> This marketing strategy furthered Guinness's profitable connections between itself and the 'Joyce Industry,' helped to restore the company's image, and created a new relationship between Joyce and commodity culture, which continues to thrive today.*

In the popular imagination Joyce's work and legacy are closely associated with alcohol (as the annual Bloomsday piss-up confirms), and the Guinness campaign from forty years ago seems to be largely responsible for that.

But as a matter of fact Joyce *did* use the phrase 'frothy freshener' in *Finnegans Wake*. It first appeared in the separately-published 'Haveth Childers Everywhere' episode, issued in pamphlet form in 1930. In it the Chapelizod publican Humphrey Chimpden Earwicker declares his love for his wife Anna Livia Plurabelle by rehearsing his achievements as a brewer:

> I brewed for my alpine plurabelle, wigwarming wench, (speakeasy!) my granvilled brandold Dublin lindub, the free, the froh, the frothy freshener, puss, puss, pussyfoot, to split the spleen of her maw.

In an intervention worthy of Hans Walter Gabler the Guinness people replaced Joyce's euphonious 'froh' (German for 'jolly') with 'flow' and dropped the artful way Dublin is mirrored in 'lindub'. (The Irish phrase for stout or porter is 'leann dubh' (literally 'black ale'), so Guinness and the city in which it is brewed share a common etymology, as 'Dublin' comes from the Irish 'dubh linn' or 'black pool'.) Joyce echoes the phrase later in the *Wake* ('the flay the flegm, the floedy fleshener') but there's no evidence to support any claim that

James Joyce Quarterly volume 48, no. 4 (Summer 2011).

he seriously proposed it to the company as an alternative to their established slogan 'Guinness is Good for You'. This appears three times in the *Wake* as 'Ghinees hies good fir yew' 'Guinness's, may I remind, were just agulp for you' and 'We have highest gratifications in announcing to pewtewr publikumst of pratician pratyusers, genghis is ghoon for you.'

The 'good for you' slogan remained in use until tighter advertising regulations forced its withdrawal. For a while it was replaced by the faintly Joycean strapline 'Guinnless isn't good for you' next to a picture of an empty glass.

When it comes to writers and booze I'm always reminded of the poet, critic and all-round man of letters Ian Hamilton. He used to hold court in a pub in Greek Street, Soho called The Pillars of Hercules, next door to the offices of *The New Review*, the monthly literary magazine which he edited. In the Pillars one lunchtime in the 1970s he invited the young poet Hugo Williams to have a second drink, no doubt in lieu of a fee, and when Williams replied that he didn't like alcohol because it tasted awful and made him feel sick, Hamilton replied wearily, as if stating a self-evident truth: 'Well none of us *likes* it.'

83. 'NEVER AGAIN BE CONTENT WITH HEMP'

Interviewed following the publication of his book *The 100 Best Novels in English* (Galileo Publishing, 2015), the journalist Robert McCrum said:

> I was reading this year's Booker Prize shortlist and every one of those feels like a footnote. They're just so trivial—each doing one thing that Joyce is probably doing a hundred times more brilliantly and in more different ways on any given page of *Ulysses*.*

That's the Booker for you, Bob. But your jaded observation prompted some thoughts that led to this essay, an attempt to answer the unanswerable questions: Why do we read, and how?

What, to take a step back from the issue, do we even mean by *literacy*?

We mean reading and writing of course, two distinct competences that go together like Guinness and oysters. But these two competences are also, in way that's either taken for granted or overlooked, opposites. This is because writing is a *productive* skill and reading a *receptive* skill.

Writing involves the ability to assemble letters into words and to organise words into sentences and sentences into texts. When we write we are usually in charge of whatever text is produced.

Reading on the other hand involves the ability to see and understand a text, whether produced by ourselves or by others. When we read we are not usually in charge of whatever text we are working with (unless, say, you're a writer editing your own work).

Writing is to a text what speaking is to speech (without getting into the Saussurean distinction between *langue* and *paroles*), so speaking and writing as productive skills go together more naturally, and in some ways more logically, than reading and writing do.

Reading is to a text what listening is to speech, so reading and listening as receptive skills go together more naturally, and in some ways more logically, than writing and speaking do.

The two productive language skills, then, are writing and speaking. The two receptive language skills are reading and listening. These

*https://fivebooks.com/best-books/best-novels-robert-mccrum

four skills are, in different combinations, the only language skills at our disposal. They're all we've got. (To be sure there are other means of communicating meaning and feeling, such as dance and mime and sign language and Morse code and so on, but what concerns me here is spoken and written language.)

Some of us have well-developed reading skills in terms of speed, accuracy, comprehension and retention, while others struggle with reading at a very basic level. Literacy, of course, is not all about literature, and illiteracy isn't just the inability to read and enjoy the works of James Joyce. A person who cannot read the destination on the front of a tram or the instructions that come with a prescription is placed at a serious disadvantage. Somebody who gives up *Ulysses* after a few pages is not placed at such a disadvantage and, come to that, joins a large and nurturing community of fellow non-readers.

We all of us give up on books for one reason or another—boredom, frustration, irritation, having something better to do—and, while it may not be for the right reason, it's usually a good reason. The reader who abandons *Ulysses* or any other book really has nothing at all to be ashamed of, but the reader who arrogantly insists that their failure to complete the novel is the author's fault is like the American visitor to Paris who complains that the menus are in French.

In an online article (which I'll be looking at again in essay 89), the American critic Stephen Marche argues that there has been a fracture in our literary culture and, to underline the point, offers for our consideration and comparison two poems, one of matchless banality by the Instagram poet Rupi Kaur (born 1992), the other a poem that opens Seamus Heaney's ninth collection *Seeing Things* (1991). Taken out of context the comparison may seem ridiculous, but Marche's aim is to show that we are currently going through a shift in literary sensibility and that the written word is in retreat, that the fight is on for meaning and that the political struggle over the use of language is ultimately about the capacity to make meaning itself. It's a high stakes game.

Rupi Kaur has four million followers on Instagram and a Wikipedia entry 1,000 words longer than that of Louis MacNeice. That doesn't make her a better poet than MacNeice or Heaney. Come to that it doesn't make her a poet at all, and if that makes me sound snobbish I'd counter that there are only a handful of things worth being snobbish about, and one of them is poetry. Marche's choice of the two poems is to illustrate the current transition in fiction between what he calls 'writers of the voice' (such as Joyce) and 'writers of the pose' (such as Sally Rooney).

This brings us back to productive and receptive skills. If you agree with me that Rupi Kaur is an absolutely negligible poet (which certainly doesn't make her a bad person) while Seamus Heaney is among the greats, it's likely that, for whatever reason, your receptive skills are, like mine, more aligned with the productive writing skills of Heaney than of Kaur. It certainly doesn't make us better or worse as people than a Kaur admirer, merely different. Readers who admire and enjoy Rupi Kaur may in time develop an appreciation of other poets, including Heaney, but Marche's point is that it's impossible to imagine a reader with tastes broad enough to respect and admire equally the work of both a Heaney and a Kaur. It's the difference between a dry martini and a Slush Puppy, and while there are no doubt some people who will insist that they enjoy drinking both, I pity and despise them.

My tastes, and my way of expressing them, are entirely a product of my particular generation, race, nationality, class, upbringing, education and privilege. My tastes are also, like everybody else's, personal, subjective, fallible, hard-won and largely non-negotiable. (Essay 50 explores some of the reasons for me turning out the way I am.) My reading skills, and choice of texts I tend to read for pleasure, likewise reflect the factors that formed me, and are an expression of the self I aim to be. I should add that this doesn't mean I read only within the narrow parameters suggested by all those factors. I like to be challenged, irritated and given beneficial shocks by the writers I encounter.

A rising generation of readers (comfortably outnumbered by non-readers) will soon replace the likes of me, of us. Should I try and keep up by attempting to engage equally with Heaney *and* Kaur, or has the former spoiled me when it comes to the latter? It's my knowledge of the works of Heaney and the other poets I admire (most of whom, I should point out, are not men) that informs any thoughts or feelings I have about Kaur, so the terms of engagement are lop-sided from the outset.

When it comes to reading contemporary fiction, Joyce likewise informs (or distorts) my tastes, standards and expectations. I'm like the hangman played by Miles Malleson in the great Ealing Studios comedy *Kind Hearts and Coronets* who, on learning that he is expected to execute a member of the aristocracy, states wistfully 'After using the silken rope . . . never again be content with hemp.'

84. BURGES/BORGESS

After the memorial service for the Poet Laureate John Betjeman in November 1984, a nervous Philip Larkin approached the critic Cyril Connolly and blurted out 'Sir—you *formed* me.' Larkin was referring to the wartime literary journal *Horizon* which Connolly had edited for its complete run of 120 monthly issues between 1939 and 1950.

I met Anthony Burgess twice, very briefly, and on both occasions wanted to stammer the same heartfelt admission but fortunately didn't, and that was because I was, on both occasions, rendered speechless by his formidable literary reputation and the baroque elaboration of his combover.

Polymath essayist, critic, cultural pundit, linguist, screenwriter, journalist, chat show stalwart, eloquent champion of Joyce and other modernist authors, composer (which he always insisted was his true vocation) and much else besides, Burgess (1917–1993) was the last great public intellectual of his generation and, one might gloomily add, the last great public intellectual full stop, at least in Britain. He loomed like an irascible schoolmaster over my impressionable late adolescence, both as a prolific author and, more generally, a powerful and respected cultural arbiter. I gobbled up his novels in the local library and sought out *The Observer* newspaper every Sunday to read his wonderfully peppery reviews; I'd make a point of reading books which featured Burgess's encomia on their covers (there seemed to be literally *hundreds* of these) and I looked out watchfully for his regular appearances on the telly—usually smoking a cheroot, sporting that astonishing combover (which seemed to begin at the hip) and always talking, talking, *talking*. He was a polyglot citizen of the world, erudite and authoritative, and seemed to me quite fantastically *cool*. This, I thought, is how an intellectual talks. Hair aside, I wanted to be like him, and talk like that.

Is he popular with younger readers these days? I hope so, but *Clockwork Orange* aside (which he dismissed as a *jeux d'esprit*), I suspect not. He's too clever, too wide-ranging and impersonal, too bombastically erudite, too much the cocksure village explainer—even meeting him half way can be an effort. His later books would have benefitted from tougher editing; they became increasingly baggy and he was prone to repeating himself, although this was hardly surprising given his prodigious output. The notorious Roger Lewis biography in 2002 both nailed and skewered him and I wondered at the time whether Burgess's reputation would ever fully recover. Lewis developed such a bilious loathing for his former literary hero that the book amounted to little more than a 500-page hatchet-job, describing Burgess as lubricious, sentimental, callous, superficial, crapulous, arcane, laborious, sanctimonious and 'essentially a fake'—and that was just in the Prologue. Perhaps he should have stuck to the books and ignored the messy life.

This hatchet-job was also, alas, an absolutely compelling page-turner, not for what it told me about Burgess (and I remain an admirer), but for what it revealed about his biographer, whose hatred for his quondam literary hero, a man he'd spent twenty years of his life researching, was clearly pathological and without limit. Lewis's level of invective at times attained a kind of epiphanic serenity. According to the reviewer Jonathan Bate in the *Telegraph*, the book was 'infuriatingly repetitive, vain and self-regarding, clever and opinionated, bloated and chaotic, quirkily learned and possibly fraudulent'. Very like Burgess, in fact.

Burgess has already featured in this book because he was for many years Joyce's representative on earth, his most eloquent, loyal and visible champion and attentive gatekeeper, offering new readers a way into the work with two essential guides. These were *Here Comes Everybody: An Introduction to James Joyce for the Ordinary Reader* (1965, published the same year in the US as *Re Joyce*) and *Joysprick: An Introduction to the Language of James Joyce* (1973) the title of which, he helpfully explained, was 'a fusion of Joycesprach, joystick, the prick that brings joy and the prick of conscience or agenbite of inwit'. He also found the time to compose *Blooms of Dublin*, a musical play commissioned by BBC Radio to celebrate the Dublin Joyce Centenary in 1982.

That was the year Burgess met his near-namesake, the Argentinian writer Jorge Luis Borges (1899–1986), in Davy Byrne's 'moral pub' at 21 Duke Street, Dublin 2, the place where Bloom has his lunch of a gorgonzola cheese sandwich and glass of burgundy. Rumour has it that the two men chatted together in Anglo-Saxon, which I think must be baloney.

I happened to be in Dublin at the time and even made it to Davy Byrne's at one point, missing this titanic literary encounter by a matter of hours. I missed a lot of things in the course of three days in Dublin, and I suppose this is a good a point as any to say something about Irish pubs, or rather (a very different proposition) Irish *theme* pubs.

In London there used to be a bar called Finnegan's Wake on Essex Road in Islington, part of a chain run by Scottish and Newcastle plc which was, according to one online reviewer, 'a poor relation of the genre'. I passed it hundreds of times over the years and never once felt an urge to go in. Not just because of that bloody apostrophe—a glimpse through the open door into the gloomy interior confirmed that the place had been assembled from a flat pack, then conscientiously cluttered up with generically 'Oirish' knick-knacks, quite possibly sourced from a warehouse in Korea. And I recall another kitsch Irish bar behind the Kremlin in Moscow, and a long afternoon in the 1990s spent sinking the most expensive pints I've ever swallowed, followed by oily vodka chasers. There was a huge television with the sound off showing (I seem to remember) Canadian ice hockey.

I get the impression that the Irish theme pub's heyday is behind us, that the 'craic' is not what it once was, although there still are— or until recently were—other Finnegan's Wake pubs (some with and some without that feckin' apostrophe) in Ealing and Edinburgh and points in between. There's a Finnegans Wake pub (without the apostrophe) in Paris and others in New York and at Delray Beach, Florida; in Rockville, Maryland; Columbus, Ohio; Walpole, Massachusetts; Springfield, Missouri; Alexandria, Los Angeles and so on, and on. In Honolulu there's an annual *Finnegans Wake* pub crawl, although as there's no pub of that name participants have to stagger between O'Toole's, Murphy's, Ferguson's and JJ Dolan's before weaving unsteadily back to O'Toole's and—in the spirit of the *Wake*—starting all over again.

There's an Irish pub in Athens called The James Joyce which opened its doors in 2007, and this one can stand for all the others. On their website they claim, unconvincingly, that it's 'a different type of Irish pub' blending 'the best of the old with the best of the new'.

> Our décor of dark wood, long bar and warm comfortable environ-
> ment evoke [*sic*] images of the great old pubs of Ireland whereas

our style of operating—our music, food and beverages—connects more so with the contemporary pubs and bars of modern Ireland.

At The James Joyce it's a place where there are no strangers, only friends you haven't met.

That last sentence, usually attributed to Yeats, conjures up a perfect nightmare of rowdy conviviality. I've never much liked the boozy take on Joyce that characterises at times the film version of *Finnegans Wake*—the tipsy chortling, the 'shoutmost shoviality' and all that. I recall my ideal Irish pub, chanced upon in the mid-1980s in Carrick-on-Shannon. It was the front room of a small terraced house in the high street which doubled as a shop selling wellington boots. A plank bar, a barrel of stout and a few bottles of whiskey, tin trays on two metal garden tables with assorted stools. A taciturn middle-aged landlady, a wireless burbling in the background. A place to drink alone, sullenly, with no risk of social intercourse. Perfect.

While we're on a pub crawl there's an online curiosity that I commend to your attention, and which brings us back, yet again, to Anthony Burgess. It's a short film made for US educational television and first broadcast as a segment in the television series Camera Three in 1973, while Burgess was a visiting professor at City College New York.*

The studio set is a mock-up Dublin bar. We hear a rumble of thunder and Burgess enters, hanging up his bone-dry raincoat to reveal a sweat-soaked grey jacket. He takes out a copy of the *Wake* from his briefcase, helps himself to a bottle of stout from behind the bar (nobody else being present) and pours it inexpertly before settling down to deliver what seems to be an extempore monologue which closely resembles his own introduction to *A Shorter Finnegans Wake*.

Burgess clearly had a hand in the script, although the credited writer is Stephan Chodarov and the director John Musilli. His monologue is interrupted by a haphazard rendering of 'The Ballad of Persse O'Reilly' and a visit to the Gents. The programme ends with the sound of a lavatory flushing as Burgess makes his way back out into the wet streets.

---

*Do watch this online—it's full of marvellous detail, such as the clock behind the bar which remains throughout at 11:32, which has a particular *Wake* significance.

85. A Bash in the Tunnel

John Ryan (1925–1992), organiser of the first Bloomsday celebration (see essay 53) attended, like Joyce, Clongowes Wood College. He later became a leading figure in mid-century Dublin as an artist, broadcaster, actor, stage designer, publisher, critic, editor, writer and—not least—publican, owner of a celebrated Dublin bar called The Bailey. He was a great bunch of lads.

Two books by Ryan, both strongly recommended, are *Remembering How We Stood* (1975) and (as editor) *A Bash in the Tunnel: James Joyce and the Irish* (1970). The former is a gossipy memoir of Bohemian Dublin in the 1950s, a time when Ryan seemed to know everyone, and everyone else as well. Here's a sample:

> A man I knew was taking a stroll down Grafton Street one day when he happened to overhear part of a discussion which three citizens were having outside Mitchell's café. The gist of their dialogue was that they were deploring the absence from the Dublin scene of any real 'characters'. They appeared to be genuinely aggrieved. They were, in fact, Myles na gCopaleen, Sean O'Sullivan and Brendan Behan.

A Bash in the Tunnel is an anthology of Irish writers which includes eight pieces originally written to mark the tenth anniversary of Joyce's death that first appeared in *The Envoy*, a literary magazine Ryan had once edited. Contributors included Samuel Beckett, Stanislaus Joyce, Patrick Kavanagh, Edna O'Brien, Aidan Higgins, Benedict Kiely and Brian O'Nolan (aka Brian Ó Nualláin, Brian Nolan, Myles na gCopaleen and, of course, Flann O'Brien). It's O'Brien's brilliant piece that gave the collection its title.

Drinking alone in The Bailey one night, O'Brien is approached by a complete stranger who 'was surprised to see a man like me drinking in a pub.' The stranger tells him that he has in his possession a 'secret key' that gives him access to the Irish State railway company's well-stocked dining cars which, shunted onto remote sidings when out of service at the weekend, are his chosen destination for a solitary all-night drinking session—or 'bash'—in one of the lavatories. What happens when the car he occupies is shunted into a tunnel and all sense of day and night is lost becomes a brilliant fable for the lot of the Irish artist:

Sitting fully dressed, innerly locked in the toilet of a locked coach where he has no right to be, resentfully drinking somebody else's whiskey, being whisked hither and thither by anonymous shunters, keeping fastidiously all the while on the outer face of his door the simple word ENGAGED!

This is an image, says O'Brien, that best fits Joyce 'particularly in his manifestation of a most Irish characteristic the transgressor's resentment with the nongressor.'

Still with Flann O'Brien, Joyce fans will know about *The Dalkey Archive*. Not to be confused with the American independent publisher of the same name, it's the title of O'Brien's fifth and final novel, published in 1964 and set mostly in the small seaside town of Dalkey south of Dublin, now a gentrified bolthole for the wealthy but back then a sleepy suburban backwater.

Much of what goes on in *The Dalkey Archive* will be familiar to admirers of O'Brien's *The Third Policeman*, which was written earlier but published later, as the author thriftily (or desperately) recycled some of the content, not least the riffs on molecular theory and the humanity of bicycles, delivered by the mad scientist De Selby. The main characters, Hackett and Mick, meet De Selby and, through him, Saint Augustine and the elderly James Joyce, employed as a curate (i.e. barman) in a local pub and emphatically denying authorship of the filthy books that wrongly bear his name. It's one of the funniest comic novels ever written, and among the first to feature Joyce as a fictional character (but see essay 56 'His Art Belongs to Dada').

86. VAN BLANC

For 45 years Ged Walsh ran a South Dublin painting and decorating company and his white Fiat van was a familiar sight around the city. It was adorned not only with his name and occupation and contact details but with lines from his favourite writers. Phrases included 'Kingstown Pier a disappointed bridge' (Stephen Dedalus's classroom quip) and 'K.M.R.I.A.' (standing for 'Kiss My Royal Irish Arse', an abbreviation taken from the 'Aeolus' episode in *Ulysses*) and Molly's 'yes I said yes I will Yes.' There was also line from Horace, unconnected with Joyce as far as I know: *et quovis lingo non fit Mercuriam* ('the god Mercury is not to be fashioned from just any piece of wood', which might be better suited to a carpenter) and the cod Latin saying *Illegitimi non carborundum* ('Don't let the bastards grind you down').

He always wanted to be a writer. After obtaining a diploma in local history from NUI Maynooth he collaborated with his publisher and illustrator Michael O'Brien to produce *On the Banks of the Dodder, An Illustrated History of Rathgar and Churchtown* (2019, O'Brien Press). The Dodder is a river that meanders through South Dublin and one illustration in Walsh's book shows 41, Brighton Square, the birthplace of James Joyce, with the author's ghost visible on the garden path.

Interviewed at the time of publication he had this to say about our man:

> James Joyce had the great capacity to write on the kitchen table while his wife worked, and the two children played around him. Alas, I didn't have that kind of concentration, nor would most people. What I needed when I started writing was peace and quiet, with perhaps a little music. So eventually I built myself a shed at the end of the garden which was to be my quiet space. When I shelved it, much to my wife's relief, I could then have all my reference books to hand. Previously they were piled up all over the house.[*]

---

[*]Taken from an interview on the Bank of Ireland website: https://www.thinkbusiness.ie/articles/how-to-write-a-book-while-running-a-company/ (14th November 2019)

A shed in the garden beats a pram in the hall. I've occasionally wondered what kind of novel Joyce would have written if his circumstances had been stabler—funds, a less chaotic domestic set-up, no kids or brother sharing two sordid rooms, the drink and so on. Could it conceivably have been even better?

87. INFORMATION SUPERHIGHWAY

Googlism.com was created as a fun tool to see what Google "thinks" of certain topics and people. Of course, the results are not really Google's opinion, they're yours, the website owners of the world. Within the Google results are thousands of your thoughts and opinions about thousands of different topics, people, names, things and places, we simply search Google and let you know what website owners think about the name or topic you suggested.

That's self-explanatory, I suppose. What you get when you punch in 'James Joyce' is a thematic babble, pulsing with chaotic life and unreason. Here's some of what came up the last time I looked, and the order it came up in, unedited:

> james joyce is fuckin' my sister
> james joyce is possibly one of ireland's most famous writers
> james joyce is that he was
> james joyce is the fullest and most readable biography
> james joyce is born to mary and john stanislaus joyce in rathgar
> james joyce is known the world over for stream of consciousness
> james joyce is reading
> james joyce is a genius in his
> james joyce is featured reading selections from his ulysses
> james joyce is the author
> james joyce is known for
> james joyce is your cup of tea
> james joyce is a typical irishman
> james joyce is also a place where college students like to meet
> james joyce is a return to the land of politics
> james joyce is one of the most revered writers of the 20th century
> james joyce is a pub with snugs
> james joyce is the most diverse
> james joyce is a genius in his own right
> james joyce is that he had renewed literature
> james joyce is remembered for his development of such literary forms as stream
> james joyce is regarded as one of the greatest literary talents of the 20th century
> james joyce is one of a series of teacher aides

james joyce is one of the key innovators of modernism
james joyce is widely regarded as one of the most distinguished writers in the english language
james joyce is the one exception
james joyce is a return journey to the land of politics
james joyce is your home from home in prague
james joyce is the new man on campus at regis university
james joyce is forever linked with that of dublin
james joyce is considered among
james joyce is one of the greatest literary masters of the 20th century
james joyce is fucking my sister i'm bitter
james joyce is that he was born in dublin
james joyce is able to combine
james joyce is overrated and exhausting to read
james joyce is like and it will open the door to other joyce classics
james joyce is considered by many as the father of modernism
james joyce is a twentieth century literary giant
james joyce is ййн van de grootste dichters en romanschrijvers die ierland heeft voortgebracht
james joyce is 15 percent better than ernest hemingway
james joyce is clearly one of these
james joyce is other people trying to write like james joyce
james joyce is a smallish pub offering standard pub fare
james joyce is one of the world's greatest authors of all time
james joyce is my favorite author
james joyce is primarily known for two of his novels
james joyce is an authentic irish pub
james joyce is arguably the most important writer in the english language in this century
james joyce is indeed a black irishman
james joyce is regarded as one of the important figures of modern literature
james joyce is well represented in the collection
james joyce is now esconced
james joyce is te vinden in het the dublin writers museum
james joyce is the absolute hero of this play
james joyce is celebrated on the 16th june each year on what is known as bloomsday

james joyce is a pitcher for paradise pisces
james joyce is discussed on streets broad and narrow
james joyce is probably one of the most famous writers to come from dublin
james joyce is best experienced read aloud rather than silently
james joyce is one of the best known novelist
james joyce is well served
james joyce is that it should send readers back to both joyce and o
james joyce is a chilling plunge into the pool of sorrow
james joyce is the author of these zero titles
james joyce is sponsoring a contest to name the pub side of the new establishment
james joyce is now known as one of the greatest writers of the twentieth century
james joyce is most renowned for having written ulysses
james joyce is "thankful for the privilege of being licensed to serve communion
james joyce is acceptable for publication in the united states
james joyce is the living proof of it
james joyce is second only to shakespeare in terms of
james joyce is most likely the best known irish writer
james joyce is te dublin geboren

And so on.

88. Fast Eddy Makes a Point

A blogger calling himself Fast Eddy can stand for that sullen multitude of readers who have never made any headway with the greatest novel in the English language and feel entitled to blame their failure to do so on the author. Here's what he wrote a few years ago:

> I have a master's degree from one of the best universities in the US. I have devoured literature all my life. I am a successful published author myself. Yet, I find *Ulysses* to be unreadable gibberish. After a few pages, my eyes glaze over. What is it about? Where is the plot? Where is the dramatic arc? Why does Joyce get to make up his own language?
>
> Why is *Ulysses* a classic and the very similar Finnegan's Wake [*sic*] a bust? They are both nonsense. It's time to put this charade into the dustbin of literature and focus on books that actually make sense.

He's perfectly entitled to his opinion, of course, and I'm equally entitled to deride it. Given his manifest accomplishments it's no surprise that Fast Eddy should insist that his failure to read *Ulysses* is entirely the author's fault. But it isn't. It's entirely Fast Eddy's fault and nobody else's, and if it's plot he's after he should stick to James Patterson. Nuts to Fast Eddy, I say. And double nuts to the anonymous *Guardian* hack who wrote (*Pass Notes*, 13th Oct 2021):

> No one—literally and literarily—has finished *Ulysses*. Unsurprisingly, James Joyce's notoriously difficult stream of consciousness novel featured in the top five abandoned classics in a handy infographic produced by Goodreads a while back.[*]

It really gets my goat when an otherwise intelligent and educated journalist with a degree of influence goes for an easy laugh with such a cretinous populist take. It's much worse when otherwise reputable critics take the same line:

> OK, I never read *Ulysses* from beginning to end, but then again, neither, I believe, has anybody else, including most of the writers and scholars who declared it the greatest English-language book of the century in that Modern Library list last year. I have read the first one hundred pages at least three times, and then, longing for a story, I never got further.

---

[*]The others? *Catch-22*, *Lord of the Rings*, *Moby-Dick* and, er . . . *Atlas Shrugged*.

'Longing for a story' my aunt Fanny. This is one Richard Bernstein, a former book critic for *The New York Times*, responding to an invitation from Jodi Kantor of the website Culturebox to name the novels he hasn't read. It's a version of the parlour game 'Humiliation', the one thing everyone recalls from David Lodge's campus novel *Changing Places* (1975), in which academics confess to their literary blind spots. It's peculiar that Bernstein admits to reading the first hundred pages before giving up, because that would have taken him as far as Mr Bloom's breakfast, at which point no reader worth their salt would dream of throwing in the towel.

Of course he may be pulling our legs—but what makes me spit feathers is his appalling arrogance in freighting the rest of us with his own personal shortcomings. He can't hack *Ulysses* so he smugly supposes that nobody else can either. Bernstein should leave such witless disparagement to the likes of Gary Butler, one of many unhappy readers giving *Ulysses* a one-star review on the Goodreads website:

> 86th book read in 2017.
>
> Number 650 out of 650 on my all time book list.
>
> Worst book I have ever read; only redeeming quality is there was a cat.*

Mkngrnao!

---

*https://www.goodreads.com/review/show/2197521630

89. CEREBRAL TENTACLES

Joyce is often described by his many non-admirers as a complicated writer and then dismissed by them as a *difficult* one. It sometimes seems to me that we've reached a point in our cultural history at which his accomplishment as a novelist counts for less, and perhaps for nothing. Here's the Spanish writer and physicist Agustín Fernández Mallo (born in 1967) interviewed in the online journal musicandliterature.org (23rd September 2021):

> Writers with a complicated prose style don't interest me, because they put themselves above the reader, they want to show they're more intelligent than them, and that to me seems like an abuse, a hangover, even, from patriarchal modes: "I've got the key to decipher this text, this hieroglyph, and I'll give it to you when I please."

If Mallo prefers to read authors who are less intelligent than him that's his choice, of course. Although he doesn't name any names, let's leap pre-emptively to the defence of our man Joyce as his likely target, because there's a lot more to the prose of *Ulysses* than 'a hangover from patriarchal modes.'

Elsewhere in the interview Mallo makes a distinction between 'complex' and 'complicated' prose. The former is good, he says, whereas the latter is bad, so perhaps he isn't thinking of Joyce at all because the multiple prose styles of *Ulysses* are generally straightforward, occasionally difficult and (in the conscientiously monotonous 'Eumaeus' episode) deliberately boring, but never complicated, in Mallo's disparaging sense. (The prose of *Finnegans Wake* is another matter.) And despite what he thinks, there's nothing inherently wrong with complicated writing, or complicated music or complicated painting or complicated performance. As an old friend of mine, the art historian David Brown, used to say: 'Art is complicated because *life* is complicated' and by that he clearly wasn't insisting that *all* art has to be complicated to have any claim on our attention, because simplicity and clarity are also great virtues. What he meant was that there must always be a place for art that engages with and speaks to the complications that we all encounter in life, and art that does so will be correspondingly complicated.

Writers such as Joyce do indeed set their readers a challenge but not, as Mallo thinks, in order to perpetuate an abusive patriarchal hegemony. As Eimear McBride said in a *Guardian* interview (6th June 2014):

> Difficulty is subjective: the demands a writer makes on a reader can be perceived as a compliment, and Joyce certainly compliments his readers in what he asks of them.

Difficulty is the main reason readers give for avoiding Joyce, but there are others. When the best-selling Irish author Marian Keyes was in London to promote her latest novel *Grown Ups* she told an audience:

> I only read women. I know that men write books. But their lives are so limited. It's such a small and narrow experience. Their literature just really can't match anything written by a woman. I just think 'fuck off'.*

Well with the greatest respect Marian Keyes can fuck off too, leaving the rest of us to make do with Tolstoy and Dostoyevsky and Proust and Dickens and Chekhov and D.H. Lawrence and Flaubert and Balzac and Thomas Mann and Kafka and Nabokov and V.S. Naipaul and Henry Fielding and Saul Bellow and Borges and Ben Okri and Henry James and Swift and Orwell and James Baldwin and Beckett and Joyce. Despite what Keyes sees as their limited lives they've all managed to keep afloat without her patronising approval, and if she wants to know how small and narrow experience can be she might try reading one of her own novels.

A few months later the Australian novelist Jessie Tu said in a *Guardian* interview (1st July 2020) that she, too, was giving up some male fiction writers, although she was more specific, and entirely reasonable:

> I probably will never read another fiction book by a straight white male author and I'm happy for you to publish that, even if that pisses people off.

Her absolutely legitimate point, in danger of being overlooked by the people she wanted to piss off, was that the writers she plans to avoid simply don't need any extra readers, and that her cultural

---

* *Daily Mail* online 7th February 2020.

allegiances lie elsewhere. I'm all for under-represented writers getting a platform, whatever their race, gender and sexuality, but I also can't help feeling any writer, whatever their race or gender or sexuality, who decides never to read novels by men (or women, come to that) would be self-sabotaging. Literature is about experiencing life through the eyes of others—the eyes of the author for starters, or the eyes of a Jewish Dubliner, a damaged Irish girl, a Somalian immigrant or (as we shall see) a sex-addicted Taiwanese violinist.

Jessie Tu was the author of a much discussed and widely derided piece about Sally Rooney in *The Sydney Morning Herald* (21st August 2021) which included a lengthy and ferocious attack on the Irish author's second novel:

> *Normal People* should be called *White People* because, in Rooney's world, people like me don't exist. In the book, Asians are mentioned only as tourists who choke the pathways of museums in Italy. 'I don't know why we're bothering with Venice—it's just full of Asians taking pictures of everything,' one of the male characters whines.

The fact that these words are spoken by a male character already established by the author as an obnoxious racist and therefore delivered *in character* does not seem to occur to her. Readers of Rooney's novel are not expected to approve of his comments, and certainly not to assume that the author shares or endorses them. How to challenge such a literal and retrogressive approach to fiction? I'm reminded of the American journalist who criticised Arthur Conan Doyle for allowing Holmes to denigrate two other fictional detectives, Dupin and Lecoq. The author responded with some waspish doggerel:

> But is it not on the verge of inanity
> To put down to me my creation's crude vanity?
> He, the created, would scoff and would sneer,
> Where I, the creator, would bow and revere.
> So please grip this fact with your cerebral tentacle:
> The doll and its maker are never identical.

Tu undermines her case by asserting that Rooney is the universally acclaimed darling of white middle-class readers the world over ('the mainstream adoration is impenetrable'), overlooking the fact that she is a divisive writer whose books have met with a mixed critical reception. For Tu the doll and its maker *are* identical, and she finds *Normal People* objectionable because it's about 'two white, able-bodied, beautiful straight people mulling about how hard it is to be white, able-bodied and straight,' which is not so very wide of the mark as a summary, but not persuasive grounds for singling out Rooney for censure because mainstream popular culture everywhere is dominated by beautiful able-bodied straight people, from South American soaps to Bollywood musicals, from the Paris catwalks to K-pop, Taiwanese movies to African graphic novels (although in this latter category I was pleased to discover that *Karmzah: The Unleashing* by Farida Bedwei features a super hero with cerebral palsy). I am not defending this universal shortcoming in culture, merely reporting it.

Tu, say her publishers, is 'a young writer with a fierce, intelligent and fearless new voice' and they describe her debut novel thus:

> *A Lonely Girl is a Dangerous Thing* is is about the awkwardness and pain of being human in an increasingly dislocated world—and how, in spite of all this, we still try to become the person we want to be.

With a title referencing Eimear McBride's 2016 debut *A Girl Is a Half-formed Thing*, Tu's novel 'explores female desire and the consequences of wanting too much and never getting it'. It's about a musician, a former child prodigy (Tu is a musician and former child prodigy) with Asian heritage (Tu's parents are Taiwanese and the family migrated to Australia when she was a child), who is addicted to sex (and I recall how justifiably irritated McBride was by crass presumptions about the link between her life and what happens to her character, an abused and damaged young woman with a violent sexual history involving self-harm and elective abjection).

'Write what you know,' writers are always being told, and isn't that what both Sally Rooney and Jessie Tu seem to be doing? It's not, you'll note, 'Write what you *are*', although for most of us there's not much difference between what we know and what we are. Writers, though, earn their place in the world by creating and inhabiting the lives of others. If Rooney wrote a novel featuring a queer disabled Taiwanese musician it would be condemned, and rightly, as an unforgivable act of cultural appropriation. And what if Jessie Tu wrote a novel about a bunch of straight white Irish girls navigating their relationships? I feel she might reasonably be cut some slack. The cards are not, to be sure, stacked against an accomplished, confident and well-connected young graduate of Trinity College Dublin as they are against many other writers.[*]

Alice, the leading character in Rooney's novel is, like her creator, a tremendously successful and wealthy young author. She is also a depressive, driven by an almost disabling social anxiety and a fierce sense of contempt for everything around her. Despite being an admirer of Rooney's first two novels, I wanted to bail out almost at once on reading her third because, with a handful of exceptions, I can't be doing with novels in which the main character is a novelist, and especially a successful one. That's a deep-seated prejudice and one I'm reluctant to abandon.

By the time you read this it's likely that we'll all have forgotten about the day back in October 2021 when Sally Rooney announced that she would not allow the Israeli publishers Modan to translate and distribute her third novel *Beautiful World Where Are You*. The company had handled her previous two books without any intervention by the author and there were predictable responses on all sides. The worst take, because it was simply untrue, was that Rooney was boycotting an entire language and people, although she had made it clear in her statement that she would welcome a Hebrew translation if it could be made in accordance with guidelines issued by the Boycott, Divestment and Sanctions movement (BDS), the Palestinian-led, anti-violence grass roots campaign calling for an economic and cultural boycott of Israel. Her decision was, she said, 'about Israeli companies and institutions in response to the apartheid system and other grave human rights violations.' She was labelled a hypocrite for not withdrawing her books from other markets where human rights are cause for concern and condemned as ignorant, attention-seeking, 'woke' and anti-Semitic. Her more aggressive detractors had clearly

---

[*]Tu's debut novel did not go unnoticed: Shortlisted Multicultural NSW Award, NSW Premier's Literary Awards 2021 AU; Longlisted Stella Prize 2021 AU; Shortlisted Matt Richell New Writer of the Year, ABIA Awards 2021 AU; Winner Literary Fiction Book of the Year, ABIA Awards 2021 AU; Longlisted Best Debut, Indie Book Awards 2021 AU; Shortlisted Readings New Australian Fiction Prize 2020 AU.

not bothered to read her statement although some, to their credit, apologised after taking the trouble to do so.

Some responses were more nuanced. Gitit Levy-Paz, a fellow at the Jewish People Policy Institute writing for the Jewish news platform *Forward*, criticised the author's decision, saying:

> The very essence of literature, its power to bring a sense of coherence and order to the world, is negated by Rooney's choice to exclude a group of readers because of their national identity.*

Is that really the essence of literature? While some novels do no doubt bring a sense of coherence and order to the world I struggle to come up with examples. Fiction explores conflict, catastrophe, loss, fear, hope, disappointment, sadness, illness and death; it navigates disrupted and damaged lives, and—so-called 'uplift' fictions aside—seldom offers readers mere consolation. Such bromides are best left to journalists and the clergy. Literature has always been as much a source of division as of consensus, as past and present critical reaction to *Ulysses* confirms. While there's always room for peace and love and sunlight and happy endings if that's your kind of thing, that's emphatically not, I'd argue, the essence of literature. 'Happiness writes white' said de Montherlant. It doesn't show up on the page.

Levy-Paz appears to be unaware that contemporary literature no longer generates many shared points of reference between genders, ages, classes, races and all the other communities that make up what we refer to as society. Literature is no longer much of a driver for social cohesion or consensus, but then of course it never was, which is what today counts against a lot of the canon, most of which fails to function intersectionally. Today the fragments shored against our ruin are simply part of the ruin; the fragments are themselves fragmented, and if anything underlines the inadequacy of literary fiction as a source of coherence and order it's the looming prospect of mass extinction brought about by climate change and the pandemic.

Following Rooney's announcement the American critic Stephen Marche tweeted patronisingly that 'Rooney finds her pose on Israel'.†

---

* 'Why won't Sally Rooney allow her latest novel to be translated into Hebrew?' By Gitit Levy-Paz, forward.com, 11th October 2021.
† @StephenMarche 8:42 PM Oct 11, 2021. He subsequently tweeted that in the author's case there was no difference between a 'pose' and a 'position' and questioned

In saying this he was quoting his own online essay (one that I have already cited in essay 61, 'Never again be content with hemp'). This was among the more thoughtful and intelligent critical takes on the author's popularity, in which Marche argued that Rooney represents the emerging division between what he calls 'writers of the voice' and 'writers of the pose'.* In the latter category he places Rooney alongside Ben Lerner and Ottessa Moshfegh. We have, he claims, reached a point at which 'the literature of the voice is dying. The literature of the pose has arrived. The basis of literary style has shifted.'

He compares Lerner (born in 1979), Moshfegh (1981) and Rooney (1991) with some of the writers he first encountered as an undergraduate in the 1990s—Toni Morrison, Martin Amis and Cormac McCarthy—each of whom had a distinctive and, to the initiated, immediately recognisable voice (or style, if you prefer). He observes—rather than complains—that the cited writers of the later generation lack this, and that while there are many contemporary authors with strong, distinctive voices, the kind of writing that most defines our time is 'the writing of the pose'. This, he says, is 'the literary product of the MFA [Master of Fine Arts] system and of Instagram in equal measure'. This makes contemporary writing part of 'the curation of the self which dominates advanced capitalist culture today'.

There certainly is an uninspiring homogeneity of style that emerges from creative writing courses, and yes, a lot of contemporary writing is self-centred. The 'curation of the self' is partly to do with social media, the commodification of the individual through Twitter and Instagram and so on, and partly to do with the triumph of the visual over the textual for a generation of writers that grew up with their noses glued to a screen. The distinction Marche makes between 'voice' and 'pose' can also be seen as the difference between writing for the page and writing for the screen.

According to Marche, what a generation of 'voice' writers had in common was a shared vision of literature, an understanding of their social function as authors and a perspective of moral certainty. In this category he bundles together Margaret Atwood, Raymond

---

the author's integrity by pointing out that 'She was the best competitive debater in Europe' and therefore, presumably, adept at adopting any pose, or position.
*'Winning the Game You Didn't Even Want to Play: On Sally Rooney and the Literature of the Pose' by Stephen Marche, lithub.com, 15th September 2021.

Carver, Joan Didion, Toni Morrison, Michael Ondaatje and Philip Roth. The same can of course be said for earlier generations of writers, and earlier literary movements, but comparing these writers with 'pose' writers—Rooney, Moshfegh and Lerner—he certainly has a point.

This love of voice is (or was) the love of the voices of *others*—women's voices, queer voices, minority voices, voices in translation. These and other voices became more culturally audible at that time, and this remains one of the period's enduring legacies. But the Atwood generation lacked what Marche calls the 'humanity-embracing openness' that is to be found in, say, *Ulysses*. Joyce and his fellow modernists were also writers of the voice, so if we are at a time of transition in literature, a shift in expectations and allegiances, are they in danger of being neglected by a new generation of readers inclined towards 'pose' writing as exemplified by Rooney?[*]

It's not simply a generational difference, and Marche points out that Zadie Smith (an exemplary 'voice' writer) and Sheila Hett (ditto for 'pose') are only a year apart in age. Nor is it a case of Boomers versus Millennials; the first group of writers Marche cites are in any case not Boomers (i.e. those born between 1946 and 1964) but members of the so-called 'Silent Generation' born between 1928 and 1944.[†] They had a range of voices at their disposal, that Silent Generation, and another word for voices is 'perspectives'. Until quite recently an author could include unpleasant characters and have them say unpleasant things from unpleasant perspectives and not be condemned by readers who lack the skill or imagination to separate the writer from their creation. In 'pose' writing there seems to be little room for differing or conflicting perspectives, and especially those perspectives which challenge the reader's sense of what is right.

Rooney is certainly a good writer, but hardly a great one, at least not yet. As a response to the way things are now her unhappiness and anger are completely genuine and understandable, and I think that is what makes her novels both necessary and interesting. I'm

---

[*]'I would like to write something as good as James Joyce's *Ulysses*, for sure, but I don't think I want to have written *Ulysses* itself, no.'—Sally Rooney in 'Books that made me' (*The Guardian*, 17th April 2020).

[†]Toni Morrison (born 1931), Philip Roth (1933), Joan Didion (1943), Raymond Carver (1938), Margaret Atwood (1939) and Michael Ondaatje (1943).

delighted that she so easily triggers right-wing commentators such as Christopher Hart who, writing in the *Daily Mail* (12th October 2021), deplored her Marxist beliefs and the fact that 'despite her wealth, she retains a strongly progressive political conscience' (which gives you an insight into his values, not hers) before gallantly describing her as ugly, verbose, pompous, a braggart, hypocritical, money-grabbing and an apologist for genocide. He is, as it happens, himself a Faber novelist and literary editor of the *Erotic Review*.

Given this bonfire of inanities, will there be any place in the future for the subtle, sophisticated and stratospherically accomplished work of Joyce? At low moments I feel that there will not. It's often been said that, in writing *Ulysses,* Joyce set out to create a new type of reader, namely the type of reader who can read *Ulysses,* a view that echoes Coleridge's much-cited opinion that a genius creates the taste by which they are judged. The same, alas, seems to apply to idiots.

90. DE MINIMIS NON SHABBY
CURATE LEX

'When I find myself in the company of scientists, I feel like a shabby curate who has strayed by mistake into a room full of dukes.'

That's W.H. Auden in *The Dyer's Hand* (1962), and I know how he feels because I'm the shabbiest of curates next to the many distinguished Joyceans past, present and future, to whom I owe a great debt. I'm thinking in particular of the writer, critic, blogger, broadcaster and Joycean *non pareil* Frank Delaney (1942–2017), whose continuing legacy is the online phenomenon that goes by the title 'Re: Joyce'.

This series of 368 five-minute podcasts, running without interruption for seven years from 2010 until its maker's death, is a fascinating and richly rewarding sequence of commentaries and reflections on particular aspects of *Ulysses*, an inexhaustible seam conscientiously and enthusiastically mined. I've listened to all of them and there are no duds.

Delaney was a model of eloquence and erudition, but we live in a world in which eloquence is held in low esteem and erudition suspect. Gormless loquacity is more highly prized, because it sounds more sincere, more artless, more *felt*. Eloquence seems too slick, too predetermined, in a culture that privileges rowdy candour. Erudition suggests expertise and we don't trust no experts, no sir.

But we desperately need broadcasters and commentators like Delaney, offering listeners reason, wisdom, clarity, insight and good judgement. If you've never signed up for Re: Joyce you really should. This, from the website:

RE:JOYCE PASSES 2 MILLION DOWNLOADS

re:joyce stats so far:

Over 2 Million Downloads
300+ Episodes
100 Hours of material
8,688 Downloads per week
1,300 Downloads per day
10+ years Estimated time the project will run
0 Kardashians in sight

A Kardashian-free zone is by now all but inconceivable, and the two million downloads have long since been exceeded. The enormous popularity of Delaney's blog offers a clobbering riposte to critics such as Jonathan Bernstein (see essay 88) who choose to doubt that anyone has ever managed to finish reading *Ulysses*. And Delaney gave it all away for free. How's this, for the last word on *Finnegans Wake* (which of course is also the first word):

> *Finnegans Wake* is not a novel . . . No! No! *Finnegans Wake* is a poem, it's a symphony by a modern atonal composer. It's an assembly of language tying together floating evanescent ideas. It's a long rapid eye movement dream, it's a marathon technicolored musing that might have been induced by mescaline or LSD or some other mind-bending substance . . . It's a massive rap, as in rapper, as in street talk, as in lingo, as in the heat of the day and the cool of the night captured dreamily and melodiously in words of all shapes and sizes. It's a mirage.

What a great guy!

91. TWO UNANSWERED QUESTIONS

Here are two unanswered questions about *Finnegans Wake* posted on the Goodreads website:

> What is the deal with the bible [*sic*] and this book. I have read that it helps if you already have read the bible to read this book. However I don't really want to, so does that help or not?

It's a good question. It used to be that a thorough knowledge of the Holy Bible—the King James Version of course—was a common currency that many Anglophone readers and writers shared. Knowing both Old and New Testaments comes in handy when looking at Renaissance art, say, or solving cryptic crossword puzzles. Joyce, schooled by the Jesuits, had just such a knowledge, which was no big deal at the time but in our secular era Bible references tend to be seen as obscure, arcane, even meaningless. Not that the Bible or any other book holds a single key to the *Wake*. That's the point, or part of it.

The second question on the Goodreads site is not in English, but I include it for the sake of completeness.

بار هر شد باعث که لذتی از ممنونم عزیز، جویس ای که بگم باید
تنها سیخ. موهام و بشه پر چشام میاد فینگاهنها بیداری اسم
رو.... تنهایی و کرد. هضم راحت خیلی میشه فینگان با رو نبودن
دالغارا.......؟ باباابا ؟ خداگونه......لذتی

I ran this through a translation engine and came up with:

> I must say that of Joyce dear, thank you for the joy that was filling up my eyes and my hair was Fyngahnha every waking name skewers. Finnegan was very comfortable not only with his digestion. And godly joy . . . alone . . .?

This didn't get me far so I shared the original Persian on social media. Not a sausage. Anyone?

92. ADVENTURES IN THE SKIN TRADE

'I don't go anywhere without a book by James Joyce called Finnegan's [*sic*] Wake' says Johnny Depp on the website brainyquote.com and the same rule applies, obviously, to his collection of tattoos. The actor has many inkings, including one on his left forearm which reads 'Silence Exile Cunning'.

You won't need reminding that the phrase is taken, more or less, from Stephen's speech to his friend Cranly towards the end of *A Portrait of the Artist as a Young Man*:

> I will try to express myself in some mode of life or art as freely as I can and as wholly as I can, using for my defence the only arms I allow myself to use—silence, exile, and cunning.

Depp's choice of an elaborate gothic font was no doubt the result of prolonged reflection and his tattooist, presumably following his clear instructions, dropped the original conjunction, removed the punctuation and added the capital letters—and why not? What interests me are the reasons behind the actor's decision to mangle this particular Joyce line, and we'll come to that in a moment.

Leafing through Eva Talmadge and Justin Taylor's *The Word Made Flesh: Literary tattoos from bookworms worldwide* (Harper Perennial, 2010) and then looking at the associated online archive, I have to admit I couldn't find many literary tattoos I liked, and there were some I couldn't even bear to look at. In the interests of balance I wanted an opposing view so I asked a good friend, who is my contemporary but, unlike me, has plenty of inkings. He's a writer in his late fifties and, along with no end of blazing skulls and broken hearts and beatnik heraldry, has 'Voyaging through strange seas of thought alone' from *The Prelude* emblazoned on his chest because (he says) it's his favourite line in English poetry and because he 'thought it was funny to have Wordsworth tattooed on oneself'.

When I asked him why he didn't quote the full line from *The Prelude* ('*A mind* voyaging . . . etc.') he replied, reasonably enough, that it wouldn't fit. Then I asked him about tattoos in general, and literary ones in particular, and he said: 'People I know see it as a continuous point of reference and don't give two hoots about being thoughtful or cultured. It's often because they want a tattoo but want to show they have a certain degree of awareness of the process.'

A casual census suggests that literary tattooing is largely confined to youngish American fans of cultish American authors (especially Vonnegut, Bukowski and Kerouac), though it's becoming more popular in Britain.

A quick online search will yield dozens of Joyce inkings on necks, wrists, forearms, shoulders and sternums, ranging from portraits of the author (some of which defy description) to scraps of text: 'shut your eyes and see', 'he lived and loved and laughed and left', 'heaventree of stars' and 'yes I said yes I will yes' (usually omitting the uppercase final affirmative as it appears in the novel). Derek Pyle of the *Waywards and Meansigns* project has had part of the *Wake*'s first thunderword ('Bababadalgharagh . . .' etc.) neatly tattooed on his forearm. It makes me wonder which phrase or sentence of Joyce's I would, if so inclined, choose to have inscribed on myself. Do I really like anything I've read, even by my favourite author, *that* much?

In the case of Johnny Depp, silence and exile are surely self-sabotaging strategies for a Hollywood leading man, although I expect cunning always comes in handy. Depp's other tattoos mostly commemorate people or events in his life: 'Lily-Rose' (his daughter's name) over his heart, 'Betty Sue' (his mother's name) on his left bicep and a sparrow flying over water with the word 'Jack' on his right forearm, a reference to his film character Jack Sparrow in *Pirates of the Caribbean*. But what prompted the choice of that particular Joyce quote?

Faye Dunaway, who co-starred with a young Johnny Depp and an old Marlon Brando in the 1995 rom-com *Don Juan DeMarco*, says in her autobiography *Looking for Gatsby* (published in the same year) that she had adopted 'Silence, exile, cunning' as a motto from the dramatist Bill Alfred (1922–1999), whose play *Hogan's Goat* provided Dunaway with her breakout role on Broadway in 1966. She says she passed the phrase on to Depp when they worked together on the 1995 movie—'we both live by it. It's meant to be the credo of an actor.'

Faye, by the way, was born in Bascom, Florida on 14th January 1941—*the day after James Joyce died*. If that doesn't strike you as worth knowing then *Multiple Joyce* really isn't the book for you.

93. Paolo Coelho is a Tw*t

> Everything that happens once can never happen again. But everything that happens twice will surely happen a third time.
>
> —Paolo Coelho, *The Alchemist* (1986).

Oh, Paolo, Paolo, *Paolo*. Think about what you said, what you wrote, just for a moment.

Paolo—before anything can happen *twice* it has to happen *once*, don't you see? I mean, things can't happen twice *once*, can they? They can only happen once, and then once again, which would make it twice. But if, as you insist, things that happen once 'can never happen again' how can anything ever, *ever* happen *twice*? Things only happen twice if they've already happened once. And there's no evidence to support your claim that simply *because* things happen twice they are necessarily bound to happen a third time. You might just as well argue that something that happens twice might then happen again, but only once. Which would be both once *and* a third time.

Paolo—you're a clot. You are also, I've decided after careful deliberation and despite a huge amount of competition, the living author I dislike the most. Am I jealous? *Of course* I'm jealous. If I could earn a fraction of your millions by churning out such silly piffle as *The Alchemist* I'd be laughing all the way to one of my many Swiss banks. I have a particular loathing for you because of something you once said to a reporter from the Brazilian newspaper *Folha de S.Paulo* (8th April 2012), reported in *The Guardian* on 6th August that year:

> One of the books that caused great harm was James Joyce's *Ulysses*, which is pure style. There is nothing there. Stripped down, *Ulysses* is a twit.

Perhaps you were misreported, Paolo. Perhaps you said 'tweet' not 'twit', but what do I know? Come to that what do *you* know? If Joyce is the Usain Bolt of literature then you're the damp towel on the locker room floor, and I say this as one damp towel to another. When it comes to Joyce we're all damp towels on the locker room floor. (But some of us are looking at the ceiling.)

Paolo, Paolo, *Paolo*. Nobody serious takes you seriously and I expect deep down you know that, and it rattles you because you clearly like to think you're very serious indeed. ('I'm modern because I make the difficult seem easy, and so I can communicate with the whole world' you say with disarming immodesty in that *Guardian* article). But you're not modern, you make the difficult facile and you don't communicate with the whole world, just your credulous readers. You're not a serious writer, you're merely immensely *popular*, which is not even the same thing as successful. Your popularity is, I freely acknowledge, on a scale that's utterly breathtaking; *The Alchemist* has been translated into more than 60 languages and has sold more than 83 million copies, holding the Guinness World Record for most translated book by any living author. I don't know why I'm telling you this as I'm sure you know it already, and it must put the snap in your celery when you wake up each morning in your jewel-encrusted boudoir, but I really can't muster the energy to tell you what a depressingly tacky and stupid book *The Alchemist* is, what a nasty mash-up of Ayn Rand and Kahil Gibran. Unlike *Ulysses,* the novel you choose so arrogantly to disparage, it's shallow, smug, infantile, pious and silly.

What's it about, *The Alchemist*?

Briefly: a young shepherd named Santiago (and you've lost me already, Paolo) travels from Spain to the Egyptian desert in search of a treasure buried—where else?—in the Pyramids, of course. But I really can't be bothered to summarise this witless farrago and will simply cut and paste the following from Wikipedia:

> No one knows what the treasure is, or if Santiago will be able to surmount the obstacles along the way. But what starts out as a journey to find worldly goods turns into a discovery of the treasure found within.

Ah! This thing that he seeks, this thing for which he is looking . . . *was in fact inside him all along*, a bathetic reveal neatly skewered by Squidward Tentacles in *Spongebob Squarepants—the Movie*. Perhaps you know it Paolo? A smart and unpretentious piece of work. I've seen it once, and then again, and then several more times.

94. HARRY POTTER AND THE ANXIETY OF INFLUENCE

'Phantom Ovaries' is a pseudonym (I sincerely hope) of the person behind the online fan fiction *Harrypottyses*, which attempts to answer the question: 'What would happen if James Joyce wrote a Harry Potter book?' He or she or they provides or provide an answer:

> Stately, pubescent, Harry Potter came down the revolving stairhead, bearing a miniature pensieve on which a wand and an enchanting charm lay crosssed [*sic*]. He held aloft the pensieve and intoned:
>
> —Specialis Revelio!

I had to look up 'pensieve', a coinage defined by the author J.K. Rowling as 'a wide and shallow dish made of metal or stone, often elaborately decorated or inlaid with precious stones, and carrying powerful and complex enchantments'. It can tap the unconscious mind to recreate memories that the owner or 'a second party' can enter and move around within. Rowling herself further elaborates:

> The name 'Pensieve' is a homonym of 'pensive', meaning deeply, seriously thoughtful; but it is also a pun, the 'sieve' part of the word alluding to the object's function of sorting meanings from a mass of thoughts or memories.

After sounding the mansplain klaxon, I 'd like to digress for a moment to consider Rowling's use of the word 'homonym'.

Homonyms are words that sound the same and are spelled the same but have different and *unrelated* meanings. 'Bear' for example, can be a verb meaning to carry or support or tolerate or withstand, or it can be a noun, meaning a bear. (Homonyms should not be confused with something similar called polysemy, which describes a word or phrase with more than one meaning. An example of which is 'book', a word with different but *related* meanings that have a shared origin, so that when you *book* a room, you're asking to have your name written down in a register, or *book*. Another example, courtesy of the poet Amy McCauley, is the sinister ambiguity of 'He gave her dog biscuits.')

Homophones, on the other hand, are words that sound the same, but *aren't* spelled the same, and have different derivations and meanings, such as 'there', 'their' and 'they're', or 'to', 'too' and 'two' or, indeed, 'pensive' and 'pensieve'. I'm not sure that I'd pronounce them the same; wouldn't the former have stress on the first syllable, the latter on the second, as in 'conceive' and 'deceive'?

I don't want to pick a fight with an author who flogs more books in a day than the rest of us do in a writing career, but these are murky linguistic waters. The Merriam-Webster website confusingly insists that homonyms can be either homophones or homographs, or both. But homographs (and the clue is in the 'graphs') refers only to written language.

A heteronym (also known as a heterophone) is a word that has the same spelling but a different pronunciation and meaning from another. Examples: record (the noun) and record (the verb). In other words a heteronym is a homograph that isn't a homophone. We could go on, but I'll simply end by observing that *Finnegans Wake* is densely populated with homonyms, polysemes, homophones, homographs and the rest, which is part of the appeal, or not, depending on taste.

'Phantom Ovaries' clearly knows his or her or their Joyce, or at least the first page of *Ulysses*, but I don't know my Harry Potter and I expect that puts me at a disadvantage. What surprises me is how few Joycean fan fictions there appear to be. A representative example is a feminist repurposing of the *Dubliners* story 'Araby' by Grace Lapointe, written when she was 19. This can be found on AO3 (Archive of Our Own), 'an open-source archive for not-for-profit fan fiction of various genres and fandoms.'

Harold Bloom coined the phrase 'the Anxiety of Influence' to describe the dilemma of poets daunted by the achievements of their precursors, those who got there first and did it better. This applies equally to novelists; Joyce can be an absolutely overwhelming influence on a writer, and not necessarily in a good way, because if the greatest novel that will ever be written has already been written, there's not much left to do. This may, however, be more of a guy thing. As Anne Enright said in a 2008 interview with the *Boston Globe*:

> It's male writers who have a problem with Joyce; they're all 'in the long shadow of Joyce, and who can step into his shoes?' I don't want any shoes, thank you very much.

She goes on to share, not too seriously, her 'very strong theory' that Joyce was actually a woman, citing as evidence that 'he wrote endlessly introspective and domestic things, which is the accusation made about women writers.' I think she's right about male writers; it took Eimear McBride to single-handedly kick-start the stalled modernist project with *A Girl Is a Half-formed Thing* in 2016, confidently co-opting Joyce into her literary back-story. No anxiety of influence there.

The poet Chris McCabe also nimbly sidestepped any authorial anxiety in *Dedalus*, his sequel to *Ulysses* (see essay 77, 'First among sequels'), and then there's John Maxwell O'Brien, whose *Aloysius the Great* (2020) is 'a seriocomic tale of an alcoholic professor who becomes resident director of an American study abroad program in England during the 1960s and finds himself on a runaway roller coaster of rebellious students, drugs, sex, liquor, and academic politics.' I haven't read O'Brien's novel, which sounds to me to owe more to J.P. Donleavy's *The Ginger Man*, but according to the author it's 'a treasure trove for admirers of James Joyce' so may be worth a punt.

Another literary response to Joyce unhampered by the author's looming presence is a novel by Jacob Appel (born 1973), an astonishingly prolific American author who, in addition to having no fewer than seven Master's degrees, is also a bioethicist, physician, lawyer and social critic, and a distinguished writer on reproductive ethics, organ donation, neuroethics and euthanasia. *The Biology of Luck* (2013), his re-telling of *Ulysses*, won the Beverly Hills Book Award the year following its publication.

The main character is a New York tourist guide called Larry Bloom who has written a book about a footloose young woman (Starshine Hart) whom he plans to take out for dinner on June 16th. The novel juxtaposes episodes from Bloom's guided tour of the city with extracts from the novel he is writing about Starshine. I've read it, and enjoyed it very much—the author has plenty of talent and energy and can be very funny but—and you must have been braced for a 'but'— no matter how good it is (and *The Biology of Luck* is *very* good) it isn't as good as *Ulysses*.

95. OUR CASTAWAY THIS WEEK . . .

The long-running BBC Radio 4 programme *Desert Island Discs* was first broadcast in 1942, hosted by the show's affable creator Roy Plomley. It has a durably simple and, no doubt for copyright reasons, unvarying format: each week a guest noted for their achievement and eminence in some field is invited to chat about their life and work and, faced with the prospect of being marooned alone indefinitely on a desert island, to select eight pieces of music, a book ('apart from the Bible, Shakespeare and big encyclopaedias') and a luxury item to keep their spirits up. That's it.

Of the 3,000 or so castaways to date the following have chosen to share their solitude with *Ulysses*: the artist Peter Blake, Edna O'Brien, the Nobel Prize-winning chemist Professor Baruch Blumberg, Seamus Heaney, David Lodge, Jimmy McGovern, Ian McEwan, the composer Peter Maxwell-Davies and the poet Derek Walcott.

The journalist Joan Bakewell shrewdly opted for—and was granted—Joyce's Collected Works. The playwright Jack Rosenthal, the fondly remembered telly zookeeper Johnny Morris and (of course) Anthony Burgess all chose *Finnegans Wake*.

It's odd that nobody apart from Joan Bakewell appears to have worked the system to their advantage when it comes to Joyce. I'd follow her lead, I think.

96. THE RAMONES OF THE DAY

If you'll gimmy your thing to me I will gamey a sing to thee.

—*Finnegans Wake*

I'm listening to a record (a proper one, made of vinyl and spin-ning on a record deck) called *Caged/Uncaged—A Rock/Experimental Homage to John Cage*. Produced by John Cale of The Velvet Under-ground, it was recorded in Italy in 1993 and features such hip lumi-naries as David Byrne, Arto Lindsay, John Zorn, Debbie Harry and Lou Reed. There's one track in particular that will snag the interest of any Joycean.

In 1942 the amateur soprano Justine Fairbank commissioned Cage (1912–1992) to compose a short piece adapted from the text of *Finnegans Wake* and the result, a two-minute work called 'The Won-derful Widow of Eighteen Springs', was premiered in May that year. Here's the Library of Congress description of the piece:

> This essentially rhythmic speech set against a patterned percussive accompaniment cannot be considered a song in the usual sense. Cage, however, is such an innovator that one often loses sight of the fact that if one does not expect conventional sounds, his music is often very well constructed.

Certainly not 'a song in the usual sense'. Cage's instructions 'for the singer' state: 'sing without vibrato, as in folk-singing. Make any transposition necessary in order to employ a low and comfortable range.'

The late Joey Ramone (1951–2001) performs the piece on *Caged/Uncaged*, the score transposed from contralto to accom-modate his baritone. He's accompanied by Don Yallach and Joe McGinty of the The Psychedelic Furs on percussion and MIDI drum pad programming, which is not quite what Cage envisaged; his score stipulated that while the singer must be accompanied by a pianist, the lid of the piano should be lowered throughout, the pianist tap-ping on the instrument's wooden casing with fingers or knuckles. But let's not quibble—it's terrific.

I've listened to it again and again. It's lovely, and now rather poignant, not least because the last time I listened voluntarily to the Ramones was almost forty years ago. I saw them play live one night in the late 1970s, in a Manchester theatre, supported by Buzzcocks. The two bands played faster than any other band I've seen or heard before or since and the audience went wild, then wilder. I loved the Ramones, and their beanpole lead singer in particular, and recall fondly his reply to the question 'Are the Ramones really brothers?' 'Yeah,' he drawled, 'but we're not each udders' brudders.'

Other composers inspired by the *Wake* include Jean Eardman, whose *The Coach with the Six Insides* (1962) was based on the character of Anna Livia Plurabelle, as was André Hodeir's jazz cantata of 1966. The American composer Samuel Barber's orchestral piece *Fadograph of a Yestern Scene* (1972) took its title from a line in the novel, and the Japanese composer Toru Takemitsu used the *Wake*'s first word for his composition *riverrun* (1984). He also took the title of his piano concerto *Far calls. Coming, far!* from the last page of the novel, and the title of his string quartet *A Way a Lone* (1981) from the very last words on that page.

You might be surprised to learn that Elvis Costello features in the *Cambridge Companion to Ulysses* (Cambridge University Press, 2014) on the strength of the lyrics of 'Battered Old Bird', a cryptic ballad from his 1986 album *Blood and Chocolate* in which Costello refers to 'the Macintosh Man' who appears at Dignam's funeral and 'burgundy, breakfast, a typewriter.'

But these are a bare handful of examples. For a massive catalogue of Joyce-related music you'll need to consult the Waywards and Meansigns website* which includes a comprehensive biographical chronology, ranging from 1850 to 2019, of all the musical works inspired by Joyce, or which inspired him. It's a huge work-in-progress compiled by Derek Pyle, Krzysztof Bartnicki, and Tess Brewer.

I've saved a favourite for the end. In 1989 the singer Kate Bush sought permission from the Joyce Estate to set some of Molly Bloom's *Ulysses* soliloquy to music, permission the Estate flatly and predictably refused to grant. So she made up her own version and recorded that instead. 'The Sensual World', the title track and first single from the album of the same name was released in September 1989 and reached number 12 on the UK Single Chart. Then for some perverse reason the Joyce Estate changed its mind and decided to grant permission, so the track was re-recorded using only words

*waywardsandmeansigns.com

taken from Molly Bloom's soliloquy as originally planned. This recording, released in 2011 as 'Flower of the Mountain', is very much better than the earlier track but less well-known. In this version Molly steps out of the pages of *Ulysses* and into the real world, our world, rather like Dorothy Gale exchanging the monochrome dustbowl of Kansas for the saturated Technicolor of Munchkinland.

Kate Bush's later recording of the song features repeatedly in the Armenian-Canadian film director Atom Egoyan's psychological thriller *Felicia's Journey* (1999) and Egoyan was among the A-list directors signed up for the ambitious *Beckett on Film* project conceived by Michael Colgan, artistic director of Dublin's Gate Theatre. Nineteen films were produced by Colgan and Alan Moloney for the Irish broadcaster RTÉ, Britain's Channel 4 and the Irish Film Board. Egoyan's version of *Krapp's Last Tape* featured John Hurt (with a Beckett haircut) in a spellbinding performance, first broadcast on television in 2001 and worth seeking out. Hurt's most direct link to Joyce is the fact that he played the role of Tristan Tzara opposite Tom Bell's Joyce in the original production of Tom Stoppard's *Travesties* in 1974 (see essay 4 'How many poets are there?').

97. *ALLEZ, SALOPARD!*

> O little oily head, sloper's brow and prickled ears!
>
> —*Finnegans Wake*

Comics in the Writings of James Joyce (2011) is a modest 14-page black-and-white publication by the cartoonist D.J. Schiff, the point of which the author explains on his website:

> As I studied *Ulysses* and *Finnegans Wake*, I began to notice citations of cartoons in Don Gifford's *Ulysses Annotated* and Roland McHugh's *Annotations for Finnegans Wake*.
>
> However, most of the time, when a cartoon was mentioned, no credit was ever given to the cartoonist. As a cartoonist myself, I was aware that many times people have no idea who creates the characters they love so well. I set about to research and track down the cartoons that were mentioned in these reference books.

What a good idea! Thanks to Schiff we can learn more about early cartoonists such as Gabriele Galantara, Charles Henry Ross, Emile de Tessier (aka Marie Duval, and more on her in a moment), William Giles Baxter, William Fletcher Thomas, Harry Conway, Bruce Bairnsfather, Elzie Crisler Segar, Russ Westover, Austin Bowen Payne and Roland Cibborn. Few of these names mean anything to me, but one of their characters still has a slight purchase on the popular imagination.

Alexander 'Ally' Sloper (*right, with brolly*) was one of the earliest British comic strip characters, first appearing in print in 1867. He was also, and very significantly, the first-ever *recurring* character in comics until his demise half a century later in 1916. A grog-nosed, work-shy schemer in a battered top hat, Sloper's name is wonderfully suggestive; he 'slopes' along alleyways, a furtive flaneur evading his creditors like Wilkins Micawber. It occurs to me that Sloper's name might derive from the Anglicised version of the French profanity '*Allez salopard!*' (roughly 'Come on, you bastard!'). There was a 19th century London tradition of doing this, as in the dismissive phrase 'san fairy ann' derived from '*ca ne fait rien*' ('it doesn't matter').

Sloper first appeared in the British magazine *Judy*, originally drawn by the artist and writer Charles H. Ross but later fully illustrated by his French wife Emilie de Tessier under the nom-de-plume

'Ally' Sloper

'Marie Duval' (Female comic strip artists of the 19th century are rare indeed). Starting in 1844 Sloper had his own comic, *Ally Sloper's Half Holiday*, and the character would later star in three feature films and many shorts. He was also the basis for a huge range of merchandising, from pocket watches to door stops. Some claim he was the model for Chaplin's 'little tramp'.

In the 'Circe' episode of *Ulysses* there's a 'hobgoblin' with 'an Ally Sloper nose,' and he puts in a second appearance in *Finnegans Wake* as an interrogative: 'Have you got me Allysloper?' Other cartoon characters appearing in *Ulysses* and the *Wake*, according to Schiff, include Mutt and Jeff, The Thimble Theater, Tillie the Toiler, Iky Moses, Pip Squeak and Wilfred and Curly Wee, each of them briefly resurrected in Schiff's booklet and each inviting further investigation.

Just as Joyce populated his work with cartoon characters, graphic artists have adapted his work for the page and the screen.

Ulysses "Seen" is—or was—the rather ungainly title of an ambitious project based around a graphic novel by the artist Rob Berry that first appeared in 2012, published by Throwaway Horse in the United States. It began as a web-based platform and was later developed in collaboration with the James Joyce Centre in Dublin, where it served for some years as the online point of entry to the Centre's *Ulysses*-related programmes. The original plan, which excited considerable interest at the time, was to complete the project in time for the 2022 centenary, but the last time I looked only four of the 18 episodes of *Ulysses* could be found there and they have now been taken down; the website* no longer seems to exist.

The project was described by its makers as 'a gateway to comprehension, exploration, and explication of the great novel', which sounds like a Good Thing. They added that their aim was to 'leverage the functionality of tablet devices in delivering visual content in a way that makes the deeper forms of content readily accessible' which meant, I guess, 'improve the way things work' but I'd already switched off. On seeing the project in action, however, all became clear.

There were three levels or layers to the text and what we saw on the screen provided an organising principle for various kinds of content, all of which appeared 'behind' or 'beneath' each page of the comic

*ulyssesseen.com

book. The three layers were as follows: on the top level the comic book itself, below that a reader's guide with 'links to online information sources, photos, videos, and other assorted bric a brac' by 'resident scholar' Mike Barsanti and finally, beneath all that, a 'user comment section' where readers could share their thoughts. A fourth layer—which had yet to appear when last I looked—would consist of 'the full text of the novel with links to scholarly resources embedded in hypertexted links.'

This structure, it was claimed, did away with the 'disruption to narrative' caused by footnotes or endnotes while providing 'an intuitive indexing function' and a searchable concordance. Speaking as somebody who first encountered the novel as a novel (there were no alternatives in that far-off analogue age), and as somebody who actually *enjoys* the disruption to narrative offered by footnotes and endnotes and all the other apparatus, I have mixed feelings about this project, as I would about plans to stage Kurosawa's *Rashomon* on ice. Whether it's done well or badly is not the point—*why do it at all?*

The graphic novel that formed the top layer of *Ulysses "Seen"* looked to me more like a storyboard for a never-to-be-made film version. The problem is that in the novel characters do little more than move around Dublin talking and thinking and—well, that's pretty much it really. A handful of moments aside there's nothing much to engage a comic book artist (or reader), so in visual terms the top layer is not particularly appealing, given the fabulous visual richness of (on the one hand) the Marvel universe and (on the other) the virtuosity and structural originality of such indie-press graphic novelists as Chris Ware. It all looks a bit dull and uninviting.

The second-layer reader's guide, or at least what I saw of it, was chatty and erratically literate (at a very basic level of spelling and punctuation) and the 'bric a brac' was, alas, far more distracting than the footnotes it claimed to replace.

Comic book fans would feel short-changed; purists would find fault and I really couldn't imagine many readers ever getting to the hypothetical fourth level, and the text of the novel proper. I hope I'm wrong, but the best reaction I can muster is equivocal. Perhaps it's my continuing belief that the word 'book' (as Anthony Burgess once noted) is an acronym for 'Box of Organised Knowledge'. When

I need to clarify something in *Ulysses* or *Finnegans Wake* (and who doesn't?), or anything else in any other book, I'll look it up, or ask around.

Ulysses "Seen" offers similar options in a different medium, but the experience of a hypothetical reader (or 'user') will be a long way from that of the person who simply picks up a printed copy of the novel and gets cracking, and (this is, I think, important) that selfsame hypothetical reader will be in closer communion with previous generations of readers, and of course with the author himself.

The James Joyce Centre still has a page referring to the project, which states:

> If you've always wanted to read ULYSSES, but have been intimidated by its size and density, this is a great way in and is a great new way in its own right to experience literature.

This portal is now firmly shut, which at least offers you the quickest way of not reading the novel in the first place.

Less ambitious in scope but of far greater interest is the conventional graphic novel *Dotter of Her Father's Eyes* by Bryan and Mary M. Talbot, published by Vintage Books in 2012, and inspired by Carol Shloss's 2003 biography of Lucia Joyce. Mary M. Talbot is a scholar best known for her work on 'synthetic sisterhood' in teenage girls' magazines (a fascinating application of Critical Discourse Analysis, a branch of Sociolinguistics). In *Dotter* she explores her own Lancashire childhood and the problematic relationship with her father, the distinguished Joyce scholar James S. Atherton (author of *The Books at the Wake*, already cited). The beautiful artwork is by the author's husband.

A Seattle-based illustrator called Stephen Crowe has for some years slowly and meticulously worked his way through the *Wake* on his 'Wake in Progress' website*, although the project currently seems to be on hold as other commitments prevail.

In 2012 the publisher One Peace Books reissued a series of 20th-century novels in the form of Japanese manga. In their version of *Ulysses* the text has been significantly shortened, radically accelerated, aggressively simplified and comically paraphrased. It has only

---

*wakeinprogress.com

the remotest connection with the original and by manga standards is a complete dud.

The best graphic novels—and they are legion—seem to me to offer an equivalent to the modernist novels of the 1920s when it comes to originality, experimentation and indifference to the commercial mainstream.* Should we compare Alan Moore, the writer behind *Watchmen* (the *Ulysses* of graphic novels), *V for Vendetta*, *Swamp Thing* and *From Hell* to Joyce? Yes, and why not? Moore's *Jerusalem* (2019), a million-word novel without graphics is his *Finnegans Wake*. It's set in his home town of Northampton and is dense, sprawling, too heavy to carry around and longer than the Bible. I haven't read it, but it's good to know that it exists. Is *Swamp Thing* a match for Earwicker, or *Promethea* for Molly Bloom? Of course not—but there's certainly room for them all.

---

*An honourable mention to Hugo Pratt (1927–1995), the Italian comic book artist who created the phenomenally popular 'Corto Maltese' series in which the eponymous sea captain encounters various real-life figures in the course of his travels, including Joyce, Hemingway, Conrad and Herman Hesse.

98. Moby Dick's hyphen

If any other work of fiction can challenge *Ulysses* for the title of the greatest novel in all of Anglophone literature it's likely to be *Moby-Dick*. The two books are, by any objective measure, the literary high points of their respective centuries. Of course there *are* no objective measures when it comes to literary judgements, but let's agree for now that they both earn their place in the world.

Despite the near-universal belief that the opening line of Melville's great novel is 'Call me Ishmael' this direct address to the reader appears only after fifty pages of what the author calls 'Front Matter', an accumulation of fragments that resemble the unsightly trash and clutter surrounding a whaling station, chunks of text roughly flensed from the body of leviathan literature. We have to pick our way carefully through these gobbets of cetacean lore before we arrive at that celebrated salutation. But those readers who skip straight to Ishmael, or who impatiently cut to the chase at the first sighting of the white whale in Chapter 133, will miss a mesmerising compendium of 'higgledy-piggledy whale statements' encompassing science, philosophy, metaphysical speculation, poetry and folk-tales, with passages from the Bible, Pliny, Plutarch, Montaigne, Rabelais, Hobbes, Bunyan, Milton—and that's just the first three pages.

The novel's actual first words are:

ETYMOLOGY

(Supplied by a late consumptive usher to a grammar school)

There follows a deflationary introduction by Melville himself, mocking the imaginary compiler as a 'mere painstaking burrower and grubworm of a poor devil of a Sub-Sub.' This is all great fun, but the editors behind my Kindle version have, quite understandably, moved all this 'Front Matter' to an appendix, realising that it's unlikely to hook the first-time reader who may feel they've downloaded another book entirely. But Melville certainly knew what he was doing, and what he was doing was something very modern, very strange and, it seems to me, in danger of being lost in this era of ebooks and indifferent editing. We'll come back to this metatextual issue later. My first concern is an apparently trivial matter, but one that has bothered me for years and might be added to the clutter of Front Matter surrounding the novel: Why is *Moby-Dick* hyphenated?

Approaching the issue by way of a digression—a very Melvillian strategy—we might recall Lewis Carroll's *Through the Looking-glass* and Alice's forest encounter with the kindly White Knight, who offers to sing to her and adds, by way of clarification: '[t]he name of the song is called "Haddocks Eyes".'

'Oh, that's the name of the song, is it?' Alice said, trying to feel interested.

'No, you don't understand,' the Knight said, looking a little vexed. 'That's what the name is called. The name really is "The Aged, Aged Man".'

'Then I ought to have said "That's what the song is called"?' Alice corrected herself.

'No you oughtn't: that's another thing. The song is called "Ways and Means" but that's only what it's *called*, you know!'

We later discover the song really *is* "A-sitting On A Gate", although the tune, needless to say, is another matter. Simply put, the hyphenated (and conventionally italicised) Moby-Dick is a book, or rather the *title* of a book; but the unhyphenated Moby Dick isn't a book at all, in the same sense that Leopold Bloom isn't a book. Moby Dick is the name of a whale in a book called *Moby-Dick*. *Moby-Dick*, not Moby Dick, is a book. although *Moby-Dick* is not really the title of the book in which Moby Dick appears but, as the White Knight would say, is only what the name of the book is called.

The real name of the book, or at least the title under which the book first appeared in America in November 1851, is *Moby-Dick; or The Whale*. In the publishers' double spaced upper case it creates a more powerful impression as

M O B Y - D I C K ; O R , T H E W H A L E

The punctuation marks are like Nantucket hooks and lances embedded in the pale flank of the title-page. That semi-colon is working hard, though not as hard as what one excitable literary blogger has declared 'the greatest hyphen in American letters'. (What are the others? Kurt Vonnegut's *Slaughterhouse-Five* and Joseph Heller's *Catch-22* come first to mind, although in both cases the hyphen merely proposes a bureaucratic continuum of other Slaughterhouses, other

Catches.) What the hyphen does to Moby Dick in *Moby-Dick* is unclear, not least because 'Dick' is not a number, not a Five or a 22, not part of any stable series, not even a suffix. But then 'Moby' isn't a prefix, as we shall see.

To muddy matters further the *first* first edition, which had been published in three volumes in Britain a month earlier, was called simply *The Whale* (or, to be precise, T H E W H A L E). In what may be the editorial gaffe of the century, Melville's Epilogue, in which Ishmael survives the climactic destruction and sinking of the Pequod, was mistakenly removed by the British publishers and the London critics pounced gleefully on the omission, pillorying the author for killing off his narrator and thus retrospectively sabotaging the entire enterprise. The critics were united in their derision: 'so much trash belonging to the worst school of Bedlam literature'; 'wantonly eccentric; outrageously bombastic'; 'bad rhetoric, involved syntax, stilted sentiment and incoherent English'; 'Mr. Melville's Quakers are the wretchedest dolts and drivellers, and his Mad Captain [. . .] is a monstrous bore'. American critics, faced with the complete text in one volume—this time including the Epilogue—tended nevertheless to follow the British critics' lead and were, if anything, even harsher.

Melville at the age of 32 now had a promising future behind him and his literary career went into a steep decline. His astonishing short story 'Bartleby the Scrivener' appeared anonymously in 1853, and the eponymous copy clerk's melancholic inertia is a reflection of the author's dilemma. Two decades of remunerative boredom were to follow when Melville took up a post as a New York City customs officer, a distraction being a visit to the Holy Land and the composition of the 16,000-line epic poem *Clarel*. His other masterpiece *Billy Budd* remained unpublished for over thirty years after the author's death at the age of 72, which went largely unremarked although the *New York Times* obituary notice (29th September 1891) referred in passing to a book called *Mobie Dick* [*sic*]. A revival of interest in his masterpiece had to wait until the 1920s when a new readership began to develop. D.H. Lawrence, an early champion, wrote in 1923: 'it is a great book, a very great book, the greatest book of the sea ever written. It moves awe in the soul.' (He had read the incomplete British version and the lack of a proper ending clearly didn't trouble him.) One scours the pages of the two first editions for revelatory differences, but although some thirty-five expurgated passages are restored to the American version there's nothing to snag the scholar's twitchy attention. What interests me, and what I hope will interest you, is the hyphen in the title and its absence in the text. What's happening there?

Confusion began before the publication of the first British edition and had its origins in an undated letter, quoted by G. Thomas Tanselle in his introduction to the Library of America edition of *Moby-Dick*, from Melville's brother Allan to the London publisher, Richard Bentley:

> Since sending proofs of my brothers [*sic*] new work [. . .] he has determined upon a new title & dedication—Enclosed you have proof of both—It is thought here that the new title will be a better selling title.

The 'enclosed' were the belated dedication to Nathaniel Hawthorne and the new title, into which Allan, erratically literate, inserted a hyphen by mistake and without his brother's knowledge. The letter arrived in time for Bentley to include the Hawthorne dedication but it was presumably too late to change the first edition title from THE WHALE, which had been used consistently in pre-publication advertising. Only 500 three-volume sets were published and they did not sell well. On the strength of the title and the first fifty pages, prospective buyers might well have mistaken the three volumes as a cetacean *vade mecum*, a non-fiction guide to the whaling industry, so the unadopted 'better selling title' might have been a belated attempt to brand the book unambiguously as a work of fiction. Melville's previous books, in common with many mid-nineteenth-century American novels, all had two-part titles: *Typee: A Peep at Polynesian Life* (1846); *Omoo: A Narrative of Adventures in the South Seas* (1847), *Mardi: And a Voyage Thither* and *Redburn: His First Voyage* (both 1849). The novel immediately preceding *Moby-Dick* was the lavishly hyphenated *White-Jacket; or, The World in a Man-of-War* (1850).

No manuscript of *Moby-Dick* is known to exist so we don't know for sure what the author had in mind. Melville's many publishers and commentators seem to share a casual indifference to the titular hyphen that, more often than not, results in references to 'Melville's Moby Dick', or (almost as bad) the italicised 'Melville's

Moby Dick'. Copies of the single-volume American first edition are quite rare—3,000 were printed and sold slowly, many being destroyed in a warehouse fire. A 'very good' copy (which all book-collectors know means 'not very good') is currently advertised online for over $40,000, and the vendor scrupulously includes the title hyphen because, for scholars, academics, bibliophiles, booksellers and pedants, *Moby-Dick* is the correct (if inconsistently employed) way to write the title, or at least part of the title, of the first American edition of the novel in which Moby Dick is the blubbery and unhyphenated protagonist.

Moby Dick's hyphen is under threat in today's electronic versions; but not only the hyphen. Crucially important aspects of layout are also endangered—numbered pagination, the indentation of new paragraphs, margins, justification, the use of italics, footnotes and almost all the long-established apparatus that (to recycle the Anthony Burgess acronym) makes BOOK a 'Box Of Organised Knowledge'. My Kindle doesn't distinguish between hyphens and dashes, but hyphens still have their place in the typesetter's toolbox, along with the various kinds of dash that serve either to bond things together or keep them apart. My ebook version of *Moby-Dick* also omits the notorious rogue hyphen that appears in the British first edition which, as Melville scholars know, is on page 609 in Chapter 133, 'The Chase—First Day':

> Accordingly, the boats now made for her, and were soon swayed up to their cranes—the two parts of the wrecked boat having been previously secured by her—and then hoisting everything to her side, and stacking her canvas high up, and sideways outstretching it with stunsails, like the double-jointed wings of an albatross; the Pequod bore down in the leeward wake of Moby-Dick.

In that first edition the first half of the whale's name in the final sentence comes at a line break, and this may have prompted a zealous typographer to add the hyphen, although its use here implies a creature elsewhere going by the single name of Mobydick, or MobyDick, the aquatic equivalent of Bono and Beyoncé. A printer's error? Or is that first sighting an early example of the conscious intertextual self-referencing beloved of postmodernist academics and the bane of the common reader? My money's on a typo.

Why *Moby* Dick anyway? What, as one wag put it, is a 'Moby'?

The name was not entirely Melville's invention but sourced in an article about the real-life capture of a notoriously violent creature called Mocha Dick, near the Pacific island of that name. The American author and explorer Jeremiah N. Reynolds published a lively account of the incident as 'Mocha Dick: Or The White Whale of the Pacific: A Leaf from a Manuscript Journal' in the May 1839 issue of *The Knickerbocker*, a New York magazine. We know that Melville obtained a copy before starting work on his novel and clearly had Reynolds' title in mind when it came to naming his own magnum opus. 'Moby' has since acquired an independent lexical value as the first part of the name of the whale, and the first part of a version of the the title of the novel in which the whale appears, *and nothing else*, unless one includes the musician Richard Melville Hall, who performs under the stage-name of Moby. (Herman was his great-great-great-granduncle, which is worth mentioning, if only for its syncopating hyphen-chain.)

Described by Reynolds as 'an old bull whale, of prodigious size and strength,' Mocha Dick was also, whether through age or some natural condition, 'as white as wool.' Melville took his cue for the name from the article, discarding the Mocha but retaining the Dick, which seems to have been a whaler's random choice selected from the anonymous triumvirate of Tom, Dick and Harry. Moby-Tom and Moby-Harry are both non-starters and 'dick' didn't come into use as a slang term for the male member until the late nineteenth century. (Whether the phallic euphemism derived indirectly from Melville is not an hypothesis under consideration here.) A plausible phonetic link to the Möbius Strip turns out to be another red herring, as this wasn't discovered until seven years after the novel was published. How 'Mocha' became 'Moby' is anyone's guess and much ingenious speculation surrounds the transformation, none of it entirely convincing. Can we suppose 'Moby' is a fictional island providing Melville with an imaginary topographical feature after which an equally fictional whale could be named?

Mocha has an afterlife in your local coffee shop, which is statistically likely to be named after the Pequod's chief mate. From its beginnings in 1971 as a single store (originally to have been named Pequod) there are now 17,000 Starbucks outlets worldwide and the Melville legacy features, dimly, in the twin-tailed mermaid logo and on their corporate website: 'The name, inspired by Moby Dick [*sic*], evoked the romance of the high seas and the seafaring tradition of the early coffee traders.' Coffee seems to have replaced whaling in what appears to be a corporate revisionist take on Moby Dick and *Moby-Dick*. There's more: 'Our mission [is] to inspire and nurture the human spirit—one person, one cup, and one neighbourhood at a time.'

But that's a mission *statement*, not a mission. Ahab has a mission, if a mission is defined as an all-consuming sense of purpose, of personal destiny, and that mission is to kill Moby Dick—one whale, one lance, and one demented monologue at a time. Ahab is a marvellous lunatic, the most exemplary monomaniac in all American literature and, unlike his literary peers Don Quixote and Falstaff, he entirely lacks innocence or charm and is undistorted by self-knowledge. Prompted by an earlier disastrous encounter into becoming the white whale's nemesis, Ahab is a hero only by default, defined by intransigence, a self-serving single-mindedness and an unslakable thirst for vengeance. He's part Long John Silver, part Flying Dutchman, part Biblical monarch (and there may be a phonetic link here—the Hebrew king Ahab's father conquered the land of *Moab*.)

Unlike Moby Dick, Ahab's vessel the Pequod, that 'fading phantom' with its crew of 'mongrel renegades, and castaways, and cannibals,' does have an etymological origin, if an obscure one. Two other fictional (and hyphenated) Nantucket ships are preparing for a three-year trip when Ishmael fetches up in Nantucket—'The Devil-Dam' and the 'Tit-bit'. Melville—via Ishmael—tells us that the ship he signs onto is named after the Native American Pequot tribe, and this was a deliberately ominous choice. Although the Pequot people have remarkably survived to this day they represented for the author an image of loss and annihilation—a 1910 census listed just 66 survivors but they were, for Melville/Ishmael, 'as extinct as the ancient Medes.' The Pequod is a ship of death, encrusted with scrimshaw, bound on a one-way necronautical odyssey.

Nothing connects the word Moby to the world except for its use by Melville. 'Moby' is an *enormous* word, a monstrous noun (or possibly adjective) but one that, despite its vastness, means nothing at all. It has—perhaps surprisingly—never developed an independent usage as an intensifier suggesting size or significance or power, like the tiresomely ubiquitous 'awesome'. Moby Dick's name really *is* awe-some, suggesting tremendous physical mass, the incarnation of all whalekind. The hyphen might fancifully be seen as a way of render-ing the natural into the cultural, a critical hook for hauling the car-cass of meaning onto the slipway of interpretation.

Moby-Dick is a literary artefact, while Moby Dick is a symbol-laden abstraction plainly drawn from nature, but greater than nature, an all-encompassing metaphor.

In terms of plot *Moby-Dick* consists almost entirely of a post-poned denouement contained in the final two chapters. Before that we are given an exhaustive account of the so-called 'fishery', an ex-tended and minutely detailed description of the business of whal-ing, a kind of 'documentary footage' that is transformed by Melville's quite astonishing powers of description and analysis into visionary reportage.

Any work of art is both functional (that is, operating on the level of its own discourse) and metaphorical. *Moby-Dick* functionally in-volves whales, and the hunting and slaughter of whales, on this level doing for the Pequod, and the now-defunct industry it serves, what Joyce does for Dublin in *Ulysses*. On the metaphorical level, W.H. Auden, in the *The Enchafèd Flood* (1950), claimed that the whole of *Moby-Dick* is 'an elaborate synecdoche' in which whale fishing be-comes an image of all our lives, teeming with parable and multiple symbolic correspondences. Auden—or his editors—regularly con-fuse the title with the creature, but that doesn't detract from a claim that the novel's universality accounts for its cultural longevity.

Almost every chapter of *Moby-Dick* begins with a precise, even pedantic, description of some aspect of whaling, and in almost every chapter the objective documentary language gradually rises to elabo-rate abstraction or a sometimes hysterical address to the reader, to all humanity, to the imminent divine. This is a maximalist fiction—one that adds to the world rather than subtracts from it—and Melville is a virtuoso maximalist. The celebrated episode in which different crew members offer elaborate and contradictory interpretations of the gold doubloon nailed by Ahab to the Pequod's mast anticipates the modernist deployment of multiple and unreliable narrators and supports the view that the novel, like the whale itself, is a *tabula rasa*, a blank upon which meaning can be inscribed. Meaning, however, that is unstable and contingent.

Even the choice of the white whale's name seems to have been a late decision. In Chapter 45 Melville lists four candidate leviathans who never make it to the final cut—Timor Jack, New Zealand Tom, Morquan and Don Miguel—none of which has the same aural resonance as Ahab's nemesis, although Jack and Tom may be first cousins to Dick. Morquan? Too weird. Don Miguel? Too Cervantean. One cannot easily conceive of novels entitled *Timor-Jack*, *New Zealand-Tom* or *Don-Miguel*. Moby trails no meaning but is, quite literally, a floating signifier. Just as there are alternative, unexplored whale stories implied by the hypothetical encounters between the three whaling ships and the four short-listed candidates, there is also an alternative Ahab in the shape of Captain Boomer, skipper of the English whaler 'Samuel Enderby'. Boomer has lost an arm in an earlier encounter with Moby Dick, and now sports an ivory prosthetic, shaped like a mallet. The two maimed captains click their artificial limbs together by way of greeting and settle down, in one of the typically rich and meandering digressions that replaces a plot, for Boomer's jocular account of his mutilation. Boomer is quite unlike Ahab—cheerful, loquacious and fond of his crew, whom he treats with bantering affection. He is dully human, and humane, unlike Ahab. That the latter is a Quaker—like the Pequod's owners and most of the Nantucket whaling community—suggests a pacific inclination that sits oddly with his scorched, obsessive and murderous nature, and his astonishing final onslaught: '[F]rom hell's heart I stab at thee; for hate's sake I spit my last breath at thee.'

Moby Dick appears by name in just three of the novel's 135 chapters. When first sighted (in Chapter 133) there is a flurry of nominal repetitions—or invocations—accompanied by the traditional fishery cry of 'There she blows' which may make us pause, because Moby Dick is elsewhere unambiguously male, a bull sperm whale of prodigious size and power and cunning. There are other distinct characteristics—the skewed or scrolled jawbone, the oddly-wrinkled brow, the scarred hide, the embedded fishing tackle, and above all the colour, or lack of it, incarnated in the snow-white hump.

Why should a *white* whale exercise such a profound and lasting purchase on our imagination? Melville's mesmerisingly strange chapter 'On the Whiteness of the Whale' has been the subject of much scholarly analysis and debate. Spectral and ineffable yet always substantial, it is above all the *meaninglessness* of such a natural anomaly, a surrealist confluence of tone and form without rhyme or reason, that most snags and troubles our attention. Moby Dick is an elusive creature that, when visible, is wholly, sensationally and unambiguously visible—not just any white whale, but *the* white whale. Melville, ranging erratically over the phenomenon of whiteness in nature and culture, unsettlingly equates it not with purity but with the opposite of everything, with oblivion, and the 'pallor of the dead.' Just as whiteness is both the sum of all colours and a lack of colour, Moby Dick is simultaneously a mass of meanings and the negation of meaning, an overwhelming accumulation of significance that adds up to everything and nothing at all. We can all of us read *Moby-Dick*, but reading Moby Dick is another matter, because Moby Dick is a symbol for everything. An ocean of rhetorical elaboration surrounds the whale, with meaning sucked in and expelled like air from a blowhole, and this instability is reflected perfectly in Melville's blend of documentary precision and pervasive metaphysical dread. The first chapter is, appropriately and portentously entitled 'Loomings'.

'The sperm whale's unique body is unlikely to be confused with any other species' says the Wikipedia entry with poker-faced understatement, but Melville insists that the whale has no body at all, consisting as it does purely of a head and a tail with no intermediate abdomen. This is followed by the author's unsettling observation that the whale has a head, *but no face*. A prodigious mass of meat and muscle, *Physeter macrocephalus* offers no concession to human understanding: the tiny eyes, the near-invisible ears, the cavernous maw—all confirm rather than vitiate the creature's absolute strangeness and inscrutability, in a way that curiously anticipates a spine-chilling moment in G.K. Chesterton's 1908 novel *The Man Who was Thursday*:

> The large face [. . .] grew larger and larger; and Syme was gripped with a fear that when he was quite close the face would be too big to be possible, and that he would scream aloud.

Moby Dick, with or without a face, is too big to be possible. Unknowable, practically unimaginable, the white whale makes our thoughts small, dwarfed both by its vast uncanny absence and its meticulously realised presence. It's unclear whether Moby Dick survives the final catastrophe—freshly wounded and with his strange cargo of Ahab's entangled corpse he simply disappears, leaving Ishmael to float away on Queequeg's empty coffin. Eventually rescued, the narrator fills a role dating back to Anglo-Saxon poetry and the 'ubi sunt' motif—that of the lone figure who lives to tell the tale of those he left behind, a not-so ancient mariner, chronically eloquent and with a leftover life to fill.

We know, up to a point, what a whale *is*, but what is it *for*? This is made vividly clear in Melville's descriptions of the process of slaughter, dismemberment and rendering down into oil, the hellishly messy and hazardous business that is the whaling-ship's *raison d'être*. We are spared no detail, from the stomach-turning retrieval of aromatic ambergris buried deep in the head to the feeding-frenzy of sharks gorging on the slung corpse. No creature has ever been so elaborately, intimately anatomised—the Brobdingnagian internal cavities, the hefty organs, the milky spermaceti, the thick layers of flensed flesh, the slicks of black blood, the unctuous oils and the textured offal of white-horse, plum-pudding, slobgollion and gurry. And what Melville did for the whale Joyce did for his native Dublin. Both authors tackle their subject—one natural, the other cultural—with encyclopedic virtuosity.

A few years ago while working abroad I re-read *Moby-Dick* on a Kindle ebook reader. Self-evident benefits of ebooks aside, I disliked the tiresome business of clicking from page to page and the inability to flick back to an earlier passage, or to riffle absent-mindedly (and *Moby-Dick* is a novel that invites riffling). The algorithmic, one-size-fits-all typography on my Kindle was a far cry from the refined custom typesetting of the best print editions. And because it didn't automatically hyphenate, the loosely-set ragged lines often failed to reach the right-hand margin, creating a so-called 'jagged right' that would horrify any professional typesetter.

Against these seismic changes in reading habits my worries about a single hyphen may seem of small account. Yet it strikes me that the ebook industry of the 21st century is a form of gung-ho exploitation not unlike Nantucket whaling in the nineteenth. Novels—bulky, cumbersome, slow-moving, rich in content and wholly exploitable—are, like whales, pursued, captured, radically commodified and made palatable to the consumer. In the process of becoming a flat grey slab, the original entity loses its physical integrity, is deprived of texture, of life. The first-time reader of *Moby-Dick* in an electronic format will have access to a reasonably reliable text but may never realise the way the short chapters alternate between narrative and analysis, between Ahab's maniac quest and Melville's own reflections. This great, unwieldy novel, electronically filleted and efficiently packaged for today's hyperkinetic lifestyles, can be dipped into over a mocha frappuccino, but still has a looming cultural presence that transcends its format. I wonder if the same can be said for the Adelaide University ebook version of *Finnegans Wake* which, in its deliberately unpaginated scroll-like format, may come closer to what Joyce intended than any print version has yet done.

Moby Dick and *Moby-Dick* surface briefly from the murky lexical depths of the *Wake* as the 'groot hwide Whalefisk' pursued by the harpooner 'queckqueck'. Joyce's last book, a behemoth to match Melville's masterpiece, also suffers at the hands of slipshod punctuators. There is, as I have tirelessly pointed out in the course of *Multiple Joyce*, never an apostrophe in *Finnegans Wake*, but there is *always* one in 'Finnegan's Wake', the Irish ballad of the 1850s composed around the time Melville was writing *Moby-Dick*. *Finnegans Wake* is a book, of sorts. 'Finnegan's Wake' is not a book at all, and never was, but this is where we came in.

Samuel Beckett's take on the *Wake*, cited earlier in this book, is worth repeating: 'His writing is not about something; it is that something itself.' Herman Melville's writing, on the other hand, *is* about something. *Moby-Dick* is a book about Moby Dick, and Moby Dick is everything.

99. 'AS IF A MAGIC LANTERN THREW THE NERVES IN PATTERNS ON A SCREEN'

Ulysses shares its centenary year with two other publishing bench-marks. One is the English translation of Wittgenstein's *Tractatus Logico-Philosophicus*, which originally appeared in German in 1921 as *Logisch-Philosophische Abhandlung*. The other is *The Waste Land*. Greater minds than mine can tackle the former, but I'd like to share some thoughts on T.S. Eliot and his poem, although Joyce is bound to elbow his way in from time to time. I particularly want to look at the connection between Eliot and Joyce and their contemporaries, and the cinema.

Recalling his first encounter with Eliot's poetry as a schoolboy, the poet Louis MacNeice (born in 1907) wrote: 'The cinema technique of quick cutting, of surprise juxtapositions, of spotting the everyday detail and making it significant, this would naturally intrigue the novelty-mad adolescent and should, like even the most experimental films, soon become easy to grasp.'*

The analogy is attractive but misleading, because the poetic tech-niques that MacNeice regarded as specifically filmic originated not in film, but in literature. Nevertheless, a presumed connection be-tween modernist writing and cinematic techniques persists to this day, although such a belief does scant justice to the achievements of the many innovators in either medium. What's more, MacNeice's view that 'it soon became easy to grasp' entirely underestimates the complexities of both modernist poetry and experimental film, as if the whole bag of tricks could be acquired and exploited without fuss or effort.

While it's perfectly reasonable for MacNeice to claim that a knowl-edge and understanding of cinema techniques informed a later gen-eration's approach to modernist writing, both as readers and as writ-ers, it is quite another matter to assume that the same knowledge and understanding informed the original authors' approach to writ-ing, because all the leading literary modernists of the 1920s grew up and came of age before cinema was established as a popular medium:

---

* *T.S. Eliot: A Symposium* edited by Tambimuttu, Conrad Aiken, Tambimuttu and Richard March (Editions Poetry London, London. 1948) p. 150.

Marcel Proust (born in 1871), Gertrude Stein (1874), Joyce, Wyndham Lewis and Virginia Woolf (all born in 1882), Ezra Pound (1885) and Eliot (1888).* While they would all, in their later years, be exposed to and unquestionably influenced by film, they were none of them in their childhood, adolescence or early maturity, able to experience, or be impressed by, what would in their lifetimes become the most powerful and ubiquitous popular art form in history.

In any case the influence of film on literary modernism was part of a cycle that began with the earlier influence of literature on the emerging medium of film. MacNeice's description of Eliot's 'cinematic' techniques ('. . . of quick cutting, of surprise juxtapositions, of spotting the everyday detail and making it significant . . .') could apply to *Moby-Dick*, *The Life and Opinions of Tristram Shandy*, *Gulliver's Travels* or almost any work of literature since Chaucer. Writers and poets had for centuries employed principles of creation, selection and organisation that were precursors of later methods in film-making.

By the time MacNeice first encountered Eliot in print, motion pictures had reached astonishing levels of technical proficiency and aesthetic sophistication, with the emergence of great directors such as Borzage, Dovzhenko, Dreyer, Eisenstein, Griffith, Hitchcock, Lang, Leni, Murnau, Pabst, Pudovkin, Renoir, Sjöström, von Sternberg, and von Stroheim. And cinema had become a cultural given for the so-called 'MacSpaunday' generation, just as the music-hall had been for Eliot.

Writers and film-makers of the 1920s were engaged in an exchange of narrative techniques, and the technique which has featured most consistently in debates about literary modernism is *montage*, the innovative organisation and juxtaposition of related and unrelated elements to create a new kind of coherence. We hardly need reminding that books came first and that silent film directors and producers had all grown up as readers, and were therefore pre-disposed to adopt and adapt literary forms familiar to them (and to a wider audience)

---

*The world's earliest surviving motion-picture film showing actual consecutive action is called *Roundhay Garden Scene*. It's very short (under 3 seconds in duration), directed by French inventor Louis Le Prince and shot in 1888. The world's first commercial movie screening was on 28th December 1895 place at the Grand Cafe in Paris, when the Lumière brothers presented their new moving-picture device, the Cinématographe. This was demonstrated in London the following year.

into cinematic techniques which would later be re-appropriated by modernist writers.

Eliot had equivocal feelings about cinema, preferring more established popular entertainments such as the music-hall, boxing and wrestling. He was nevertheless quite a film buff, admiring Laurel and Hardy, Charlie Chaplin, the Marx Brothers (especially Groucho, with whom he maintained an intermittent correspondence) as well as crowd-pleasing westerns and slapstick comedies. He shared such lowbrow tastes with Ludwig Wittgenstein (1889–1951), who enjoyed cowboy shoot-'em-ups and raucous Betty Grable musicals, which he used to watch intently from the front row of the Cambridge Arts Theatre.*

Eliot was also a founding member of the London Film Society and as such had signed up to the ideals of an emerging, largely European film culture with an intellectual following. Established in 1925, the Film Society was the first of its kind in Britain and screened mostly foreign movies, early silents, avant-garde work and documentaries, its members-only policy circumventing the defenders of decency at the British Board of Film Censors. Membership was priced beyond the means of most working people, but the weekly audiences were encouragingly large.

The popular press derided the Society's intellectual pretensions but it was an immediate success, soon moving from the 1,400 seat New Gallery Kinema to the Tivoli Palace in the Strand, which could—and did—accommodate well-heeled audiences of up to 3,000. As well as so-called 'resurrection' screenings of early silents, there was an emphasis on the continental avant-garde and films from Germany, Russia and France tended to dominate each season. One programme, consisting entirely of films made by women, featured Germaine Dulac's *La Coquille et le Clergyman* (1926), memorably rejected by the British censors as 'so cryptic as to be almost meaningless. If there is a meaning, it is doubtless objectionable.'

---

*Eliot's second wife Valerie, interviewed by Timothy Wilson for *Esquire* magazine, 'produced a scrapbook she'd kept of theatre and film programs in which he'd written comments. I noticed a long appreciative piece on Kurosawa's adaptation of Macbeth, which Eliot called "the best film I've ever seen." ('The Wife of the Father of The Waste Land', *Esquire* May 1972) This was in fact *Kumonosu-jō* (1957) Akira Kurosawa's re-imagining of *Macbeth* set in feudal Japan, better known in English as *Throne of Blood*.

In the silent era, films were truly international, with equal or closely comparable cultural weight and impact and value whatever their country or language of origin, and wherever they were screened. Any inter titles offering exposition or essential dialogue would be translated into the local language and inserted into the reel for projection (a fairly complex process that involved split-second timing and a good deal of labour). But the films themselves circulated in virtually identical prints wherever they were shown, which is how Chaplin swiftly became the most famous man in the world, and the highest-paid performer in history. Film, unlike literature, and even more unlike poetry, did not—inter titles aside—depend for its transmission and reception on translation, and was immediately legible and overwhelmingly popular. No wonder many writers born in the previous century were sceptical about this upstart new medium, and responded with a condescension and disdain that is still in evidence today.

Another Film Society member was Eliot's friend Virginia Woolf, who spent the afternoon of Sunday 14th March 1926 at the fifth screening of the Society's first season, when the main feature was Robert Wiene's expressionist masterpiece *The Cabinet of Dr. Caligari* (1920). We know what the 44-year-old Woolf made of this because she wrote a magazine piece entitled 'The Cinema' which appeared in the New York journal *Arts* in June.* In it she describes a revelatory moment:

> [A]t a performance of *Dr Caligari* the other day, a shadow shaped like a tadpole suddenly appeared at one corner of the screen. [. . .] For a moment it seemed as though thought could be conveyed by shape more effectively than by words.

Woolf's epiphany, prompted by a flaw in the print (or possibly in the projector), recalls Proust's memory, in the opening pages of *Du côté de chez Swann* (1913), the first volume of *À la recherche du temps perdu*, of a nursery magic lantern projecting an image that morphs around the surfaces of a billowing curtain or bedroom doorknob.

---

*The essay appeared first in the New York journal *Arts* in June 1926 and in the *Nation and Athenaeum* the following month. The quotations are from David Trotter's excellent essay *Virginia Woolf and Cinema* (Film Studies Issue 6, Manchester University Press, Summer 2005). Most of the newsreel footage seen and described by Woolf can be found on the British Pathé website.

Earlier in the article Woolf describes her response to different kinds of film, starting with newsreel: '[A]t first sight, the art of the cinema seems simple, even stupid,' then reflects on the mutability of banal events caught by the camera, and capturing something of the melancholy that permeates cinema:

> Further, all this happened ten years ago, we are told. We are behold-ing a world which has gone beneath the waves. Brides are emerging from the abbey—they are now mothers; ushers are ardent—they are now silent; mothers are tearful, guests are joyful; this has been won and that has been lost, and it is over and done with.

'Ten years ago'? Woolf is making a point by using the future sub-junctive, i.e. 'all this will have happened ten years ago, we shall in time come to realise.' In a spellbinding passage she reflects on the ephemeral nature of the image:

> We behold them as they are when we are not there. We see life as it is when we have no part in it. As we gaze we seem to be re-moved from the pettiness of actual existence. [. . .] From this point of vantage, as we watch the antics of our kind, we have time to feel pity and amusement, to generalize, to endow one man with the at-tributes of the race. Watching the boat sail and the wave break, we have time to open our minds wide to beauty and register on top of it the queer sensation—this beauty will continue, and this beauty will flourish whether we behold it or not.

It is the viewer then, and not the spectacle that is spectral, as film has an objective existence independent of the spectator's gaze. The spectator is thus demoted, erased even, in an act that anticipates Roland Barthes' declaration of the death of the author. It is a mod-ernist take on a perennial aesthetic consideration.

She foresees a time when film will actually *supplant* literature, when the movies will replace the text as the main medium of cul-tural dissemination. In a sense that has already happened, at least if one chooses to compare box office receipts for the latest James Bond blockbuster against annual sales of *Mrs Dalloway*. To be sure this was always the case; compare sales of *The Waste Land* in 1922, of which only a thousand copies of the Boni and Liveright edition were pub-lished in New York.

Woolf's description of that 'shadow shaped like a tadpole' may re-mind us of the line in *The Love Song of J. Alfred Prufrock* (1915):

But as if a magic lantern threw the nerves in patterns on a screen[.]

'the nerves in patterns on a screen'

A magic lantern was a predecessor of the cinema projector and this line is an instance of Eliot (or Prufrock, as the young poet's ageing mouthpiece) employing a self-consciously old-fashioned word for a near-obsolete technology, as one might with some affectation (and affection) say 'wireless' or 'gramophone' today when referring to a radio or CD player, and we may also be reminded of Eliot's nostalgic reference to 'Daguerreotypes and silhouettes' in 'A Cooking Egg' (*Poems*, *1920*). More significantly, it was this earlier form of visual spectacle, already slightly archaic, that appears to inform Eliot's later poetic practice; *The Waste Land* in particular seems to me to owe much of its form and content to the magic lantern presentations that were hugely popular antecedents to cinema, and certain to have been a feature of Eliot's childhood.*

Magic lanterns date back to the seventeenth century and belong to the pre-history of cinema, but were still being manufactured in

---

*A memorable horror in *Prufrock* is the image of the formulated subject 'sprawling on a pin [. . .] pinned and wriggling on a wall' which, like the projection of nerves upon a screen, is a moment of involuntary revelation coupled with a nightmarish loss of agency.

the 1920s, by which time cinema had entirely replaced them as a form of public spectacle. They remained popular as home entertainments in middle-class households and also as a means of viewing pornography.* Before the widespread introduction of overhead projectors in the 1960s (which had their origins as 'vertical lanterns' in the 1880s and which have now been entirely superseded by Powerpoint and the like), magic lanterns remained in common everyday use for briefing and educational purposes for at least three decades after the Second World War. In classroom and lecture hall they were capable of projecting—among other things—microscopic images of bacteria on a wall or screen, often using photographs taken from illustrated text books.

The one reference to magic lanterns in Joyce's fiction I can find is the moment in the *Dubliners* short story 'Grace' in which the alcoholic Mr Kernan, following a drunken tumble down a pub staircase, is visited by three friends, Power, M'Coy, and Cunningham, concerned about his health. The four men have a rambling, error-laden conversation about religion and attempt to persuade Kernan to take part in a Jesuit retreat as a means of putting his life in order. He eventually agrees but has doubts about certain aspects of Catholic ritual:

> 'I bar the candles,' said Mr Kernan, conscious of having created an effect on his audience and continuing to shake his head to and fro. 'I bar the magic-lantern business.'
>
> Everyone laughed heartily.
>
> 'There's a nice Catholic for you!' said his wife.

Kernan's irreverent dismissal of established practice is typical of the anti-clerical tone that characterises many of the stories. Priests in *Dubliners* are often 'the object of Joyce's wit, ridicule, sarcasm, and

---

*The Mutascope was a pre-cinematic device consisting of photographs mounted on a cylinder, a version of the flicker books still in circulation today. Sometimes known as 'What the Butler Saw', Mutascopes were popular end-of-the pier attractions offering viewers mildly pornographic short films for a penny. Bloom recalls one in the 'Nausciaa' episode of *Ulysses*: 'Ah, yes. Mutoscope pictures in Capel street: for men only. Peeping Tom. Willy's hat and what the girls did with it. Do they snapshot those girls or is it all a fake?'

contempt [,] harbingers of darkness rather than bringers of light'.* Each of the first four stories in the collection features uninspiring, incompetent clerics: Father Flynn in 'The Sisters', Father Butler in 'An Encounter' and the nameless clerics in 'Araby' and 'Eveline'. That even the unprepossessing drunkard Kernan can see through the theatrical bells and smells of Jesuit ceremony, that he compares the solemn ritual to a nursery toy or lowbrow public entertainment, is telling.

Whether in domestic or public settings, magic lantern presentations were rarely a single coherent aesthetic experience and in this respect they anticipated the behaviour of today's 'channel-hopping' cable television viewer, clicking promiscuously across providers from one programme to another. A lantern programme might feature fairy tales, sports, visual illusions, travelogues, religious images and (from the 1860s onwards) a combination of painted and photographic images.

In more sophisticated public presentations several lanterns might be employed, with dissolves between images, moving slides, musical accompaniment and the recitation of a prepared commentary.

The origins of many magic lantern projections lay in illustrated books, and such well-known images as George Cruikshank's 'Oliver Asks for More' in Dickens's *Oliver Twist* not only formed the basis for later theatrical versions but also circulated via other media such as stereoscopes, *cartes-de-visit*, picture postcards (a craze for collecting which began on the continent at the turn of the century), cigarette cards, advertisements and, ultimately, cinema. Taken together these manifestations constitute what the philosopher Steve Neale calls an 'intertextual relay' independent of the original narrative text, which may remind us of *The Waste Land*'s accumulation of heterogenous images and fragments sourced in drama, poetry and foreign languages.

Magic lantern shows offered audiences a spectacle of the world in fragments and their popularity made them every bit as influential as photography as a cultural mediator between 19th century pictorial representations and the emergence of British cinema in the late

---

*Lachtman, Howard: 'The Magic Lantern Business: James Joyce's Ecclesiastical Satire in Dubliners' in *James Joyce Quarterly* Vol. 7, No. 2 (Winter, 1970), pp. 82–92. Published by University of Tulsa.

19th and early 20th centuries.* An especially popular subject was the aristocratic itinerary of The Grand Tour, which served to shrink the world (squeezing the universe into a ball) while at the same time expanding the viewer's horizons. In their disconnected heterogenous content, in their heap of broken images, magic lantern displays offer a cultural link and visual correlative to the culminating, deracinated fragments of *The Waste Land*:

> London Bridge is falling down falling down falling down
> *Poi s'ascose nel foco che gli affina*
> *Quando fiam ceu chelidon*—O swallow swallow
> *Le Prince d'Aquitaine à la tour abolie*
> These fragments I have shored against my ruins
> Why then Ile fit you. Hieronymo's mad againe.
> Datta. Dayadhvam. Damyata.
>   Shantih shantih shantih.

Earlier in the poem we may be reminded of the rapid and, as it were, 'unpunctuated' dissolves between lantern lecture slides of capital cities:

> Jerusalem Athens Alexandria
> Vienna London
> Unreal

The Waste Land's many lexical lists—of Tarot cards, of London districts (Highbury, Richmond, Kew, Moorgate), of street names (King William Street, Lower Thames Street) and buildings (the Canon Street Hotel, the Metropole)—are part of a more general accumulation, at the humblest level of heterogenous nouns: sunsets, dooryards, sprinkled streets, novels, teacups, skirts that trail along the floor and so on, just as a magic lantern lecture would comprise an

---

*See Christine Gledhill *Reframing British Cinema 1918–28: Between Restraint and Passion* (London: BFI Publishing, 2003), pp. 48–50. Gledhill argues that magic lantern shows 'contribut[ed] to the circulation of affective and cognitive perception from one social arena to another.' According to Stephen Humphries, India 'inspired more more lantern sequences than any other in the late nineteenth century.' See *Victorian Britain Through the Magic Lantern* (London: Sidgwick & Jackson, 1989) p. 49. It is tempting to see Eliot's use of lines from the Upanishads at the end of *The Waste Land* as an unconscious nod in this direction.

accumulation of songs, hymns, stories, recitations, religious services, lectures and comic subjects.*

Following Slavoj Žižek's approach in *The Hitchcockian Blot* we can interpret the image of a magic lantern capable of projecting images of the subjects 'nerves' in terms of the oral, anal and phallic dimensions that Žižek applies to film.[†]

In the case of a cinematic image, Žižek defines the 'oral' stage as the 'zero degree' of film making—a simple uninflected shot of an event (of the newsreel kind noted by Virginia Woolf) or of an object. Montage, if applied in this case, has no effect on the narrative and appears in the 'anal' stage when the action is fragmented, cut up, multiplied, and the illusion of coherence is lost (though not necessarily the illusion of spatial and temporal continuity); a new *metaphorical* meaning emerges which may have no relation to the component parts assembled in the 'oral' stage. Finally there is the 'phallic' stage, in which the image is in some way problematised, its meaning destabilised. Virginia Woolf, struck by the sudden appearance of a shadowy blob on the screen, recognised and responded to this accidental 'phallic' stage, which had in turn been anticipated by Eliot's image of the nerves projected on a screen. And it is surely their appearance in a *pattern*, something symmetrical, artificial, decorative and somehow therefore denatured, that adds to the sense of helpless passivity; the subject having no control over either the projection, the pattern or the response elicited from the audience. The Hitchcockian Blot is the term used by Žižek to describe the 'eruption of the chaos world' in a Hitchcock film, the uncanny moment when we become aware of the plane dusting crops where there ain't no crops to dust; when a windmill's sails turn in the wrong direction, or a murder suspect sits in a dark room with only the light of his glowing cigar visible. We are unnerved by the patterns on the screen, and frightened.

---

*Is it too fanciful to see the phonetic and topographical elision from 'Moorgate' to 'Margate' as the aural equivalent of a dissolve between two magic lantern slides? And between the two four-syllable phrases 'at Moorgate, and . . .' to 'On Margate Sands . . .'? This contrasts with the sudden, violent 'cut' from Margate to Carthage, as if unrelated slides have suddenly been jumbled together.

[†]*The Trouble with Harry*: The corpse that wouldn't die' by Slavoj Žižek (translated by Richard Miller) in *October* Vol. 38 (Autumn, 1986), pp. 99–111 (The MIT Press). Originally appearing in *Hitchcock* (Ljubljana, DDU Univerzum, collection Analecta, 1984), co-edited by Žižek and Mladen Dolar.

In Eliot's case it is the pattern of nerves thrown onto a screen that provides the phallic jolt. Not least because we have the impression (established in the first lines of *Prufrock* when the evening sky is compared to an etherized patent on a table) of some futuristic medical apparatus, somehow capable of projecting the subject's nervous system—and by implication his unconscious mind—onto a screen for an audience to inspect, a screen that in shape and perhaps size resembles the aforementioned table. There is an echo of the lecture hall rather than the cinema, suggesting an auditorium packed with medical students and prurient members of the public. There is also an underlying fear of a *literal* public exposure, as the subject's most intimate secrets are made luminously manifest. If, that is, the nerves projected on the screen are actually *his*—there is no possessive pronoun connecting these nerves to any individual, and they may as well belong to another anaesthetised patient, or be sourced in an illustrated medical textbook. Whatever the case, there is a darkly foreboding sense of some as-yet unimaginable technology that would render such a 'live' projection possible.*

But this may not be merely a concocted simile. In an unpublished lecture the critic Eric Griffiths cites Robert Crawford who, in *The Savage and the City in the Work of T.S. Eliot* (1991), refers to an illustration in an 1897 issue of the *St. Louis Daily Globe-Democrat*, a newspaper Eliot's father took, accompanying an article on X-rays which claimed that X-raying the brain literally meant 'having one's thoughts read.' Griffiths chortlingly refers to Cambridge in the 1920s, when I.A. Richards' *Principles of Literary Criticism* contained 'a diagrammatic representation of events which take place when we read a poem.'†

Did Eliot read *L'homme Machine (Man a Machine)* by the 18th-century French physician and philosopher Julien Offray de La Mettrie? In it he observed that the body and soul were united in sleep, that 'diverse states of the soul are always correlated with those of the body' and that therefore

*A friend of mine saw Eliot lecture at the Italian Cultural Institute in London in the late 1950s and, in response to a question from a member of the audience about how he came to settle on the image of three white leopards in 'Ash Wednesday', the poet mildly replied: 'That would be a matter for a *neurologist*.'

†The fourth in a series of eight lectures delivered to the English faculty at Sheffield University in the early 1990s.

> judgment, reason, and memory are not absolute parts of the soul,
> but merely modifications of this kind of medullary screen upon
> which images of the objects painted in the eye are projected as by
> a magic lantern.*

That 'projected' is the translator's astute take on 'renvoyés'. It's note-worthy that de la Mettrie appears to affirm the Platonic idea that vi-sion is the result of beams emitted from the eyes, and we'll come back to that in a moment.

The *Prufrock* projection is a form of public exposure, a violation of the private, the intimate, the internal. Eliot's line is also quite literal—magic lanterns raised at the back of the auditorium projected (i.e. 'threw') images above the audience's heads and onto the screen, a process quite unlike the digital technologies of today, in which films are projected from *behind* the screen.

Magic lantern projections rarely included much in the way of text, apart from hymns or songs and occasional topical news stories. Rather, projected slides were accompanied by the spoken word, usu-ally delivered to an audience by the 'professor' or 'projectionist'.

Something magic lantern displays and early silent cinema shared is the role played by inter titles—the explanatory phrases appearing on screen briefly between sequences to identify characters, locations and plot points, or to render dialogue. And, in the case of the movies, what dialogue! 'Some excellent judges think that I resemble Satan' (from *The Penalty*, 1920); 'Give me something sentimental about a cat—or get out!' (*La bohème*, 1926); ALL STORIES HAVE AN END (Hitchcock's *The Lodger, a Story of the London Fog*, 1927) and THAT NIGHT THE FIRST OF A STRANGE SERIES OF MURDERS OC-CURRED (*The Cabinet of Dr. Caligari*, 1920). The latter film, with its *guignol* quality, the whiff of the uncanny and the nocturnal settings, has many alignments with Eliot's poetic sensibility.

There is no shortage of evidence to confirm the impact of inter ti-tles on modernist writing—the 'Aeolus' episode in *Ulysses* is broken up by newspaper headlines which in many cases could serve equally as film inter titles and some of which are unambiguously cinematic,

---

*[L]e jugement, le raisonnement, la mémoire ne sont que des parties de l'âme nulle-ment absolues, mais de véritables modifications de cette espèce de toile médullaire, sur laquelle les objets peints dans l'œil sont renvoyés, comme d'une lanterne mag-ique. English translation by Gertrude C. Bussey, rev. by Mary Whiton Calkins (1912).

such as the 'establishing shot' of 'IN THE HEART OF THE HIBER-
NIAN METROPOLIS', documentary cues ('HOW A GREAT DAILY
ORGAN IS TURNED OUT') and the introduction of new characters ('WILLIAM BRAYDEN, ESQUIRE, OF OAKLANDS, SANDY-
MOUNT'). Likewise Wyndham Lewis's Vorticist drama *Enemy of the
Stars* (1914) takes the form of a film script (but could never be produced as a conventional theatrical piece or, come to that, as a film),
and John Dos Passos regularly employed a Newsreel technique in
1919, the second volume of his U.S.A. trilogy published in 1932.

The melodramatic headings for each of the five sections of *The
Waste Land* also resemble title cards, each setting the scene for what
follows, if cryptically. They could almost be read as elements making
up a wide-ranging magic lantern programme:

I. THE BURIAL OF THE DEAD
II. A GAME OF CHESS
III. THE FIRE SERMON
IV. DEATH BY WATER
V. WHAT THE THUNDER SAID

A more explicitly *cinematic* image can be found in these lines from
Prelude III of *Prufrock*:

You dozed, and watched the night revealing
The thousand sordid images
Of which your soul was constituted;
They flickered against the ceiling.

Eliot knew his Kipling and, as Christopher Ricks has observed,[*]
may well have been thinking of these lines from 'Gentlemen-
Rankers', a poem that appeared in *Barrack-Room Ballads, and Other
Verses* (1892):

Every secret, self-revealing on the aching whitewashed ceiling,
Do you wonder that we drug ourselves from pain?

Both passages imply a supine figure; a squaddie on his bed in the
barracks or a patient (unetherised) upon a table. In Eliot's lines, dis-
turbingly, the figure sleeps while the sordid images that constitute

[*]Christopher Ricks, *Along Heroic Lines* (Oxford University Press 2021) ch. 13 'Heroic
Work by Samuel Johnson and Samuel Beckett' p. 309

his soul flicker above, as if projected from within, the ceiling serving as a screen. The ancients believed this is how sight worked—Plato's view was that visual perception was achieved through beams emitted by the eyes, through so-called 'extromissionism', a theory challenged by Socrates but which remained in circulation until the Renaissance. In both cases the unconscious figure is the source of the projected imagery, a magic lantern made of flesh and blood, and with no more agency than the subject whose nerves are thrown in pattern on a screen.

Early motion pictures were known as 'flickers' as the projection of hand-cranked prints had an intermittent quality which has been lost in today's digitalised versions of the originals. Flickering also suggests a contingent and discontinuous approximation of the projected consciousness, anticipating the 'nerves in pattern on a screen' in the collection's title poem.

Eliot as a poet is both cameraman and editor (or rather 'cutter' as the humbler practical role was known), assembling pre-existing fragments (the literary equivalent of 'library footage') into new combinations and juxtapositions, then introducing new, 'freshly-shot' material to contextualise that footage. These fragments, once combined, *are* the ruins.

Eliot's professed love of music hall, like the relentlessly scatological King Bolo verses he inflicted on his friend Bonamy Dobrée, is at odds with his austere, buttoned-up High Anglican Tory Royalist persona. The psychological tension between Apollo and Dionysus (mentioned earlier in my essay on Auden and Joyce) has long been a fruitful source for artists and writers, and in Eliot's case both positions were masks put on to meet the faces that he met.

Not all of Eliot's contemporaries were impressed. 'The aim of the music hall is to cheer up the lower classes by showing them a life uglier and more sordid than their own' wrote Max Beerbohm (1872–1956), although one might be inclined to see this as a positive quality. By the turn of the century, and certainly by the time Eliot started frequenting London's music halls, things had become far more refined under the management of a few reputable theatrical entrepreneurs and the critical scrutiny of such bodies as the National Vigilance Association. Sanitised acts toured a nationwide circuit controlled by Moss Empires, the largest music hall chain with fifty theatres scattered throughout the country. But by the 1920s the music-hall culture so admired by Eliot was on its last legs, not least because its traditional audiences were migrating to the new picture houses. Eliot's music hall was bowdlerised, and the vulgarity he so admired was by now a much-diluted version of a more energetic, more obscene, more subversive cultural tradition. Just as the magic lantern shows of his boyhood were now largely redundant spectacles confined to nursery, church hall and smoking-room, the music hall, drained of its vibrancy, was a reduced and emasculated version of its earlier self. A cultural Prufrock, if you will.

In *The Possibility of Poetic Drama* (included in *The Sacred Wood* (1922)), Eliot had written that 'the moment an idea has been transferred from its pure state in order that it may become comprehensible to the inferior intelligence it has lost contact with art.'* With a fastidious shudder Eliot rejects the idea of silent cinema as a form of mute theatre, although at the time of writing cinema had become a very sophisticated form of dumb-show, with luminously beautiful silver nitrate film stock creating and recording the supernatural radiance of stars such as Garbo, Fairbanks, Valentino and Dietrich. That such films were, in Eliot's chilly phrase, 'comprehensible to the inferior intelligence' is a criticism less of the medium than the content, but it also suggests that the popular appeal of cinema was, for Eliot, a bad thing in and of itself, although his rather hypocritical condescen-

---

*Eliot makes a rare on-screen appearance in the 1936 documentary *Cover to Cover* (directed by Alexander Shaw). Sponsored by The National Book Council and with a commentary written by the wonderfully-named Igenlode Wordsmith, it depicts the production of an imaginary novel from the completion of the manuscript to its arrival in a bookshop. Eliot aside (as the only poet and modernist) the film features Dame Rebecca West ('It is quite true that great writers have more often been men than women. But then, you see, women have other work to do.'), Somerset Maugham (then the most famous living writer in the English-speaking world) and the *Punch* humorist A.P. Herbert, all three embodiments of the non-experimental, anti-modernist tendency in English letters. Eliot's brief contribution to this film is not widely known, and here it is:

> It's no more use trying to be traditional than it is trying to be original. Nobody invents very much, but there is one thing to be said for contemporary poetry that can't be said in favour of any other, and that is that it is written by our contemporaries.

Of course 'contemporary' and 'modern' are very different things, in that everything is contemporary at some point but not necessarily modern, either in a literary sense or metaphysically. Eliot's bland observation was made at a time when many contemporary poets were not engaged in writing modern poetry and were, indeed, fiercely opposed to such wild practices.

sion did not extend to music-hall and boxing-matches, both spectacles equally comprehensible to 'the inferior intelligence'.

Eliot would in time come to revise this view. He would later in his career have direct experience of the commercial and technical realities of film production through working on the screen version of *Murder in the Cathedral* (1951), a turgidly faithful rendering of his stage play directed by George Hoellering (1897–1980), produced in connection with the Festival of Britain. Eliot himself (uncredited) provided the voice of the Fourth Tempter.

David Trotter has argued that Eliot's 'understanding of film technique was thoroughly up-to-date, and a good deal more sophisticated than that shown by cinephile writers such as Franz Kafka.'* We must hesitate, however, before concluding that Eliot in the early 1920s owed any particular debt to cinema, as suggested by Louis Mac-Neice, as opposed to a sensibility delicately attuned to the didactic and pictorial tropes of the magic lantern with its discontinuities, its accumulation of fragments, its intersection of the private and public domains. Michael Wood has argued that the 'principle of montage [is] quintessentially modernist' and, while this is a reasonable perspective, any view of *The Waste Land* as a modern montage poem is one we can challenge, because at the time of the poem's composition the intellectual discussion of montage had yet to begin outside of the Soviet Union, and Eliot hadn't been exposed to the kind of Russian propaganda productions that would become a mainstay of Film Society screenings from 1925 onwards.

Eliot has himself influenced contemporary cinema in a range of ways, some of them surprising, such as the conclusion of Francis Ford Coppola's Vietnam epic *Apocalypse Now* (1979), with Marlon Brando as the demented Kurtz mumbling lines from *The Hollow Men*. The International Movie Database (IMDB) lists an impressive number of Eliot-related productions, not confined to documentary but including cinema and television versions of the plays. We should also take into account the numberless appearances, mostly unofficial, that Eliot and his works now make on the internet, and particularly on YouTube, the magic lantern *de nos jours*.

***T.S. Eliot and Cinema* by David Trotter, published in *Modernism/modernity*, Volume 13, Number 2, April 2006, pp. 237–265, Johns Hopkins University Press.

100. MULTIPLE JOYCE

I'll tell you a test. But you must sit still. Will you hold your peace
and listen well to what I am going to say now?

—*Finnegans Wake*

Anticipating the modern trend for online crowdfunding, Sylvia
Beach sent a prospectus to various cultural movers and shakers
inviting them to subscribe to the publication of *Ulysses* a year ahead
of its appearance. This prompted a ferocious typewritten response
(dated 11th June 1921) from George Bernard Shaw (1856–1950):

> I have read several fragments of *Ulysses* in its serial form. It is a re-
> volting record of a disgusting phase of civilisation; but it is a truth-
> ful one; and I should like to put a cordon round Dublin; round up
> every male person in it between the ages of 15 and 30; force them to
> read it; and ask them whether on reflection they could see anything
> amusing in all that fouled mouthed, foul minded derision and ob-
> scenity. To you, possibly, it may appeal as art: you are probably (you
> see I don't know you) a young barbarian—beglamoured by the ex-
> citements and enthusiasms that art stirs up in passionate material;
> but to me it is all hideously real: I have walked those streets and
> know those shops and have heard and taken part in those conver-
> sations. I escaped from them to England at the age of twenty and
> forty years later have learned from the books of Mister Joyce that
> Dublin is still what it was, and young men are still drivelling in
> slackjawed blackguardism just as they were in 1870 . . .

He goes on a bit longer in this vein, comparing Joyce's work to a
cat having its nose rubbed in its own shit, before signing off with a
flourish:

> I must add, as the prospectus implies an invitation to purchase,
> that I am an elderly Irish gentleman; and if you imagine that any
> Irishman, much less an elderly one, would pay 150 francs for a book,
> you little know my countrymen.

Joyce found Shaw's response very amusing and had a copy of the
letter made to share with his patron Harriet Shaw Weaver. (Shaw
himself would eventually declare *Ulysses* a work of genius, but that
wasn't until 1939.)

Most writers worth their salt have an opinion about Joyce, and here are some more of them. Opinions, that is. And writers of course. To ginger things up a little I've made each statement anonymous and what you have to do is guess in each case which of the four writers said or wrote each of the following two dozen comments. The answers are on page 352. A mark for each one you get correct, but there are no prizes.

1. 'Mr. James Joyce is a great man who is entirely without taste.'

   (a) E.M. Forster
   (b) Rebecca West
   (c) Edith Sitwell
   (d) Cyril Connolly

2. 'And Joyce was a poor sick fucker who probably died with his balls somewhere up around his navel. None of that for me, thanks.'

   (a) Ernest Hemingway
   (b) Norman Mailer
   (c) Hunter S. Thompson
   (d) Gore Vidal

3. 'I guess the man's a genius, but what a dirty mind he has, hasn't he?'

   (a) W.H. Auden
   (b) Flannery O'Connor
   (c) Edna O'Brien
   (d) Nora Barnacle

4. 'I declare to god, if I hear that name Joyce one more time I will surely froth at the gob.'

   (a) F.R. Leavis
   (b) Oliver St. John Gogarty
   (c) Brendan Behan
   (d) Flann O'Brien

5. 'Joyce is good. He is a good writer. People like him because he is incomprehensible and anybody can understand him. But who came first, Gertrude Stein or James Joyce? [. . .] Joyce has done something. His influence, however, is local. Like Synge, another Irish writer, he has had his day.'

    (a) Maurice Bowra
    (b) Alice B. Toklas
    (c) Gertrude Stein
    (d) Ernest Hemingway

6. '*Ulysses* could have done with a good editor.'

    (a) Lucy Ellmann
    (b) Roddy Doyle
    (c) Todd McEwen
    (d) Gordon Lish

7. '[*Ulysses*] will remain, eternally cathartic, a monument like a record diarrhoea . . . He collected like a cistern in his youth the last stagnant pumpings of Victorian Anglo-Irish life. This he held steadfastly intact for fifteen years or more—then when he was ripe, as it were, he discharged it, in a dense mass, to his eternal glory. That was *Ulysses*.'

    (a) Ford Madox Ford
    (b) Djuna Barnes
    (c) Nancy Cunard
    (d) Wyndham Lewis

8. 'A poor dotty Irishman called James Joyce, who was thought to be a great influence in my youth . . . wrote absolute rot.'

    (a) Christopher Isherwood
    (b) P.G. Wodehouse
    (c) Evelyn Waugh
    (d) Aldous Huxley

9. 'Why don't you write books people can read?'

    (a) Giorgio Joyce
    (b) Nora Barnacle
    (c) Stanislaus Joyce
    (d) Lucia Joyce

10. '[*Ulysses* is] a turgid welter of pornography . . . & unformed & unimportant drivel. Until the raw ingredients of a pudding make a pudding, I shall never believe that the raw material of sensation & thought can make a work of art without the cook's intervening.'

(a) Wyndham Lewis
(b) Edith Wharton
(c) Rebecca West
(d) Cyril Connolly

11. 'As for Joyce, he treated people invariably as his equals, whether they were writers, children, waiters, princesses, or charladies. What anybody had to say interested him; he told me that he had never met a bore.'

(a) Ezra Pound
(b) H.G. Wells
(c) Sylvia Beach
(d) Ford Madox Ford

12. 'Joyce is always in my mind, I carry him everywhere with me.'

(a) Salman Rushdie
(b) Eimear McBride
(c) V.S. Pritchett
(d) Terry Pratchett

13. 'Joyce has a most goddamn wonderful book. It'll probably reach you in time. Meantime the report is that he and all his family are starving but you can find the whole celtic crew of them every night in Michaud's where Binney and I can only afford to go about once a week . . . The damned Irish, they have to moan about something or other.'

(a) Jack Kerouac
(b) Ernest Hemingway
(c) Paul Bowles
(d) F. Scott Fitzgerald

14. 'Oh, yes, let people compare me to Joyce by all means, but my English is pat ball to Joyce's champion game.'

(a) Philip Roth
(b) Saul Bellow
(c) Joseph Heller
(d) Vladimir Nabokov

15. 'James Joyce was a synthesizer, trying to bring in as much as he could. I am an analyzer, trying to leave out as much as I can.'

(a) Ann Quinn
(b) B.S. Johnson
(c) Samuel Beckett
(d) Brigid Brophy

16. 'Shakespeare said pretty well everything and what he left out, James Joyce, with a nudge from meself, put in.'

(a) James Stephens
(b) J.P. Donleavy
(c) Flann O'Brien
(d) Brendan Behan

17. 'If our society should go to smash tomorrow (which, as Joyce implies, it may) one could find all the pieces, together with the forces that broke them, in *Finnegans Wake*.'

(a) Joseph Campbell
(b) Richard Ellmann
(c) Jack B. Yeats
(d) Alberto Giacometti

18. 'When his work comes to be judged according to its true value, as posterity will judge it, it will appear overwhelming, if only because of the crushing labour that it obviously represents, and one man's life will seem to have been conceived on too small a scale in comparison with the immensity of the effort involved.'

(a) Sylvia Beach
(b) T.S. Eliot
(c) Italo Svevo
(d) Paul Leon

19. 'James Joyce—an essentially private man who wished his total indifference to public notice to be universally recognized.'

(a) Eugene Jolas
(b) Harold Pinter
(c) Alan Bennett
(d) Tom Stoppard

20. 'He single-handedly killed the 19th century.'

    (a) T.S. Eliot
    (b) Stephen Spender
    (c) W.H. Auden
    (d) William Empson

21. '*Ulysses* is not mainstream, nor was it ever meant to be. When people claim Joyce had his eye on posterity, that is true, but it was intellectual posterity he was after, not mass approval.'

    (a) Jacques Derrida
    (b) John Banville
    (c) Paolo Coelho
    (d) Jacques Lacan

22. 'People say of James Joyce that he looks both sad and tired. He does look sad and he does look tired, but it is the sadness of a man who has procured some medieval permission to sorrow out of time and and in no place; the weariness of one self-subjected to the creation and overabundance in the limited.'

    (a) Nancy Cunard
    (b) Djuna Barnes
    (c) Virginia Woolf
    (d) William Plomer

23. 'To call this man angry is too temperate a word, he was volcanic.'

    (a) Maeve Brennan
    (b) Edna O'Brien
    (c) Susan Sontag
    (d) Éilis Ní Dhuíbhne

24. 'When I read *Ulysses* and then come back to my own work, I feel like a eunuch who has taken a course in voice production and can pass himself off fairly well as a bass or a baritone, but if you listen closely you can hear the good old squeak just the same as ever.'

    (a) Julian Barnes
    (b) Ian McEwan
    (c) George Orwell
    (d) Martin Amis

Answers

1. Rebecca West
2. Hunter S. Thompson
3. Nora Joyce
4. Flann O'Brien
5. Gertrude Stein
6. Roddy Doyle
7. Wyndham Lewis
8. Evelyn Waugh
9. Nora again
10. Edith Wharton
11. Sylvia Beach
12. Salman Rushdie
13. Ernest Hemingway
14. Vladimir Nabokov
15. Samuel Beckett
16. Brendan Behan
17. Joseph Campbell
18. Paul Leon
19. Tom Stoppard
20. T.S. Eliot (on *Ulysses*)
21. John Banville
22. Djuna Barnes
23. Edna O'Brien
24. George Orwell

AFTERWORD

We'll meet again, we'll part once more. The spot I'll seek if the hour
you'll find. My chart shines high where the blue milk's upset. For-
givemequick, I'm going!

—*Finnegans Wake*

When I settled on these valedictory lines from the *Wake* to open this
Afterword I was unaware of the American composer and music theorist Benjamin Boretz (b. 1934), who got there first with his 1976 piece
entitled *(". . . my chart shines high where the blue milk's upset . . .")*
(for Milton Babbitt at 60), a hauntingly minimalist work so airy and
pared down that it's almost not there. I'm playing it now as part of a
self-imposed Oulipian constraint because, with notes to hand, I aim
to write this Afterword (and so complete this book) within the time
it takes the pianist Michael Fowler to perform the 31-minute work.
Because if I don't do it now I'll keep putting it off and fiddling with
the rest of the text. This is a deadline I need.

So. It's nearly 6:30am on a Saturday in late October 2021 and I'm
starting from scratch, *now*.

Finnegan Wake™ sits next to my laptop on my desk, gazing at me
blankly from his flamespoked wheelchair. As my constant companion throughout the writing of this book, and as its unwitting inspiration, it seems both appropriate and in the circular spirit of the *Wake*
to end where we began, with him.

His time is now past. He is no longer in circulation either as a
cartoon or as a plaything, and was never in any case the type of
toy Roland Barthes thought represented a microcosm of adult life,
despite embodying and articulating many positive values. Children
born in the early part of this century who owned him, or yearned
to, are now entering early adulthood. Nothing, I fear, not even the
ghouls of *Monster High*, has prepared them for what they will face
now and in the future.

Essay 50, at the mid-point in this book, explained how I was raised
to believe the world would come to an end in 1975, when God would
judge all humankind and Jehovah's Witnesses alone would find a
place in an earthly paradise while the rest of humanity would face
oblivion. Those crackpot millennial convictions are now becoming
unsettlingly literal—the world is falling apart.

Faced with the catastrophes of climate change, the COVID-19 pandemic, the collapse of social institutions and the anti-intellectualism that accompanies populism and neo-fascism, as well as all the other challenges that we are certain to confront as individuals and as nations and as a race, being told repeatedly that there's no evidence to support the likelihood of 'near-term human extinction' is not reassuring. The ghouls of the Watchtower, Bible and Tract Society of Pennsylvania likewise did nothing to prepare me for the life I chose to lead in the real world, but they also used up all my fear of extinction. In a sense they did for me what the Jesuits did for Joyce—they supplied, unwittingly, the resources for flight and exile.

The continuing existence of life on earth mattered more to Joyce as a humanist with skin in the game than it did to the High Anglican T.S. Eliot with his belief in the Christian afterlife. Joyce's take on his own posthumous career was both secular and pragmatic; when the French translator Jacques Benoist-Mechin asked him to reveal the scheme of *Ulysses*, Joyce said: 'If I gave it all up immediately I'd lose my immortality. I've put in so many enigmas and puzzles that it will keep the professors busy for centuries arguing over what I meant, and that's the only way of insuring [*sic*] one's immortality.'

But any writer's afterlife depends on attracting and retaining the attention of readers, not just professors, and my concern is that Joyce's literary reputation in the future will depend on a dwindling community of literary folk—serious readers all—who may, by the middle of the 21st century, in just thirty years' time, be as few in number as the audience for magic lantern lectures is today. Thirty years! That's the difference between the 1950s and 1980s, which is enough to make you think. Three decades that saw, not just the beginning of sexual intercourse and the Beatles' first LP, but also a cultural paradigm shift in the change from analogue to digital technologies.

For now, and thanks largely to the internet, the works of Joyce continue to offer both readers and non-readers a portal to . . . well, everything, it seems. I chanced upon the Boretz piano composition, playing in the background as I type this, when looking up a *Wake* quote online, and this opened the way to other musical discoveries. One of the ways in which Joyce continues to make his presence felt is as a prompt to further investigation and discovery. His cultural aura is all-pervasive.

Unlike Finnegan Wake™, *Finnegans Wake* has not been consigned to what the art critic Robert Hughes called 'the mausoleum of the nearly new'. Joyce and his works still have an active presence in our culture, and in other cultures. A couple of days before I sat down to write this, the first Swedish translation of *Finnegans Wake* by Leif Høghaug appeared, the culmination of a project started by his colleague Bertil Falk in 1954:

> flodflöde, förbi Eva och Adams, från strandens sväng till buktens böj, för oss via en behändig ström av återcirkulering tillbaka till Howth Castle och Environs.

It's now nearly 7am and this Afterword is now complete, with two minutes to spare. So *Multiple Joyce* is also complete, and ready to submit to Jacob, my publisher in New York. I hope he likes it, and you will too, my reader. My mute unblinking muse, Finnegan Wake™, continues to gaze at me blankly as I wait for the music to come to an end, or simply stop.

It's very quiet, apart from these last padded taps on my laptop keyboard and, far off, a barking dog, a siren, a distant church bell striking seven. The sounds of a waking city. I have nothing more to say and so, with acknowledgements to Joyce, I'll end this book in the middle of the

ACKNOWLEDGEMENTS

My first thanks are to my publisher Jacob Smullyan of Sagging Meniscus Press for his support and patience, to Guillermo Stitch (a fine writer from Dublin) for introducing us and to Rónán Hession (another fine writer from Dublin) for his friendship, and for providing a very generous foreword.

Peter Chrisp, author, Joyce scholar and Wake blogger *non pareil*, kindly read and commented on the manuscript, making many constructive suggestions, corrections and expansions. My thanks to him and may we long be as chummy as two mashed spuds.

I am especially grateful for generous contributions from two authors I count as friends.

Susan Tomaselli gave permission for me to include in full her editorial 'Where the Dead Voices Gather' which originally appeared in the first issue of *gorse*, (8th June 2014), the Dublin literary journal she founded and edits. *Når vi døde vågner* is the Norwegian title of Ibsen's final play *When We Dead Awaken*.

Ray Davis kindly provided some eloquent thoughts on W.N.P. Barbellion (essay 61), and I add my thanks to Jake Goldsmith for creating the prize that honours Barbellion's name, work and legacy.

Lisa Jewell and her colleagues at Poetry Ireland offered helpful suggestions when it came to calculating the number of poets in Ireland for essay 4 'How many poets are there?'.

My thanks to Jacob Trunk for permission to include two of his illustrations in essays 11 and 12, and to Peter Wheatley for letting me include his note on Larry O'Rourke's pub from his monograph *dark and true and tender* (CB editions, 2012) in essay 14 'The Fall of the House of Usher'.

Sasha Dugdale kindly shared with me the letter from John Keats quoted in essay 19 'Crayoning achievement'; David McCallister gave his permission for me to repeat his undergraduate exchange with Professor John Sutherland (essay 20 'The Buck stopped there').

I am grateful to Peter Bowen-Walsh, John Day, Joe McKeowan, Donnachadh Ó Mórdha, Peter Rigney, Richard Yudin and members of the Railway Preservation Society of Ireland for sharing information about Dublin tramways (essay 22 'Tramways and sigla').

Natasha Lehrer kindly shared her thoughts on two *Ulysses* translations (essay 24 'Mrkgnao!'). Professor Finn Fordham of University College London and his *Finnegans Wake* reading group offered me a warm welcome and a night to remember (essay 36 'Time Management').

My Dublin friend Alan Crilly undertook some spirited research into Hispano-Suiza motor cars (essay 54 'Sexcaliber hrosspower') and the Volta cinema (essay 65 'In camera') and was also an early and constructively critical reader. The book takes the form it does thanks to his thoughtful interventions.

Details of the Split Pea Press box set edition of seven 'Work in Progress' pamphlets in essay 67 ('The Cats of Copenhagen and Finn's Hotel') were kindly provided by the publisher Ian Gunn and designer Owen Griffith.

For essay 78 ('And words. They are not in my dictionary') Toby Litt kindly allowed me to quote from his piece 'From "Acedia" to "Zeitgeist": Auden in the 2nd Edition of the OED', which first appeared in *The W.H. Auden Society Newsletter* in October 1989.

Essay 89 'Never again be content with hemp' owes a particular debt to Stephen Marche's essay 'Winning the Game You Didn't Even Want to Play: On Sally Rooney and the Literature of the Pose' which appeared on the Literary Hub website on 15th September 2021.

For essay 91 ('Adventures in the skin game') Derek Pyle of the 'Waywords and Meansigns' website confirmed details of his forearm thunderclap tattoo and my old friend David Holzer shared some personal thoughts on literary tattoos.

The lines from W.H. Auden's essay 'James Joyce and Richard Wagner' in essay 79 'Out of the Audenry' appear with permission of the Estate of W.H. Auden with thanks to Professor Edward Mendelson.

Professor John Haffenden kindly read and commented on essay 99 'As if a magic lantern threw the nerves in patterns on a screen' and Dr Freya Johnston of St. Anne's College Oxford generously supplied the lecture notes by Eric Griffiths quoted therein. Professor David Chinitz of Loyola University Chicago confirmed the source of the claim that one of T.S. Eliot's favourite films was Kurosawa's *Throne of Blood*.

Several of these essays owe a debt to Glenn Johnston, whose frequent tweets about Joyce via @johnstonglenn have been and remain a regular source of delight and inspiration. Many other essays are indebted to the huge community of Joyce scholars past and present. I thank them all.

Quotations from Richard Ellmann's *James Joyce* (1959) courtesy of Lucy Ellmann. Extract from *Peregrine Prykke's Pilgrimage through the London Literary World* in essay 6 'Their Hospitality' and the poem 'A Gesture Towards James Joyce' in essay 38 'Caught gesture' are both © The Estate of Clive James and reproduced by permission. Quotations from 'The Love Song of J. Alfred Prufrock' and *The Waste Land* in the final essay © The Estate of T.S. Eliot.

Part of 'Dubliners 100' (essay 13) originally appeared in my book *About a Girl: a reader's guide to Eimear McBride's* A Girl Is a Half-formed Thing (CB editions, 2018); part of 'His art belongs to Dada' (essay 56) originally appeared in the *Times Literary Supplement* (15th 2014) and a version of 'First among sequels' (essay 77) appeared in the *Literary Review* (August 2018).

'Moby Dick's Hyphen' (essay 98), first published in *Sonofabook* (CB editions, 2016), appears here in revised form. My thanks to the respective editors for their permission to include them.

I am profoundly grateful to Sara Baume, Kevin and Georgia Boniface, Marie-Elsa Bragg, Charles Boyle, Susanna Crossman, Kevin Davey, Emma Devlin, Sharon Duggal, Will Eaves, Lauren Elkin, Stephanie Ellyne, Wendy Erskine, Tim Etchells, Andrew Gallix, Rachel Genn, Jonathan Gibbs, Niven Govinden, Neil Griffiths, Philip Hancock, M. John Harrison, David and Ping Henningham, Caroline Hett, Jen Hodgson, Vlatka Horvat, Michael Hughes, Paulette Jonguitud, Sam Jordison, Riva Lehrer, Linda Mannheim, Eimear McBride, Melissa McCarthy, Amy McCauley, Eloise Miller, Sam Mills, J.O. Morgan, Dan O'Brien, Declan O'Driscoll, Helen Ottaway, Melanie Pappenheim, C.D. Rose, Paul Stanbridge, Julian Stannard, Joanna Walsh, Aea Varfis-van Warmelo, Tony White, Lisa Wolfe and Natalia Zagorska-Thomas, to name but some, and add my warmest thanks to all of those who, in one way or another, as contributors or audience members, took part in my online gatherings *A Leap in the Dark* and *Carthorse Orchestra* between March 2020 and October 2021.

My heartfelt thanks to Laura who makes everything possible, and probable, and to Frank for putting up with us both.

And finally, for my dear son Edwin: this book is for you, with my love.
DC
London, October 2021

David Collard writes for print and online publications including the *Times Literary Supplement, Literary Review, 3:AM Magazine, gorse, Exacting Clam, White Review* and others. *About a Girl: a Reader's Guide to Eimear McBride's* A Girl Is a Half-formed Thing was published by CB editions and he contributed to the recent anthologies *We'll Never Have Paris* and *Love Bites*.

He lives in London, where he organises cultish online literary gatherings. He has a website.

Rónán Hession is a writer, musician and civil servant from Dublin. His debut novel *Leonard and Hungry Paul* (published by Bluemoose Books in 2019) was nominated for the Irish Book Awards, British Book Awards, the BAMB awards, and long-listed for the Republic of Consciousness prize. His third album *Dictionary Crimes* was nominated for the Choice Music Prize for Irish Album of the Year. His second novel *Panenka* was published by Bluemoose in 2021 and a third, *Ghost Mountain*, will appear in 2023.

Lightning Source UK Ltd.
Milton Keynes UK
UKHW012214020622
403923UK00002B/82

9 781952 386329